INEQUALITY

Opposing Viewpoints® in Social Problems

INEQUALITY

Opposing Viewpoints® in Social Problems

David L. Bender, *Publisher*
Bruno Leone, *Executive Editor*
Bonnie Szumski, *Editorial Director*
Lori Shein, *Book Editor*

Greenhaven Press, Inc., San Diego, CA

Every effort has been made to trace the owners of copyrighted material. The articles in this volume may have been edited for content, length, and/or reading level. The titles have been changed to enhance the editorial purpose of the Opposing Viewpoints® concept. Those interested in locating the original source will find the complete citation at the end of each article.

Library of Congress Cataloging-in-Publication Data

Inequality : opposing viewpoints in social problems /
Lori Shein, book editor.
    p. cm.—Opposing viewpoints series
  Includes bibliographical references and index.
  ISBN 1-56510-736-5 (pbk.). — ISBN 1-56510-737-3 (lib.)
  1. Equality—United States. 2. Social problems—United States.
3. Social classes—United States. 4. Racism—United States.
5. Poverty—United States. 6. Sex discrimination—United States.
7. United States—Social conditions. 8. United States—
Economic conditions. 9. United States—Race relations.
I. Shein, Lori, 1957–   . II. Opposing viewpoints series (Unnumbered)
HN79.S6I53   1998
305'.0973—dc21   97-40016
                                                                CIP

Cover Art: JoAnn Kopanny

©1998 by Greenhaven Press, Inc., PO Box 289009,
San Diego, CA 92198-9009
Printed in the U.S.A.

Contents

Chapter 8: Can Government Solve Social Problems?

Preface

The American dream signifies the hope that one's lifestyle can be improved and that following generations will share even greater success than that of their parents. But the American dream often does not mirror the American reality. Though the ideals persist, many people in the United States today feel that they are denied the fruits of the American dream. To them, equal opportunity is a myth. Factors such as race, gender, ethnicity, age, education, and economic status divide the population and deter some segments from achieving the success of their fellow citizens. In a nation built on the premise that all men are created equal, few men and women seem to enjoy the benefits of that equality.

The topic of inequality has always been of interest to students of sociology because it is at the root of many of society's most troubling and insoluble problems. Designed as a supplementary reader for introductory sociology courses, *Inequality: Opposing Viewpoints in Social Problems* examines many vestiges of inequality in the United States and the impact they have on institutions such as law, business, and education. The opposing viewpoints format allows students to see that these topics are seldom clear-cut and that they evade simple solutions.

Many students will confront these issues for the first time. They will encounter arguments that will challenge, and perhaps cause them to question, deeply held beliefs. The aim of this text, however, is not to persuade students, but to encourage them to think critically and become more discerning readers. To facilitate this, the selections in this text are accompanied by active reading questions. General discussion questions at the end of the book provide fodder for further contemplation and discussion. Finally, complete bibliographies aid students in conducting more in-depth research.

As inequality continues to haunt the economic system, the welfare system, the criminal justice system, and other sectors of American society, students of sociology will often be faced with the complexity of this topic. *Inequality: Opposing Viewpoints in Social Problems* offers inroads to the most current debates. Whether to provide a thought-provoking basis for class discussion or to spur research for papers and projects, this book will well serve instructors and students of today's important social concerns.

Charles Howard, MSW, LSW

Introduction

"America, in the assembly of nations, has uniformly spoken among them the language of equal liberty, equal justice, and equal rights."
John Quincy Adams, 1767–1848

The United States is just one of many countries born of the violence of revolution. Unlike many nations, however, the United States has consistently attempted to sustain the ideals chiseled from the revolutionary past. Justice, liberty, and equality remain American goals. Every schoolchild can recite Abraham Lincoln's moving words that bind equality inextricably with the goals of our nation: "Fourscore and seven years ago, our fathers brought forth on this continent a new nation, conceived in Liberty and dedicated to the proposition that all men are created equal." This idealism places America at the center of a basic dilemma: If equal justice is guaranteed to all American citizens, how can Americans allow unequal conditions to exist?

In order to eradicate unequal conditions, the U.S. government has played in the past, and continues to play, a substantial role. Social security, the New Deal, affirmative action, and the civil rights amendments are all examples of a government attempting to assure equal justice, the final aim being for America to exist both in reality and in philosophy as the country that places the quality of individuals above all else.

However, government attempts to remove social inequities through regulation and legislation have often proven controversial. After all, it is argued, America is the land of opportunity, and as such, individuals should be able to achieve their goals without the aid of government. In the middle of the nineteenth century, Horatio Alger's popular stories showed ordinary people succeeding in America simply by displaying industry and other allegedly positive personal qualities. Alger's "Match Stick" boy, Mark, rose above his humble beginnings by hard work, resolve, and cleverness. By becoming a self-made millionaire, Mark informed countless legions of American readers that success, acceptance, and equality could be achieved by personal, not governmental, initiative.

Not everyone agrees with Alger's optimism. Alexis de Tocqueville, for example, believed inequality to be a natural state, one that people, government, and laws are unable to alter. He wrote over a century ago in

Democracy in America, "People will never succeed in reducing all the conditions of society to a perfect level; and even if they unhappily attained that absolute and complete equality, inequality of minds would still remain." In contrast, Abraham Lincoln believed equality should be something "constantly looked to, constantly labored for and even though never perfectly attained, constantly approximated and thereby constantly spreading." He challenged Americans to strive toward the perfection of equality at all times.

Inequality: Opposing Viewpoints in Social Problems is a compilation of articles related to America's most troubling problem. Authors in this volume, including sociologists, political commentators, and laypersons, debate individuals' access to the American dream. The topics in this book reflect the deeper and broader issue of how America can live up to the ideals upon which it was founded and create a society in which all people are truly equal.

CHAPTER 1

Is Inequality Inherent in American Society?

Chapter Preface

The U.S has one of the highest standards of living in the world, with a 1986 median family income of $29,460. This high standard of living attracts hundreds of thousands of immigrants to America every year. Some immigrants come with excessive expectations—like those immigrants who came in the 1800s after hearing a rumor that America's streets were paved with gold. Although they soon found that this was untrue, they and later immigrants nonetheless discovered economic opportunities in the U.S. that existed in few other countries.

Many people believe that America is still the land of opportunity. They maintain that America's economic system is the best at distributing wealth and goods fairly—those who work hardest in the system are most likely to succeed. Because the U.S. government does not maintain strict control over the economy, they contend, Americans have the freedom to participate and succeed as they choose.

Others, however, say that America's high standard of living does not reflect a land of opportunity. They maintain that although some Americans who work hard may be rewarded, those who are disadvantaged in any way are punished. The disabled, the ill, and those born into poverty all suffer under America's economy. As evidence these critics point out that in America, 1 percent of the people own 50 percent of the wealth; 20 percent of the children live in poverty; and half a million citizens are homeless. America's economy provides opportunities only for the fortunate, many believe. They argue that few opportunities exist for the less fortunate.

America has long been known as the land of economic opportunity. Many people question whether this is still true. The authors in the following chapter discuss this issue and debate whether inequality is inherent in American society.

America's Economic System Depends on Inequality

by Sheila Collins

Sheila Collins is associate professor of political science at William Paterson College in New Jersey. In the following viewpoint, Collins contends that inequality is as fundamental to capitalism as capitalism is to the American way of life. Capitalism, she argues, is built on a myth of a classless society in which upward mobility can be achieved by anyone willing to work for it. This widely accepted view of American life belies the gross inequities in wealth and income that form the very foundation of capitalism, she argues. These inequities both reinforce and result from a class system in which the wealthy hold political and economic power and the rest of the population labors to enrich the wealthy and help them maintain their hold on power.

"Capitalism needs inequality in order to function and continuously reproduces inequalities as part of its normal operation."

The United States is a deeply divided society. The movements that erupted over the last thirty years exposed the unacknowledged (but ever-present) fault lines of color, gender, and sexual orientation. But there is another source of division that cross-cuts all of these—that of class.

The concept of "class" is used by sociologists and economists to describe differences between people that are based on economic position—income and wealth, occupational group, etc. Class differences imply differences in power. Yet one rarely hears the term mentioned in this country except in relation to the *middle class*. In fact, some have called *class* the most taboo subject in the United States. This is not so in Europe or in many other parts of the world, where the reality of class is openly acknowledged and political parties and campaigns are forged around class interests. For example, if my parents had lived in England, they would have belonged to the Labor Party. In Italy, they might have voted for the Communist Party, which in that country claimed a huge base among ordinary workers during the post-World War II era. Instead, they considered it natural to back the Democratic Party, which can claim the loyalty of organized labor along with that of super-rich and powerful corporate types.

It should be obvious that differences in income and wealth go a long way in determining our life chances: where we live; how much we have to spend on luxuries; the kind of health care and education we receive; the amount of leisure we can enjoy; the amount of control we have over our work; and what kind of recognition we can expect from public officials. People here, like everywhere, are grouped in society by all these factors, as well as by how we survive—whether on wages, salaries, or access to accumulated wealth. We all take our place in society as part of one or another class, know it or not, like it or not.

The government's own statistics on income distribution say a lot about the nature of class inequality. Each year, the Census Bureau surveys a representative sample of 60,000 households, both families and individuals, asking them questions about their pre-tax incomes.[1] From this sample all kinds of information are derived, such as the gender, racial, age, and geographical distribution of income, the sizes of families dependent on certain levels of income, and so on. The government currently includes as income not only wages and salaries, but money from dividends, interest, royalties, net rental income, Social Security, welfare payments, pensions, and such other miscellaneous sources as alimony. It excludes such sources as inheritances, gifts, capital gains or losses, the value of fringe benefits, in-kind income such as free meals, or the value of government transfer payments such as food stamps or Medicaid/Medicare.

There are two ways that the Census Bureau measures the distribution of income, and therefore income inequality. The first is by ranking all households (or families) from lowest to highest on the basis of income and then dividing the population into equal groups, called *quintiles*, each representing 20 percent of the total.[2] The aggregate income of each group is then divided by the overall income to determine each quintile's share. This picture of income shares gives us a fairly adequate (though not completely accurate) measure of income inequality in the United States.[3]

The second method of measuring income inequality involves incorporating more detailed income data into a single statistic, called the *Gini index*. This statistic summarizes how all income shares are dispersed across society's whole income distribution, using a standard of total equality as its measure. The Gini index ranges from zero (perfect equality), where the total income is shared equally by everyone, to one, which indicates perfect inequality—where all the income is received by only one recipient. The Gini index is normally neither zero nor one, but somewhere in between. In 1993 the measurement for the nation's households was .447.[4] This index is most useful in measuring long-term changes in income inequality and in comparing inequality across geographical boundaries. Both these ways of measuring inequality provide important information about the structure of U.S. society and the relative amounts of power held by various groups.

Figure 1-1 illustrates how lopsided income distribution in the United States is. The top 20 percent of households receive almost half of all the nation's household income, while the bottom 20 percent receive a

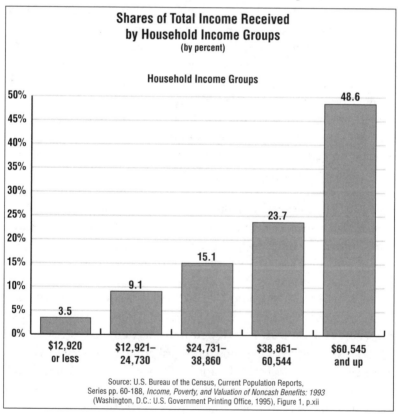

**Shares of Total Income Received
by Household Income Groups**
(by percent)

Household Income Groups

Source: U.S. Bureau of the Census, Current Population Reports,
Series pp. 60-188, *Income, Poverty, and Valuation of Noncash Benefits: 1993*
(Washington, D.C.: U.S. Government Printing Office, 1995), Figure 1, p.xii

16

minuscule 3.5 percent! What's more, the top 5 percent of the population ($99,372 income and up) receive over five times the share of the bottom 20 percent. . . .

Wealth and Inequality

Income levels alone don't tell the whole story about inequality. Wealth is also important, not only because it provides financial stability in the face of sudden loss of income, but because it enables those who hold it to get richer and to control the labor and credit of others. Wealth offers access to enormous political power.

"Them that's got shall get, them that's not shall lose" sang Billie Holiday. Wealth, as both security and power, takes a number of forms held by various groups in our society. Wealth consists of assets that, although not available immediately as money, could be turned into money. People with similar incomes in any given year could have very different levels of wealth, because most wealth is either inherited or accumulated over a lifetime—although those with more income do tend to have more wealth as well.

Most Americans with assets have them invested in such consumer durables as homes and cars. Among the truly rich, however, types of assets change dramatically from physical items to paper assets—mainly stocks and bonds.[5]

In 1989, 89 percent of the financial assets in the country—the type of wealth that generates more income—was held by the richest 10 percent, while the bottom 90 percent of the population held only about 10.6 percent. For all the cheerleading in government and media for entrepreneurial spirit and small business, business ownership figures show that the wealthiest 1 percent owned *over half of all business assets*, while the great majority (90 percent) owned only 18.8 percent![6]

According to researchers at the Federal Reserve Board and the Internal Revenue Service, in 1989 the top 1 percent of households was worth more than the bottom 90 percent. The richest 1 percent commanded 38.3 percent of total net worth (all assets, including real estate, stocks and bonds, checking and savings accounts, etc., minus debts), while the richest 10 percent commanded almost 70 percent of the country's net worth. The remaining 90 percent owned only a little over 30 percent of total net worth![7]

Based on these and earlier findings, researchers Lawrence Mishel and Jared Bernstein speculate that more than half of all U.S. families are living from paycheck to paycheck with little or nothing in the bank in case of a serious financial emergency.[8] . . .

Trends in Inequality

Even though people in the United States are not locked by birth into their class positions, great inequality has been a constant feature of life. In the country's founding days, a small elite of white male doctors, merchants, bankers, lawyers, and slaveholders wrote a constitution that excluded the vast majority of the population from its protections.

This majority included all women, indigenous peoples, African slaves, and all men without property. One historian concluded that "the wealth inequalities in the thirteen colonies were about on a par with those in the United States nearly two hundred years later."[9]

While the disparities have remained in place, there was a move toward greater equality beginning in the 1950s and continuing through the 1960s, when a unique spurt of economic growth coupled with low inflation was followed by President Johnson's "War on Poverty." However, that period was to be short-lived. By the early 1970s, the Gini index had begun to move up again, and in the 1980s it accelerated its upward pace. Between 1967 and 1993, the Gini index moved closer to perfect inequality by about 15 percent, erasing whatever gains had been made in reducing inequality in the previous decades.

Increasing inequality returned with a vengeance, driven by changes in both the general economy and government policy. For the average worker, this meant more permanent unemployment and underemployment—the result of changes in the structure of the labor market rather than the usual cause, cyclical ups and downs in the economy. For those who still had a job, it meant declining *real* (inflation-adjusted) wages.

The Census Bureau reported in 1994, for example, that the percentage of all Americans who work full-time but earn less than the poverty level for a family of four rose by 50 percent in thirteen years, and this trend has affected every group in our society.[10] People who work in the same field and are of similar age and education, regardless of race or gender, are finding that their wages, once very close, are now spread over a much wider range. "Inequality is going up in nearly every occupation," according to Lawrence Katz, a Harvard labor economist. For example, in 1980 young lawyers just starting out in the field of pension law could expect to earn similar salaries. By 1990, the wage spread for such a position was as large as $68,000. Before, people could expect to receive roughly the same pay if they switched jobs—but not any more.[11]

The very rich, on the other hand, saw their incomes skyrocket during this time. According to the Internal Revenue Service, from 1980 to 1990 incomes for those making over $1 million a year increased by 2,184 percent, while incomes for those making $200,000 to $1 million increased by 697 percent.[12]

Some writers have identified a decline of the middle class. The Census Bureau found that between 1968 and 1993, the top fifth of the population gained 5.4 percent of total income, the middle three fifths lost 4.8 percent, and the bottom fifth lost 0.6 percent. But within the top fifth, however, more than half of the gains (almost 60 percent) went to the top 5 percent.[13] Even more startling changes appeared in pre- and post-tax incomes between 1977 and 1989 based on tax returns. More than two thirds of the growth in average pretax incomes went to the wealthiest 1 percent of families. After-tax income inequality was slightly reduced: the super-rich gained a mere 60 percent of the total growth.[14]

The wealth of the affluent (largely in stocks and bonds) rose in the 1980s to what one economist labeled "Great Gatsby levels," that is, from merely well-to-do to spectacular.[15] By 1989 all of that increase in wealth had gone to those at the very top of the heap.[16]

"Modern Horatio Algers notwithstanding, a wave of recent studies shows that rags-to-riches remains the exception, not the rule," the *New York Times* reported. If anything, the climb out of poverty has become more difficult, especially for the young, the unskilled, and the undereducated. According to economist Gary Solon, a child whose father is in the bottom 5 percent of earners has only one chance in twenty of making it into the top 20 percent of families. The same child has a one-in-four chance of rising above the median wealth and a two-in-five chance of staying poor or near poor.[17]

While some may take one step up or one step back, precious few fall from or rise to great heights. Lady Day's economic analysis still applies: "God bless the child that's got his own."

Even as four-fifths of all Americans saw both their incomes and their wealth decline during the 1980s and early 1990s, African-Americans as a whole (with the exception of a small group of athletes, movie stars, and CEOs) experienced a deeper downward turn than whites. Job status for young African-American males fell relative to whites—even within the same industry and with the same educational levels and work experience.[18] This was contrary to the period between 1967 and 1991, when African-Americans had begun to move modestly toward greater parity. The height of that modest gain was reached in 1988, when per capita black income measured 59.5 percent of per capita white income. Since then, the gap has widened.

What's more, increasing numbers of African-Americans have been reduced to poverty (33.1 percent in 1993) and permanent unemployment. For African-Americans, the Urban League has reported, "the entire period has been characterized by conditions that would be considered depression level if they were experienced by all Americans."[19] Census results show that conditions are especially desperate for young African-Americans, who may be just starting out to raise families.[20]

Although this decline in both absolute and relative status has taken place in a period of moderate economic expansion, there has been no effort to make social programs help those caught in the downward spiral. In fact . . . such programs have been steadily reduced or eliminated.

During the same years, the proportion of whites living in poverty declined from 12.8 percent to 12.2 percent.[21] That trend, however, did not hold for the very young, white or black. After a period of decreasing poverty in the late 1960s, the poverty rate for children began to climb again in 1974 and is back at roughly the level it was at in 1963.

On paper, there has been more parity between male and female incomes since the 1960s. Median income for females in 1967 was 32.4 percent of males', and in 1993 it was 52 percent. The closing of this gap in the earlier years can be traced to women's entry into previously male-dominated fields, as well as enforcement of anti-discrimination laws. But most of the gains since 1980 are due to declines in real male wages, rather than to any improvements in the workplace for women!

The Myth of Classlessness

Far from being one big classless society, the United States is a nation of stark contrasts. Deep and unrelenting economic deprivation and humiliation coexist with wealth that would make the kings and queens of old look like middle-class shop-owners. During the Reagan, Bush, and Clinton years, under the guise of carrying out their promise to cut taxes for the middle class, congressional Republicans and Democrats have presided over one of history's largest transfers of wealth to the already wealthy.

Yet the myth of a classless United States persists, even as so many admire and aspire to "lifestyles of the rich and famous." This social schizophrenia—a constant state of confusion between fantasy and reality—may be the only way to make "common sense" of the blatantly unfair and destructive situation that confronts everyone on a daily basis.

The logic of the myth of classlessness—of unlimited upward mobility for anyone who is willing to work for it—reinforces the belief that our economic system distributes its rewards according to merit. Those who don't succeed, it is constantly explained, haven't made the effort, or are by character or by genetic makeup incapable of making it. In other words, failure is the fault of the individual. During times of widespread economic distress, such as depressions and recessions, the cause of such failures is often shifted to "outside" forces, such as oil crises, natural disasters, or "government interference."[22]

But not only is upward mobility a mirage for the majority, its promise blurs some hard realities. In fact . . . capitalism *needs* inequality in order to function and continuously reproduces inequalities as part of its normal operation.

The myth serves the system in several ways. It offers an incentive to work harder—often in jobs that are dull, repetitive, and economically unrewarding—in the hopes of achieving the ever-elusive American Dream. And it pits the lure of individual success against a range of options involving collective action. In short, it is a form of social control.

Economic power and political power are intricately linked. However much we pride ourselves on our political democracy, those with the most wealth ultimately have the most to say about politics most of the time—especially about those policies that affect economic life. The poorest are, for all intents and purposes, disenfranchised. Bernie Sanders of Vermont, the only member of Congress to be elected as an independent on a specifically pro–working class platform, has described the U.S. political system as an *oligarchy* (rule by a few).

> Oligarchy refers not just to the unfair distribution of wealth, but to the fact that the decisions that shape our consciousness and affect our lives are made by a very small and powerful group of people. . . . The mass media (television, radio, newspapers, magazines, publishers, movie and video companies), for example, are largely controlled by a few multi-national corporations that determine the news and programming we see, hear and read—and, ultimately, what we believe. While violence, scandal, horror, sports, and Rush Limbaugh are given much attention, we are provided with virtually no in-depth analysis of the problems facing working people, or their possible solutions. . . . Economic decisions that wreck the lives of millions of American families are made by a handful of CEOs. While these corporate leaders bemoan the breakdown of "morality" and "law and order," they close down profitable companies, cut wages and benefits, deny retired workers their pensions and transport our jobs to Third World countries. American workers, who have often given decades of their lives to these companies, have absolutely no say as to what happens to them on the job. They are powerless and expendable, which is what oligarchy is all about.[23]

Politicians, who owe their political careers either to their own fortunes or to others with big money, get the rest of us to vote for them by promising to reduce taxes for the middle class, or to get tough on "welfare cheats," criminals, and other outsiders. They present themselves as ordinary people who rose out of the middle class through talent and hard work, living proof that anyone can make it to the top.

Yet historically, when the political rhetoric says "one big happy family," the strategies and tactics call for cynical manipulation of feelings of powerlessness, economic insecurity, and loss of status—feelings that are part of living in a class system.

One direct result of the denial of social inequality is the outbreak of personal crises brought on by self-blame. Social psychologists have documented self-blame in increased rates of alcoholism, drug abuse, suicides, and domestic violence, and in stress-related illnesses such as heart disease and cancer.[24] Many people find convenient targets for pent-up rage and frustration in scapegoats, such as racial minorities, immigrants, and "welfare cheats." Recruits to neofascist organizations are mostly young white men who are either unemployed or underemployed. The majority of victims of street crime and drug violence are, like the perpetrators, poor people.

Meanwhile, with the rise of anti-union sentiment that accompanies the fear of economic insecurity, the public's organized lines of defense are collapsing. The trade union movement is eroding quickly—down from 32.5 percent of the labor force in 1953 to 15.8 percent in 1992 (11.5 percent in the private sector), another consequence of the decline of solidarity among employed and unemployed workers. Employers are freed to step up benefit cuts: strong and enforceable health and safety protections for workers, adequate minimum wage, parental leave policies, adequate employment compensation, and other basic services are deemed excessive. Workers find little or no support among lawmakers.

Democracy is another casualty. The United States has the lowest voter turnout of any major industrialized country. While the Republicans and Democrats argue over who really represents the middle class, the same moneyed interests give to both parties, hedging their bets. Candidates or parties who express explicitly pro–working class themes are branded as "fringe elements" or "special interests" and excluded from media and party platforms through which they might make their case to the people. In 1984, Jesse Jackson was belittled by the mainstream press and politicians as being too liberal for most Americans. His campaign was effectively blocked, even though most of his campaign themes were closer than his opponents' to public sentiments expressed in numerous opinion polls.[25]

In electoral politics and in interest group campaigning, money talks—so loudly it is nearly impossible to be heard over the noise it makes. Corporations are spending hundreds of millions on advertising, lobbying, and fake "grassroots" campaigns organized to support their interests. The result is an electorate that is heavily skewed to the high end of the economic heap, with the natural effect that elected officials show more and more open disdain, and even hostility, toward the poor and "lower middle." Small wonder, then, that in the last several presidential elections non-voters have made up the largest part of the electorate.

Notes

1. The latest collection of this data is found in U.S. Bureau of the Census, *Current Population Reports*, Series P60–184, *Money Income of Households, Families and Persons in the United States: 1992* (Washington D.C.: U.S. Government Printing Office, 1993).
2. The Census Bureau defines a household as consisting of all persons who occupy a housing unit whether related or unrelated. The occupants live and eat together and enter the unit through a separate entrance.
3. Although the Census Bureau carefully constructs its population sample so as to be scientifically representative of the total population of the United States, it can never be totally accurate and suffers from several distortions. Estimates from a sample may differ from figures from a complete census using the same questionnaires, instructions and enumerators. Nonsampling errors may result from inability to obtain information about all cases in the sample; vague definitions; differences in the interpretation of questions; confusion, poor memory, or sabotage by respondents; errors made in data collection such as in recording or coding the data; errors made in processing data; errors made in estimating values for missing data; and failure to represent all units with the sample. See U.S. Bureau of the Census, *Current Population Reports*, Series P60–184, *Money Income of Households, Families, and Persons in the United States: 1992* (Washington, D.C.: U.S. Government Printing Office, 1993), pp. D-2–D-3.
4. U.S. Bureau of the Census, *Current Population Reports*, Series P60–188, *Income, Power and Valuation of Noncash Benefits: 1993*, p. xii.
5. Lars Osberg, *Economic Inequality in the United States* (Armonk, NY: M.E. Sharpe, 1984), pp. 38–49.
6. Lawrence Mishel and Jared Bernstein, *The State of Working America, 1992–93* (Washington, D.C.: Economic Policy Institute; Armonk, NY: M.E. Sharpe, 1993), Table 5.3, p. 256.
7. Sylvia Nasar, "Fed Gives New Evidence of 80's Gains by Richest," *New York Times*, 21 April 1992, p. 1. The Federal Reserve survey from which these data were taken was conducted on a sample of 3,143 households, concentrating especially on families with very high incomes who are typically undercounted in most surveys. The top 1 percent of households—834,000—was worth about $5.7 trillion, while the bottom 90 percent—84 million households—was worth $4.8 trillion. However, because of the difficulty in getting accurate data on wealth and potential sampling error, researchers issued several caveats about accepting the validity of the data. See also Mishel and Bernstein, *The State of Working America, 1992–93*, p. 255.
8. Mishel and Bernstein, p. 255.
9. A.H. Jones, *Wealth of a Nation to Be: The American Colonies on the Eve of Revolution* (New York: Columbia University Press, 1980), p.317.
10. Jason DeParle, "Sharp Increase Along the Border of Poverty," *New York Times*, 31 March 1994, p. A18.
11. Christopher Jencks, a sociologist who has studied poverty, has conjectured

that on the basis of such data, more people may be becoming so discouraged that they are dropping out of the labor market. See Louis Uchitelle, "Unequal Pay Widespread in the U.S.," *New York Times*, 14 August 1990, p. D1.

12. Donald Barlett and James Steele, "Rules Shaping the Economy Stacked Against Middle Class," *Charlotte Observer*, 24 November 1991, p.1A.

13. U.S. Bureau of the Census, *Current Population Reports*, Series P-60, No. 177, *Trends in Relative Income: 1964–1989* (Washington, D.C.: U.S. Government Printing Office, 1991), p. 3. Cited in Frederick R. Strobel, *Upward Dreams, Downward Mobility*, p. 47.

14. Sylvia Nasar, "The 1980's: A Very Good Time for the Very Rich," *New York Times*, 5 March 1992, p. 1.

15. Robert Pear, "Rich Got Richer in 80's; Others Held Even," *New York Times*, 11 January 1991, p.1.

16. Paul R. Krugman, economist at the Massachusetts Institute of Technology, quoted in Sylvia Nasar, "Fed Gives New Evidence of 80's Gains by Richest," *New York Times*, 21 April 1992, p. 1.

17. Sylvia Nasar, "Those Born Wealthy or Poor Usually Stay So, Studies Say," *New York Times*, 18 May 1992, p.1.

18. John Bound and Richard B. Freeman, "What Went Wrong? The Erosion of Relative Earnings and Employment Among Young Black Men in the 1980s," *Quarterly Journal of Economics, 1992*, cited in Marc Breslow, "The Racial Divide Widens: Why African Americans Have Lost Ground," *Dollars and Sense*, No. 197 (January/February, 1995), p. 11.

19. Davide H. Swinton, "The Economic Status of African Americans During the Reagan-Bush Era: Withered Opportunities, Limited Outcomes, and Uncertain Outlook," *The State of Black America, 1993*, p. 135.

20. U.S. Bureau of the Census, *Current Population Reports*, Series P60–184, *Money Income of Households, Families, and Persons in the United States: 1992*, Table 22.

21. U.S. Bureau of the Census, *Current Population Reports*, Series P-60–185, *Poverty in the United States: 1992* (Washington, D.C.: U.S. Government Printing Office, 1993), Table 3.

22. Michael D. Yates, *Longer Hours, Fewer Jobs: Employment and Unemployment in the United States* (New York: Monthly Review Press, 1994), p. 84.

23. Bernard Sanders, "Whither American Democracy," Congressional reprint. First published in the *Los Angeles Times*, 16 January 1994.

24. Lillian Breslow Rubin has described the effects on working-class families of such internalized self-doubt and alienation in *Worlds of Pain: Life in the Working Class Family* (New York: Basic Books, 1977). Dr. Harvey Brenner of Johns Hopkins University has, over the last twenty years, documented rises in the unemployment level (economic failure experienced as individual failure) with increased rates of heart attacks, alcoholism, and other stress-related diseases. See M. Harvey Brenner, "Economy, Society and Health," paper prepared for the Conference on Society and Health, Harvard School of Public Health, 16 October 1992.

25. Sheila Collins, *The Rainbow Challenge: The Jackson Campaign and the Future of U.S. Politics* (New York: Monthly Review Press, 1987); see especially Chapter 8, pp. 228–253.

Inequality Is the Result of Human Limitations

by Thomas Sowell

Thomas Sowell is a senior fellow at the Hoover Institution, a public policy research center dedicated to understanding the causes and consequences of economic, political, and social change. In the following viewpoint, Sowell contends that political and intellectual elites, whom he calls "the anointed," have given reasons for inequality among individuals that have undermined the United States. Sowell argues that "the anointed" blame most evils on outside forces such as capitalism, racism, and sexism while rejecting the view that human beings have limitations and that moral and intellectual inadequacies are often the cause of inequality. Those who hold the latter view Sowell calls "the benighted." Sowell argues that the prevailing vision, which characterizes the failure of society as the primary cause of America's problems, is flawed in that it is based on sweeping assumptions that cannot be supported by evidence.

"Individual sufferings and social evils are inherent in the innate deficiencies of all human beings, whether these deficiencies are in knowledge, wisdom, morality, or courage."

The vision of the anointed may stand out in sharper relief when it is contrasted with the opposing vision, a vision whose reasoning begins with the tragedy of the human condition. By tragedy here is not meant simply unhappiness, but tragedy in the ancient Greek sense, inescapable fate inherent in the nature of things, rather than unhappiness due simply to villainy or callousness. The two visions differ in their respective conceptions of the nature of man, the nature of the world and the nature of causation, knowledge, power, and justice. These differences can be presented schematically, as below:

	The Tragic Vision	The Vision of the Anointed
Human capability	severely and inherently limited for all	vast for the anointed
Social possibilities	trade-offs that leave many "unmet needs"	solutions to problems
Social causation	systemic	deliberate
Freedom	exemption from the power of others	ability to achieve goals
Justice	process rules with just characteristics	just (equalized) chances or results
Knowledge	consists largely of the unarticulated experiences of the many	consists largely of the articulated intelligence of the more educated few
Specialization	highly desirable	highly questionable
Motivation	incentives	dispositions
Process costs	crucial	incidental
Decision-making mechanism preferred	systemic processes that convey the experiences and revealed preferences of the many	deliberate plans that utilize the special talents and more advanced views of the few
Kinds of decisions preferred	incremental	categorical

These differences are not random happenstances. They are systematic differences that follow logically from fundamental differences in underlying assumptions, beginning with assumptions about the nature of human beings and the range of possibilities open to them. All these particular differences between the two visions turn ultimately on differences about human limitations and their corollaries. The more ambitious definitions of freedom and of justice, for example, in the vi-

26

sion of the anointed are consistent with the expansive sweep of human capabilities they assume. By the same token, the emphasis on specialization by those with the tragic vision reflects their sense of the inherent limitations of the human mind and the corresponding dangers in attempting to bite off more than anyone can chew. It is not merely that the engineer cannot perform surgery, the judge in his decisions cannot venture very far beyond his narrow expertise in the law without precipitating disasters when he attempts to become a social philosopher who can make law the instrument of some grander vision of the world.

The Underlying Vision

The conflicts between those with the tragic vision and those with the vision of the anointed are virtually inevitable. Clearly, those who assume a larger set of options are unlikely to be satisfied with results deriving from a smaller set of options. Thus, those with the vision of the anointed, who assume an expansive range of choices, repeatedly find themselves in conflict with those who have the tragic vision and who consequently assume a much smaller set of choices. While these conflicts pervade contemporary ideological politics, they are not peculiar to our times. Both visions have a long history, encompassing many individuals of historic stature. Those with the vision of the anointed are particularly prone to think of their own philosophy as new, and therefore as adapted to contemporary society, but their framework of assumptions goes back at least two centuries—as does the framework of those with the tragic vision.

Both visions also have internal coherence. Those who follow the assumptions of a particular vision as regards law tend also to follow that vision as regards economics. Thus Judge David L. Bazelon . . . believed in the socioeconomic sphere that "inequality of riches in our affluent society" was one of "a host of inequities,"[1] that government should provide people's "basic needs as rights," that income, education, and medical care should be "matters of right, not of grace."[2] Conversely, Adam Smith not only had opposite views from Judge Bazelon on government's role in the economy, but also on the application of the criminal law. For Smith, "mercy to the guilty is cruelty to the innocent."[3] A similar coherence of vision is found across many other issues, with environmentalists and their opponents often taking opposite positions on military defense as well, for example. As a contemporary writer has noted:

> Liberalism in America and worldwide has great faith in modifying human behavior by adjusting "underlying social conditions" to make people desire the right thing instead of the

wrong thing. In its clearest form, this is the response to crime control by liberals, who are not much interested in tougher sentences, improved security devices, better-armed and equipped police, more escape-proof prisons—they seek to change society or the malefactors, so that people will not want to commit crime. This is also the form of the liberal solution to most foreign policy problems—we should behave in a better manner and reorder the world so that the urge to war will be reduced, and mankind will live in better harmony.[4]

Police, prisons, etc., represent only trade-offs, while creating a society in which crime is prevented from arising in the first place is a solution. Hence the former approach is consistent with the tragic vision and the latter approach is in keeping with the vision of the anointed. Not only today, but for more than two centuries, both crime and war have been seen, by those with the vision of the anointed, as things to be deterred by changing people's dispositions rather than by confronting them with retaliatory capabilities that provide incentives against crime or war. William Godwin's 1793 treatise, *Enquiry Concerning Political Justice*, remains one of the most systematic elaborations of the vision of the anointed and in it crime and war are approached in precisely the same way as among 1960s liberals and their later followers. Dispositions and understanding are seen by the anointed as the key to crime control, for example: "It is impossible that a man would perpetrate a crime, in the moment when he sees it in all its enormity,"[5] according to Godwin, just as Ramsey Clark was to say in the twentieth century, "healthy, rational people will not injure others."[6] In both cases, it is the failure of "society" that causes crime, with the criminal being the victim of circumstances. . . .

Innate Limitations Versus Unwise Social Policy

In the tragic vision, individual sufferings and social evils are inherent in the innate deficiencies of all human beings, whether these deficiencies are in knowledge, wisdom, morality, or courage. Moreover, the available resources are always inadequate to fulfill all the desires of all the people. Thus there are no "solutions" in the tragic vision, but only trade-offs that still leave many desires unfulfilled and much unhappiness in the world. What is needed in this vision is a prudent sense of how to make the best trade-offs from the limited options available, and a realization that "unmet needs" will necessarily remain—that attempting to fully meet these needs *seriatim* only deprives other people of other things, so that a society pursuing such a policy is like a dog chasing its tail. Given this vision, particular

28

solutions to particular problems are far less important than having and maintaining the right processes for making trade-offs and correcting inevitable mistakes. To those with the tragic vision, the integrity of processes is crucial—much more so than particular causes. As Jean-François Revel put it, in a free society "there is no single just *cause*, only just *methods*."[7]

The vision of the anointed begins with entirely different premises. Here it is not the innate limitations of human beings, or the inherent limitations of resources, which create unhappiness but the fact that social institutions and social policies are not as wisely crafted as the anointed would have crafted them. As John Stuart Mill put it, the "present wretched education, and wretched social arrangements, are the only real hindrance" to happiness being widespread.[8] Mill's view in many ways epitomized the vision of the anointed.[9] When he spoke of "the best and wisest,"[10] it was with none of the sense of irony that the phrase "the brightest and the best" has acquired in our time. Great things could be achieved, Mill said, "if the superior spirits would but join with each other" for social betterment.[11] He called upon the universities to "send forth into society a succession of minds, not the creatures of their age, but capable of being its improvers and regenerators. . . ."[12]

The Human Condition

To those whose reasoning begins with the tragedy of the human condition, evil is diffused throughout humanity, while those with the vision of the anointed tend to see evils more localized in particular "oppressors" of one sort or another, as expressed in "white racism," "male domination," or "capitalist exploitation," for example. This second set of evils, however severe, is more remediable than the kind of evil implied in the remark: "We have met the enemy and it is us." The logic of the two visions almost inevitably puts them at odds as to how much improvement can be expected from the political process. At the extreme, a revolutionary cannot believe in the tragic vision, for that would imply that all the sacrifices and sufferings incident to a revolution could easily result in largely cosmetic changes in personnel and style—or might even bring to power a worse despot. Conversely, it would be unconscionable to be conservative if that meant passively accepting unnecessary evils and *simultaneously* preventable sufferings.

To those with the tragic vision, institutions, traditions, laws, and policies are to be judged by how well they cope with the intellectual and moral inadequacies of human beings, so as to limit the damage they do, and to coordinate the society in such a way as to maximize the use of its scattered fragments of knowledge, as well as to correct inevitable mistakes as quickly as possible. But to those with the less constrained vision of the anointed, the goal is the liberation of human beings from unnecessary social inhibitions, so as to allow repressed creativity to emerge and the vast knowledge and talent already available to be applied to existing problems.

For the anointed, traditions are likely to be seen as the dead hand of the past, relics of a less enlightened age, and not as the distilled experience of millions who faced similar human vicissitudes before. Moreover, the applicability of past experience is further discounted in the vision of the anointed, because of the great changes that have taken place since "earlier and simpler times." Here the two visions clash again, for those with the tragic vision see no great changes in the fundamental intellectual or moral capacities of human beings, however much the material world may have changed or various institutions and customs may have developed through trial and error.

Justice Holmes saw modern man as being very much like his barbarian ancestors,[13] with the different conditions of life today being due to economic and social developments based on the very institutions, traditions, and laws which those with the vision of the anointed are anxious to supersede with untested theories. As Edmund Burke put it, we "should approach to the faults of the state as to the wounds of a father," with "awe and trembling solicitude"[14]—not as an "exciting" opportunity for experimentation. Beginning, like Holmes, with a vision of human nature little changing in its basic essentials, Burke expected no great benefit from speculative theories as a basis for public policy:

> We know that *we* have made no discoveries, and we think that no discoveries are to be made, in morality; nor many in the great principles of government, nor in the ideas of liberty.[15]

To those with the tragic vision, barbarism is not some distant stage of evolution, but an ever-present threat when the civilizing institutions are weakened or undermined:

> Civilization is not inherited; it has to be learned and earned by each generation anew; if the transmission should be interrupted for one century, civilization would die, and we should be savages again.[16]

A similar sense of the fragility of civilization led Edmund Burke to regard the promotion of social experimentation and atomistic reason as a dangerous playing with fire:

> We are afraid to put men to live and trade each on his own private stock of reason; because we suspect that this stock in each man is small, and that the individuals would do better to avail

30

themselves of the general bank and capital of nations and of ages.[17]

Neither Burke nor others in the tradition of the tragic vision were opposed to change, per se, and many of them in fact advocated major changes in their own day. The authors of *The Federalist Papers* were, after all, not only establishing a new government after overthrowing the old, but were also establishing a radically new *kind* of government, in a world ruled by monarchs. What made them different from those who led the French revolution was that their vision of human beings was radically different. The French revolution operated on assumptions much closer to those of the vision of the anointed.

Where the American revolution deliberately created a government of elaborate checks and balances, to constrain the evils inherent in human beings, the French revolution concentrated vast powers in its leadership, so as to allow those who were presumably wise and benevolent to effect sweeping changes with little hindrance. Condorcet, as an intellectual supporter of the French revolution, could see no reason for the American system of checks and balances, in which society was to be "jostled between opposing powers" or to be held back by the "inertia" of its constitution.[18] Indeed, even after the revolutionaries turned against him and threw him into prison, Condorcet still seemed not to understand the reason for limitations on government power. . . .

Social Causation

Those with the tragic vision and those with the vision of the anointed not only have different conceptions of the limitations of human beings and of the limitations of resources, relative to the insatiable desires of people, but also have very different conceptions of cause and effect as it operates in social processes.

In the vision of the anointed, it is the dispositions, wisdom, intentions, talents, will, and commitment of social decision makers which are crucial. In the tragic vision, where human knowledge and foresight are very limited *for all*, causation more often operates in systemic ways, with innumerable interactions producing results controlled by no given individual or group, but falling into a pattern determined by the incentives and constraints inherent in the logic of the circumstances, rather than as a consequence of specifically articulated, syllogistic rationality.

Systemic causation operates in a wide spectrum of circumstances, whether in the world of nature or in human societies. Vegetation on a mountainside may fall into a pattern, not because any of the plants or trees sought to produce such a pattern, but because different temperatures at different heights favor the survival of different species. Even where human volition is involved, the overall pattern that emerges need not reflect anyone's volition. The Dow Jones industrial average may stand at 4086, not because anyone planned it that way, but because that was the net result of innumerable transactions by innumerable people seeking only their own individual advantage on the particular stocks they were trading.

More broadly, language arises out of gropings, accidents, experiences, and historical borrowings and corruptions of other languages. *No wise individual or council sat down and designed language*—either as a general concept or as specific languages, except for artificial languages like Esperanto, which have languished in disuse. The richness, complexity, and subtleties of language have arisen systemically, from the experiences and interactions of millions of ordinary human beings, not from a top-down "plan" formulated by some elite. From time to time, linguistic practices are codified or modified by intellectuals, but this is an incidental part of a vast drama.

Systemic causation creates an order which arises as a consequence of individual interactions directed toward various and conflicting ends, not toward the creation of this order itself. The characteristics of such an order can be analyzed, even if they cannot be created—and this order may, in particular instances or in general, be superior to what can be created, as the case of artificial versus naturally evolving language suggests. The eighteenth-century school of French economists called the Physiocrats coined the term *laissez-faire* to express their view that "the natural order" that would emerge in a market economy was both discernible and more beneficial than attempts to control such complex interactions from the top. That has likewise been the central theme of the twentieth-century writings of Friedrich Hayek, who has sharply distinguished an emergent "order" from a contrived "design."[19] In short, systemic causation has been an enduring feature of the tragic vision, whether among economists, legal analysts, or social thinkers in various other fields.

Experience or Rationality?

Systemic causation takes many forms. Legal traditions, family ties, social customs, and price fluctuations in an economy are all systemic ways in which the experiences and preferences of millions of people powerfully influence the decisions of millions of other people. Where the tragic vision and the vision of the anointed differ most fundamentally is on the reality and validity of such systemic processes, which utilize the experiences of the many, rather than the articulated rationality of a talented few. Related to this difference is a sharp difference in the role of dispositions, intentions, or goals in the two visions.

The very terms of discourse among those with the vision of the anointed have historically reflected their preoccupation with dispositions, intentions, goals, whether these were "liberty, equality, fraternity" in the eighteenth century or "social justice," "compassion," or "women's liberation" today. By contrast, those with the tragic vision have emphasized process characteristics, often treating the dispositions, intentions, or goals of those operating within these processes as incidental or irrelevant. For example, although Adam Smith regarded the intentions of businessmen as selfish and anti-social,[20] he saw the systemic consequences of their competition as being far more beneficial to society than well-intentioned government regulation.[21]

Although the overall results of systemic interactions are not directly controlled by anyone, they are neither random nor unfathomable. Otherwise, there could be no such thing as economic analysis of market competition or scientific analysis of ecological or evolutionary patterns. Determining the particular characteristics of particular kinds of systems of reciprocal interaction can be a demanding task—but it is a task seldom undertaken by those with the vision of the anointed, who see little standing between intention and result, other than such subjective factors as compassion or commitment. Thus, systemic causation seldom plays a major role in the prevailing vision of the anointed, however important it may be in the tragic vision. Where the world is conceived in the tragic vision as a system of innumerable and reciprocal interactions, all constrained within the confines of natural and human limitations, individual problems cannot be solved one by one without adding to other problems elsewhere, if only by using up the resources available to deal with them. . . .

Contrived Explanations of Social Phenomena

Within the framework of systemic causation, proclamations of high principles and deep compassion are irrelevant distractions which promote a dangerous confusion between what you would like and what is likely to happen if what you advocate is put into practice. But those with the vision of the anointed tend automatically to attribute statistical differences between groups to intentional reasons (discrimination) or to dispositional reasons (racism, sexism), with seldom a serious thought about systemic reasons, such as age differences, cultural differences, or differences associated with childbearing and homemaking. It is considered an act of generosity if the latter reasons are not dismissed out of hand but are accorded a "perhaps"—and all this without a speck of evidence being used to distinguish between these possibilities and those possibilities whose only superior claims are based on their being part of the intentional and dispositional reasons at the heart of the vision of the anointed.

Nowhere does the difference between systemic causation and intentional causation show up more dramatically than in discussions of racial issues. With such negative phenomena as racism, as with such positive phenomena as compassion, *systemic* causation does not depend simply on whether these dispositions exist but on the situational incentives and constraints within which they exist. An owner of a professional basketball team and an owner of a symphony orchestra may be equally racist, but it would be financially suicidal for the former to refuse to hire black basketball players, while the relatively few black symphonic musicians could be denied jobs with much less effect on the overall quality of a symphony orchestra or its financial viability. . . .

Systemic causation does not presuppose perfect rationality on the part of human beings. On the contrary, its rationality is a systemic rationality, such that any professional basketball team owner who refused to hire black players under competitive market conditions would simply not continue to survive as an owner. Similarly, systemic causation would not explain the highly varying proportions of female employees in different industries and occupations by the subjective attitudes of men in those particular industries and occupations, but by the varying situations in those sectors of the economy where women are prevalent or rare. It would, in fact, be an incredible coincidence if men's attitudes toward women should continue to be radically different from one industry to another, over a span of time sufficient for a complete turnover of the men in all the industries.

The point here is not to resolve issues involving women or minorities in the labor market. The point is to illustrate the difference between seeking systemic explanations of social phenomena and presupposing that subjective dispositions provide a sufficient causal explanation. A spectrum of subjective responses to any situation is virtually inevitable and these responses will almost invariably include both wise and foolish reactions, as well as reactions well articulated and clumsily expressed. Nothing would be easier, *on any issue*, than to seize upon foolish, malign, or confused statements or actions, in order to present a social problem as due to subjective dispositions which differ from the superior dispositions of the anointed. But, if causation is seen as systemic rather than dispositional, then the task is to discover the underlying reality behind the varied subjective expressions. Perceptions are like mirrors which reflect the real world with varying degrees of distortion, but proving distortion does not disprove the existence of a reality which cannot be talked away. . . .

The Preferences of the Anointed

The language of politics, and especially of ideological politics, is often categorical language about "rights," about *eliminating* certain evils, *guaranteeing* certain benefits, or *protecting* certain habitats and species. In short, it is the language of solutions and of the unconstrained vision behind solutions, the vision of the anointed. Indirectly but inexorably, this language says that the preferences of the anointed are to supersede the preferences of everyone else—that the particular dangers they fear are to be avoided at all costs and the particular benefits they seek are to be obtained at all costs. Their attempts to remove these decisions from both the democratic process and the market process, and to vest them in obscure commissions, unelected judges, and insulated bureaucracies, are in keeping with the logic of what they are attempting. They are not seeking trade-offs based on the varying preferences of millions of other people, but solutions based on their own presumably superior knowledge and virtue.

Notes

1. David L. Bazelon, *Questioning Authority: Justice and Criminal Law* (New York: Knopf, 1988), pp. 196–197.
2. Ibid., p. 295.
3. Adam Smith, *The Theory of Moral Sentiments* (Indianapolis: Liberty Classics, 1976), p. 170.
4. B. Bruce-Briggs, *The War Against the Automobile* (New York: E.P. Hutton, 1977), p. 125.
5. William Godwin, *Enquiry Concerning Political Justice and Its Influence on Morals and Happiness* (Toronto: University of Toronto Press, 1969), Vol. I, p. 276.
6. Ramsey Clark, *Crime in America: Observations on Its Nature, Causes, Prevention and Control* (New York: Simon & Schuster, 1970), p. 220.
7. Jean-François Revel, *The Flight from Truth: The Reign of Deceit in the Age of Information* (New York: Random House, 1991), p. 142.
8. John Stuart Mill, "Utilitarianism," *Collected Works of John Stuart Mill*, Vol. X: *Essays on Ethics, Religion and Society* (Toronto: University of Toronto Press, 1969), p. 215.
9. However, Mill's inconsistencies often had him contradicting his assertions with his provisos. See, for example, Thomas Sowell, *A Conflict of Visions* (New York: Morrow, 1987), pp. 111–112. For similar inconsistencies in Mill's discussions of technical economic issues, see Thomas Sowell, *Say's Law: An Historical Analysis* (Princeton, N.J.: Princeton University Press, 1972), Chapter 5.
10. John Stuart Mill, "Civilization," *Collected Works of John Stuart Mill*, Vol. XVIII: *Essays on Politics and Society* (Toronto: University of Toronto Press, 1977), p. 139.
11. John Stuart Mill, "De Tocqueville on Democracy in America [I]," ibid., p. 86.

12. John Stuart Mill, "Civilization," ibid., p. 128.
13. Oliver Wendell Holmes, Jr., *The Common Law* (Boston: Little, Brown, 1976), p. 2.
14. Edmund Burke, *Reflections on the Revolution in France* (London: J.M. Dent & Sons, Ltd., 1967), p. 93.
15. Ibid., p. 83.
16. Will and Ariel Durant, *The Lessons of History* (New York: Simon & Schuster, 1968), p. 101.
17. Ibid., p. 84.
18. Keith Michael Baker, editor, *Condorcet: Selected Writings* (Indianapolis: Bobbs-Merrill, 1976), pp. 87, 157.
19. F.A. Hayek, *Studies in Philosophy, Politics and Economics* (New York: Simon & Schuster, 1969), pp. 96–105; F.A. Hayek, *Law, Legislation and Liberty*, Vol. I (Chicago: University of Chicago Press, 1973), pp. 35–54.
20 Adam Smith, *The Wealth of Nations* (New York: Modern Library, 1937), pp. 128, 249–250, 460, 537.
21. Ibid., p. 423.

Systemic Racism Underlies All Inequality in the United States

by Doris Y. Wilkinson

Doris Y. Wilkinson is professor of sociology at the University of Kentucky in Lexington. She writes frequently on issues of race and race relations. In the following viewpoint, Wilkinson contends that all forms of inequality in America stem from the "ingrained, systemic, and pervasive" influence of race and racism. Other influences, such as gender and class discrimination, play a part in inequality, Wilkinson argues, but none outweigh the profound impact of racism. Unequal economic, occupational, residential, and health outcomes between whites and blacks all result from racial division and discrimination that pervades America's cultural and economic landscapes, she states.

"Despite the growing concern with diversity . . . race remains a principal determinant of social organization, affecting every aspect of employment, educational opportunity, health, and justice."

> *In every society there are at least two groups of people, besides the Negroes, who are characterized by high social visibility expressed in physical appearance, dress, and patterns of behavior, and who have been "suppressed." We refer to women and children. Their present status, as well as their history and their problems in society, reveal striking similarities to those of the Negroes. . . . It will, therefore, give perspective to the Negro problem and prevent faulty interpretations to*

37

*sketch some of the important similarities between the Negro problem
and the women's problem.*[1]

In the perceptive appendix to *An American Dilemma*, Gunnar Myrdal
clarified the meaning of "A Parallel to the Negro Problem." Concentrating on historical placement, status differentiation, and accompanying socially constructed attributes and behaviors, he interpreted what
"marked" Americans of African ancestry in the United States. He observed that their position in the country's racially framed stratification
system was analogous to that of free white women since both were under the control of a white male patriarchy. Taking into account the historically racialized social location and treatment of African slaves,
without making gender distinctions among them, Myrdal noted that the
ironic paternalistic conception of the slave as a family member "placed
him beside women and children. The parallel goes, however, considerably deeper than being only a structural part in the defense ideology
built up around slaves. Women [during the era of slavery] lacked a number of rights otherwise belonging to all free white citizens of full age."[2]
Emphasizing the social position of white women, Myrdal recognized at
the outset that

> a tremendous difference existed both in actual status of these
> different groups and in the tone of sentiment in the respective
> relations. In the decades before the Civil War, in the conservative and increasingly antiquarian ideology of the American
> South, woman was elevated as an ornament and looked upon
> with pride, while the Negro slave became increasingly a chattel
> and a ward. . . . [Yet,] from the very beginning, the fight in
> America for the liberation of the Negro slaves was, therefore,
> closely coordinated with the fight for women's emancipation.[3]

This essay will address aspects of this situation as applicable to the
present racialized political arena in which "black-white" relations remain significant and polarized. Despite the growing concern with diversity—with all that is implied by the contemporary multiculturalism
movement—race remains a principal determinant of social organization, affecting every aspect of employment, educational opportunity,
health, and justice.

The Paradoxes of Race in a Gendered Society

In these last decades of the twentieth century, both intellectual discourse
and academic scholarship are being greatly altered, indeed transformed,

through the introduction of feminist perspectives, with a gender-balanced view providing new interpretations of the structure of postindustrial society.[4] New and reconstructed theoretical paradigms, deriving from poststructuralism, hermeneutics, and postmodernism, are modifying the ways in which contemporary political, economic, and social realities are viewed. Where the humanities, the social sciences, and the natural sciences dwell increasingly on gender identities and emphasize the diverse conditions of oppression experienced by women, inequality in opportunity based on race tends to receive considerably less attention.

In academic discussions of inequality based on gender, considerable attention is given to women's traditional roles, the numerous workplace barriers that preclude upward mobility, and the disproportionately high male representation in many professional hierarchies, not least within the corporate world. Women are clearly underrepresented in the sciences; the "glass ceiling" restricts their movement into managerial positions in that domain and elsewhere. While there have been large changes in the labor force—in what women are now employed to do—and while housework is now seen, by some at least, as a form of employment, even if still uncompensated, there is increasing attention to problems created by sexual harassment in the workplace, conventional sexual stereotypes, and family violence, all adversely affecting the daily lives of women.[5]

In the contemporary, postmodern culture, gender is given a very considerable salience; social class and race are not thought to be equally important as determinants of inequality. Where individuality, perceptions of self-worth, and patterns of interaction are weighed so heavily, the social stratification based on racial distinctions and race-based animosities figures less prominently. Women, because of today's characteristic role stereotyping and the resulting gender imbalance in the work force, are reduced to subordinate places, and there is no denying this obvious fact.[6] Within academic and corporate settings, this inequality is constantly alluded to, and it is significant that such analysis is more commonly made by white female scholars and behavioral scientists than by those of African American descent or by their white male colleagues. In status ascription, identity, and group consciousness, gender description figures prominently. So long as race is not seen as the central element in defining the nation's opportunity structure, there can be no understanding of why the American race-based democracy continues to be confronted by the "dilemma" that Gunnar Myrdal so insightfully portrayed.

The salience of gendered differentiation in daily interaction and in the structure of society has contributed a meaningful dimension to intellectual dialogue and to scholarly descriptions and interpretations of status arrangements.[7] Examining the importance of gender has enabled a more functional explication of the beliefs and customs that frame our complex political culture. At the same time, translating the ingrained, systemic, and pervasive influence of race and racism in the country's institutions and ideologies permits greater understanding of the construction and perpetuation of all forms of inequality. Delineating race as the central element in opportunity and in status arrangements provides an explanation for the permanence of an "American dilemma" within a race-based democracy.[8]

Events of the early 1940s, in the years just before Myrdal's classic work, provide a context for examining the premises of this discussion. The examples which follow focus on the prominence of race and the relatively inconsequential impact of gender in the persistence of structural inequality. Neither gender nor class has been significantly deterministic in the historical patterns of racial exclusion, segregation, and discrimination experienced by African Americans.

The Structure of Race Relations in the 1940s

When Gunnar Myrdal, a Swedish economist and social activist, wrote *An American Dilemma*, the United States was confronting a rapid transformation of its political culture and system of stratification. The Depression had ended and World War II was nearing its final phases. What was observed then about a democratic nation facing a moral paradox over its treatment of former African slaves remains salient today. It is, therefore, instructive to reexamine Myrdal's work.

In 1944, Myrdal, Richard Sterner, and Arnold Rose wrote that "segregation is now becoming so complete that the white Southerner practically never sees a Negro except as his servant and in other standardized and formalized caste situations." Both ecological separation and racial distance were entrenched in the fabric of the nation's beliefs, values, and social class hierarchy. All housing, private and public, was segregated by custom and by law. In fact, the Federal Housing Administration assumed "the policy of segregation used by private institutions, like banks, mortgage companies, building and loan associations, and real estate companies." Myrdal commented on this dilemma: "It is one thing when private tenants, property owners, and financial institutions maintain and extend patterns of racial segregation in housing. It is quite another matter when a federal agency chooses to side with the segregationists."[9] Thus, interracial separation, spatial isolation, and all forms of ecological discrimination were among the myriad of racial restrictions confronting "the American Negro" and the country as a whole. Yet, the ideological dissonance Myrdal perceived as a phenomenon of white America was not a part of the oppressive circumstances or the cognitive understanding of the descendants of African slaves. Similarly, gender segregation was obliterated as an issue with equivalent meaning to the spatial and economic segregation and political disenfranchisement of Americans of African descent.

As the decade of the 1940s unfolded, an estimated 13 million Americans of African heritage were residing in the United States, representing 9.8 percent of the population. Most of the foreign-born Americans of African descent were from the West Indies. Although the descendants of former slaves and free persons were living in an evolving industrial country founded on democratic principles, their historical conditions, daily interactions, and life chances were vastly different from those of Euro-American men and women. As Myrdal observed, blacks and whites never encountered each other except in subordinated-superiorized role relationships.

Furthermore, there were no parallels in the social position of white women, slaves, or free blacks in the class system, nor were there parallels in their health status, and the conditions of oppression endured. Demographic data for 1940 show that a wider gap existed in life expectancy with regard to race than to gender. For example, life expectancy for white females was approximately 66.6 years, 62.1 years for white males, 54.9 years for African American females, and 51.5 years for African American or nonwhite males.[10] These comparative statistics, at that time as today, were empirical indicators of a major consequence of structural inequality based principally on a single ascriptive variable. Within racial categories today, significant variations persist in life expectancy. Life expectancy remains unequal for African American women and men, and throughout the 1940s infant and maternal mortality rates were predictably higher for nonwhites, most of whom were African American, than for whites. Racial inequality, not gender, is the foundation of these dissimilarities in life chances.

In spite of the organization of racial segregation in the country a half century ago, race and gender were systemic in the distribution of employment, privileges, and forms of opportunity throughout the North and the South. Data on the representation of African American workers among various types of occupations in the United States by region in 1940 vividly reveal the differential occupations and unequal economic situation of black men and women vis-a-vis white men and women. A disproportionate number of African American women worked in the service sector. Over one-half of employed black males were in nonfarm labor with the majority in unskilled jobs, service work, or in machine operative positions. In addition, the weight of race and gender in unemployment figures was relatively constant; throughout the decade, the unemployment rate for white males remained less than that for African American males. A wide racial gap also existed for women—unemployment rates for white women were much lower than those for black women. This racially determined gender inequity characterized employment in Northern industrial cities, in the Midwest, and in the South, where vast disparities in employment rates and occupational statuses prevailed.[11]

In addition, housing discrimination was also normative and schools were separate and unequal. Race, not gender, was the principal determinant of this legislated inequality. Patterns of exclusion and isolation in the lives of African American women were the complete opposite of those encountered by Euro-American women. Black and white families lived in racially divided communities in all parts of the country; they were segregated by physical and socially constructed barriers. This racial distance occurred even when historical dwelling units and housing patterns dictated that they live on the same street. Myrdal felt that this ecological reality crystallized the "American dilemma."

Following the Civil War and throughout the mid–twentieth century, racial customs and laws were interconnected in denying voting privileges, housing, and educational opportunities to African American families. Economic class was not the main component in the definitions of status, benefits, or advantages at any time between 1940 and 1970. Virtually not since slavery have economic class and gender affected where Americans of African ancestry would live, work, attend school, or worship. As previously noted, the Federal Housing Administration assented to the deliberate exclusion of "the Negro" from federal housing and even mandated the adoption of restrictive covenants for new housing based solely on race.[12] In addition, the Federal Housing Administration did not require that builders sell to African Americans.

Residential separation remains today. It is reinforced by lending institutions as well as real estate companies, and it is based on traditional customs and racial preferences. Gender is not a factor in housing discrimination based on race. While the masses of ethnic families in the United States live in ecologically distinct neighborhoods and communities, only African Americans remain spatially isolated and practically restricted to low income or predominantly black areas. Because of the variability in the amenities that accrue to those in particular residential communities, the salience of race linked to class transcends gender in interpretations of this form of inequality.

The economic conditions and health outcomes for African Americans just prior to and immediately following World War II and the Korean War negated the notion of a quandary in the consciousness of Euro-Americans. Merging with institutionalized, federally supported, and racially-based preferential treatment, the system of justice also stood squarely against the descendants of African slaves. For them, gender was not a basis for the inequities encountered in the administration of justice. Specifically, the death penalty was applied with greater frequency to blacks than to whites convicted of capital crimes. In the 1990s, this tacitly approved practice of the differential allocation of fairness under the law has been relatively unchanged.[13] Any regional variations in police behavior and in judicial outcomes merely show the pervasiveness of a race-based political culture.

The Primacy of Race in a Gendered Social Order

The primary sociodemographic forces underlying inequality in the United States and in many other parts of the world, especially South Africa and England, are race and class. In order to understand the interrelations among status arrangements, the nature of social inequality, and the dynamics of the culture, these two stratifying factors require explication. A racially framed economy creates nearly permanent disenfranchised and disempowered strata almost independently of the interactive effects of gender and class. Therefore, any discussion of gender and structural differentiation exclusive of race leaves a much greater void in our knowledge base and hence in our comprehension of racialized realities.

Today gender is recognized as a crucial variable in the mapping of life experiences. Nonetheless, it is understandable why sex and gender discrimination were not examined extensively at the time *An American Dilemma* was written. The changing status of women and the gendering of society had not progressed as critical aspects of the transformation of American social organization and culture. At the same time, sexism has prevailed as an ideological force that has affected our values, beliefs, politics, the economy, the health sector, and other institutions. Given our country's multifaceted heritage, race has always been a far more fundamental basis of placement and intergroup exchange than has gender. Since Myrdal's analysis, economic class has emerged as a highly complex multidimensional variable and is somewhat more difficult to extricate from its interdependency with race.[14]

A half century after *An American Dilemma* and the *Brown v. Board of Education of Topeka, Kansas* decision, racial division continues to produce unequal economic, occupational, residential, and health outcomes be-

43

tween whites and blacks, as documented in labor force participation rates and health statistics for African American and Euro-American women between 1890 and 1960. This period spanned unparalleled changes in the country's political economy from one of slave-driven agricultural production and eventually complete racial exclusion, or "Jim Crowism," to an industrial order permeated by slowly evolving quasi-integration.

With rapid industrial growth and the diversification of the society, structural inequality evolved along gender and racial lines. Non-gender-specific placement characterized the employment of Americans of African descent. Their restricted occupational outlets gave rise to a "secondary labor market." The original source for this employment discrimination was slavery. Racism provided the ideological justification for restricting opportunities and stratifying labor on the basis of race.

> The institution of slavery in the United States set apart the work and employment privileges of African American males and females from those of European heritage. . . . In the process of equalizing the positions of African American men and women, enslavement embedded in the organization of work a virtually permanent caste-like component up to the mid–twentieth century. By establishing and legally validating rigid separation between the races, the institution generated vastly disparate ranking in the class system. Thus, it was inevitable that the descendants of slaves would inherit this structural pattern.[15]

While political and economic inequities mirror sex differences and gender roles, and while these link with class placement in the framing of U.S. culture, racial ascription is far more pervasive in its impact, extent, intensity, historical meaning, and durability. Reflecting on Myrdal's thinking, the issue of class position does raise perplexing questions. However, the United States is guided in its customs, status hierarchies, beliefs, and normative domain by class domination intertwined with the injurious ideologies of racism and sexism. Whenever race is a part of the mosaic, it outweighs all other potential influences.

Racial Oppression in the 1990s and Beyond

The *Brown* decision of 1954 recast the structural paradoxes surrounding education in the United States. Following that historic decision, the latent puzzles and concealed passions of race began to surface. Gender identity and sexual orientation were not at the forefront of the African American quest. Their central preoccupations were with the elimination

44

of housing discrimination and restrictive covenants, access to quality health care, walking the streets without fear of police or other group harassment, the right to serve on juries and to receive justice in the courts, being treated with respect and dignity, being able to work, having voting privileges, and having the chance to secure an education, including having quality schools for their children.

Regardless of socioeconomic status and gender identity, segregation, discrimination, and restricted access have delimited the life experiences of all African Americans since the founding of the country and throughout most of the twentieth century. As shifts in the social class structure began to occur in the 1960s, African Americans who were successful or educated were seen as the enemies of the lower classes and of all "politically correct thinking" blacks. The notion was also propagated that Jews were the enemies of blacks, even though they had helped to build schools, had supported the NAACP, had participated in other Civil Rights organizations, and had marched alongside them in their struggle for freedom and equal protection under the Constitution.

In this century, race is the foundation of inequality for African Americans in all phases of life. White men and women in any social stratum, regardless of education, skills, ideological convictions, ethnic affiliations, gender, or sexual orientation, are aware that American society favors them over all African Americans. An example involving a Southern university in the 1990s will clarify this point. In one nonacademic unit of the university, all of the supervisors, secretaries, and mid-level managers are white. Not one has a college degree. The "runners"—those who run back and forth across the campus to pick up the mail—are often black men with college degrees. In this unit, when a college educated African American female data entry clerk wanted to take some college classes, rules were passed stipulating that one could no longer take extensive breaks or enroll in more than one course. This attempt to prohibit a black female from continuing her education is an example of institutionalized racism. And yet, this practice is sanctioned at all levels of the division's administrative hierarchy.

Awareness of privilege associated with socially constructed status is a major dimension of group affiliation and shared behaviors. Independent of educational achievements and economic class, poor white men and women know that the entire social system treats them preferentially over blacks. Middle-class white males and females are aware that judges, lawyers, health professionals, Congress, legislators at local and state levels, and college and university administrators of predominantly white colleges and universities, among others, support and uphold their rights above all Americans of African descent. Being white in America, regardless of gender, means being supported over Black Americans in all actions by "the system." This "system," anchored in the nation's cultural matrix, is an interlocking directorate and hierarchy dominated and controlled by men of one race. Myrdal and his associates recognized this phenomenon.

Gender contributes significantly to social inequalities. However, the United States is racially organized and hence its class structure is racially designed. White racism, along with class oppression and sexism, pervades the boundaries of the culture. Throughout this country's history and ensuing political economy, the extensiveness and permanence of the ideology of racism has been sustained. Recently, African American heterosexual women have been targeted as being the carriers, perpetrators, and/or victims of the acquired immune deficiency syndrome (AIDS). This politically contrived racist stereotyping will inevitably affect the life chances, family functioning, employment options, and the entire future of African Americans. The direct link between race, not gender, and social inferiorization is evident in this politicization of a world-wide health crisis. The shift in categorization of a disease that was disproportionately concentrated among homosexual men to heterosexual black females negates all logic. This attempt to reconstruct the origins and victims of the current pandemic clearly demonstrates the profound impact of race over gender *and* class in the United States.

We live in a social system where race endures as a politically charged attribute and where racism is a paramount belief configuration that reinforces a particular form of status domination and economic oppression. The ideology of racism determines, legitimizes, and reinforces the interlocking character of the race-class-gender triad. Myrdal was too early in his interpretations and descriptions to grasp this fundamental reality.

Notes

1. Gunnar Myrdal, *An American Dilemma: The Negro Problem and Modern Democracy* (New York: Harper & Brothers, 1944), 1073.
2. Ibid.
3. Ibid.
4. Doris Wilkinson, Maxine Baca Zinn, and Esther Chow, eds., "Race, Class and Gender," *Gender and Society* 6 (September 1992).
5. Paula S. Rothenberg, ed., *Race, Class and Gender in the United States: An Integrated Study*, 2d ed. (New York: St. Martin's Press, 1992).
6. Ibid.
7. Marietta Morrissey, *Slave Women in the New World: Gender Stratification in the Caribbean* (Lawrence, Kans.: University Press of Kansas, 1989).
8. Frances Beale, "Double Jeopardy: To Be Black and Female," in Toni Cade,

ed., *The Black Woman: An Anthology* (New York: New American Library, 1970), 190. Jacquelyne Jackson, "A Critique of Lerner's Work on Black Women and Further Thoughts," *Journal of Social and Behavioral Sciences* 21 (Winter 1975): 63–89. Deborah K. King, "Multiple Jeopardies, Multiple Consciousness: The Context of a Black Feminist Ideology," *Signs: Journal of Women in Culture and Society* 14 (1988): 42–72.

9. Myrdal, *An American Dilemma*, 349–50. James E. Blackwell, *The Black Community: Diversity and Unity* (New York: Harper & Row, 1985).

10. Peter M. Bergman and Mort N. Bergman, *The Chronological History of the Negro in America* (New York: Harper & Row, 1969), 486–93.

11. Doris Wilkinson, "The Segmented Labor Market and African American Women from 1890–1960: A Social History Interpretation," *Race and Ethnic Relations* 6 (1991): 85–104.

12. Blackwell, *The Black Community*, 151–52.

13. Thomas J. Keil and Gennaro F. Vito, "Race and the Death Penalty in Kentucky Murder Trials: 1976–1991: A Study of Racial Bias as a Factor in Capital Sentencing," paper presented at the "Variations in Capital Punishment" panel, Academy of Criminal Justice Science, Chicago, Ill., 11 March 1994. Raymond Paternoster, "Prosecutorial Discretion in Requesting the Death Penalty: A Case of Victim-Based Racial Discrimination," *Law and Society Review* 18 (1984): 437–78. M. Dwayne Smith, "Patterns of Discrimination in Assessments of the Death Penalty: The Case of Louisiana," *Journal of Criminal Justice* 15 (1987): 279–86.

14. William J. Wilson, *The Declining Significance of Race* (Chicago, Ill.: University of Chicago Press, 1978).

15. Wilkinson, "The Segmented Labor Market and African American Women from 1890–1960," 88. See also Elizabeth Ross Haynes, "Negroes in Domestic Service in the United States," *Journal of Negro History* 8 (October 1928): 389–421.

From Doris Wilkinson, "Gender and Social Inequality: The Prevailing Significance of Race," reprinted, with permission, from *An American Dilemma Revisited: Race Relations in a Changing World*, edited by Obie Clayton Jr.; © 1996 Russell Sage Foundation, New York.

Racism Is Not Always the Cause of Inequality

by William A. Henry III

Before his death in June 1994, William A. Henry III was a culture critic for *Time* magazine. His writing earned two Pulitzer Prizes, one for criticism and one for coverage of school desegregation in Boston. In the following viewpoint, Henry argues that racism unarguably played a historic role in preventing blacks from enjoying economic advancement. However, racism cannot still be blamed for all inequalities, he contends. Efforts to achieve an equal stake in contemporary life are hampered more by continued identification of blacks as a single category and by ameliorative mechanisms that enshrine the notion of inequality than by America's racist past. Henry argues that equality will result only when blacks are allowed to rise or fall as individuals, achieving success or experiencing failure as a result of individual performance rather than group identity.

"Without resolving whether racial prejudice is still holding blacks down or whether preference quotas are buoying them up . . . or whether any one person's talent is equal to his appointed task, we can say that . . . the real problem has less to do with race than with the culture of poverty."

The most basic fact of American life is this: Sometime within the next fifty or so years, non-Hispanic white people will become demographically just another minority group. They will be collectively outnumbered by Hispanics of all races, blacks, Asians, Indians (in both vernacular meanings), and assorted other ethnic groups not associated with western Europe. Within the work force, this shift to a no-majority America will happen substantially sooner. Whites already tend to be older than other ethnic groups and to reproduce less prolifically. Moreover, immigration, legal and otherwise, is bringing in a disproportionate share of Hispanics and nonwhites. Among the school age population, the new America is already showing itself. By 1990, non-Hispanic whites accounted for less than half of public school enrollment, grades kindergarten through twelve, in the entire state of California. The same will be true in New York State a few years hence, with Texas and Florida, among other places, poised to follow soon after.

This ethnic evolution provides the underlying significance to the national debate over multiculturalism. The pressure for change in how America defines itself is philosophical and ideological, but it is above all political in the most basic way. The new arrivals at the table want to reslice the pie. While some opponents of the new order are genuinely concerned with the preservation of intellectual traditions and competitive values, many others are symbolically protesting the change in America's face and character. They want to ensure the longevity of a nation resembling the one they grew up in. To them, fuss and feathers about the place of Plato in the syllabuses of the better colleges is all well and good for getting the adrenaline racing in the bloodstream of traditionalists. They see sincere reasons to protest the manipulation of the elementary and secondary school curriculum. They do not wish to celebrate primitive cultures or to castigate the leadership cadres of the past for brutalities wholly normal for those times.

Ethnic Anxiety

But they also feel an ethnic anxiety uncomfortably close to racism. During the later 1970s, evangelist-politician Pat Robertson built a following for his *The 700 Club* that eventually launched him into a 1988 presidential campaign and ongoing political manipulations far afield of his Virginia headquarters. (For example, he put up a slate of endorsed candidates during New York City's 1993 school board elections and, appallingly, got quite a few of them elected.) While Robertson tends to speak in more discreet code language now, in earlier days he preached that a vital reason to oppose abortion was racial power. In the absence of sufficient white fecundity, he warned on air, within a couple of generations the majority of the United States population would derive from Asia, Africa, and Latin America and would "lack our Anglo-Saxon heritage and values." Many of his loyal constituents heard rhetoric like that back then and are still hearing it in their mind's ears now.

Robertson is not, alas, a lone nut preaching in the wilderness. When I wrote a 1990 cover story for *Time* laying out the demographic facts of the American future and sketching some of the implications—illustrated by a cover image of the American flag in browns and yellows, emblazoned with the words "America's changing colors"—readers sent in more than a thousand letters. About half were fiercely disapproving. They divided more or less equally between people who favored this change in America but feared that we would slow it by calling attention to it and people who opposed the change and worried that we would legitimize it by paying it notice. The latter group included not a few who implied that a nonwhite America could not be a "real" America. The two sides agreed on nothing except the worrisome preference for silence over open debate—and, of course, the inescapable notion that a multiracial America will be very different from a white-dominated one.

Plenty of nonracists, like Arthur Schlesinger, Jr., as quoted above, are fretful over the impact of the ethnic evolution. They recognize that a different racial identity will to a considerable degree redefine the nation's future. At the core of the many battles over multiculturalism is the deeper and emotionally more explosive reality that racial change is already redefining the nation's past. Traditional judgments about what America has meant to its own people and to the world get radically altered when someone new does the interpreting, from a different perspective and often with a chip on the shoulder. Historians and cultural scholars who see the American experience as the world's most successful experiment in governance and creativity are being jostled aside by those with a grudge against the past and present. Some are feminists, some are gay liberationists, and not a few are unregenerate Marxists who refuse to regard the breakup of the Soviet empire as any kind of definitive judgment on the intellectual bankruptcy of socialist egalitarianism.

Supplanting American Values

The most potent threats, however, come from thinkers with a racial agenda. Women's rights and gay rights can be integrated within the American mainstream, and to an astonishing degree already have been. Racial scholars, however, often seek not to expand traditional American values but to supplant them. . . .

American multiculturalism of the present day embraces six basic elements that impinge to varying degrees on elitism. First is the unexamined notion that "fair" competition would automatically result in demographically proportional sharing of society's rewards, and that any deviation from such sharing is ipso facto proof of unfairness. Second is the notion of the equivalency of cultures. Third is a generalized skepticism toward, if not outright rejection of, the European heritage respon-

50

sible for most of mankind's freedom and medical and material progress. Fourth is a disbelief in the value of linguistic standardization, and thus a validation both of the multigenerational preservation of Spanish as the primary tongue in growing parts of this country and also of the glorification of substandard, subliterate speech as authentic dialect or idiom ("black English"). Fifth is the wicked idea that drug dealing, gang crime, violence, and retreat from schools and learning should be regarded as natural, sensible, valid responses among the urban poor to the difficulty of their situation. Sixth is the sickeningly prevalent notion among young urban blacks that speaking standard English, getting good grades in school, and succeeding amounts to "acting white"—an equation of blackness with ignorant failure that is more racially suppressive than anything ever spoken by the Ku Klux Klan.

As this list above implies, the troublesome aspect of multiculturalism is not the opening of "our Anglo-Saxon heritage and values" to the recognition of other achievements. It is the systematic validation of black failure and Hispanic racial isolation, accompanied by a rationale that forbids polite society from labeling those things as what they are. . . .

Blame and Injustice

The basic political aim of much multicultural scholarship is to explain away the lack of success of groups designated (in the case of blacks, with undeniable validity) as victims. However artful and diverting the phrasing, the purpose is to blame their failure on the people who have succeeded, turning that success from a legitimate source of pride into proof positive of blame. Underlying this effort is an unexamined assumption that talent is distributed absolutely evenly across lines of class, race, and gender and that differences in performance reflect only differences in opportunity, not differences in ability. . . .

Most of the past two decades of civil rights litigation have depended on the assumption that unequal results in the allocation of society's goodies automatically prove that the process for allotting them is unjust. If researchers demonstrated that racial or gender differences exist (I personally suspect they don't, but who really knows?), that rationale would obviously be invalidated. What would be the next step? To adjust the quotas downward by some debatable percentage? To throw them out altogether? To create some vast improvement scheme for minorities and women (or for white men, if it turns out they are the weaker performers)? Or perhaps, in keeping with the egalitarian spirit of our age, to declare that ability is not the prime criterion for employment anyway?

Without resolving whether racial prejudice is still holding blacks down or whether preference quotas are buoying them up—both are probably true, sometimes for the same individual—or whether any one person's talent is equal to his appointed task, we can say that a closer analysis of black economic experience suggests that the real problem has less to do with race than with the culture of poverty. In *Paved With Good Intentions: The Failure of Race Relations in Contemporary America*, Jared Taylor reports on economic research demonstrating that blacks and whites "who grew up under the same circumstances and went on to get similar educations show no difference in their average incomes." Among others, Taylor cites black scholar Walter Williams of George Mason University, who says that data about the comparable earnings of black and white women college graduates are "one of the best-kept secrets of all times and virtually totally ignored in the literature on racial differences." Taylor quotes Thomas Sowell, a black economist at the Hoover Institution, who says, "There is a positive hostility to analyses of black success if they suggest that racism may not be the cause of black failure." Taylor notes that while the black population doubled between 1950 and 1990, the number of black white-collar workers went up ninefold. He adds: "The number of blacks that are 'affluent' (earning more than $50,000 in inflation-adjusted dollars) went from one in seventeen in 1967 to one in seven in 1989." Of course many of these statistics reflect broader social trends in the United States; nonetheless, blacks were able to share in those improvements.

Troublingly, even as economic statistics demonstrate that things are getting better for black Americans, the black perception is that things are getting worse. In a May 1994 survey of more than a thousand blacks by Michael Dawson, a political science professor at the University of Chicago, some sixty-five percent said they did not expect racial equality to come within their lifetimes, and twenty-two percent say they did not expect it to come ever. Dawson found "a more radical black America than existed even five years ago," with burgeoning support for black nationalism or separatism. Sixty-two percent favored the creation of all-male public schools for blacks, sixty-eight percent favored black control of government in majority-black areas, seventy-four percent called for black economic control in those areas, and eighty-one percent said blacks deserved a better chance legally, socially, and economically. Those sentiments were most pronounced among the young and poor, who appear to have given up hope of mainstream advancement.

At a deeper level, these blacks who do not participate in this economic rise may indeed be deemed victims of racism, for it surely played a major role in immersing them in the ghetto and poverty culture from which they find it so difficult to escape. But only historically is the underclass a product of racism; now it is the underclass primarily because it is culturally imprinted with the failings of the underclass.

Dispelling Assumptions of Black Inferiority

The programs devised to deal with this grim reality generally do so by taking on the rather easier business of advancing privileged, middle-class blacks into the upper echelons of the mainstream. The most conspicuous have to do with college and graduate school admission, for which a dual standard exists virtually everywhere. Taylor reports that in most years, blacks who are admitted to medical school have lower average scores than whites who are rejected. The situation is almost as extreme in law schools. At the University of Texas, for example, white applicants generally need scores of approximately the ninety-second percentile on the nationally administered Law School Aptitude Test, while blacks scoring as low as the fifty-fifth percentile get in.

In the arts and sciences, the recruitment situation is especially dire. In 1986, Taylor notes, of some eight thousand doctorates awarded in the physical sciences and engineering, only thirty-nine went to blacks. Indeed, in that year there were only 820 doctorates awarded to blacks altogether. Half were in education, and there were none whatsoever in geology, aerospace engineering, astronomy, geometry, astrophysics, theoretical chemistry, European history, architecture, Russian, Spanish, German, or the classics. No wonder that so many academic departments fail to meet their affirmative action quotas.

The natural response to such troubling statistics is to redouble efforts to recruit black students into the top tier. But the Hoover Institution's Sowell says that may be self-defeating. Noting that two thirds of blacks at the University of California at Berkeley fail to graduate—including many who might have prospered at less competitive schools—Sowell urges that schools apply uniform admissions standards and let black students settle in at whatever level is comfortable. This would presumably increase their individual contentment and their collective rate of success. Says Sowell: "The issue is not whether minority students are 'qualified' to be in college, law schools, etc., but whether they are systematically mismatched with the particular institutions they are attending." A better match of circumstances would benefit not only them but white society as well. The best way to dispel assumptions of black inferiority is to observe black success firsthand. Watching an affirmative action beneficiary struggle to (not quite) keep up has the opposite effect.

Affirmative Action and Mediocrity

In theory, as opposed to often ham-handed practice, affirmative action is not anti-elitist. It presupposes that blacks and whites are equally talented but unequally treated due to racism present and past. Its promoters even promise that on some future (and increasingly distant) day, the program will die away for lack of need. In truth, it is likely to die away whether or not blacks catch up in performance, because other racial and ethnic groups who do not share in white guilt are bound to be less and less willing to see blacks given a built-in advantage. Already blacks are less than half of the total minority population. Early in the next century, if it has not happened already, they will be bypassed by Hispanics as the largest single minority group. This is already true in cities such as Miami, Los Angeles, and New York, where the burgeoning Hispanic populations are demanding their proportional share. "It's the ultimate nightmare of affirmative action," says Ricky Gaull Silberman, vice chair of the federal Equal Employment Opportunities Commission, as quoted in a January 1994 report from the Newhouse News Service. "It is the Achilles' heel." Mamie Grant, who heads the organization representing black city workers in Los Angeles, protests about Hispanics: "They're trying to siphon off all our gains." Her counterpart in representing black workers countywide, Clyde Johnson, correctly says, "When you think of affirmative action, you think of black and white. All the laws were really directed specifically at eliminating patterns of discrimination against blacks." He adds with some bitterness, "All the others are latecomers and bandwagon jumpers." But as Latino activist Xavier Hermosilla of Los Angeles is quoted as saying, "They shall overcome. We shall *overwhelm*."

For now, however, affirmative action is alive and well, and its operation is profoundly anti-elitist, not just against white candidates who lose out, but against the ablest blacks. The practical effect of affirmative action is to give places to mediocrities while causing white (and, for that matter, nonwhite) colleagues to view with suspicion the talents and credentials of all blacks newly given authority. . . .

The Measure of a Just Society

In truth, not very many sophisticated employers will be unaware of the double standard. They know full well that credentials of minority alumni may come with an invisible asterisk denoting the dual set of rules. So who is most apt to be victimized? Again, the minority candidate who could make it on a level playing field but whose accomplishments are initially, and perhaps always, suspect. That is the double bind of affirmative action. It begins with a presumption that all groups are equal, so their results in life should be equal. It then employs ameliorative mechanisms that end by enshrining the notion that the groups are

54

not equal and probably never will be. As applied to the upper intellectual reaches of society, affirmative action is an idea that subverts its own aims.

Indeed there is now a sizable body of thought, not all of it conservative or white, that questions the wisdom of continuing affirmative action unchanged. . . .

[I]n a society sans affirmative action, somewhat fewer blacks than whites would go to college, fewer would become lawyers or doctors, fewer would run large corporations. Would it matter? Arguably not, as long as everyone who is qualified has a chance and more than a few minority candidates actually continue to make it. America's doors will never again be closed to blacks. Perhaps it is time to stop thinking of blacks—and having them think of themselves—as a category. Let them rise or fall as individuals. That would be, in the moral and metaphysical sense, an affirmative action. The measure of a just society is not whether a demographically proportional share of any group succeeds, but whether any individual of talent can succeed regardless of what group he belongs to. If all groups seek to belong to an elite, let us have an elite based once again on elitism.

A Flight from Reality

The second great multicultural threat to elitism, the notion of the interchangeability or at least comparability of cultures, has roots closely related to affirmative action. Quotas are meant to guide blacks to equality in the present. Multicultural theory is meant to give them a sense of equality about their past. This is often a flight from reality, no more valid for being wholly understandable. If Africa was indeed the womb of civilization, as many Afrocentric scholars assert, it certainly has not been so for a thousand years, maybe twice that long. And when it was a true world power, in the heyday of pharaonic Egypt, the peak creativity arose in a civilization far removed in place as well as time from the ancestral lands of most American blacks. It is unlikely that Egyptians did, as many Afrocentrists claim, master glided flight or invent electrical batteries and electroplating or discover the principles of quantum mechanics, Darwinian evolution, gravity, and the wave-particle duality of light. Even if they did, how does that ennoble sub-Saharan black Africans? They were not Egyptian rulers. They were subjugated people, in the United States, in Latin America, in the Caribbean, in Europe. Even more painfully for blacks who see Islam as their appropriate religion, Africans were a subjugated people in Arabia. Some Africans were trapped by slavers because they were not quick enough or cunning enough to get away. Some were sold into slavery by fellow blacks, either marauding native tribes or on occasion their own kinsmen. Slavery was a moral blot on its white perpetrators. It was a blot on many black tribes as well.

As for African cultural achievements, they are real enough. Anyone who has visited the splendid (if ill-maintained) African art collection in the museum in Dakar, capital of Senegal, or surveyed the Benin bronzes at the Smithsonian in Washington can perceive the beauty, craftsmanship, and sophistication of African art. Like most great art of the past, it found its inspiration in religion, which is natural enough—religion, like art, is based on metaphor. The great pyramids of ancient Zimbabwe bespeak both an esthetic vision and an ambitious and enduring empire. The long and arduous trade routes of ancient Africans, along trails that daunted Burton, Livingstone, and other European explorers, are evidence of social organization and economic awareness. In politics and warfare, tales of empire abound. The Zulus were sufficiently disciplined and shrewd to fight English forces in South Africa to a virtual standstill.

All this is of value to anyone interested in the making of the modern world. So are more contemporary studies of tribal political organization, trade routes, nomadic ecology, and the subtleties of rhythm structure in African music. Indeed, in a perverse way there is something to be gained in studying why so many African women willingly, even eagerly, continue to submit their daughters to the horrific mutilation of the clitoris and vulva euphemized as "female circumcision." Without joining the appalling number of Afrocentrist scholars who try to defend this as indigenous tradition, one can recognize that here is a way of coming to grips with a truly alien world.

But that does not mean that studying African culture is any kind of substitute for studying Euro-American culture, even for American children of African descent. . . .

Individual Performance Versus Group Identity

No reasonable person can argue that African culture was materially superior to European; the reasons range from enslavement to illiteracy. But that does not make Americans of African descent inferior to Americans of European or any other descent. The error is in looking for a group basis, a categorical basis, for pride. One's worth and self-regard ought to come from individual competitive performance, not from group identity. Pride based on clan or tribal connections is atavistic. It appeals to people who fear they cannot succeed as individuals, and by diverting their energies it all but ensures that they *will* not succeed as individuals. . . .

Perhaps it is unfair to blame on multicultural scholars a range of behavior that some of them would likely discourage. Their aim, after all, is to call attention to black achievements, real or asserted. Some of them doubtless feel they are promoting a kind of elitism, too, albeit in a different context. Yet when all is said and done, the answer to black, Hispanic, or any other sense of exclusion from the mainstream must be to bolster boldness and self-confidence, not to concoct alternative scholarship or install alternative institutions. America has many races. It needs only one culture, the more inclusive the better.

From *In Defense of Elitism* by William A. Henry III. Copyright © 1994 by William A. Henry III. Used by permission of Doubleday, a division of Bantam Doubleday Dell Publishing Group, Inc.

Equality Is Incompatible with a Free Society

by Llewellyn H. Rockwell Jr.

Llewellyn H. Rockwell Jr. is president of the Ludwig von Mises Institute, an educational organization that stresses a free market economy and private property rights. In the following viewpoint, Rockwell argues that liberty and equality cannot coexist because one always comes at the expense of the other. All attempts to impose equality of result or opportunity, he argues, destroy individual liberty. Government efforts to forbid discrimination, for example, only create other forms of discrimination and ultimately violate the freedom of association. Rockwell argues that efforts to force equality "endanger the foundation of capitalism and civilization itself."

"The free market offers not an unstratified society, but something of real value: liberty itself."

The Fabian Society of Britain believed in three central doctrines of political economy. First, every country must create its own form of socialism. Second, socialism imposed slowly is more permanent than the revolutionary form. And third, socialism is not likely to succeed in Western countries if it appears undemocratic or authoritarian. On all these points, the Fabian Marxists disagreed with Marxist-Leninists.

And just as the Fabians recommended, today's America is under the spell of a peculiar form of socialism, designed for our political and demographic conditions.

Under Fabian influence, Britain's piecemeal socialism was marked by nationalized industries, soft planning, extreme labor union privileges, middle-class income redistribution, and a government-run medical industry.

Here in the United States, on the other hand, we have little reason to fear nationalized industries or comprehensive planning. Labor union power seems to be on the decline. Americans bristle at any hint of direct controls over production decisions. Our semi-socialized medicine resists change toward greater government control, or less, with the conservative Republican leadership dedicated to "saving" Medicare. But our labor markets, though increasingly devoid of direct union control, are more frozen and regulated than Britain's were at the height of union power.

Socialism, U.S. Style

What accounts for this? American socialism is a carefully tailored product. First, it is designed to fit with America's excessive devotion to abstractions like democracy and equality. Second, it is designed to exploit the radical heterogeneity of our population. Third, its implementation relies on America's traditionally sanguine view of centralized executive power.

We could argue about when American socialism first took root. Many say it began with the Great Society. Others trace it to the New Deal. There's a good case to be made that it began in the Lincoln presidency and the Reconstruction era, which used the language of democracy and egalitarianism, exploited our radical heterogeneity, and dramatically centralized power in an imperial executive. That period also provided a test run for inflationary monetary policy and income taxation, two institutions that the Progressive Era entrenched and which provide the fuel for American socialism today.

The symptoms of American socialism are easy to identify. They appear in legislation like the Americans with Disabilities Act [ADA], the limitless amendments to the Civil Rights Acts, the Community Reinvestment Act, in the egregious behavior of the Equal Employment Opportunity Commission [EEOC], and in all manner of interference with the freedom of association. In addition, executive-branch agencies issue tens of thousands of regulations each year to manage the private lives of citizens and the conduct of private business, including the Department of Housing and Urban Development [HUD], the banking regulators at the Federal Reserve, and the bureaucrats at the EEOC.

The result has been tyranny. Civil rights lawsuits have shut down thousands of businesses. Many potential capitalists decide not to open businesses at all for fear of the race, sex, and disability police. Small companies routinely do anything within the law to avoid advertising for new positions. Why? Because government now sends out "testers" to entrap business in the crime of hiring the most qualified person for a job. Pity the poor real estate agent and the owner of rental units, who walk the civil rights minefield every day. If any of these people demonstrate more loyalty to the customers than to the government, they risk bringing their businesses to financial ruin.

The restaurants Denny's and Shoney's, two wonderful examples of capitalism in action, know all about this. In the last few years, they were both hit with class action suits alleging discrimination. It didn't matter that the plaintiffs were all trumped up and the specific cases cited were patently fraudulent. For example, one plaintiff found a foreign object in her hashbrowns and claimed it was put there on grounds of her race. Both companies decided to settle out of court, establish extensive quota programs, pay off all plaintiffs, and set up new highly subsidized, minority-owned franchises. They did so not because they were guilty, but because the so-called justice system is stacked against them.

Denying the Obvious

The courts enforce an egalitarianism that tolerates no acknowledgment of the differences among people, especially not when they express themselves along group lines. But this denies the obvious. People do differ radically in their talents and weaknesses, their determinations to succeed, their mental facilities, their attitudes and character, their physical abilities, and their physical makeup. Moreover, these differences appear not only in individuals but also systematically in groups.

Men as a group, for example, are different from women as a group. Northerners are different from Southerners. Californians are different from Texans. Catholics are different from Baptists. Blacks are different from whites. Immigrants are different from natives. The rich are different from the poor. The evidence for these propositions is all around us and should be celebrated. As Ludwig von Mises pointed out, radical *in*equality is the key fact about the human race, and thank goodness. If we were all the same, there could be no division of labor.

Yet our central government attempts to abolish these differences by forcing individuals and businesses to act as if they did not exist. The primary means has been the criminalization of our most serious secular sin: discrimination. There can be no action in American life—save the decision of whom to marry—that discriminates on the grounds of any number of criteria as defined by the government. If anyone commits this sin, the penalty is cash to the government and the special interests, with a bundle going to the left-wing lawyers who arrange the transfer.

To see just how serious the government takes this sin, and how ab-

surd the result, consider disabilities law. The EEOC has effectively defined disability as any physical or mental limitation. Along with other
civil rights laws, this robs business of any operational discretion in the
treatment of employees, how much they are paid, if they are promoted,
or whether they are hired at all.

If you have hired a salesman who can't remember names, he's got a
mental disability. You cannot demote him, much less fire him, because
that would be discrimination.

Since the ADA went into effect, tens of thousands of complaints,
which are threatened lawsuits, have been filed with the Equal Employment Opportunity Commission. Drunkards are suing for their right not
to show up to work and still get paid. Students are suing for their right
not to study and take tests. The government is siding with every con-
ceivable complaint, from men who want to work as waitresses in restaurants with all-women workforces to people in wheelchairs who want to
dance on stage.

The number of private complaints against employers in which no
suits are filed but result in settlements would be impossible to count.
The amount of lost wealth is vast and growing. With the ADA, there is
eventually no way to comply, because there is no way to prepare for
every possible contingency, every possible lawsuit or government ploy.

The Myth of the Level Playing Field

The ADA illustrates an important point about anti-discrimination law,
the central pillar of American socialism. Contrary to myth, rules against
discrimination never create a level playing field. Forbidding one form of
discrimination must necessarily compel another. If a person is forbidden
to discriminate in hiring on grounds of sex or race, the government can
only discover a violation of the law by looking at who is hired. This
compels active discrimination *against* people on grounds of their sex or
race. It is a zero-sum game where one person's winnings come from another's losses. The only way to end this is through the repeal of all anti-
discrimination laws, and all other laws that violate the freedom of
association.

Until that happens, whole institutions are being destroyed in the
name of stamping out discrimination. The banking sector has been
racked by complaints that it discriminates against minorities in its grant-
ing of loans. You might think the regulators would consider that minorities have relatively weaker credit ratings and fewer assets. In fact,
that doesn't matter, since the executive agencies enforcing equality care
only for the numbers.

In the banking sector, tens of billions have been doled out to satisfy interest groups who cry discrimination. Fleet Financial Group surrendered to an extortionist who used complaints of group victimology. Decatur Savings & Loan in Atlanta was put out of business by a federal lawsuit. Sovran Bank had to buy its right to become Nationsbank by handing out welfare checks to the politically correct.

Danger of Limiting Rights and Privileges

This campaign has only just begun. Some people on the political left propose an explicit quota program for lending, which would effectively require banks to give loans to minorities regardless of credit history, job history, or assets. The pool of loanable funds has become a convenient substitute for direct welfare benefits, and it's just as redistributionary.

The same is true in other sectors of the economy. Consider two recent government housing programs: Moving to Opportunity, which is administered by HUD, and residential integration, which is administered by the Justice Department. In both cases, the government has declared that all voluntary group associations resulting in racial disproportionalities are segregationist by definition. That term no longer refers to *de jure* action but to the *de facto* results of voluntary behavior. To remedy the non-problem that people tend to group themselves by their similarities, HUD has a program to give minorities in city slums the financial means to move to middle-class suburbs.

An incident in Vidor, Texas, illustrates something about the use of force. The Justice Department and HUD orchestrated a propaganda blitz against this insular and peaceful community, painting it as thoroughly racist. This paved the way for federal marshals to install some new minority residents into a housing complex whose residents wanted to be left alone. And this is representative of what is happening to every business in the country.

In many respects, a firm is much like a community. It has its own internal culture that best develops and thrives in the context of liberty. Whether the federal bureaucrats are invading Denny's, Decatur Savings & Loan, or Vidor, the effect is the same: to snuff the very life out of the business world and the communities around the country.

The media and the government imply that because one firm hasn't hired and promoted a member of every politically represented group then no firm is going to. This reveals a misunderstanding of the nature of competition. In a free market, competition is not only between laborers but also between whole firms and communities of firms. We must allow diversity between firms, even if it does not exist within them.

Free markets and private property are all of a piece. We cannot have free labor markets so long as we don't have the freedom to hire and fire. It is as essential that women's health clubs be allowed to exclude men as it is for Korean restaurants to be able to hire and promote only Koreans. These are the rights and privileges that come with private property. If we limit them, we endanger the foundation of capitalism and civilization itself.

Forced Equality

America's peculiar version of socialism is just as coercive as any other form. Yet because it is more expansively egalitarian than others have been, the ill-effects are made worse by the demographic differences in the American population. Forced equality has no chance of success in any country, but especially not here. The attempt has wrought destruction, and if extended much further, will create a reign of terror.

America' s fascination with equality stretches back to the Declaration of Independence, when Mr. Jefferson penned the obvious untruth that all men are created equal. He couldn't have meant it literally or in the way it is used today. In the very same document, Jefferson accuses the King of exciting insurrections among the "merciless Indian savages, whose known rule of warfare is an undistinguished destruction of all ages, sexes, and conditions."

In those two statements, we find the essential contradiction of the American democratic faith. We are supposed to want people to be equal. We are supposed to want the president to insure it to be so.

If we are ever to reverse our current course, we must pay closer attention to the wisdom of Alexis de Tocqueville, John C. Calhoun, John Randolph of Roanoke, Lord Acton, Helmut Schoeck, Bertrand de Jouvenal, Ludwig von Mises, Murray N. Rothbard, and all the others who have taught us that liberty and equality are incompatible goals. One always comes at the expense of the other. Equal protection of life and private property from violent transgressions is the only ideal of equality that is consistent with individual liberty.

The free market economy has a record like no other of offering economic advancement for everyone no matter what his station in life. But it does not offer equality of result or equality of opportunity. How can opportunity be equated between the quick-witted and simple-minded, between the energetic and the lazy? The free market offers not an unstratified society, but something of real value: liberty itself. And civil rights laws violate that liberty.

Libertarian philosophers have long pointed out that the conventional separation between human rights and property rights is a false one. If property rights are violated, so are human rights. If property rights are protected, so are human rights.

The same logic applies to civil rights. If they are invoked at the expense of private property—which they are by definition in the U.S. legal context—they violate rights. What Herbert Spencer called the "law of equal freedom"—in which a person has property rights and no special privileges—means a society in which people can discriminate or not discriminate, i.e., make choices, on any grounds of their choosing.

Sometimes those who think that civil rights have gone too far see the problem in terms of quotas. This is a misdirection of intellectual energy. Under a pure property regime, people are free to impose quotas if they desire. Even the alleged dream of a perfectly integrated society could be achieved if that is what market actors chose. It is also the case that a "separated" society could result.

Based on experience, what we are likely to see in a regime of pure property rights is authentic diversity, rather than the trumped-up form imagined by government bureaucrats. Some firms, companies, and communities would be homogeneous, while others would be heterogeneous. But the more important goals of social peace and prosperity would be met in a demographic free market.

But would vulnerable populations be helped? Yes, but not as a result of special rights and coercion. The division of labor finds a place for all sorts of people, and encourages a culture of productivity, which would eventually replace the no-win culture of envy and victimology.

As the Fabians recognized, there are as many varieties of socialism as there are nations. We are cursed with a particularly vicious sort that denies the right of association, rejects essential aspects of the freedom of enterprise, and combats natural inequalities as if they represented a disease on the body politic.

As executive agencies acquire ever more power and money, and run roughshod over all aspects of private life, we are encouraged to look the other way. At this rate, we may eventually disprove the old Fabian teaching that socialism in Western countries cannot succeed if it appears undemocratic or authoritarian.

Anyone familiar with Joseph Schumpeter's paradoxical prediction that socialism would win out over capitalism might also think that the retreat of socialist governments in 1989 disproved him. In light of our present situation, let's revisit Schumpeter. In *Capitalism, Socialism and Democracy* he defines his terms very carefully.

The capitalist or commercial society, he says, is defined by two elements: first, private property in the means of production; second, regulation of the productive process by private contract, management, and initiative. By Schumpeter's definition, we only have capitalism in the first sense. We have private property, but no longer can we govern the productive process by private contract, management, and initiative. The government exercises veto power over all matters of economic management.

By socialist society, he further writes, he means an institutional pattern in which the control over the means of production itself is vested with a central authority, or as a matter of principle, the economic affairs of society belong to the public and not to the private sphere.

Which does our society most closely resemble: Schumpeter's commercial society or Schumpeter's socialist society? Certainly we know where the trend line is pointing. And we know what to do about it: eliminate all violent intervention in the market, and allow for the flourishing of freedom of contract and association, and the protection of private property.

That is the only way to dig ourselves out of the pit of this peculiarly American form of socialism called civil rights.

From "Civil Rights Socialism" by Llewellyn H. Rockwell Jr., *Freeman*, May 1996. Copyright © 1996 by the Foundation for Economic Education. Reprinted by permission of the *Freeman*.

A Humane Society Must Compensate for Inherent Inequalities

by John Kenneth Galbraith

John Kenneth Galbraith is Paul M. Warburg Professor of Economics Emeritus at Harvard University. In the following viewpoint, Galbraith argues that while absolute egalitarianism is not a realistic goal, a humane society must offer access to a rewarding life for all. But, he contends, the modern market economy limits access by according wealth and distributing income in an unequal and damaging fashion. He argues that a humane society must give "a better break" to those at the bottom by committing to a support system for the poor, by ensuring honesty in the financial world's transactions, and by instituting a fully progressive tax system.

"What is necessary are strong ameliorating actions that reflect and address the inherent and damaging inequality."

The good society does not seek equality in the distribution of income. Equality is not consistent with either human nature or the character and motivation of the modern economic system. As all know, people differ radically in their commitment to making money and also in their competence in doing so. And some of the energy and initiative on which the modern economy depends comes not only from the desire for money but also from the urge to excel in its acquisition. This last is a test of social excellence, a major source of public prestige.

A strong current of social expression and thought has held that there is, or could be, a higher level of motivation if there were an egalitarian level of reward—"From each according to his abilities, to each according to his needs." This hope, one that spread far beyond Marx, has been shown by both history and human experience to be irrelevant. For better or for worse, human beings do not rise to such heights. Generations of socialists and socially oriented leaders have learned this to their disappointment and more often to their sorrow. The basic fact is clear: the good society must accept men and women as they are. However, this does not lessen the need for a clear view of the forces controlling the distribution of income and of the factors forming attitudes thereon. And of how, in a wholly practical way, policy on income distribution should be framed.

Inequality Is a Hallmark of the Market Economy

There is, first, the inescapable fact that the modern market economy (in the now-approved terminology) accords wealth and distributes income in a highly unequal, socially adverse and also functionally damaging fashion. In the United States, now the extreme case among the major industrial countries, the Federal Reserve, an impeccable source said, as reported in the *New York Times*, that the top 1 percent of American households owned nearly 40 percent of the nation's wealth in 1989, the top 20 percent more than 80 percent. The lowest-earning 20 percent of Americans had 5.7 percent of all after-tax income; the best-rewarded 20 percent had 55 percent. By 1992, the top 5 percent were getting an estimated 18 percent, a share that in more recent years has become substantially larger, as that of those in the poorest brackets has been diminishing. This, the good society cannot accept. Nor can it accept intellectually the justification, more precisely the contrivance, that defends this inequality. The latter is one of the most assiduously cultivated exercises in economic thought. Never, however, does it quite conceal the fact that the economic and social doctrine involved is subordinate to the pecuniary purpose (and forthright greed) that it serves.

Specifically, it is held that there is a moral entitlement: the man or woman in question has the right to receive what he or she earns or, more precisely, what he or she receives. This can be asserted with emphasis, on occasion with asperity and often with righteous indignation. It encounters opposition, however, in both history and hard fact.

Much income and wealth comes with slight or no social justification, little or no economic service on the part of the recipient. Inheritance is an obvious case. So also the endowments, accidents and perversions of the financial world. And the rewards that, from its personal empowerment, modern corporate management bestows on itself. As noted, the modern corporate management is committed, as in all orthodox economic doctrine, to profit maximization. Because it is exempt to a substantial degree from stockholder control or restraint, it extensively maximizes return on its own behalf. With compliant boards of directors of its own selection it effectively sets its own salary, provides its own stock options, establishes its own golden parachutes. That such return is unrelated in any plausible fashion to social or economic function is largely accepted. The frequent and sometimes fervid assertion of such function is a cover story for the patently improbable.

The rich have a certain reluctance in defending their wealth and income as a social, moral or divine right, so their only possible resort is the functional justification. From the undisturbed and admittedly unequal distribution of income comes the incentive to effort and innovation that is in the service of all. And from the income so distributed come the saving and investment that are for the advantage of all. The rich and the affluent do not speak in defense of their own good fortune; they speak as the benign servitors of the common good. Some may even be embarrassed as to their worldly reward, but they suffer it, nonetheless, as a service to the general well-being. Social and economic purpose is adjusted to personal comfort and convenience. This, all in the good society will recognize.

Further, there is the protection that the peculiar class structure of the United States accords the affluent and the rich. All reputable reference concerning class structure emphasizes the middle class. There is an upper and a lower class, but these are back in the shadows. Although it is rarely so designated, for practical purposes we have a three-class system consisting of only one class, an arithmetic novelty. And the middle class, which is so dominant, then provides protective cover for the rich. Tax reduction on behalf of the middle class extends on to the very affluent. The upper class does not, in such discussion and action, separately exist. Such is the political attitude. There is a strong functional effect here as regards the working of the economy.

As to the income going to the very rich, there is, to repeat, the exercise of, in the economist's term, liquidity preference—the choice between consumer expenditure and investment in real capital or merely holding the money in one or another form of effective idleness. This is a choice as to the use of income that the individual or family of modest means cannot exercise. They are under the pressure of more urgent need; that they will spend the money they receive is thus certain. Accordingly, income that is widely distributed is economically serviceable, for it helps to ensure a steady flow of aggregate demand. There is a strong chance that the more unequal the distribution of income, the more dysfunctional it becomes.

A Better Break for Those at the Bottom

What, then, is the right course as regards the distribution of income? There can be no fixed rule, no acceptable multiple as between what is received by the rich and what goes to the poor. Or, indeed, as between what is earned by management at the top and what is earned on the shop floor. The basic character of the system is here involved. It does not lend itself to arbitrary rules. What is necessary are strong ameliorating actions that reflect and address the inherent and damaging inequality.

There is, first, the support system for the poor. The attack on inequality begins with a better break for those at the bottom. . . .

There is, second, . . . the need to deal with the dominant tendencies of the financial world. Insider trading, false information in investment promotion, deviant investment behavior as in the case of the great savings-and-loan disaster, the corporate takeovers and the recurrent episodes of speculative insanity, all unfavorably affect income distribution. Measures that ensure elementary honesty in financial transactions and a better understanding of the speculative episode have a useful leveling effect.

There is, third, the need for stockholder and informed public criticism to address the personal income maximization of corporate management. Independent of such stockholder and public restraint, the corporate managerial take has, as already noted, become a major cause of socially adverse income distribution. The only answer here is united action by the stockholder owners who are thus disadvantaged. The chance for such action is, it must be conceded, not great. Those who own the modern corporation are notably passive as regards their personal exploitation.

There remain two lines of affirmative public action looking toward a more equitable income distribution, one of which is of decisive importance.

The first is for the government to remove the present tax and expenditure concessions to the affluent. In recent times these have achieved a measure of recognition under the cognomen of corporate welfare. Included here are diverse business subsidies and tax breaks; support to agricultural producers who are already in the higher income brackets, especially a lavishly endowed sugar monopoly and subsidies to tobacco production; export subsidies, including those for arms exports; and, bulking largest of all, the vast payments to the now recidivist weapons producers. . . .

69

However, the most effective instrument for achieving a greater measure of income equality remains the progressive income tax. This has the central role in accomplishing a reasonable, even civilized, distribution of income. Nothing else, it may be added, is subject to such highly motivated and wholly predictable attack. The good society, on the other hand, affirms its purpose; it also assumes that there will be strong, articulate, even eloquent resistance from those so taxed. They will especially allege the deleterious effect of the tax on incentives. As earlier suggested, it could be claimed with equal improbability that a strongly progressive income tax causes the rich and the affluent to work harder, more imaginatively, in order to sustain their after-tax income. Referring to past experience, it can, indeed, be pointed out that the American economy had one of its highest rates of growth, its highest levels of employment and in some years a substantial budget surplus in the period immediately following World War II, when the marginal rates on the personal income tax were at a record level.

The basic need, however, is to accept the principle that a more equitable distribution of income must be a fundamental tenet of modern public policy in the good society, and to this end progressive taxation is central.

The Distribution of Income and Power

The distribution of income in the modern economy derives ultimately from the distribution of power. This, in turn, is both a cause and a consequence of the way income is shared. Power serves the acquisition of income; income accords power over the pecuniary reward of others. The good society recognizes and seeks to respond to this traditionally closed circle.

Its response is the empowerment and public protection of the powerless. In the market economy the natural focus of power is the employer, most often the business firm. The right of workers to join together and assert a countervailing authority must be central and accepted. As those who organize to invest enjoy the protection that the state accords the corporate structure, so those who organize to enhance income or improve working conditions should have a broadly equivalent protection for their organization.

In modern times, especially in the United States, the empowerment of workers has been diminishing in its general effect. Trade union membership as a proportion of all workers has sharply declined, partly in consequence of the decline in mass-production, mass-employment industry, partly because of the aged lethargy of the trade union movement

70

itself. The good society seeks, where possible, to reverse this decline in trade union power, for worker organization remains a major civilizing factor in modern economic life.

For many workers, however, organization is not now a practical solution. This is especially true in the widely dispersed service industries. As was once the case with the employment of women and children, direct action by the state on behalf of those in need outside the unions is required, including provision for health insurance and unemployment compensation and, currently most important, a socially adequate minimum wage. In the good society the last is an absolute essential. That it will diminish employment opportunity, the argument most commonly made in opposition, may be dismissed out of hand, for that is, invariably, the special plea of those who do not wish to pay the wage, and it is without any empirical support. (Even were it at cost to the employment of the few, it would still be justified as the protection of the many.) Along with a basic safety net the good society must also protect the working income of its least favored members.

CHAPTER 2

Is Societal Inequity a Cause of Poverty?

Chapter Preface

Statistics show that poverty rates in the United States are much higher among certain groups than for the population as a whole. They reveal that one in five American children (one in four under the age of six) lives in poverty, usually with a single mother. While the general unemployment rate has gone up and down, for more than thirty years unemployment levels for blacks have held fairly steady at twice the rate for whites. Many Native American tribes suffer devastating rates of poverty; for instance, the poorest county in the country—Shannon County, South Dakota—is home to the Oglala Sioux.

However, being a single mother, Native American, black, or a member of any other minority in the United States is not in itself a sentence of poverty: All of these groups are represented in the wealthy and middle classes. Statistics can only suggest a correlation between poverty and certain demographic characteristics. They do not conclusively show whether individual behavior or structural inequities lead to poverty. They do not show whether being a member of a given group brings into play external factors, such as racial discrimination, or internal factors, such as lack of self-esteem or a solid work ethic; they do not show causes. And those causes are the subject of often heated debate, as the following viewpoints demonstrate.

Perhaps in considering these causes, we should heed Christopher Jencks, author of *Rethinking Social Policy: Race, Poverty, and the Underclass*, who ventured this opinion on the effects of racism on poverty: "Isn't it obvious that both sides are right? Whenever we talk about race, it almost always boils down to either-or: a matter of justice or a matter of effort. It's time to start thinking in terms of both-and."

Structural Inequities Contribute to Poverty in Single-Parent Families

by Sanford F. Schram

Sanford F. Schram is a visiting professor at the Graduate School of Social Work and Social Research at Bryn Mawr College in Bryn Mawr, Pennsylvania. He writes often on poverty and welfare issues. In the following viewpoint, Schram contends that single-parent families are not the cause of their own poverty. The cause can be found, he argues, in the culturally biased social policies and programs that favor two-parent families and deny adequate help to poor, female-headed families. Those policies punish poor single mothers and reinforce their inferior status by offering benefits that do little to help them become self-sufficient. In this way, Schram contends, public policy and social programs help create the poverty they purport to eliminate.

"Blaming female-headed families for growing poverty provides a convenient and culturally ascendant way to deflect attention from the deleterious effects of the changing economy on the poorer segments of society."

A cultural "backlash" against feminism is afoot, with reverberations for social policy.[1] Electoral politics has provided conservatives with a forum for suggesting that the problems of increased crime, unemployment, low school performance, family deterioration, and welfare dependency can be blamed on a decadent cultural or "media" elite who support the alleged feminist moves implied in such television sitcoms as *Murphy Brown* and tolerate, if not glorify, the formation of mother-only families. By April 1993, although the Republicans may have lost the election, they seemed to have won the debate in the popular press when the *Atlantic*'s cover story on the deleterious effects of family breakup was headlined "Dan Quayle Was Right."[2]

This propagandizing of the two-parent family no doubt oversells its advantages and discounts its limitations in ways that make it harder to promote social policies that will treat alternative families more equitably. Yet what is most critical for understanding contemporary social policy is not so much how cultural value conflicts help influence social policy. Instead, the growing preoccupation with mother-only families in the current period highlights how social policy itself is a cultural force working to reinforce advantages for the traditional two-parent family over others.[3]

Much has been made in the past of how welfare benefits as material resources are largely available only for one-parent families and therefore are a disincentive to the creation and maintenance of two-parent families.[4] However, this stress on the materiality of welfare overlooks how it operates as a cultural force, reinforcing the two-parent family through the negative symbolic significance attached to welfare taking by female-headed families. Welfare as a cultural formation provides female-headed families benefits but does so under punitive and stigmatizing conditions that reinforce the denigration of female-headed families and help rationalize popular resistance to state efforts on their behalf.

In this viewpoint I want to suggest that the statistically documented trend of the "feminization of poverty" can be profitably characterized as an established social policy reflecting the inadequacy of welfare, both as material benefits and as cultural standard. Following a review of the statistical evidence regarding why mother-only families predominate among the officially defined poor, I interrogate contemporary welfare policy so as to highlight how it has been a critical constitutive factor in reproducing poverty in these families. The goal is to promote a destabilization of increasingly insistent and anachronistic distinctions of welfare policy discourse so that we can increase the chances of making public policy in a more democratic way that is more tolerant of the variety of families and the diversity of circumstances.

The Self-Fulfilling Prophesy of Welfare Policy

The cultural significance of welfare policy is better appreciated when it is seen not as a response to a preexisting problem but instead as something central to the problem's formulation. Political scientists have for some time toyed with inverting the linear, rational problem-policy re-

75

sponse paradigm. E.E. Schattschneider long ago noted that "new policies create a new politics." Aaron Wildavsky years later stressed that "policy becomes its own cause" in the sense that, once in place, public policies inevitably are administered in ways that legitimate the need to expand and develop them. Margaret Weir has emphasized how the evolution of policy is contingent upon how previous policies have served to reinforce a prevailing ideational context such that former policies prefigure future policies, sometimes irrespective of the ostensible problems to be attacked. Frances Fox Piven has reminded us that programs create political constituencies at least as much as the other way around.[5] Yet there is a latent literalism in many attempts to invert the positivistic policy paradigm. They underestimate the extent to which policy is partly constitutive of the reality against which it is directed.[6] Policy, therefore, as an ensemble of discursive practices, does not just create its own politics or become its own cause, but it is a critical contributing factor in making up the reality it confronts.[7] Anne Schneider and Helen Ingram have written:

> Social constructions become embedded in policy as messages that are absorbed by citizens and affect their orientations and participation patterns. Policy sends messages about what government is supposed to do, which citizens are deserving (and which not), and what kinds of attitudes and participatory patterns are appropriate in a democratic society. Different target populations, however, receive quite different messages. Policies that have detrimental impacts on . . . target populations may not produce citizen participation directed toward policy change because the messages received by these target populations encourage withdrawal or passivity. Other target populations, however, receive messages that encourage them to combat policies detrimental to them through various avenues of political participation.[8]

For the most part, only in this most ironic sense is there something in the right-wing view that welfare causes poverty. The inadequacy of welfare policy for poor women with children is therefore part of a self-fulfilling prophesy that makes it hard for these families to be successful. This paradox consequently reinforces the idea that these families are the cause of their own problems. In its perpetuation of the blind commitment to the two-parent family as a fundamental constitutive element of the market system, welfare policy resists providing assistance to alternative families. These practices are likely to continue the bias in favor of the two-parent family as the route out of poverty and are just as likely to accelerate the trend toward the "feminization of poverty.". . .

Materializing Family Structure as Impoverishing

A critical dimension to welfare policy discourse is the presumption that two-parent families have at least the potential for being "self-sufficient" and are therefore "deserving," whereas mother-only families are "dependent" largely for reasons for which they must assume responsibility, and therefore are not deserving of as much support. Invidious distinctions of self-sufficiency/dependency, deserving/undeserving, responsible/promiscuous are deployed in gendered ways. The symbolic significance of welfare lies in its denigration of mother-only families in the name of affirming two-parent families. Welfare policy as a system of symbolic signification serves to reduce the extent to which social institutions, markets, and state policies feel pressure to structure their practices to accommodate mother-only families. The main way it does this is by reinforcing the idea that mother-only families are the cause of their own problems.

Conservatives argue that two-parent families are better than one-parent families for a variety of reasons, including greater ability to provide necessary parental attention to children and the presence of a male role model, specifically for young boys.[9] This argument is particularly a concern for poor minority families, which have distinctively high rates of female-headship, and these themes have in fact been emphasized by moderate and conservative African American politicians, such as Sharon Pratt Kelly, the former mayor of Washington, D.C., and Douglas Wilder, former governor of Virginia.[10] Others have suggested that it will be extremely difficult to build political coalitions with the white working class unless there is a shared commitment to valuing the two-parent family.[11] Yet the growth of female-headed families among whites has also been a cause for concern in recent years.[12]

The growth of poor female-headed families among both whites and blacks is indeed a troubling development in certain respects, most significantly in that it poses increased risks for children regarding such matters as schooling completed, earnings potential, out-of-wedlock childbearing, and future welfare dependency.[13] There is evidence that children in two-parent families are much less likely to be poor, and that the growth in female-headed families is strongly associated with sharp increases in child poverty, especially among minorities.[14] Yet the genesis and implications of the growth of female-headed families are more complicated than universal condemnations suggest. . . .

An Invidious Notion

The feminization of poverty occurs not because two-parent families are better or will always prove a more effective institutional structure for escaping poverty. The trend to single-parent families is the product of a confluence of factors, some negative and others positive, and some quite complicated, including the trend toward leaving abusive marital relationships and the increase in pregnancies outside of marriage.[15] The problem is the reverse of what pro-family values advocates wish to suggest: it is as often the case that poverty creates female-headed families than that female-headed families create poverty. A number of recent studies have documented that teen pregnancy and out-of-wedlock childbearing are most common among children who have been raised in low-income, less educated, more mobile families.[16] Poverty often leads, among young males as well as females, to a lack of information about birth control, a lack of understanding about skills in parenting, and a general sense of hopelessness that might make having a child attractive even to an unmarried teenager. Young poor males who father children may be reluctant to form two-parent families because of the lack of economic opportunities available for them.[17] Yet, as long as the prevailing discourse helps re-create the idea that family structure causes poverty, rather than the other way around, many people will continue to accept the invidious notion that single-parent families are the cause of their own poverty.[18]

Welfare Policy Re-Creates Its Own Reality

Existing social policies are implicated in this problem. They have helped construct female-headed, single-parent families as the marginal "other" and set them up for inferior benefits and punitive therapeutic practices.[19] From this perspective, it is a mistake to see the growth in female-headed families as an autonomous "pathology" generated independent of policy and social institutions. Instead, it is more important to address how welfare policy is a critical constitutive factor reproducing the female-headed family as a stigmatized and disadvantaged social formation.[20]

Linda Gordon emphasizes that public assistance is founded on a "family wage" system based on the assumption that families have two parents and the male is the breadwinner.[21] Diana Pearce argues that even the public assistance program that primarily serves women with children—Aid to Families with Dependent Children—continues to be organized along the lines of the "male pauper model," which assumes that welfare benefits should be low enough so they do not discourage family heads from taking even the lowest-paying jobs as a means of supporting a family.[22] Under these circumstances, two-parent families are more likely to benefit from such varying phenomena as economic growth and jobs programs, which tend to be designed with the two-parent family in mind. Although neither males nor females are likely to do well in a labor market that increasingly consists of low-wage jobs, women with children will lag behind as they struggle to make do with policies and programs not designed to accommodate their particular needs and circumstances as single mothers.[23]

Policies geared toward women with children tend to offer inferior benefits or are lacking in commitment to the services and strategies, such as child care and pay equity, women need in order to become self-sufficient.[24] In particular, a major reason for the increased poverty of women with children is that AFDC has been less effective than programs such as social security and unemployment compensation in lifting families out of poverty.[25] The debased value of public assistance programs focused on poor women with children is a major factor in explaining the sharp increases in their poverty rate in recent years. The average cash benefit in constant dollars received from all public assistance programs over the 1973–87 period declined dramatically. Also, benefits to female-headed families have flagged relative to those going to other families: female-headed households went in real terms from a mean cash transfer (in 1987 $s) of approximately $7,000 in 1973 to $4,400 in 1987, or a 37 percent decline, compared with a corresponding drop from approximately $8,000 to $6,000, or a 25 percent decline, for male-headed families.[26]

These trends exacerbate a historic divide. Programs focused on poor women with children have historically been inadequate to lift their recipients out of poverty. Sheldon D. Danziger and Jonathan S. Stern have examined the rate at which families and the elderly are lifted over the official poverty line by cash assistance. They have found that whereas the elderly's rate is quite high, because of social security, female-headed families have a very low rate, with no more than 10 percent escaping poverty today through government transfers.[27] This discrepancy is almost entirely the result of the extent to which welfare programs focused on these families continue to offer benefits well below the poverty level for most families.[28]

Whether it was because public assistance was tied to the "family wage" system that promoted women's dependence on a male breadwinner or because it was tied to a market logic that sought to ensure that benefits were below the lowest wages, women on welfare have been denied adequate benefits under invasive treatment.[29] There is a need to highlight how welfare policies designed to be consonant with the low-wage labor market work together to promote more poverty. During a time of decreased welfare benefits, deterioration of job opportunities for the relatively unskilled, and increases in the numbers of female-headed families, the growth of female-headed families in poverty is symptomatic of the cultural biases embedded in social policy. Social policy operates to disadvantage women with children, materially as well as symbolically. Reinforcing their inferior status, social policy logically provides them inferior benefits.[30]

Welfare Policy as a Culture in Denial

The foregoing analysis is not meant to suggest that change will flow easily once welfare politics comes to be a cultural politics centered on what welfare signifies about families. Given its active involvement in promoting two-parent families, the welfare state has vested interests in perpetuating its own cultural construction.[31] Therefore, welfare policy discourse continues to construct poverty as a problem of family structure and seeks to find its solution in the two-parent family. In fact, discursive moves on behalf of the two-parent family wage system intensify especially as that ideal becomes harder to sustain. Insisting that family breakdown is a cause rather than a symptom of growing poverty allows social policy to continue to legitimate itself in spite of the failure of social policy to address the collapse of the family wage system. To be sure, blaming female-headed families for growing poverty provides a convenient and culturally ascendant way to deflect attention from the deleterious effects of the changing economy on the poorer segments of society.[32] The scapegoating of family structure for problems embedded in the sexist, racist, and economic exclusionary practices of the "contemporary postindustrial society of economic decline" propels popular resistance to public assistance and aggressively silences attempts to articulate a family policy that could ensure that all families have the resources to avoid poverty. Moving from a "culture of poverty" argument, which blames the poor for their problems, policy discourse has hit upon a "culture of single motherhood" to promote a punitive approach to punishing poor women with children that obviates the need to address the dwindling economic opportunities associated with the current economic transition.[33]

Social policy then becomes ever more easily and explicitly dedicated to supporting only the two-parent family, blaming one-parent families for their problems, punishing women with children who fail to marry, refusing to address problems of sexism, exploitation, and abuse within the two-parent family, and so on. Overall, public assistance becomes less readily available, more temporary, more contingent on moral and social regulation, more premised on state surveillance of sexual, medical, social, and parental practices, and more attached to work requirements that move recipients from welfare to work irrespective of the lack of improvement in their economic condition. Even the outright abolition of welfare now gains ascendancy in policy circles, and some states pass legislation promising to do just that.[34]

Many of these changes overlook that family structure is in all likelihood far less significant in determining the economic well-being of family members than it is often made out to be. Most important, there is a tendency to emphasize the deleterious effects of family breakup while neglecting the fact that poverty itself is a major factor undermining the two-parent family among the poor. Also lost is the possibility that improved schooling, enhanced employment prospects, less sexism and racism in both areas, improved sex education, and a generally more hopeful horizon for poor children, especially from minority communities, would go a long way toward minimizing the significance of family structure and reducing the welfare burden on the state. Relatively stable marriages would likely increase among disadvantaged populations and alternative families that did form would be less likely to pose high welfare costs. Yet, in the current period, the incentive grows to blame symptoms, such as changing family patterns, rather than address the cultural biases that social policies actively reinforce.[35]

Confronting a Harsh Reality

The feminization of poverty is an important phenomenon in need of increased attention; however, it is not new and its growing visibility is an artifact of bad statistics. The feminization of poverty is a manifestation of how welfare policy has historically served to create its own reality—stigmatizing female-headed families in order to reinforce two-parent families. The inadequacy of welfare policy for poor women with children is part of a self-fulfilling prophesy that makes it hard for these families to be successful and, consequently, reinforces the idea that these families are the cause of their own problems.

Women heading these families do not have access to other programs, often for no other reason than that their spouses chose to leave them rather than died, became disabled, or ended up out of work. Reflecting the biases of the broader society, the welfare state is not structured to provide such women with "family insurance" or "divorce insurance" policies that could correspond to programs that protect families when the primary wage earner dies, becomes disabled, or becomes unemployed. Cultural biases persist in perpetuating a welfare state that will insure families against some hazards but not others.

In spite of, and actually because of, rising numbers of single-parent families, society continues to resist the idea that women need to be protected from the risks of bearing and raising children on their own. Alternative arguments stress holding women responsible, getting "dead-beat dads" to pay child support, or some combination of both.[36] Yet, why is it that the risk of bearing and raising children on one's own is still considered largely a private responsibility, when coping with losing a job, becoming disabled, or losing a wage-earning spouse through death is accepted as a state that makes one deserving of support by government-sanctioned and funded "insurance" programs? Gender biases persist in relegation of women's risks to the private realm and prevent us from seriously confronting the need to guarantee all families minimally adequate resources after private sources of support, such as alimony and child support, have been tapped. Instead, poor women with children who do not qualify for the more generous types of assistance must confront the harsh reality of an underfunded and punitive welfare system. They are seen as "dependent" welfare recipients, whereas others can claim the name of "beneficiaries" or "insurees." Until we recognize that these women are just as deserving on average as recipients of the benefits from other programs, the biases of the existing welfare state and its failure to provide women either equality of treatment or special protection are likely to endure. . . .[37]

Until we are ready to commit to women with children and value women's reproductive work as integral to the well-being of society, these families will not receive support in any way commensurate with that received by the retired, disabled, and unemployed. In other words, until women's attempts at independence are valued as much as anyone else's, the feminization of poverty will remain established policy.

Notes

1. Susan Faludi, *Backlash: The Undeclared War against American Women* (New York: Crown, 1991).
2. Barbara Dafoe Whitehead, "Dan Quayle Was Right," *Atlantic*, April 1993, 47–84.
3. For analysis of how propagandizing the two-parent family accentuates the post–World War II boom in the nuclear family to the neglect of how that was an exceptional countertrend of the past 150 years, see Stephanie Coontz, *The Way We Never Were: Family and the Nostalgia Trap* (New York: Basic Books, 1993).
4. See Charles Murray, "The Coming White Underclass," *Wall Street Journal*, October 29, 1993, A14; Charles Murray, *Losing Ground: American Social Policy* (New York: Basic Books, 1984).
5. E.E. Schattschneider, *Politics, Pressure and the Tariff* (Englewood Cliffs, N.J.: Prentice Hall, 1935); Aaron Wildavsky, *Speaking Truth to Power: The Art and Craft of Policy Analysis* (Boston: Little, Brown, 1979), 62–83; Margaret Weir, *Politics and Jobs: The Boundaries of Employment Policy in the United States*

(Princeton, N.J.: Princeton University Press, 1992), 19–26; Frances Fox Piven, "Reforming the Welfare State," *Socialist Review* 22 (July–September, 1992): 78. A similar point is made by Theda Skocpol in *Protecting Soldiers and Mothers: The Political Origins of Social Policy in the United States* (Cambridge: Harvard University Press, Belknap Press, 1992), 58: "We must make social policies the starting points as well as the end points of analysis. As politics creates policies, policies also remake politics."

6. For discussion on this issue, see Mary Hawkesworth, *Theoretical Issues in Policy Analysis* (Albany: State University of New York Press, 1988), 190–94; Deborah A. Stone, *Policy Paradox and Political Reason* (Boston: Harper-Collins, 1988), 4–10.

7. See Stone, *Policy Paradox and Political Reason*, 106–206; Murray Edelman, *Constructing the Political Spectacle* (Chicago: University of Chicago Press, 1988); Murray Edelman, *Political Language: Words That Succeed and Policies That Fail* (New York: Academic Press, 1977).

8. Anne Schneider and Helen Ingram, "Social Construction of Target Populations: Implications for Politics and Policy," *American Political Science Review*, 87 (June 1993): 334.

9. See Whitehead, "Dan Quayle Was Right"; Murray, "The Coming White Underclass."

10. See "Mayor Dixon's Call for Action," *Washington Post*, November 29, 1991, A30.

11. Thomas Byrne Edsall with Mary D. Edsall, *Chain Reaction: The Impact of Race, Rights and Taxes on American Politics* (New York: W.W. Norton, 1991), 256–88.

12. Murray, "The Coming White Underclass."

13. Christopher Jencks, "Is the American Underclass Growing?" in *The Urban Underclass*, ed. Christopher Jencks and Paul Peterson (Washington, D.C.: Brookings Institution, 1991).

14. David J. Eggebeen and Daniel T. Lichter, "Race, Family Structure, and Changing Poverty among American Children," *American Sociological Review* 56 (1991): 801–17.

15. See Maxine Baca Zinn, "Family, Race, and Poverty in the Eighties," *Signs*, 14 (1989).

16. For a literature review, see Chong-Bum An, Robert Haveman, and Barbara Wolfe, "Reducing Teen Out-of-Wedlock Births: The Role of Parental Education and Family Stability," discussion paper 944–91, Institute for Research on Poverty, Madison, Wis., 1991.

17. See William Julius Wilson, "Public Policy Research and the Truly Disadvantaged," in *The Urban Underclass*, ed. Christopher Jencks and Paul Peterson (Washington D.C.: Brookings Institution, 1991), 460–81.

18. See Michael B. Katz, *The Undeserving Poor: From the War on Poverty to the War on Welfare* (New York: Pantheon, 1989), 215–23.

19. Linda Gordon, "Welfare Reform: A History Lesson," *Dissent* (Summer 1994): 323–28; Evelyn Z. Brodkin, "The Making of an Enemy: How Welfare Policies Construct the Poor," *Law and Social Inquiry* 18 (Fall 1993): 647–70. Brodkin is paraphrasing Joel F. Handler and Yeheskel Hasenfeld, *The Moral Construction of Poverty: Welfare Reform in America* (Newbury Park, Calif.: Sage, 1991).

20. See Diana Pearce, "Welfare Is *Not* for Women: Why the War on Poverty Cannot Conquer the Feminization of Poverty," in *Women, The State, and*

Welfare, ed. Linda Gordon (Madison: University of Wisconsin Press, 1990), 265.

21. Linda Gordon, "What Does Welfare Regulate?" *Social Research* 55 (1988): 609–30.

22. Pearce, "Welfare Is *Not* for Women."

23. See Fraser, *Unruly Practices*, 144–87; Nancy Fraser, "Clintonism, Welfare, and the Antisocial Wage: The Emergence of a Neoliberal Political Imaginary," *Rethinking Marxism* 6 (Spring 1993): 9–23.

24. Gordon, "What Does Welfare Regulate?"

25. Barbara J. Nelson, "The Origins of the Two-Channel Welfare State: Workmen's Compensation and Mothers' Aid," in *Women, the State, and Welfare*, ed. Linda Gordon (Madison: University of Wisconsin Press, 1990),123–51; Mimi Abramovitz, *Regulating the Lives of Women: Social Welfare Policy from Colonial Times to the Present* (Boston: South End, 1989).

26. Sheldon Danziger and Jonathan Stern, *The Causes and Consequences of Child Poverty in the United States*, research report no. 90-194 (Ann Arbor: University of Michigan, Population Studies Center, 1990).

27. Ibid.

28. See Gordon, "What Does Welfare Regulate?"; Nelson, "The Origins of the Two-Channel Welfare State." For a view that recognizes but de-emphasizes the significance of differences between programs concentrated on female-headed families and male-identified programs, see Theda Skocpol, *Protecting Soldiers and Mothers*, 525–39; Ann S. Orloff, "Gender and the Social Rights of Citizenship: The Comparative Analysis of Gender Relations and Welfare States," *American Sociological Review* 58 (June 1993): 303–28.

29. For a debate over whether welfare was more in service of sexist subordination of women than of capitalist subordination of workers, see Gordon, "What Does Welfare Regulate?"; Frances Fox Piven and Richard A. Cloward, "Welfare Doesn't Shore Up Traditional Family Roles: A Reply to Linda Gordon," *Social Research* 55 (Winter 1988): 631–45.

30. For a summation of a convincing analysis of how the federalization of welfare programs since the New Deal has served to construct welfare recipients as second-class citizens, see Linda Gordon, *Pitied but Not Entitled: Single Mothers and the History of Welfare* (New York: Free Press, 1994), 293–306.

31. See Joan Tronto, *Moral Boundaries: A Political Argument for an Ethic of Care* (New York: Routledge, 1993), 165–66. Tronto argues that the breadwinner system of a family wage is premised on the work ethic in a way that marginalizes the care ethic so as to devalue women's responsibility, competence, and productivity as members of society.

32. See, for instance, Murray, "The Coming White Underclass."

33. See Susan L.Thomas, "From the Culture of Poverty to the Culture of Single Motherhood: A New Poverty Paradigm," paper prepared for the annual meeting of the Western Political Science Association, San Francisco, March 19–22, 1992.

34. There has been what seems to be growing acceptance of the calls by Charles Murray for the outright abolition of public assistance. The increased interest in the Clinton two-year time limit for receipt of welfare is one indicator. See Murray, "The Coming White Underclass." Wisconsin has adopted legislation calling for the abolition of public assistance by 1999. For a polemic on behalf of this legislation from Charles Murray of Wisconsin, see Charles J. Sykes, "Good Reasons to Kill Welfare," *Isthmus*, December 3, 1993, 12.

35. See William E. Connolly, *Identity/Difference: Democratic Negotiations of Political Paradox* (Ithaca, N.Y.: Cornell University Press, 1991), 206–10.

36. Improvements in child support collection and a growing interest in getting unemployed noncustodial parents into work programs, including the nationwide experimental project Parents' Fair Share, are laudable developments that should not be overrated. Many poor absent fathers lack not only employment but the skills that would enable them to get jobs that would provide enough child support to remove their families from welfare. See Jean Hopfensperger, "Anoka, Dakota Counties Target 'Welfare Dads' in New Jobs Program," *Minneapolis Star Tribune*, March 21, 1994, 1A, 7A. For a plan to replace welfare with an assured child support system that routinely collects child support payments, works to improve the earnings of noncustodial parents, and supplements support payments of the low-income with government assistance, see Irwin Garfinkel, *Assuring Child Support: An Extension of Social Security* (New York: Russell Sage Foundation, 1992).

37. For analyses of how treating women the same and treating them differently—providing equality *and* protection, in the parlance of social policy—are not mutually exclusive and can be combined in ways that protect women against risks special to them as equally as men are insured by the state, see Wendy Sarvasy, "Postsuffrage Feminism, Citizenship, and the Quest for a Feminist Welfare State," *Signs* 17 (Summer 1992): 329–62; Orloff, "Gender and the Social Rights of Citizenship," 322–24.

Excerpted from chapter eight of *Words of Welfare: The Poverty of Social Science and the Social Science of Poverty* by Sanford F. Schram (Minneapolis: University of Minnesota Press, 1995). An earlier version of this material appeared as "Postmodern Policy Analysis: Discourse and Identity in Welfare Policy," *Policy Sciences*, vol. 26, no. 3 (1993), pages 249–70. Reprinted by permission of the author and Kluwer Academic Publishers.

Fatherlessness Is to Blame for Poverty in Single-Parent Families

by David Blankenhorn

David Blankenhorn is president of the Institute for American Values, a family advocacy organization in New York City. In the following viewpoint, Blankenhorn contends that poverty and its various spin-offs, including violence and teen pregnancy, all result from the absence of a father in the family. Children who grow up without fathers, he states, lose out on important guidance and role modeling and are statistically more likely to move down than up the socioeconomic ladder. The tie between fatherless families and poverty is so clear, Blankenhorn states, that the spread of fatherlessness will soon constitute a new source of social and economic inequality: the haves being those who had fathers and the have-nots being those who did not.

"Fatherlessness has become the single most powerful determinant of child poverty— more important than race, region, or the educational attainment of the mother."

Fatherhood is a social role that obligates men to their biological off-spring. For two reasons, it is society's most important role for men. First, fatherhood, more than any other male activity, helps men to become good men: more likely to obey the law, to be good citizens, and to think about the needs of others. Put more abstractly, fatherhood bends maleness—in particular, male aggression—toward prosocial purposes.[1] Second, fatherhood privileges children. In this respect, fatherhood is a social invention designed to supplement maternal investment in children with paternal investment in children.

Paternal investment enriches children in four ways. First, it provides them with a father's physical protection. Second, it provides them with a father's money and other material resources. Third, and probably most important, it provides them with what might be termed paternal cultural transmission: a father's distinctive capacity to contribute to the identity, character, and competence of his children. Fourth, and most obviously, paternal investment provides children with the day-to-day nurturing— feeding them, playing with them, telling them a story—that they want and need from both of their parents. In virtually all human societies, children's well-being depends decisively upon a relatively high level of paternal investment.

Indeed, many anthropologists view the rise of fatherhood as the key to the emergence of the human family and, ultimately, of human civilization. As Jane and Chet Lancaster put it:

> In the course of evolution, the keystone in the foundation of the human family was the capturing of male energy into the nurturance of the young. . . . The human family is a complex organizational structure for the garnering of energy to be transformed into the production of the next generation, and its most essential feature is the collaboration of the male and female parent in the division of labor.[2]

In short, the key for men is to be fathers. The key for children is to have fathers. The key for society is to create fathers. For society, the primary results of fatherhood are right-doing males and better outcomes for children. Conversely, the primary consequences of fatherlessness are rising male violence and declining child well-being. In the United States at the close of the twentieth century, paternal disinvestment has become the major cause of declining child well-being[3] and the underlying source of our most important social problems, especially those rooted in violence. . . .

Youth Violence

In 1994, the Carnegie Corporation devoted an entire issue of the *Carnegie Quarterly* to the topic of "Saving Youth from Violence." In summarizing recent research on the sources of, and solutions for, youth violence, the Carnegie Corporation came up with this list of factors that contribute to youth violence: frustration, lack of social skills, being labeled as "dumb," poverty, drug and alcohol abuse, physical abuse and neglect, violence on television and in video games, school days that are too short, the availability of guns, the failure to use antiviolence and conflict-resolution curricula in school classrooms and child-care centers, inadequate health care programs, the shortage of community-based life skills training programs, and the absence of effective mentoring programs for at-risk young people.[4]

As something approaching panic about the problem of youth violence erupted across the nation during 1993 and 1994—"Teen Violence: Wild in the Streets," announced the cover of *Newsweek* in August 1993—numerous prestigious institutions and scholars emphasized the same basic themes presented by the Carnegie Corporation. For example, the American Psychological Association's Commission on Violence and Youth issued a 1993 report on *Youth and Violence*. The report attributes the rise of youth violence to the following factors: access to guns, involvement in gangs and mobs, exposure to violence in the mass media, lack of parental supervision, physical punishment, substance abuse, social and economic inequality, prejudice and discrimination, and the lack of antiviolence programs and psychological services in schools and communities.[5] Along with just about everyone else, the commission calls for a comprehensive, multiapproach solution to the problem.

But what is wrong with these lists? Surely, all these "factors" can and do, at least indirectly, contribute to youth violence. Yet the single most obvious factor—the one, moreover, most likely to produce the other factors—is conspicuously absent from these reports and recommendations and from countless others like them. . . .

Put simply, we have too many boys with guns primarily because we have too few fathers. If we want fewer of the former, we must have more of the latter. There is little evidence to suggest that any other strategy will work. Social workers, psychologists, mentors, and life skills instructors can frequently help [troubled] children . . . , but they cannot even begin to do the work of a father. And despite our current policy of spending ever-larger sums of money on prison construction, our capacity to build new prisons is being far outstripped by our capacity to produce violent young men. We are generating male violence much faster than we can incarcerate it.

Prisons cannot replace fathers. At best, new prisons constitute an expensive endgame strategy for quarantining some of the consequences of fatherlessness. In this sense, locking up [a violent child] . . . , might make us feel better and it might make us safer. But putting this child in jail is not an act of justice. It is an admission of failure, a symbol of our retreat. . . .

The Rise of Child Poverty

If the most immediately frightening societal consequence of fatherlessness is the rise of male violence, the most easily measurable is the rise of child poverty. Across history and cultures, the foundational tasks of fatherhood have been twofold: protection and provision. The first is about violence. The second is about money.[6] For the child, fatherlessness means more of the former and less of the latter.

A blizzard of statistics and studies confirms the relationship between fatherlessness and child poverty, but here, at least arguably, are the three most revealing comparisons. In married-couple homes in the United States in 1992, about 13 percent of all children under the age of six lived in poverty; in single-mother families, about 66 percent of young children lived in poverty—a ratio of 5 to 1.[7] In married-couple homes with preschool children, median family income in 1992 was approximately $41,000; in single-mother homes with young children, median income was about $9,000—a ratio of more than 4 to 1.[8] Of all married-couple families in the nation in 1992, about 6 percent lived in poverty; of all female-headed families, about 35 percent lived in poverty—a ratio of almost 6 to 1.[9]

One more comparison, regarding the economic well-being of African-American children. Of all black married couples with children under age eighteen in 1992, about 15 percent lived in poverty; of all black mother-headed homes with children, about 57 percent lived in poverty—a ratio of almost 4 to 1.[10]

In *Single Mothers and Their Children*, Irwin Garfinkel and Sara S. McLanahan succinctly summarize the evidence: "Families headed by single women with children are the poorest of all major demographic groups regardless of how poverty is measured."[11] In *Poor Support*, David T. Ellwood similarly concludes that "the vast majority of children who are raised entirely in a two-parent home will never be poor during childhood. By contrast, the vast majority of children who spend time in a single-parent home will experience poverty."[12]

Most scholars now agree that this link between family structure and child poverty is not simply a statistical correlation. It is a causal relationship. Fatherlessness causes child poverty. Indeed, according to numerous scholars, fatherlessness has become the single most powerful determinant of child poverty—more important than race, region, or the educational attainment of the mother. As William Julius Wilson and Kathryn M. Neckerman put it, "sex and marital status of the head are the most important determinants of poverty status for families."[13]

Similarly, Leif Jensen, David J. Eggebeen, and Daniel T. Lichter, analyzing a national child poverty rate that jumped from 14 percent in 1969 to 20.6 percent in 1990, despite much more social spending on children, attribute most of this surge to "the demographic shift of children living in married-couple families to 'high-risk' single-parent families." Echoing other scholars, they suggest that "changing family structure is the greatest long term threat to U.S. children."[14]

In his careful review of the evidence, William A. Galston, currently the deputy assistant to the president for domestic public policy, concludes that current research findings "suggest that the best anti-poverty program for children is a stable, intact family."[15] He might just as easily have said: a married father on the premises.

Paternal Disinvestment

In 1986, our society crossed an important threshold. That year, for the first time in our nation's history, a majority of all poor families were father-absent.[16] Historically, for most poor children, poverty stemmed primarily from fathers being unemployed or receiving low wages. For most poor children today, poverty stems primarily from not having a father in the home.

In strict economic terms, this trend can be understood as paternal disinvestment: the growing refusal of fathers to spend their resources on their offspring. This trend helps to explain an apparent paradox. Public spending on children in the United States has never been higher. At the same time, child poverty is spreading and child well-being is declining.[17] The explanation is that our rising public investment in children has been far outweighed by our private disinvestment, primarily paternal disinvestment.

Certainly, the clearest economic consequence of paternal disinvestment is rising child poverty, a condition that, in 1992, afflicted 22 percent of all children under age eighteen and 25 percent of all children under age six.[18] But paternal disinvestment also produces an economic ripple effect that extends well beyond the official definition of poverty. For even when fatherlessness does not consign children to poverty, it commonly consigns them to a childhood—and frequently an early adulthood as well—marked by persistent economic insecurity.

For example, divorce typically means lower living standards for women and children. One study estimates that, in the year following divorce, average income for women drops by approximately 30 percent.[19] Even the best postdivorce economic arrangements, in which fathers regularly pay child support, almost always mean less money and more insecurity for children—including fewer traditional childhood activities such as athletics, summer camp, vacations, school trips, and swimming lessons. A 1991 study concludes: "other than paying child support and buying gifts, the majority of [divorced] fathers have never provided assistance to their children."[20]

A New Source of Social Inequality

Moreover, millions of children in our society—from those who have never seen their fathers to those whose absent fathers visit regularly and pay child support—fail to receive any financial support from their fathers precisely when they need it the most: when they are crossing the threshold of adulthood. As they enter their late teens and early twenties, these young people will want to buy a car. They will want to go to college, or make a down payment on a house, or buy furniture for an apartment, or find a cosigner for a bank loan. But, unlike previous generations, these young people will get no help from their fathers. Even among divorced fathers who pay child support, the end of the support order, usually when the child reaches age eighteen, usually signals the end of support. In her study of paternal support following divorce, Judith S. Wallerstein was dismayed to find that many fathers

> who had maintained contact with their children over the decade, who had supported them with regularity, and who were well able to continue supporting them financially, failed to do so at the time when their youngsters' economic and educational preparation for adulthood was at stake.[21]

For many young people, this paternal disinvestment in young adulthood contributes to downward social mobility. Although many children manage to do well without a father's help, those who grow up without fathers are far more likely to move down, not up, the socioeconomic ladder. Sons are especially affected, since they are the traditional beneficiaries of a father's occupational guidance and role modeling.[22]

In a larger sense, the cessation of the intergenerational transfer of paternal wealth—from father to child and from paternal grandparents to grandchild—is likely to emerge by the early years of the next century not only as a growing determinant of individual economic well-being but also as a new source of social inequality. For as fatherlessness spreads, the economic difference between America's haves and have-nots will increasingly revolve around a basic question: Which of us had fathers?

Adolescent Childbearing

After protection and provision, the central task of fatherhood is cultural transmission. In many respects, the single most consequential development in the story of human fatherhood, powerfully portrayed in classic texts such as the Bible's Book of Genesis, is the movement of males toward understanding their paternity not simply as biological insemination, nor even primarily as providing resources and warding off danger, but also—and perhaps most important—as "manhandling" their offspring: making sure not only that the child survives, but also that the child grows up to be a certain kind of person.

Here we see the essential difference between biological paternity and fatherhood. The former helps to produce a child. The latter helps to produce an adult. In the broadest sense, cultural transmission can be understood as fathers and mothers, in overlapping but distinctive ways, teaching their children a way of life. The result of effective cultural transmission is the development of competence and character in children.

Fatherlessness—the absence of paternal transmission—contributes to a decline of character and competence in children. Today, a growing characterological deficit among children is widely evident in our society, affecting countless aspects of children's behavior and mental health, from school misconduct to eating disorders to the decline of politeness and manners.[23] For this reason, characterological disinvestment by fathers is harder to quantify than economic disinvestment, but it is far more important. For children, doing without a father's money is the easy part. Money influences what you have and what you can do. Fathers shape who you are.

For boys, the most socially acute manifestation of paternal disinvestment is juvenile violence. For girls, it is juvenile and out-of-wedlock childbearing. One primary result of growing fatherlessness is more boys with guns. Another is more girls with babies. . . .

Many studies confirm that girls who grow up without fathers are at much greater risk for early sexual activity, adolescent childbearing, divorce, and lack of sexual confidence and orgasmic satisfaction.[24] These problems do not stem primarily from economic status. Scholars have studied this issue carefully, documenting the effects on girls of fatherless homes while controlling for income—that is, eliminating income as a dependent variable in the studies. They have concluded that father absence, not money absence, is the core issue.

For example, Garfinkel and McLanahan, in their careful summary of the research on the many "intergenerational consequences" of fatherless homes, place special emphasis on the "family formation behavior" of girls who grow up without fathers. Among white families, one study finds that "daughters of single parents are 53 percent more likely to marry as teenagers, 111 percent more likely to have children as teenagers, 164 percent more likely to have a premarital birth, and 92 percent more likely to dissolve their own marriages."[25] . . .

The Crisis of Fatherlessness

From a societal perspective, this particular consequence of fatherlessness is very much like most others. It is not remediable. Paternal disinvestment cannot be offset by either maternal investment or public investment. As a society, we will not solve our crisis of fatherlessness with prison cells, mentoring programs, antiviolence curricula, boyfriends, antistalking laws, children's advocates, income transfers, self-esteem initiatives, or even mothers. We will solve it only with fathers.

Notes

1. The most recent empirical confirmation of this thesis, drawing upon a four-decade study of fathers and their children, can be found in John Snarey, *How Fathers Care for the Next Generation* (Cambridge, Mass.: Harvard University Press, 1993), 84–119. Perhaps the most well-known statement of this theme comes from Erik H. Erikson's discussion of "generativity" in *Childhood and Society*, 2d ed. (New York: Norton, 1963), 266, passim.
2. Jane B. Lancaster and Chet S. Lancaster, "The Watershed: Change in Parental-Investment and Family Formation Strategies in the Course of Human Evolution," in Jane B. Lancaster et al., eds., *Parenting Across the Life Span: Biosocial Dimensions* (New York: Aldine de Gruyter, 1987), 189.
3. The leading cause of the decline of child well-being is the steady breakup of the mother-father child-raising unit. This proposition, for years the subject of heated scholarly and public debate, is now increasingly supported by the weight of scholarly evidence. This evidence has been summarized in recent years by numerous bipartisan national commissions. For example, see *Starting Points: Meeting the Needs of Our Youngest Children* (New York: Carnegie Corporation, 1994); *Families First: Report of the National Commission on America's Urban Families* (Washington, D.C.: U.S. Government Printing Office, (1993); and National Commission on Children, *Beyond Rhetoric: A New American Agenda for Children and Families* (Washington, D.C.: U.S. Government Printing Office, 1991). See also Ronald J. Angel and Jacqueline L. Angel, *Painful Inheritance: Health and the New Generation of Fatherless Children* (Madison: University of Wisconsin Press, 1993).
4. "Saving Youth from Violence," *Carnegie Quarterly* 39, no. 1 (winter 1994): 1–15.
5. *Youth and Violence: Psychology's Response*, vol. 1 (Washington, D.C.: American Psychological Association Commission on Violence and Youth, 1993). See also Barbara Kantrowitz, "Wild in the Streets," *Newsweek*, August 2, 1993, 40.

   For two additional scholarly examples of this basic understanding of the problem, see *Call for Violence Prevention and Intervention on Behalf of Very Young Children* (Arlington, Va.: Violence Study Group of the National Center for Clinical Infant Programs, 1993); and Deborah Prothrow-Stith, *Deadly Consequences: How Violence Is Destroying Our Teenage Population and a Plan to Begin Solving the Problem* (New York: HarperCollins, 1993).

   Throughout this national discussion of youth violence, special emphasis has been placed on new ways for teachers and other professionals to help children both avoid and cope with violence. For example, in 1993, the Erikson Institute for Advanced Study in Child Development published *Let's Talk About Living in a World with Violence*, an activity book for schoolchildren designed to "help children process their feelings and experiences about violence." See *Erikson* (fall/winter 1993): 25. See also Daniel Goleman, "Schools Try to Tame Violent Pupils, One Punch and One Taunt at a Time," *New York Times*, August 19, 1993, 12.

6. Much contemporary writing on fatherhood dwells almost exclusively on what might be termed the affective potential of paternity: the need for fathers to become more sensitive, more communicative, more nurturing, more egalitarian, and more emotionally accessible. This concern is important; but we misunderstand the issue if we isolate it from the larger context of male behavior in families and society.

Yes, paternal behavior includes an important affective dimension. Yet in all human societies, for better or worse, paternal behavior (and maternal behavior, too, for that matter) ranges well beyond the affective dimension, with great social consequences for children and society. The evidence is fairly clear: There is more to the male animal than its potential for nurturing.

Consider two of the harder truths about male behavior. Men compete with one another, often violently, over money, status, and sex. The overwhelming majority of violent acts in our increasingly disordered society are committed by men. Although the gap is lessening, men still earn and control most of the money in our society.

These are basic things that men do. They are not small matters. They can change, but they will not disappear anytime soon. Such enduring male problems are related to issues of emotional sensitivity and nurturant behavior, but they also extend well beyond them, pointing us toward the problematic essence of what it means to be a man. Moreover, these core dilemmas of masculinity—including the ultimate question of whether male behavior can be guided toward prosocial ends—are inextricably linked to the status of fatherhood. Consequently, a serious analysis of fatherhood must directly confront these primary questions concerning violence and money.

7. U.S. Bureau of the Census, "Poverty in the United States: 1992," Current Population Reports, series P-60, no. 185 (Washington, D.C.: U.S. Government Printing Office, September 1993), x.

8. U.S. Bureau of the Census, "Money Income of Households, Families, and Persons in the United States: 1992," Current Population Reports, series P-60, no. 184 (Washington, D.C.: U.S. Government Printing Office, September 1993), 68–69.

9. U.S. Bureau of the Census, "Poverty in the United States: 1992," xv.

10. Ibid., table 4, p. 8.

11. Irwin Garfinkel and Sara S. McLanahan, *Single Mothers and Their Children: A New American Dilemma* (Washington, D.C.: Urban Institute, 1986), 11.

12. David T. Ellwood, *Poor Support: Poverty in the American Family* (New York: Basic Books, 1988), 46.

13. William Julius Wilson and Kathryn M. Neckerman, "Poverty and Family Structure: The Widening Gap Between Evidence and Public Policy Issues," in Sheldon H. Danziger and Daniel H. Weinberg, eds., *Fighting Poverty: What Works and What Doesn't* (Cambridge, Mass.: Harvard University Press, 1986), 240.

14. Leif Jensen, David J. Eggebeen, and Daniel T. Lichter, "Child Poverty and the Ameliorative Effects of Public Assistance," *Social Science Quarterly* 74, no. 3 (September 1993): 542, 544.

The increase in child poverty during the past two decades reverses the progress made in the years between 1949 and 1973, when child poverty dropped dramatically. From close to 50 percent in 1949, the child poverty rate was halved by 1959, and almost halved again by 1973. But then it began to rise. By 1991, the child poverty rate had climbed back nearly to the level of 1965, the year that President Lyndon Johnson announced the War on Poverty.

Moreover, in looking at the historical trends, what stands out most clearly is the growing income gap between two-parent and single-parent homes, regardless of race. For example, two-parent black families today are economically better off than white single-parent families. Indeed, the poverty rate for two-parent black families has fallen substantially since 1969. As a predictor of poverty, the influence of race is declining; the influence of family structure is rising. See Sandra K. Danziger and Sheldon Danziger, "Child Poverty and Public Policy: Toward a Comprehensive Antipoverty Agenda," *Daedalus* 122, no. 1 (winter 1993): 59–61.

15. William A. Galston, "Causes of Declining Well-Being Among U.S. Children," *Aspen Institute Quarterly* 5, no. 1 (winter 1993): 68.

16. U.S. Bureau of the Census, "Poverty in the United States: 1992," xvi.

17. The contrast of rising public spending on children and declining child well-being is examined in Victor R. Fuchs and Diane M. Reklis, "America's Children: Economic Perspectives and Policy Options," *Science* 255, no. 3 (January 1992): 41–46; Peter Uhlenberg and David Eggebeen, "The Declining Well-Being of American Adolescents," *The Public Interest*, no. 82 (winter 1986): 25–38; Uhlenberg and Eggebeen, "Hard Times for American Youth: A Look at the Reasons," *National Association of Secondary School Principals Bulletin* 72, no. 508 (May 1988): 47–51; and Jensen, Eggebeen, and Lichter, "Child Poverty."

18. U.S. Bureau of the Census, "Poverty in the United States: 1992," x.

19. Saul D. Hoffman and Greg J. Duncan, "What Are the Economic Consequences of Divorce?" *Demography* 25, no. 4 (November 1988): 641.

20. Jay D. Teachman, "Contributions to Children by Divorced Fathers," *Social Problems* 38, no.3 (August 1991): 368.

21. Judith S. Wallerstein and Shauna B. Corbin, "Father-Child Relationships After Divorce: Child Support and Educational Opportunity," *Family Law Quarterly* 20, no. 2 (summer 1986): 110.

22. See Timothy J. Biblarz and Adrian E. Raftery, "The Effects of Family Disruption on Social Mobility," *American Sociological Review* 58, no. 1 (February 1993): 97–109. They conclude: "Family disruption affects occupational mobility in contemporary American society in two ways. First is the direct effect of family disruption: Men from nonintact family backgrounds have greater odds of entering low status occupations as opposed to high status occupations. Second is the conditional effect of family disruption: Family disruption weakens intergenerational inheritance and resemblance, even after the disruption's direct effects are taken into account. Hence, including family structure in studies of social mobility adds to our understanding of the present distribution of occupations" (p. 107). See also Jiang Hong Li and Roger A. Wojtkiewicz, "A New Look at the Effects of Family Structure on Status Attainment," *Social Science Quarterly* 73, no. 3 (September 1992): 581–95.

23. Urie Bronfenbrenner of Cornell University, one of the nation's leading family scholars, powerfully underscores this point: "Controlling for associated factors such as low income, children growing up in such [female-headed] households are at greater risk for experiencing a variety of behavioral and educational problems, including extremes of hyperactivity

or withdrawal, lack of attentiveness in the classroom, difficulty in deferring gratification, impaired academic achievement, school misbehavior, absenteeism, dropping out, involvement in socially alienated peer groups, and especially, the so-called 'teenage syndrome' of behaviors that tend to hang together—smoking, drinking, early and frequent sexual experience, and, in the more extreme cases, drugs, suicide, vandalism, violence, and criminal acts." See Urie Bronfenbrenner, "Discovering What Families Do," in David Blankenhorn, Steven Bayme, and Jean Bethke Elshtain, eds., *Rebuilding the Nest: A New Commitment to the American Family* (Milwaukee: Family Service America, 1990), 34.

24. Interestingly, the research on sexual satisfaction challenges the belief that, for daughters, fathers simply reinforce sexual inhibition. In this common view, a father's influence on his daughter's sexuality is essentially restrictive rather than empowering. The father's goal for his daughter is sexual modesty, not pleasurable sexual experiences. Yet research on female sexual satisfaction suggests that, in addition to lowering the risk for precocious sexual behavior and adolescent childbearing, effective fatherhood contributes significantly to the later sexual happiness of daughters. For example, Seymour Fisher, in his research on the psychological aspects of orgasmic difficulties in women, concludes that "the greater the difficulty women had in becoming orgiastically excited the more anxiously preoccupied they were about loss." What kind of loss? In Fisher's study, preoccupation with loss among low-orgasmic women—anxiety about losing something that is love giving but undependable—stems in large measure from nonexistent or highly tenuous father-daughter relationships. Other studies confirm the importance of father loss as a foundation of female sexual anxiety about "loss of love." Moreover, "in contrast to the confluence of findings affirming the role of fear of loss in inhibiting orgasm, largely negative results have emerged from the study of many other variables. Orgasm consistency has proven to be unrelated to such diverse factors as early dating history, reaction to first menstrual period, anxiety about sexual stimuli, mode of expressing hostility, masochism, anxiety level, achievement drive, sense of humor, amount of use of alcohol and cigarettes, various personality traits, and political conservatism-liberalism. The positive findings pinpointing the significance of concern about loss stand out in an otherwise largely negative array." See Seymour Fisher, *Sexual Images of the Self* (Hillsdale, N.J.: Lawrence Erlbaum, 1989), 43–44, 46.

25. Garfinkel and McLanahan, *Single Mothers and Their Children*, 30–31.

Societal Biases Perpetuate Child Poverty

by Herbert J. Gans

Herbert J. Gans is the Robert S. Lynd Professor of Sociology at Columbia University. In the following viewpoint, Gans argues that commonly used pejorative behavioral labels may prevent poor children and their families from escaping poverty by negatively influencing the behavior of poor people and public attitudes towards them. Labels such as "underclass," literally banish the poor from the class hierarchy, designate the poor as undeserving of help, and distract the public from the core causes of poverty. Other labels, usually based on stereotypes, become self-fulfilling prophecy for the labeled, Gans states. Teachers who label low-income students as unable to learn, for example, may devote less effort to teaching them. Even if this is unintentional, Gans argues, these students will become less able to learn and will never acquire the tools that might provide a way out of poverty.

"The danger common to all behavioral labels . . . is that they focus on behavior that hides the poverty causing it, and substitutes as its cause moral or cultural or genetic failures."

One of America's popular pejorative labels is "slum," which characterizes low-income dwellings and neighborhoods as harmful to their poor occupants and the rest of the community.[1] In the nineteenth century, slums were often faulted for turning the deserving poor into the undeserving poor, but in the twentieth century the causality was sometimes reversed, so that poor people with "slum-dweller hearts" were accused of destroying viable buildings and neighborhoods.

After World War II, "slum" and "slum dweller" as well as "blight" all became more or less official labels when the federal government, egged on by a variety of builder and realty pressure groups, started handing out sizeable sums for the "clearance" of low-income neighborhoods unfortunate enough to fit these terms as they were defined in the 1949 U.S. Housing Act.[2] Although by and large only slums located in areas where private enterprise could build luxury and other profitable housing were torn down, more than a million poor households lost their homes in the next twenty years, with almost nothing done for the people displaced from them.

This viewpoint is written with that much-told history in mind, in order to suggest that the underclass label—as well as all but the most neutrally formulated behavioral term—can have dangerous effects for the poor and for antipoverty policy. While the emphasis will be on "underclass," the dangers of related labels will be discussed as well.

Labels may be only words, but they are judgmental or normative words, which can stir institutions and individuals to punitive actions. The dangers from such labels are many, but the danger common to all behavioral labels and terms is that they focus on behavior that hides the poverty causing it, and substitutes as its cause moral or cultural or genetic failures.[3]

"The Underclass" as Code Word

The term "underclass" has developed an attention-getting power that constitutes its first danger. The word has a technical aura that enables it to serve as a euphemism or code word to be used for labeling.[4] Users of the label can thus hide their disapproval of the poor behind an impressively academic term. "Underclass" has also become morally ambiguous, and as it is often left undefined, people can understand it in any way they choose, including as a label.

Because "underclass" is a code word that places some of the poor *under* society and implies that they are not or should not be *in* society, users of the term can therefore favor excluding them from the rest of society without saying so.[5] Once whites thought of slaves, "primitives," and wartime enemies as the inhuman "other," but placing some people under society may not be altogether different.[6]

A subtler yet in some ways more insidious version of the exclusionary mechanism is the use of "underclass" as a synonym for the poor, deserving and undeserving. While not excluding anyone from society, it increases the social distance of the poor from everyone else. This distance is increased further by the contemporary tendency of elected officials and journalists to rename and upgrade the working class as the lower middle class—or even the middle class.

Because "underclass" is also used as a racial and even ethnic code word, it is a convenient device for hiding antiblack or anti-Latino feelings. As such a code word, "underclass" accommodates contemporary taboos against overt prejudice, not to mention hate speech. Such taboos sometimes paper over—and even repress—racial antagonisms that people do not want to express openly.

Ironically, the racial code word also hides the existence of very poor whites who suffer from many of the same problems as poor blacks. When used as a racial term, "underclass" blurs the extent to which the troubles of whites and blacks alike are generated by the economy and by classism or class discrimination and require class-based as well as race-based solutions.

Like other code words, "underclass" may interfere with public discussion. Disapproval of the actions of others is part of democracy, but code words make covert what needs to be overt in order for the disapproval to be questioned and debated. If openly critical terms such as "bums" and "pauper" were still in use, and if umbrella terms such as "underclass" were replaced with specific ones such as "beggars" or "welfare dependents," upset citizens could indicate clearly the faults of which they want to accuse poor people. In that case, public discussion might be able to deal more openly with the feelings the more fortunate classes hold about the poor, the actual facts about the poor, and the policy issues having to do with poverty and poverty-related behavior. . . .

The Reification of the Label

A further source of danger is the reification of the label, which takes place when a definition is awarded the gift of life and label users believe there to be an actually existing and homogeneous underclass that is composed of whatever poor people are currently defined as underclass. Reification, which turns a definition into an actual set of people, hides the reality that the underclass is an imagined group that has been constructed in the minds of its definers. Once a stigmatized label is reified, however, visible signs to identify it are sure to be demanded sooner or later, and then invented, so that people bearing the signs can be harassed more easily.

Furthermore, once the signs are in place so that imagined groups can be made actual, the labels run the danger of being treated as causal mechanisms. As a result, the better-off classes may decide that being in the underclass is a cause of becoming homeless or turning to street crime. Homelessness then becomes a symptom of underclass member-ship, with the additional danger of the hidden policy implication: that the elimination of the underclass would end homelessness, thereby avoiding the need for affordable housing or for jobs and income grants for the homeless.

Even purely descriptive terms referring to actual people, such as "welfare recipients," can be reified and turned into causal labels. People may thus persuade themselves to believe that being on welfare is a cause of poverty, or of single-parent families. Once so persuaded, they can propose to eliminate both effects by ending welfare, and without ap-pearing to be inhumane—which is what conservative politicians running for office, and the intellectuals supporting them, have been doing since the early 1990s. They ignore the fact that in the real world the causal ar-row goes in the other direction, but they achieve their political aim, even if they also harm poor mothers and their children.

Since popular causal thinking is almost always moral as well as em-pirical, the reification of a label like the "underclass" usually leads to the assignment of *moral* causality. If the underclass is the cause of behavior that deviates from mainstream norms, the solution is moral condemna-tion, behavioral modification, or punishment by the elimination of fi-nancial aid. Thus people are blamed who are more often than not victims instead of perpetrators, which ignores the empirical causes, say, of street crime, and interferes with the development of effective anti-crime policy. Blaming people may allow blamers to feel better by blow-ing off the steam of righteous (and in the case of crime, perfectly justified) indignation, but even justified blaming does not constitute or lead to policy for ending street crime.[7] . . .

The Dangers of the Umbrella Effect

Since "underclass" is an umbrella label that can include in its definition all the various behavioral and moral faults that label-makers and users choose to associate with it, two further dangers accrue to those it labels.

The sheer breadth of the umbrella label seems to attract alarmist writers who magnify the many kinds of moral and behavioral harmful-ness attributed to people it names. A correlate of the umbrella effect is amnesia on the part of writers about the extreme and usually persistent poverty of the labeled. Thus, the more widely people believe in the va-lidity of the underclass label, and the broader its umbrella becomes, the more likely it is that political conditions will not allow for reinstituting effective antipoverty policy. If the underclass is dangerous, and danger-ous in so many different ways, it follows that the government's responsibility is to beef up the police, increase the punishments courts can demand, and create other punitive agencies that try to protect the rest of society from this dangerous class.

Umbrella labels also do harm when they lump into a single term a variety of diverse people with different problems.[8] This ignores the reality that the people who are assigned the underclass label have in common only that their actual or imagined behaviors upset the mainstream population, or the politicians who claim to speak in its name. Using this single characteristic to classify people under one label can be disastrous, especially if politicians and voters should ever start talking about comprehensive "underclass policies," or what Christopher Jencks has called "meta solutions."[9] For one thing, many of the people who are tagged with the label have not even deviated from mainstream norms, and yet others have done nothing illegal. An underclass policy would thus be a drastic violation of civil rights and civil liberties.

At this writing, electioneering politicians as well as angry voters still remain content with policies that harm the people who bear specific labels, such as welfare recipients, illegal immigrants, and the homeless. . . .

Even a thoughtful underclass policy would be dangerous, because the people forced under the underclass umbrella suffer from different kinds of poverty and, in some cases, poverty-related problems, which may require different solutions. Reducing poverty for able-bodied workers requires labor market policy change; reducing it for people who cannot work calls for a humane income grant program. Enabling and encouraging young people to stay in school requires different policies than the elimination of homelessness, and ending substance abuse or street crime demand yet others. Labelers or experts who claim one policy can do it all are simply wrong.

The Human Dangers of Labeling

Most immediately, the underclass label poses a danger for poor people in that the agencies with which they must deal can hurt clients who are so labeled.[10] For one thing, agencies for the poor sometimes build labels into their operating procedures and apply them to all of their clients. As a result, either evidence about actual clients is not collected, or the label is assumed to fit regardless of evidence to the contrary. Agencies responsible for public safety typically resort to this procedure as a crime prevention or deterrence measure, especially when those labeled have little legal or political power. For example, in 1993, the Denver police department compiled a roster of suspected gang members based on "clothing choices," "flashing of gang signals," or associating with known gang members. The list included two-thirds of the city's young black men, of whom only a small percentage were actual gang members.[11]

Labeling also creates direct punitive effects of several kinds. Bruce Link's studies of people labeled as mentally ill have found that the labeling act itself can lead to depression and demoralization, which prevent those labeled from being at their best in job interviews and other competitive situations.[12] Likewise, when poor youngsters who hang out on street corners are treated as "loiterers," they may end up with an arrest record that hurts them in later life—which is probably why middle-class teenagers who also hang out are rarely accused of loitering.

Some effects of labels are felt even earlier in children's lives. Teachers treat students differently if they think they come from broken homes.[13] A long-term study of working-class London has found that labeling effects may even be intergenerational. Labeling of parents as delinquent makes it more likely that their children will also be labeled, adding to the numbers in both generations who are accused of delinquent or criminal behavior.[14]

Sometimes the effect of labeling is more indirect: agencies cut off opportunities and the label turns into a self-fulfilling prophecy. When teachers label low-income or very dark-skinned students as unable to learn, they may reduce their efforts to teach them—often unintentionally, but even so students then become less able to learn. If poor youngsters accused of loitering are assumed to have grown up without the self-control thought to be supplied by male supervision, they may be harassed—sometimes to tease and entrap them into an angry response. The arrests and arrest records that inevitably follow may deprive youngsters from fatherless families of legal job opportunities, and help force them into delinquent ones. In all these cases, the self-fulfilling prophecy is used to declare the labeled guilty without evidence of misconduct. . . .

Labels Hurt Many People

The labels that have produced these effects are not created solely from overheated mainstream fears or imaginations. Like all stereotypes, such labels are built around a small core of truth, or apply "to a few bad apples," as lay psychology puts it. Labeling, however, punishes not only the bad apples but everybody in the population to whom the label is applied. By labeling poor young black males as potential street criminals, for example, the white and black populations fearful of being attacked may feel that they protect themselves, but at the cost of hurting and antagonizing the large majority of poor young black males who are innocent. Inevitably, however, a proportion of the innocent will react angrily to the label, and find ways of getting even with those who have labeled them. In the end, then, everyone loses, the label users as well as the labeled.

Nonetheless, labeling is only a by-product of a larger structural process that cannot be ignored. In any population that lacks enough legitimate opportunities, illegitimate ones will be created and someone will take them. When the jobs for which the poor are eligible pay such a low wage that even some of the employed will turn to drug selling or other crime to increase their incomes, the labeling process is set in motion that finally hurts many more people, poor and nonpoor, whether or not they are guilty or innocent. Still, the real guilt has to be laid at the door of the employers that pay insufficient wages and the market conditions that may give some of them little other choice.

The Inaccuracies of Labels

Last but not least, labels are dangerous simply because they are inaccurate. "Underclass" is inaccurate if interpreted literally, because there can be no class that exists *under* society, as the class hierarchy extends from the top of society to its very bottom. Indeed, "underclass" is like "underworld," which is also part of society, and in fact could not long exist if it were not supplying demanded goods or services to an "overworld."[15]

"Underclass" is also an inaccurate label because it so vague that there is no agreement on a single or simple definition. Several other labels, however, which have evolved from descriptive terms about which there is widespread consensus, offer good illustrations of how much the portraits of the labeled vary from data on actual people.

"Welfare dependent," "single-parent family," "teenage mother" and "the homeless" are relevant examples. "Welfare dependent" is a corruption of "welfare recipient," which assumes that recipients become dependent on the government by virtue of obtaining welfare. In fact, however, only 30 percent of all recipients who begin a period on welfare will stay on for more than two years, and only 7 percent will be on more than eight years, although some of those who leave it also return to it later.[16] Further, about 20 percent of all welfare recipients report non-AFDC income, although if off-the-books employment is counted, nearly half of all recipients are working.[17]

Some recipients would leave welfare and take their chances in the labor market if they could obtain medical insurance for their children. Still, many poor women clearly rely on AFDC and are thus dependent on the government program; what is noted less often is that often they are even more dependent on staying in the good graces of their welfare agency, which can decide to cut them off arbitrarily without a great deal of accountability.

Ironically enough, only welfare recipients are accused of being dependents; others who are subsidized by government without adding something to the economy in exchange for their subsidy are not so labeled. Students with government fellowships, home owners who receive federal tax and mortgage interest deductions, corporations that receive subsidies to stay in existence, as well as unproductive civil servants and the workers on superfluous military bases kept open to prevent the elimination of jobs, are not thought of as being dependent. Thus the economic dependency of welfare recipients is not the real issue, and the label is misnamed as well as partly inaccurate.

"Single-parent family," or at least the label, is also partly or wholly incorrect. For one thing, some families have a man in or near the household de facto if not de jure; more are embedded in an extended family in which mothers, grandmothers, and others share the parenting.[18]

The notion that the children of such families are subject to undue school leaving, joblessness, and poverty, as well as crime and various pathologies, because they did not grow up in two-parent households is similarly incorrect. Since the modern family is not an economically productive institution, single-parenthood per se cannot logically cause poverty in the next generation, any more than growing up in a two-parent family can cause affluence. This helps to explain why well-off single parents are rarely accused of raising children who will grow up with economic or other problems. And since single-parent households are almost always poorer than other poor households, at least when their economic condition is measured properly, whatever economic effects children from such households suffer can be traced to their more extreme poverty or greater economic insecurity.

In addition, while the children of happy two-parent families are best off, all other things being equal, the children of single parents are sometimes emotionally and otherwise better off than the children of two parents who are in constant conflict.[19] If parental conflict is more detrimental to children's well-being and performance than is single parenthood, it would explain the results of studies concluding that children of divorced parents are not uniformly worse off than those from intact families.[20] Since the scarcity of money is a major cause of conflict—and spouse battering—among poor parents, this also helps to explain further the unwillingness of pregnant young women to marry their partners if they are jobless. None of this argues that poor single-parent families are desirable and should be encouraged, because if there is only one parent, the economic and other burdens on her and the children are often too great, and all may suffer. But the single-parent family structure and the burdens that come with it are usually the result of poverty. . . .

Labels Express Mainstream Discontent

Labels, whether applied to welfare recipients, the homeless, and other poor people, cannot ever describe the labeled, because labels mainly describe their imagined behavioral and moral deviations from an assumed mainstream. Justified or not, labels express the discontents of the mainstream and those speaking for it, not the characteristics and conditions of the labeled themselves. When label users are discontented and seek people on whom they can project their frustrations, the accuracy of the resultant labels is not a major consideration. In fact, accuracy may get in the way if frustrated people want to be enraged by poor people and thus able to blame them.

Ultimately, however, even accurate labels for the poor are dangerous because the labels cannot end poverty or the criminal and offending poverty-related behavior of some of the poor, or the fear, anger, and unhappiness of the labelers. In the long run, these latter may be the most dangerous effects of labels.

Notes

1. This viewpoint is a drastically revised version of my "Deconstructing the Underclass: The Term's Dangers as a Planning Concept," *Journal of the American Planning Association* 52 (Summer 1990): 271–77; and chapter 21 of my *People, Plans and Policies* (New York: Columbia University Press, 1991, 1994). I am indebted to Michael B. Katz and Sharon Zukin for comments on these versions, and to the long list of scholars who wrote about the dangers of the term "underclass" before I did, among them Robert B. Hill, Richard McGahey, Jewelle T. Gibbs, and Michael B. Katz.
2. They deserve to be called official labels because the criteria by which federal government described slums and blight had as much to do with the undesirability of their poor inhabitants as with the condition of the housing in which they lived.
3. This is of course one of the virtues of labels for cultural and political conservatives who prefer not to acknowledge the existence of poverty.
4. Irving Lewis Allen distinguishes between euphemisms, which are innocently substituted for labels, and code words, which are intentional substitutes, but empirical researchers will have to discover whether people are willing to discuss the intent involved in Allen's distinction (Irving Lewis Allen, *Unkind Words: Ethnic Languages from Redskin to WASP* [New York: Bergin and Garvey, 1990], chap. 8).
5. European analysts have developed the phrase "social exclusion" to describe both economically excluded native-born people and immigrants who are excluded on ethnic, racial, or citizenship grounds. For a comprehensive

analysis, see Hilary Silver, "Social Exclusion and Social Solidarity: Three Paradigms" (Geneva: International Institute for Labour Studies, DP/69, 1994).

While the European phrase is a scholarly concept used for studies concerned with ending exclusion, it is possible to imagine redefinitions, particularly in America, in which the phrase becomes a popular label to condemn the excluded.

6. The prefix "under-" has often been pejorative in America, as in "underhanded," "underworld," and even the untranslated but occasionally used *Untermensch*.

7. Blaming poor people may help lead to their imprisonment, since prisons exist in part to isolate the blamed, but imprisonment does not seem to be an effective policy against street crime either.

8. William Kornblum, "Lumping the Poor: What *Is* the Underclass?" *Dissent* (Sept. 1984): 295–302.

9. Christopher Jencks, *Rethinking Social Policy: Race, Poverty and the Underclass* (Cambridge, Mass.: Harvard University Press, 1992), p. 202.

10. Such labeling is class-blind; it can hurt rich or poor, and it need not even be pejorative in intent. See, for instance, "A Disabilities Program that Got Out of Hand," *New York Times*, Apr. 8, 1994, pp. Al, B6, which describes the effects of special education experts labeling preschool children at one of New York City's most prestigious private schools.

11. Dirk Johnson, "Two of Three Young Black Men in Denver Listed by Police as Suspected Gangsters," *New York Times*, Dec. 11, 1993, p. B8. This procedure is akin to the one many police department "red squads" once used to list alleged communists.

12. Bruce Link, "Understanding Labeling Effects in the Area of Mental Disorders: An Assessment of the Effects of Expectations of Rejection," *American Sociological Review* 52 (Feb. 1987): 96–112.

13. Nan M. Astone and Sarah McLanahan, "Family Structure and High School Completion," (Madison, Wisconsin: Institute for Research on Poverty, discussion paper 905–9, 1989).

14. John Hagan and Alberto Palloni, "The Social Reproduction of a Criminal Class in Working-Class London," *American Journal of Sociology* 96 (Sept. 1990): 265–99.

15. The demanded goods and services the underclass supplies to the better-off are described in my discussion of the functions of the undeserving poor in chapter 4 of *The War Against the Poor*, by Herbert J. Gans.

16. Committee on Ways and Means, U.S. House of Representatives, *1993 Green Book* (Washington, D.C.: U.S. Government Printing Office, 1993), p. 716. At any given time, however, the majority on AFDC are long-term recipients who also take up most of the resources.

17. *1993 Green Book*, p. 706, and Jencks, *Rethinking Social Policy*, p. 208. Most worked part-time, and only prostitutes earned a high income.

18. See, for instance, Linda Burton, "Teenage Children as an Alternative Life Course Strategy in Multigeneration Black Families," *Human Nature* 1, no. 2 (1990): 123–43.

19. See, for instance, Helen J. and Vernon J. Raschke, "Family Conflict and Children's Self-Concepts: A Comparison of Intact and Single-Parent Families," *Journal of Marriage and the Family* 41 (1979): 367–74; and James Peterson and Nicholas Zill, "Marital Disruption, Parent-Child Relationships and Behav-

ior Problems in Children," *Journal of Marriage and the Family* 48 (1986): 295–307.

20. See, for instance, P. R. Amato and B. Keith, "Parental Divorce and the Well-Being of Children: A Meta-Analysis," *Psychological Bulletin* 110, no. 1 (1991): 26–46.

VIEWPOINT 4

Self-Defeating Values and Attitudes Perpetuate Child Poverty

by Myron Magnet

Myron Magnet is a member of the board of editors of *Fortune* magazine and a fellow of the Manhattan Institute for Policy Research. In the following viewpoint, Magnet argues that American society includes an underclass of people who are unwilling to work their way out of poverty. This underclass, he contends, is characterized by impoverished intellectual and emotional development and a lack of "inner resources" to take advantage of opportunities. These deficiencies are not of their own making; rather, they are the result of the 1960s cultural revolution which, Magnet argues, robbed the poor of responsibility for their fate and taught them to view themselves as victims of an unjust society. Blameless though the underclass may be in the creation of this mindset, Magnet states, they perpetuate it—and poverty—by passing on to their children a "self-defeating set of values and attitudes."

"The key to the mystery of why, despite opportunity, the poorest poor don't work is that their poverty is less an economic matter than a cultural one."

Weren't dizzying contrasts of wealth and poverty supposed to have gone out with Dickensian London? What are they doing flagrantly alive again, deeply ingrained in the basic texture of today's American cities?

The daily juxtapositions are so bizarre that they strain belief, however numbingly familiar they grow. In New York City, directly under the windows of the treasure-crammed five-million-dollar apartments that loom over glittering Fifth Avenue, for instance, sleep the homeless, one

108

and sometimes two to a park bench, haggard, usually ill, huddled in rags turned dead gray with dirt and wear. In a gentrified neighborhood across town, bustling with upper-middle-class professionals, only a thickness of brick separates a building where staid burghers have paid upwards of three quarters of a million dollars for an apartment from the squalid crack house next door.

Not far away, for the last few Christmas seasons, the line of fur-coated holidaymakers jovially filing into a luxury food store to buy caviar advertised at "only" $260 a pound has adjoined the sullen line of ravaged paupers waiting for the soup kitchen to open at the church around the corner. Downtown, in the suave, postmodern towers that house health clubs, power lunches, and automated teller machines, grimy derelicts looking like leftovers from the Depression haunt the gleaming atriums for warmth and safety, while above sit dapper invest-ment bankers, some of whom made seven-figure incomes rearranging the industrial order before they were forty. As for the urban parks and pillared train stations that speak of a once-confident civic pride and prosperity, how often are they now—graffitied, vandalized, reeking of human waste—but dreary gauntlets of beggary?

Or worse: think of the savage 1989 rape of a twenty-eight-year-old jog-ger by a "wilding" pack of Harlem teenagers in New York's Central Park. What starker contrast of Haves and Have-Nots could be found than be-tween the victim, a Wall Street investment banker ambitious to excel in every pursuit, and her brutal attackers, unregenerate beneficiaries of a wide array of social programs designed to uplift the "disadvantaged"?

"Nobody's Mistreated Dependents"

Like Death interrupting the dumbstruck banquet, the poverty and vice that pervade America's cities appall the prosperous. What's wrong with the country, they worry, that such problems are everywhere? Does the same system that enriches the Haves simultaneously degrade the Have-Nots? Does the comfort of the prosperous somehow rest upon the de-basement of their poorest fellow citizens, the homeless and the underclass? Are the prosperous *responsible* for the condition of the poor?

When the Haves think about their relation to the poor, the images that come to mind feed their anxiety and sense of guilt: their brother's keeper . . . the biblical grandee Dives with the beggar Lazarus at his mansion gates . . . the religious duty to aid the poor. They think of Dick-ens's *Christmas Carol* or of "Good King Wenceslas," embodiments of that Victorian paternalist ethic that holds masters responsible for the condition of their dependents. Who doesn't remember how utterly a hard Scrooge devastates exploited Bob Cratchit and his family; how a reformed Scrooge, with the administration of a timely dose of paternalist generosity, gives Tiny Tim life? Exemplifying right treatment of the poor, Good King Wenceslas, his charity stronger than the fury of wild nature, carries a feast to his needy subject through a blizzard, proving himself worthy of God's blessing by blessing the poor.

But happily, modern society isn't hierarchical in Victorian fashion. Today's Haves aren't the "betters" or the "masters" of the Have-Nots, and today's worst-off poor are nobody's mistreated dependents or exploited employees: they are radically disconnected from the larger society, and they don't work. Victorian philanthropy isn't equal to their plight.

Impersonal and economic, rather than intimate and moral like the Victorian notions, modern theories hold the prosperous, as a class, responsible for the condition of the poor, as a class. Take Jesse Jackson's much-trumpeted theory of "economic violence," holding that the Reagan administration mindset that unfettered the rich simultaneously immiserated the poor by unraveling the social safety net. The rich got a tax break, leaving less revenue to go to the poor. A more sophisticated formulation holds that in the eighties the Haves created a world economy that handsomely rewards themselves while constricting opportunity for the Have-Nots.

The eloquent fact that means-tested federal welfare spending rose 44 percent between 1980 and 1987, however, explodes a theory like Jackson's. And further refuting this whole line of thought, the eighties boom that enriched the tycoons created an astonishing 18.4 million new jobs, both skilled and unskilled, offering a way out of poverty to almost any poor person with the willingness and discipline to work.

So even if the economic developments of the eighties did increase the disparity in income between the rich and the poor, I will argue . . . that those developments don't explain why we have an underclass or why the homeless haunt the streets. Since low-skill jobs exist in profusion, since work today will normally lift people above the poverty line, and since opportunity for further advancement is open to those with the ambition and energy to seize it, for the able-bodied poverty in America is no longer an utterly ineluctable fate: one can choose to try to escape, by legitimate rather than criminal paths, with a good chance of success.

Why Do the Poor Stay Poor?

But in that case, America's deepest-rooted poverty starts to look more than a little mysterious. If jobs do exist, as they did throughout the eighties, why do large numbers of very poor people remain in poverty? The emblem of this mystery, ubiquitous in big cities, is the panhandler begging outside McDonald's, right under the *Help Wanted* sign.

This viewpoint will suggest that the key to the mystery of why, despite opportunity, the poorest poor don't work is that their poverty is less an economic matter than a cultural one. In many cases . . . the Have-Nots lack the inner resources to seize their chance, and they pass on to their children a self-defeating set of values and attitudes, along with an impoverished intellectual and emotional development, that generally imprisons them in failure as well. Three, sometimes four generations have made the pathology that locks them in—school-leaving, nonwork, welfare dependency, crime, drug abuse, and the like—drearily familiar.

But the underclass culture they live in is far from being wholly of their own invention. Underclass culture has its own very distinct inflection, to be sure; but for all its idiosyncratic peculiarity it is a dialect, so to speak, shaped more by the culture as a whole, and by the singular history of underclass communities within that culture, than by any independent, internal dynamic.

An Honorable Aim

That's why the prosperous are indeed implicated in the poverty of the poor, even though they don't extract their BMWs from the hides of the underclass the way mine owners squeezed profits out of abused children in the early days of the Industrial Revolution, when "economic violence" was more than rhetoric. This viewpoint's central argument is that the Haves are implicated because over the last thirty years they radically remade American culture, turning it inside out and upside down to accomplish a cultural revolution whose most mangled victims turned out to be the Have-Nots.

This was the precise opposite of what was supposed to happen. For when the Haves began their cultural revolution a generation ago, they acted in the name of two related liberations. Above all, impelled by the fervor of the civil rights movement, they sought the political and economic liberation of the Have-Nots, the poor and the black. The ideal that guided them was a vision of democracy; their honorable aim was to complete democracy's work, to realize democratic values fully by making American society more open and inclusive. Out of this democratic impulse sprang the War on Poverty, welfare benefit increases, court-ordered school busing, more public housing projects, affirmative action, job-training programs, drug treatment programs, special education, *The Other America*, Archie Bunker, *Roots*, countless editorials and magazine articles and TV specials, black studies programs, multicultural curricula, new textbooks, all-black college dorms, sensitivity courses, minority set-asides, Martin Luther King Day, and the political correctness movement at col-

111

leges, to name only some of the almost endless manifestations.

The deep changes in the majority culture's beliefs about the nature of democratic society and the poor's place within it had momentous consequences for the worst-off. . . . But in addition to trying to liberate the poor and excluded from their marginality, the cultural revolution sought a second, even more spectacular liberation, which also shaped the fate of the poor, indirectly but far-reachingly.

This was the personal liberation that the Haves sought for themselves. Chafing against what the avant-garde writers and "sick" comedians of the fifties lambasted, only sometimes correctly, as that era's life-denying repression and conventionality, the Haves yearned to free themselves from a sense of anxious, stifling conformity, to claim a larger, more fulfilling life than that of an Organization Man or Man in the Gray Flannel Suit, or as a faceless atom in a Lonely Crowd, as titles of some of the era's influential texts had it.

That longing found two epochal expressions. The first was the sexual revolution, whose attitudes, diffused throughout the culture by advertising, movies, popular music, and television, so transformed values and behavior that they ultimately reshaped family life, increasing divorce, illegitimacy, and female-headed families on all levels of society.

The second manifestation was the sixties counterculture. As its name announced, the counterculture rejected traditional bourgeois culture as sick, repressive, and destructive. Bourgeois culture's sexual mores, based on guilt, marriage, and the perverse belief that present gratification should be deferred to achieve future goals, were symptoms of its pathology. Its sobriety and decorum were mere slavish, hypocritical conformism; its industriousness betokened an upside-down, materialistic value system; its family life was yet another arena of coercion and guilt. This culture went hand in hand with an inherently unjust capitalist economic order, and a political order whose murderousness was plainly revealed by "Amerika's" war in Vietnam.

By contrast, "letting it all hang out," expressing yourself, acting upon what you really feel, "doing it"—all this constituted authentic, liberated selfhood, healthy and life-affirming. Such free expressiveness would get you closer to the counterculture's cherished ideal of a guilt-free, undivided selfhood, described in the therapeutic language of psychoanalysis as filtered through counterculture gurus like Norman O. Brown and Herbert Marcuse.

No-Fault Social Policy

Consistent with that ideal, you didn't have to live by the disciplines of work and family and citizenship but could drop out from one or all, forging your own "alternative life-style," as the phrase went, more valid and authentic, and certainly more communitarian, than the conventional one. Moreover, you would get closer to authentic selfhood by kicking free of mechanical rationality and opening yourself to altered states of consciousness—drug-induced or not—that would let you behold truths deeper than reason reveals.

Just as you didn't have to frequent singles bars to be affected by the sexual revolution, you didn't have to live in a commune and eat mushrooms to be affected by the counterculture's quest for personal liberation. The new adversary stance toward conventional beliefs and ideals, breathlessly reported by the press and diffused almost instantly among the young, quickly put traditional values on the defensive, making them newly problematic even for those who continued to hold them.

And because the counterculture belonged to the young, its influence has persisted into the present, as the original Aquarians have matured into middle age and assumed positions of influence. That's what accounts for the dreams of so many Silicon Valley entrepreneurs that they'll drop out before long, or for the widespread use of cocaine in Hollywood and on Wall Street until recently. What you believe at twenty, as one historian has remarked, has a way of leaving its stamp on your worldview for life.

The cultural revolution's yoking together of personal and political liberations had a curious effect. It dignified the purely personal, making self-cherishing seem unselfish, almost civic-minded. Conversely, the irresponsibility that could mark the quest for personal liberation sometimes got carried over into social policy, too. The career of Senator Edward Kennedy exaggeratedly, almost parodically, exemplifies this process: as columnist Joe Klein has observed, the no-fault way in which he has conducted his personal life is mirrored by his no-fault social policy, all rights and entitlements without responsibilities.

A New Intractable Poverty

Partly because of this confusion of the selfish and the civic, the cultural revolution failed in devastating ways in both of its two large intentions. Instead of ending poverty for the Have-Nots—despite the civil rights movement, despite the War on Poverty—the new cultural order fostered, in the underclass and the homeless, a new, intractable poverty that shocked and dismayed, that seemed to belong more to the era of ragged chimney sweeps than to modern America, that went beyond the economic realm into the realm of pathology. Poverty turned pathological . . . because the new culture that the Haves invented—their remade system of beliefs, norms, and institutions—permitted, even celebrated, behavior that, when poor people practice it, will imprison them inextricably in poverty. It's hard to persuade ghetto fifteen-year-olds not to get pregnant, for instance, when the entire culture, from rock music to upscale perfume commercials to highbrow books, is intoxicated with the joy of what before AIDS was called "recreational" sex.

Worse, during the sixties and seventies, the new culture of the Haves, in its quest for personal liberation, withdrew respect from the behavior and attitudes that have traditionally boosted people up the economic ladder—deferral of gratification, sobriety, thrift, dogged industry, and so on through the whole catalogue of antique-sounding bourgeois virtues. As social thinker Irving Kristol puts it, "It's hard to rise above poverty if society keeps deriding the human qualities that allow you to escape from it."

Moreover . . . the new culture held the poor back from advancement by robbing them of responsibility for their fate and thus further squelching their initiative and energy. Instead of telling them to take wholehearted advantage of opportunities that were rapidly opening, the new culture told the Have-Nots that they were victims of an unjust society and, if they were black, that they were entitled to restitution, including advancement on the basis of racial preference rather than mere personal striving and merit. It told them that the traditional standards of the larger community, already under attack by the counterculture, often didn't apply to them, that their wrongdoing might well be justified rebellion or the expression of yet another legitimate "alternative lifestyle." It told them that, if they were mentally ill, they were really just marching to a different drummer and should be free to do their marching in the streets—which is where many of them ended up, homeless.

The new culture . . . allowed the neighborhoods of the Have-Nots to turn into anarchy, and it ruined the Have-Nots' schools by making racial balance, students' rights, and a "multicultural" curriculum more important than the genuine education vitally needed to rise. In all this, too, the new culture hinted to the Have-Nots that they must be slightly defective, or they wouldn't need such extraordinary measures. Otherwise—went the implication—if the Have-Nots hadn't been truly damaged by their deprivation, a simple opening of opportunity would have been enough to liberate them.

It wasn't only that the new cultural program failed the Have-Nots in important ways, as evidenced by the increase of the underclass and the homeless. The Haves harmed themselves with the new cultural order they brought into being. It was supposed to make their lives happier, more meaningful, more just. The personal liberation aspect of it was supposed to allow them to live more authentically, more intensely, with a larger area of pleasure and spontaneity in their lives. Instead, the personal freedom they claimed weakened families and communities, diluting the authority they had once had to invest individual life with meaning and solidity.

Even the aspect of the cultural revolution aiming to liberate the Have-Nots was also intended to increase the pleasure the Haves took in their own lives. It gave them an ennobling cause, larger than themselves and worth fighting for. They would make good on the long-imperfect American promise of doing justice to the poor and most especially by righting the historic wrongs done to blacks, finally creating the fully just, fully democratic society. Surely that part of the effort would allow the Haves to feel that their lives had moral substance and dignity. Were they inclined to use the language of religion, they might say it would show that they were justified. For the revolution was a kind of secular crusade, with the most elevated, sincere moral aims, for which the appropriate marching music might be "The Battle Hymn of the Republic."

Dubious Measures Led to Failure

For a generation, the moral intensity of these worthy aims gave social policy questions something of the aspect of faith. It invested policies designed to achieve these aims with the zeal that charged the aims themselves. Yet however creditable, that zeal made it hard to argue against the wisdom or efficacy of the specific policies. How could one argue against benevolence and goodwill? And if one asked if the policies were really working, the faith that can look beyond the mere appearances of things—the faith that is proof against the doubts of reason—would reply: how could they fail?

But very often they did fail, not merely leaving conditions for the Have-Nots unimproved but making them worse. And failure was the harder to confront because, beyond liberating the Have-Nots, the policies had the additional, unspoken aim of confirming the Haves in their sense of self-worth and moral excellence.

It was the harder to confront because of the price the Haves had been willing to pay to achieve success. For paradoxically, in the name of more perfect democracy, the cultural revolution trampled underfoot key democratic values. In order to gain laudable ethical ends, the Haves acquiesced in dubious and ultimately destructive measures such as the parceling out of rewards on the basis of race . . . or the excusing of criminals as themselves victims . . . or . . . the lifetime public support of able-bodied women whose only career was the production of illegitimate and mostly ill-parented children.

Countenancing these measures . . . subverted the fundamental democratic principles from which Americans derive their strongest sense of national identity and unity. However temporary, for however good a purpose, what most Americans knew to be wrong—imposing racial quotas, say, or freeing violent criminals on trivial technicalities—became officially right in the service of a supposedly higher value. When the evidence of their senses proclaimed the inevitable bad results of these measures, many even came to mistrust their senses.

A Crisis of Values

No wonder that their heads swam, that their ethical judgments became guarded and tentative, that they came to view moral assertions with wary cynicism. No wonder that so many complain that America is undergoing a crisis of values. That crisis—real enough—is not caused by greed, contrary to what is often alleged. . . . It is the unsurprising result of three decades of holding basic beliefs in abeyance and using questionable means to try to achieve a worthy social end. It is the result of making a democratic cultural revolution that ended—tragically—by making a travesty of the democratic values it had set out to uphold.

Before examining how waves of change in the elite culture rippled outward across American life and thought and engulfed the underclass, we need to focus . . . on the power of cultural forces to shape the material and institutional reality in which people live their lives. Then we need to examine the underclass and the homeless more precisely. . . . But first . . . let me add two brief general observations.

First, the cultural revolution was made by an elite of opinion makers, policymakers, and mythmakers—lawyers, judges, professors, political staffers, journalists, writers, TV and movie honchos, clergymen—and it was overwhelmingly a liberal, left-of-center elite. Thus for the last thirty years, the dominant American culture has been liberal culture; notwithstanding Republican presidents in the White House, the ideas and values that have come to Americans from their newspapers and network news programs, their university (and increasingly their grammar and high school) classrooms, their pulpits, their novels and movies and television sitcoms, their magazines and advertisements and popular music, their courtrooms and their Congress, have added up to a liberal, left-of-center worldview.

By no means did everyone embrace this culture, but it became the norm for a generation, and it formed the set of assumptions out of which social policy sprang. It became powerful enough to put those who didn't endorse it on the defensive. They came to look upon their own opposing views, however strongly held, as old-fashioned, no longer in the cultural mainstream, no longer utterable with the same intellectual and moral authority.

Most of those who did buy into the new culture, of course, didn't adopt it after careful study and analysis. Participating in a *Zeitgeist* is more a matter of sympathy, unexamined assumption, fashion, and political correctness. As a result, many of the Haves who bought into the new culture did so only partially, with reservations, in some cases without relinquishing diametrically opposed ideas. Consequently, at its farthest reaches the new culture was beset with strains; it wasn't a unitary system. When it came to such extreme practical embodiments of the cultural revolution as busing and especially affirmative action, many Haves grew restive and uncomfortable. But such was the power of the new culture that dissent became hard to express. Often enough, doubt manifested itself as a willful suspension of disbelief.

Second, when the Haves ask what responsibility they bear for the plight of the poor, they ask because they earnestly want to help. It would debase their lives, they feel, to be implicated in degradation they didn't try to relieve. What more, they wonder, should they be doing? "The emotional problem for the middle class is very real," political scientist Charles Murray once remarked, "but unrelated to the actual problem."

The bitter paradox that is so hard to face is that most of what the Haves have already done to help the poor—out of decent and generous motives—is part of the problem. Like gas pumped into a flooded engine, the more help they bestow, the less able do the poor become to help themselves. The problem isn't that the Haves haven't done enough but that they've done the diametrically wrong thing. "If people could just stop making things worse," concludes economist Thomas Sowell ruefully, "it would be an enormously greater contribution than they're likely to make any other way."

Excerpted from pages 13–23 of *The Dream and the Nightmare* by Myron Magnet. Copyright © 1993 by Myron Magnet. Reprinted by permission of William Morrow & Company, Inc.

CHAPTER 3

Is the Criminal Justice System Fair?

Chapter Preface

Dehundra Caldwell, a black seventeen-year-old honor student at Upson-Lee High School in Thomaston, Georgia, had no criminal record prior to August 1993. Neither did Sylvia Reed, a fifty-two-year-old white woman and chief financial officer for Alternative Schools Network in Chicago. Caldwell was convicted of burglary after he admitted accompanying two other boys who broke into the high school in July 1993 and stole a box of ice cream bars worth $20. He was sentenced to three years in prison. Reed admitted to stealing $180,000 from her employer in August 1993. Her sentence was probation and one thousand hours of community service.

Many blacks assert that the differences in the sentences between Caldwell and Reed illustrate the racism that is rampant in the American criminal justice system. Statistics show that although blacks represent only 12 percent of the U.S. population, they make up half the population in the nation's prisons. And a study released in October 1995 by the Sentencing Project, a Washington, D.C.–based organization that studies criminal justice issues and sentencing reform, found that 32.2 percent of black Americans are under the supervision of the criminal justice system. The Sentencing Project maintains that racism is a factor in the convictions of blacks on drug charges: "Blacks are arrested and confined in numbers grossly out of line with their use or sale of drugs," the report states.

While the criminal justice system may have discriminated against blacks in the past, it does not do so now, maintains Patrick A. Langan, a senior statistician with the U.S. Department of Justice's Bureau of Justice Statistics. He contends that a defendant's prior record and the seriousness of the offense have more of an influence on his or her arrest, prosecution, conviction, and sentencing than does the defendant's race. A study conducted by his department in 1993 found no significant disparities between the rates of prosecution and conviction of blacks and whites. Although this same study showed that more blacks were sentenced to prison than were whites, blacks committed more violent crimes and were more often repeat offenders, factors that judges strongly consider when handing down sentences.

Is the death penalty applied unfairly to blacks? Would harsher sentencing laws serve the cause of justice or weaken it? Should jurors use their verdicts to correct perceived inequities in the justice system? The authors in the following chapter examine fairness and inequities in the criminal justice system.

The Death Penalty Is Applied Unfairly to Blacks

by Jesse Jackson

The Rev. Jesse Jackson is president of the Rainbow Coalition, an economic justice and human rights alliance, and founder of Operation PUSH, an organization that works toward educational and economic equity for blacks and others in American society. He speaks and writes frequently on civil rights issues. In the following viewpoint, Jackson contends that the American justice system is institutionally racist, especially where the death penalty is concerned. Race, he states, is the determining factor in death penalty cases. African Americans, he says, are more likely to receive the death penalty than are whites charged with similar crimes. The race of the victim also influences who lives and who dies, Jackson argues, in that blacks who kill whites are more likely to receive a death sentence than are those who kill nonwhites.

"Bias and discrimination warp our nation's judicial system at the very time it matters most—in matters of life and death."

W ho receives the death penalty has less to do with the violence of the crime than with the color of the criminal's skin or, more often, the color of the victim's skin. Murder—always tragic—seems to be a more heinous and despicable crime in some states than in others. Women who kill and who are killed are judged by different standards than are men who are murderers and victims.

The death penalty is essentially an arbitrary punishment. There are no objective rules or guidelines for when a prosecutor should seek the death penalty, when a jury should recommend it, and when a judge should give it. This lack of objective, measurable standards ensures that the application of the death penalty will be discriminatory against racial, gender, and ethnic groups.

The majority of Americans who support the death penalty believe, or wish to believe, that legitimate factors such as the violence and cruelty with which the crime was committed, a defendant's culpability or history of violence, and the number of victims involved determine who is sentenced to life in prison and who receives the ultimate punishment. The numbers, however, tell a different story. They confirm the terrible truth that bias and discrimination warp our nation's judicial system at the very time it matters most—in matters of life and death. The factors that determine who will live and who will die—race, sex, and geography—are the very same ones that blind justice was meant to ignore. This prejudicial distribution should be a moral outrage to every American.

The Where and How of Executions

On September 1, 1995, legislation reinstituting the death penalty went into effect in New York, bringing the total of states with the death penalty to 38. Sadly, the list of states that do not employ capital punishment seems woefully short: Alaska, Hawaii, Iowa, Maine, Massachusetts, Michigan, Minnesota, North Dakota, Rhode Island, Vermont, West Virginia, Wisconsin, and the District of Columbia remain the only jurisdictions that have not adopted legal murder.

Between 1976, when the Supreme Court reinstated the use of capital punishment, and June 1996, 330 death row inmates have been executed. Over that period, the number of executions per year has generally risen. After a slow start—there were no executions in 1976 and only one in 1977—the rate started rising rapidly. Every year since 1984, the number of condemned prisoners executed has been in the double digits, with a high of 56 in 1995. With concerted efforts in the states and in Congress to cut off death row appeals, it appears that each new year will see a new record for executions. . . .

The Disproportionate Number of Blacks on Death Row

The relationship between race and capital punishment is much more complex than most people suppose. One surprise for many people is that more white defendants than black defendants have been executed. Since 1976, according to the Death Penalty Information Center, 56 percent of the condemned prisoners executed have been white, 38 percent have been black, and 6 percent have been Hispanic, Native American, or Asian. And death row population statistics reflect similar percentages. As of January 1996, 48 percent of the inmates on death row were white, 41 percent were black, 7.5 percent were Hispanic, and 3.5 percent were listed as "other." (See *Death Row, U.S.A.*, NAACP Legal Defense Fund.)

These statistics are simply the beginning of a chain that is not generally reported by the media, and so is not known by the public. Numerous researchers have shown conclusively that African American defendants are far more likely to receive the death penalty than are white defendants charged with the same crime. For instance, African Americans make up 25 percent of Alabama's population, yet of Alabama's 117 death row inmates, 43 percent are black. Indeed, 71 percent of the people executed there since the resumption of capital punishment have been black.

The population of Georgia's Middle Judicial Circuit is 40 percent black, but 77 percent of the circuit's capital decisions have been found against black defendants. The Ocmulgee Judicial Circuit posts remarkably similar numbers. In 79 percent of the cases in which the district attorney sought the death penalty, the defendant was black, despite the fact that only 44 percent of the circuit's population is black. More ominously, in the cases where black defendants faced capital prosecution, 90 percent of the district attorney's peremptory strikes were used to keep African Americans off the juries.

And this disproportion in capital sentencing is not just a Southern problem, for the results of the 1988 federal law providing for a death penalty for drug kingpins are telling. In 1993, all nine defendants approved for capital prosecution were African Americans. Of the first 36 cases in which prosecutors sought the death penalty under this new legislation, four of the defendants were white, four were Hispanic, and 28 were black. (See the Racial Justice Act, Y1.1/8 103–458.)

It's Not That You Kill, It's Who You Kill

It is not just the race of the defendant that affects the state's decision of whether to seek the death penalty and whether it is meted out. The race of the victim—more specifically, whether or not the victim was white—can have an even stronger influence.

Dr. David Baldus of the University of Iowa has studied over 2,500 Georgia murder cases. Controlling for 230 nonracial factors in the cases, he found that defendants accused of murdering a white victim are 4.3 times more likely to receive the death penalty than defendants accused of killing blacks. Baldus determined that the race of the murderer was less important than the race of the victim. Fewer than 40 percent of the homicide victims in Georgia are white, yet fully 87 percent of the cases resulting in the death penalty involved white victims.

Baldus cited one judicial circuit in Georgia where, despite the fact that 65 percent of the homicide cases involved African American victims, 85 percent of the cases in which the district attorney sought the death penalty were against murderers of whites. Overall, this particular district attorney sought the death penalty in 34 percent of the cases involving white victims but a mere 5.8 percent of the cases in which the victim was black. (See the Racial Justice Act, Y1.1/8 103–458.)

The Victim's Skin Color Matters

Georgia is not the only state where the color of the victim's skin can mean the difference between life and death. Nationwide, even though 50 percent of murder victims are African American, says the Death Penalty Information Center, almost 85 percent of the victims in death penalty cases are white. And in their 1989 book *Death and Discrimination: Racial Disparities in Capital Sentencing*, Samuel Gross and Robert Mauro analyzed sentencing in capital cases in Arkansas, Florida, Georgia, Illinois, Mississippi, North Carolina, Oklahoma, and Virginia during a period when these states accounted for 379 of the 1,011 death penalties nationwide. They found widespread discrepancies in sentencing based on the *victim's* race in all eight states.

Defendants in Florida, for example, who killed whites received the death penalty eight times more often than those defendants convicted of killing African Americans. In Bay County, blacks are the victims of 40 percent of the murders, yet in all 17 cases between 1975 and 1987 in which a death sentence was handed down, the victims were white.

As one study after another confirmed the correlation between the race of the homicide victim and whether the defendant would receive a capital sentence, the evidence became so overwhelming that Congress's General Accounting Office decided to take up the question itself. In its February 1990 report *Death Penalty Sentencing*, the GAO reviewed 28 studies based on 23 sets of data and concluded, "In eighty-two percent of the studies, race of the victim was found to influence the likelihood of being charged with capital murder or receiving the death penalty, i.e., those who murdered whites were found more likely to be sentenced to death than those who murdered blacks."

And when a case involves interracial murder, the bias against black homicide defendants multiplies the effects of the bias against the murderers of white victims. Since 1976, only four white defendants have

124

been executed for killing a black person, yet 75 back defendants have been executed for murdering a white person. Astoundingly, African Americans who murder whites are *19 times as likely to be executed* as whites who kill blacks.

A Pattern of Discrimination

In 1987, Warren McCleskey, a black man armed with formidable evidence linking the victim's race with the distribution of the death penalty, appealed to the Supreme Court to overturn his death sentence. He argued that the fact his victim was white played an important role in his sentencing. Although the Court acknowledged that the correlation of the victim's race and the imposition of the death penalty was "statistically significant in the system as a whole" (*McCleskey v. Kemp*, 481 U.S. 279), it denied McCleskey's petition saying that the burden is on the defendant to prove his individual sentence was based on his victim's race. (See Smolowe, "Race and the Death Penalty," *Time*, April 29, 1991.) McCleskey was executed on September 25, 1991.

In response to the *McCleskey* decision, the Racial Justice Act was introduced in Congress in 1994. The purpose of the act was to allow condemned prisoners to appeal their death sentences using evidence of past discriminatory sentencing—the kind of evidence that failed to save McCleskey. After passing in the House 217-212, the bill failed in the Senate. To date, there has been no precedent set for citing biased sentencing patterns to successfully appeal a death sentence.

Blatant Racism

With black men nearly eight times more likely to be victims of homicide than white men, could there be a more blatant message from the criminal justice system that it values some lives more highly than others? Not in a loud voice that would attract undue attention, but quietly and methodically, one prosecution at a time, our judicial system is telling us that African American life is less important than white life, and its annihilation less tragic. Our judicial system is demonstrably, institutionally racist in the end result, and the end result—killing a disproportionate number of black males—matters. . . .

We are confronted with the undeniable evidence that the death penalty is handed down unjustly. The reaction of most state governments to this evidence has been to assert that the death penalty is still necessary, and that what is needed is a way of ensuring that it is distributed fairly and handed down for the right reasons. At this time, the

Supreme Court agrees with the majority of the states. The goal of implementing a fair system for imposing the death penalty, however, has proved very elusive. And the statistics that are proving the failure of this policy have been produced under the supposedly stricter post-*Furman* laws.

Thirty-five years in the civil rights struggle has taught me that you can't legislate acceptance, objectivity, or morality. How then, at the moment between life and death, is society to erase a lifetime of social conditioning, assumptions, and attitudes the judges and jurors may not even realize they hold? There is no way the states, the federal government, or the judicial system can ensure that every prosecuting attorney, every jury member, and every judge involved in every homicide case is impartial and unbiased. And in the case of the death penalty, the stakes are just too high for even one life to be lost to prejudice and hatred.

Excerpted from *Legal Lynching: Racism, Injustice, and the Death Penalty* by Jesse Jackson (New York: Marlowe, 1996; published in association with National Press Books). Copyright © 1996 by Jesse Jackson. Reprented by permission of the publishers.

The Death Penalty Is Not Applied Unfairly to Blacks

by Stanley Rothman and Stephen Powers

Stanley Rothman is director of the Center for the Study of Social and Political Change at Smith College in Northampton, Massachusetts. Stephen Powers is a research assistant at the center. In the following viewpoint, Rothman and Powers contend that the racial biases that influenced death penalty cases in the past do not persist today. They argue that black criminals receive a disproportionate share of death sentences, not because of racism but because of the nature of the crimes they commit. Additionally, they state, black on white murders often include the aggravating circumstances that merit the death penalty, whereas black on black murders usually do not.

"When a number of legal factors are taken into account, the relationship between a defendant's race and the likelihood of execution tends to disappear."

The employment of the death penalty as the ultimate criminal sanction has been the subject of enormous debate. Execution has been challenged not only on moral and religious grounds, but more recently on constitutional grounds—as a violation of the Eighth Amendment's protection against cruel and unusual punishment. Opponents of the death penalty contend that it is employed so arbitrarily as to amount to a game of state-sponsored Russian roulette. While the Supreme Court has not ruled capital punishment to be unconstitutional, in 1972 it held that the death penalty was unconstitutional as then practiced, finding evidence of arbitrariness sufficient to require that states overhaul death sentencing procedures.

One of the most controversial aspects of the arbitrariness claim is the charge—leveled by numerous activists and social scientists—that the death penalty has been applied in a manner unfair to blacks. In *Furman vs. Georgia* (1972), several members of the Court observed that racial discrimination had produced different patterns of sentencing and rates of execution for blacks and whites. Indeed, numerous studies of the late 1800s and early 1900s have found that blacks were executed in disproportionate numbers, particularly when the victims of their crimes were white. . . .

But is death sentencing truly discriminatory? The truth is complicated by a number of factors that opponents of the death penalty have tended to discount or ignore. There appear to be legitimate reasons for racially disparate sentencing. Indeed, a number of social scientists have argued that racial prejudice is not a significant determinant of execution rates. These social scientists have demonstrated that when a number of legal factors are taken into account, the relationship between a defendant's race and the likelihood of execution tends to disappear. Why, we must ask, in spite of the questionable validity of the discrimination thesis, does the death penalty continue to be assailed as one of the most repugnant manifestations of American racism? . . .

Who Kills Whom and Why

The vast majority of murderers who receive the death penalty are involved in intra-racial offenses—that is, in cases of whites killing whites or blacks killing blacks. Most analysts agree that between 92 and 97 percent of homicides are intra-racial. In the much smaller number of cases in which blacks kill whites, the circumstances surrounding the crimes appear to be substantially different. (The number of cases in which whites kill blacks is usually too small to be factored into analyses.)

Black on black homicides are most likely to occur during altercations between persons who know one another. On the other hand, black on white homicides (and to a somewhat lesser extent, white on white) are often committed during the course of a felony or by a multiple offender. In fact, these are examples of aggravating conditions that the Supreme Court has held to be valid criteria in determining sentence severity. Yet while judges and juries take these factors into account, sociological studies often do not. Lest one think the motivation of judges and juries is racism, these factors are given consideration in societies all over the world, whatever their racial composition. They are seen universally as both fair and conducive to public order.

The key issue, then, is whether blacks convicted of killing whites are more likely to be executed because of the racial identity of their victims or because of qualitative differences in the nature of their crimes. In fact, the latter is clearly the case and would appear to explain much of the racial disparity in death sentencing.

The McCleskey Case

One of the most effective challenges to the claim of racial discrimination actually arose in a court case that supporters of the discrimination thesis had hoped would prove their point. In the 1980s, the National Association for the Advancement of Colored People (NAACP) funded a major study of the effect of race on criminal sentencing. The study, directed by university professors David Baldus, Charles Pulaski, and C. George Woodworth, gained notoriety when it was used in the defense of Warren McCleskey, a black man sentenced to death for the shooting of a white police officer in Georgia. Defense attorneys relied on the Baldus study to substantiate their claim of systemic discrimination against black defendants. The study showed that in cases of mid-range aggravation, blacks who killed whites were more likely to receive the death penalty than whites who killed whites. (In cases of low and high aggravation, the study found race to be an insignificant factor.) The authors of the study argued that racial bias occurred because prosecutors and juries were prejudiced.

The attorneys prosecuting McCleskey countered by hiring an expert methodologist, Joseph Katz, who analyzed the NAACP study and found a number of conceptual and methodological problems. For one, it turned out that police reports often did not include some of the case circumstances that were supposed to have been weighted in the study. In these instances, the researchers recorded that the circumstances were not present, when, in fact, that was not possible to determine. Katz also pointed out that the researchers frequently weighted aggravating conditions in subjective ways. Most importantly, he argued that the researchers had not accounted satisfactorily for the fact that black offender–white victim homicides were often quite different from intraracial homicides. Katz showed that black on white murders tended to be the most aggravated of all, and frequently were combined with armed robbery, as McCleskey's was. Katz also testified that by Baldus's own measures, McCleskey's was not a mid-range case but a highly aggravated one, and that in such cases the death penalty was as likely to be applied to whites as blacks.

The Race of the Victim

The Supreme Court ended up rejecting the McCleskey defense, and ruled that statistical models alone do not provide sufficient evidence of discrimination. Later, Katz testified before the Senate Judiciary Committee, and offered further evidence of the differences between homicides in which blacks kill blacks and blacks kill whites. Katz reported that the reason why 11 percent of blacks who killed whites in Georgia received the death penalty—as opposed to only 1 percent of blacks who killed blacks—was that the killings of whites more often involved armed robbery (67 percent of the black on white cases, compared with only 7 percent of the black on black cases). In addition, black on white murders more frequently involved kidnapping and rape, mutilations, execution-style murders, tortures, and beatings. These are all aggravating circumstances that increase the likelihood of a death sentence.

By contrast, 73 percent of the black victim homicides were precipitated by a dispute or fight, circumstances viewed by the courts as mitigating. Katz also observed that 95 percent of black victim homicides were committed by black offenders, and that there were so few white on black cases that no distinctive homicide pattern could even be ascertained. Among the fewer than thirty Georgia cases identified by Katz as white on black, mitigating circumstances seemed to outweigh aggravating. These crimes rarely involved a contemporaneous felony and often were precipitated by a fight. This pattern may or may not hold outside of Georgia, but as of Summer 1994 there has been no detailed national study of white on black crime. (Research has also shown that death sentences are especially likely in cases in which police officers are killed in the line of duty, and that 85 percent of police officers killed are white.)

No Evidence of Discrimination

Some findings suggest that blacks may actually be treated more leniently than whites. Analysts at the Bureau of Justice Statistics have pointed out that the percentage of inmates on death row who are black (42 percent) is lower than the percentage of criminals charged with murder or non-negligent manslaughter who are black (48 percent). If the legal system still discriminates against blacks, why do they make up a higher percentage of those charged with murder than those executed for murder?

Some critics reply that the police may be more likely to arrest and charge blacks than whites. Yet we have found few data that support this assertion. In fact, Patrick Langan, a senior statistician at the Bureau of Justice Statistics, investigated the possibility of such discrimination and found little evidence of it. Langan based his research on victims' reports of the race of offenders, and found that blacks were sentenced at rates similar to those one would expect given the reports of victims. Obviously, this kind of research could not be conducted for murder cases (because the victims are dead) but the research suggests that the discriminatory arrest argument is highly problematic.

In the federal courts, the discrimination argument has found little support. In a number of cases, judges have concluded that the evidence of systemic bias is extremely weak. Rather than order an overhaul of the legal system on the basis of highly problematic and conflicting social science research, judges have preferred to adjudicate discriminatory sentencing claims on a case by case basis. The preferred corrective has been procedural reforms. A number of states have adopted clearer sentencing standards, various provisions to remove extra-legal influences, and the judicial review of death sentences.

Ideology Prevails

Why, then, have some researchers continued to find evidence of racial discrimination? One possible explanation is that while the sociologists who design death penalty studies are most interested in and competent to measure such variables as the demographic characteristics of groups, these sociologists are ill-equipped to assess the importance of the legal variables that influence the operation of the criminal justice system. In the past, researchers did not bother to control for even the most obvious of legal variables.

Yet despite the crudeness of their methods, sociologists have concluded confidently that racism in the legal system is rampant. Mindful of the history of racial discrimination in capital cases, sociologists perhaps are predisposed to conclude that discrimination persists today. It seems obvious.

An additional difficulty with many of the sociologists is that their assumptions concerning discrimination are often overly idealistic—for example, the belief that extra-legal variables must be entirely absent from the criminal justice system for it to be legitimate, and the assumption that complete objectivity is even possible. Taken to their logical extremes, these kinds of utopian beliefs would require us to condemn virtually every legal system in the history of the world. At best, legal systems are imperfect institutions, reflecting community standards of fairness and objectivity. The jury system and judicial discretion are indispensable instruments of social justice, which permit broad principles to be tailored to the particulars of each case. Without these instruments, and the attendant margin of error or abuse that all free exercises of judgment hazard, the legal system would be doomed either to excessive punishments or to a forbearance that placed innocent individuals at great risk.

While there is justification for the claim that discriminatory capital sentencing and execution occurred in the past, the charge that they persist today lacks support. The best available evidence indicates that disproportionate numbers of blacks commit murder, and that in those cases in which the victims are white the crimes generally are aggravated. . . .

Politics and the Death Penalty

Clearly there are reasons other than statistical analysis for the continued belief that the legal system discriminates against black defendants. Those who oppose the death penalty on principle, for example, tend to incorporate the discrimination argument into their litany of protest. These critics perceive capital punishment as a vestige of an outmoded, barbaric, and irrational penal code. Black elites, meanwhile, often perceive discrimination in places others do not. They are joined by members of the white cultural establishment, who are quick to sympathize with those who allege racial unfairness.

This may sound like a harsh indictment, but how else are we to explain the facts? For decades, those who argued that the death penalty was administered in a biased manner maintained that the fact that more blacks were executed than whites revealed a lack of concern for black lives. When this argument became untenable—when it became clear that white murderers were actually more likely to be executed than black murderers—these same critics turned to other, equally unsatisfactory arguments. Now, however, they reject the implication of their previous view—that the execution of a larger percentage of whites than blacks must reveal a lack of concern for white lives. The only issue now is the race of the criminal's victim. These critics rationalize their position, but, we submit, their stance can be explained only by a need to find racism everywhere. One is reminded of the wolf in Aesop's fable. The wolf insisted that the lamb was injuring him, and was quick to change his story each time the lamb pointed out the factual errors in his claims. Finally, the wolf killed and ate the lamb anyway, proving that desire can overcome the failure of rationalization.

If the controversy over racial discrimination and the death penalty turned on the merits of the research, politicians would have to concede that death penalty discrimination has been virtually eliminated. Alas, the news media have done little to clarify matters. Most reporting on the issue is inaccurate. An article that appeared in the *New York Times* on April 21, 1994, is typical. The article concluded as follows:

> That some bias occurs is not much at issue. Many studies show that juries mete out the death penalty to black and other minority defendants in a disproportionate number of murder cases, particularly when the victims are white and especially in states and counties that have a history of racial problems.

In fact, as we have shown, these comments are patently false.

From "Execution by Quota?" by Stanley Rothman and Stephen Powers, *Public Interest*, no. 116, Summer 1994, pp. 3–16. Reprinted with permission of the authors and the *Public Interest;* © 1994 by National Affairs, Inc.

VIEWPOINT 3

Harsh Sentencing Laws Further the Cause of Justice

by Mary Kate Cary

Mary Kate Cary is director of the First Freedom Coalition, a group that advocates strengthening the U.S. criminal justice system. She is former deputy director of the Justice Department's Office of Policy and Communications. In the following viewpoint, Cary argues that the public suffers as a result of sentencing laws that fail to deliver punishment that is swift, certain, and severe. Such laws, she states, are especially unfair to the most beleaguered segment of American society—inner-city, largely minority residents who are also most often the victims of violent crime. She cites mandatory minimum sentences as one way for the public to demonstrate its intolerance of chronic, violent crime.

"The first duty of government is to protect its citizens."

Violent crime remains at intolerably high levels. Gang violence is spreading across the country. And juveniles are committing more and more serious crimes. At the same time, crime is becoming more ruthless and wanton. Too many Americans—especially residents of the inner cities—have become prisoners in their homes, behind bars and chains. It is not surprising, therefore, that the strongest support for tougher law enforcement is found among inner-city, largely minority residents.

Despite this plague, a powerful bloc of liberal lawmakers in Congress prevented the passage of tough anti-crime measures proposed by the

[George] Bush Administration. If President Clinton is to launch a war on crime, he will have to overcome this resistance on Capitol Hill.

As Bill Clinton prepares his own initiatives on crime, he would be wise to examine the recommendations of the report released in 1992 by former Attorney General William P. Barr. The report, entitled "Combatting Violent Crime," focuses on actions which can be taken at the state and local levels. President Clinton should call on governors and state legislators to act on the recommendations, and he should frame federal legislation and policies to complement the proposals.

Federal and State Partnership

When the federal government works with state authorities, the combined assault on crime can yield real results. Working with local police under "Operation Triggerlock," for example, federal prosecutors were able to charge over 10,000 dangerous criminals who used firearms in the operation's first eighteen months alone (Summer 1991–Winter 1992). The average sentence for three-time felons was eighteen years without parole. In another operation, 300 FBI agents were transferred from counterespionage to anti-gang squads in 39 cities across the country, and the federal RICO (Racketeer Influenced Corrupt Organizations) statutes were used in many cases to dismember violent gangs. Under the innovative "Operation Weed and Seed," law enforcement resources were combined with social programs at the local level to reduce crime in 20 targeted cities. And U.S. Marshals, in one ten-week period, rounded up thousands of dangerous fugitives in a massive manhunt named "Operation Gunsmoke."

The Clinton Administration should continue to assist state and local law enforcement officials in these ways. At the same time President Clinton should build upon the progress made by Presidents Ronald Reagan and George Bush in strengthening the federal criminal justice system. During the 1980s, federal legislation reformed bail laws to establish pretrial detention for dangerous offenders; sentencing guidelines were initiated to ensure firm and consistent punishment; mandatory minimum sentences were created and federal parole was abolished to bring the amount of time served closer to the amount of time imposed in criminal cases. In addition, substantial resources were invested in federal law enforcement. The number of prosecutors and federal law enforcement officials increased significantly, and President Bush doubled federal prison capacity in just three years.

Nevertheless, the impact of federal policy necessarily is limited, since 95 percent of crimes fall within the jurisdiction of state and local governments. But state and local law enforcement agencies, with limited resources, are under great strain to deal effectively with the increase of violence in this country. To fight violent crime on the state and local levels, Attorney General Barr made 24 recommendations in his report. Developed in partnership with a broad array of non-partisan law enforcement officials, these recommendations are a sound framework for state and local policy makers seeking tough action on crime. And if the Clinton Administration should fail to follow through on candidate Clinton's anti-crime rhetoric, or weaken existing law enforcement programs through the appointment of liberal jurists to the federal bench, it will be all the more important for state and local officials to strengthen law enforcement in their jurisdictions. . . .

State officials must address a simple fact: The United States is in the grip of a violent crime wave. The number of violent crimes has jumped dramatically in the last thirty years, over three times the rate in the 1990s as in 1960. Measuring the increase in terms of population over the same time period, the U.S. population has increased by 41 percent, while the violent crime rate has increased by more than 500 percent. As Heritage Foundation Distinguished Fellow William J. Bennett, former National Drug Control Policy Director, observes, "The rate of violent crime in the U.S. is worse than in any other industrialized country."

The victims of violent crime tend to be disproportionately poor and members of racial and ethnic minorities, particularly blacks. "Given current crime rates," observes Bennett, "eight out of every ten Americans can expect to be a victim of violent crime at least once in their lives."

Most of the criminal violence in American society is committed by a very small group of chronic, violent offenders—hardened criminals who commit many violent crimes whenever they are out on the streets. They begin committing crimes as juveniles, and they go right on committing crimes as adults, even when on bail, probation, or parole.

The first duty of government is to protect its citizens. If law enforcement officials are to make any progress in reducing violent crime, their top priority must be to identify, target, and incarcerate these hard-core, chronic offenders.

The Barr report indicates ways in which state legislatures can take decisive action to protect citizens.

Pretrial Detention of Dangerous Defendants

Every state should grant statutory and, if necessary, state constitutional authority to its trial judges to hold, without bail, those defendants who are a danger to witnesses, victims, or the community at large—both before trial and pending appeal.

A study by the Department of Justice's Bureau of Justice Statistics (BJS) of individuals on pretrial release in 75 of the nation's most populous counties found that 18 percent of released defendants were known to have been rearrested for the commission of a felony while on pretrial release. Two-thirds of those rearrested while on release were again released.

This revolving door justice adds significantly to crime and destroys public confidence in the criminal justice system. Law-abiding citizens understandably are reluctant to inform police of criminal activities when they know that those arrested will be back on the street in a few days, or even in a few hours. Citizens fear retaliation, intimidation, and harassment by returning criminals if they help police.

At the federal level, the Bail Reform Act of 1984 grants federal judges the authority to deny bail or pretrial release to defendants who pose a danger to specific individuals or to the community in general. Under the Act, criminal defendants with serious records, including the commission of crimes while on release and those charged with serious drug felonies, are presumed to be a danger to the community and therefore unsuitable for release. The Act also creates a strong presumption that a convicted offender will remain imprisoned during any post-conviction appeal.

Pretrial detention has helped federal prosecutors cripple organized crime and drug rings. When pretrial detention is foregone, defendants have the opportunity to intimidate or harm witnesses before their trials. But when pretrial detention is enforced, dangerous defendants are put behind bars until trial, where they are unable to obstruct justice or pose a threat. Pretrial detention also increases the protection afforded to witnesses and victims of crimes.

The Statute's Proven Effectiveness

Despite the proven effectiveness of the federal statute, and its soundness as federal constitutional law (the Supreme Court rejected a constitutional challenge to the pretrial detention provisions of the Bail Reform Act in *United States v. Salerno*, 481 U.S. 739 [1987]), only a few states have effective pretrial detention provisions. In many states, pretrial detention is not currently possible because of an absolute right to bail in the state constitution. Thus where state constitutional reform is necessary to remedy this, it should be enacted.

States also should consider other key provisions of the Bail Reform Act of 1984, such as the serious penalties for jumping bail and enhanced penalties for crimes committed while on release.

In Philadelphia in 1986, for example, a judge placed a limit on the number of criminals that could be housed in the Philadelphia jail, in order to prevent overcrowding. Released because of this order were dangerous arrestees who otherwise would be held without bail or on very high bond. The result was an increase in violent crimes committed by the releasees. In the face of this crisis, the federal government stepped in to use federal pretrial detention in cooperation with state authorities. Over 600 gang members, who would have been turned loose by state judges because there was no room to hold them, were placed in federal facilities under federal law while awaiting trial. The homicide rate in Philadelphia declined as a result.

Imprisoning the hard-core population of chronic, violent offenders will reduce the level of violent crime in America. The reason: When these criminals are on the streets, they are victimizing citizens; when they are in prison, they are not committing crimes against the public. While liberals may question the deterrent and rehabilitative aspects of imprisonment, one thing is beyond debate: Prison incapacitates chronic, repeat offenders.

Consider the American experience of the last three decades. In the 1960s and early 1970s, incarceration rates dropped and violent crime rates skyrocketed. Conversely, when incarceration rates jumped in the 1980s, the rate of increase of crime was substantially reduced. This is all the more impressive, considering the mid-1980s "crack" drug epidemic and its associated violence.

The best way to reduce crime is to identify, prosecute, and incarcerate hard-core criminals. Study after study shows that a relatively small portion of the population is responsible for the lion's share of criminal violence in this country. For example, one California study found that 3.8 percent of a group of more than 236,000 men born in 1956 were responsible for 55.5 percent of all serious felonies committed by the study group.

Putting chronic offenders in prison for long periods, especially upon second and third convictions, is the most effective way to reduce violent crime.

An axiom of effective law enforcement is that punishment should be swift, certain, and severe. Yet in too many jurisdictions, it is none of these. In fact, most violent offenders who are sent to state prison serve only a small fraction of their sentences. According to the Bureau of Justice Statistics, analysis of release practices in 36 states and the District of Columbia in 1988 shows that although violent offenders received an average sentence of seven years and eleven months imprisonment, they served an average of only two years and eleven months in prison—or 37 percent of their imposed sentence. Overall, 51 percent of the violent offenders in the survey were discharged from prison in two years or less, and 76 percent were out in four years or less.

The Failure of Parole

This huge gap between the nominal sentence given and the real time served is dishonest, and it is bad policy. It is dishonest because the public—especially victims of crime—is often under the impression that the sentence will be served in full, when in fact no such thing happens. It is bad policy because it puts the public at risk.

There are several reasons why states should restrict parole practices. First, parole is based on the mistaken idea that the primary reason for incarceration is rehabilitation (prisoners can be released as soon as they are rehabilitated, so the argument goes), and ignores the deterrent, incapacitative, and retributive reasons for imprisonment. A clear and truthful sentence increases the certainty of punishment, and both its deterrent and incapacitative effects.

Second, in too many cases parole simply does not work. Studies of the continuing failure of parole obscure the terrible human cost to law-abiding citizens. For example, Suzanne Harrison, an eighteen-year-old honor student, three weeks from graduation, left her home in Texas with two friends, nineteen and twenty years old, on May 4, 1986. Her body was found the next day. She had been raped, beaten, and strangled. Her two companions were shot to death, and their bodies were found ten days later in a ditch.

Their killer, Jerry Walter McFadden (who calls himself "Animal"), had been convicted previously of two 1973 rapes, and sentenced to two fifteen-year sentences in the Texas Penitentiary. Paroled in 1978, he was again sentenced to fifteen years in 1981 for a crime spree in which he kidnapped, raped, and sodomized a Texas woman. Despite the fact that his record now contained three sex-related convictions and two prison terms, he was released again on parole in July 1985. McFadden's crime spree finally came to an end when he was convicted of the capital murder of Suzanne Harrison and sentenced to death in 1987. McFadden raped and killed Harrison and killed her two friends less than a year after being released on parole. This tragic example is all too common, and the cost of failed parole practices to the public safety is all too high.

Enact Mandatory Minimum Sentences

Parole sometimes is used as an answer to prison overcrowding. This is hardly a reasonable justification for the premature release of violent criminals into the community. The answer to a lack of prison space is to build more prisons, not to release dangerous criminals.

Until recently, the Texas prison system was not expanding rapidly enough to house that state's criminals. Under federal court order to remain at a maximum of 95 percent of capacity, the Texas prison system responded by increasing the number of inmates released on parole. The number of felons on parole increased by 430 percent during the 1980s, and inmates served an average of only sixty-two days for each year of their sentence. As a result, reported crime rates in Texas increased 29 percent in the 1980s, according to the FBI, while they fell for the nation as a whole.

States should enact "truth in sentencing." Parole should be restricted so that the sentence served more closely matches the sentence imposed. While "good behavior" incentives may be used to control prisoners, the mechanism should not exceed federal standards requiring 85 percent of sentence to be served.

In many states, sentences for violent crimes are too short. To many criminals, jail time is little more than a brief cost of doing business. For example, in 1988, of an estimated 100,000 persons convicted in state courts of murder, rape, robbery, and aggravated assault, some 17 percent—or about 17,000 violent criminals—received sentences that included no prison time at all.

State legislators should enact mandatory minimum sentences for aggravated crimes of violence, and for such crimes committed by repeat offenders. Every state should follow the example of federal law, which mandates imprisonment where a firearm is used or possessed in the commission of certain serious felonies.

Every state should also enact laws similar to the federal armed career criminal statute, which targets repeat violent criminals who possess a gun. Under federal law, any person who has been convicted of three violent felonies or serious drug offenses, and who illegally possesses a firearm, is sentenced to at least fifteen years imprisonment without possibility of parole. There are graduated, lesser penalties for those who have been convicted of one or more prior felonies and illegally possess a gun. . . .

On the federal level, President Clinton should use the power of his office to continue the federal effort against crime. In so doing, he should build upon the progress of his predecessors, Presidents Reagan and Bush, in strengthening the criminal justice system.

At the same time, state legislators and judicial officials can and should take concrete steps to make America safer. Concerned citizens, victims of crime, and law enforcement leaders are working to strengthen the criminal justice system. Law-abiding citizens, however, are asking if their state and local public safety laws are as effective as those of the federal government and the more rigorous states. They want police and prosecutors to have the tools they need to combat gangs, drug dealers, and chronic violent offenders. They want states to ensure that dangerous criminals are in prison, not in their neighborhood. And they want victims of crime to have the same say as the criminals do in the system.

Excerpted from "How States Can Fight Violent Crime: Two Dozen Steps to a Safer America" by Mary Kate Cary, *Backgrounder*, June 7, 1993. Reprinted by permission of the Heritage Foundation.

Harsh Sentencing Laws Impede the Cause of Justice

by Chi Chi Sileo

Chi Chi Sileo is a contributing editor to *Insight on the News*, a weekly newsmagazine published by the *Washington Times*. In the following viewpoint, Sileo cites mandatory minimum sentences as a prime example of harsh sentencing laws gone awry. The original intent of such laws was to end sentencing disparities based on family connections, race, and other factors. In practice, he states, the laws have reintroduced sentencing disparities and led to overly harsh—and profoundly unfair—punishments for many nonviolent offenses. Sileo contends that such laws do not serve the cause of justice—for the public or the offenders—in that they eliminate alternative sentences for many nonviolent offenders who, studies show, have a high rate of rehabilitation.

"Mandatory minimums are increasingly being attacked . . . as frustrating, draconian, unjust, racist and completely ineffective."

Laura Graser, a Portland, Ore., defense lawyer, is under no illusions about her clients. Known as a tough, law-and-order type, Graser believes in harsh punishment and describes the average drug dealer as a "selfish, whiny jerk." But ask her about Michael Irish and she says, without hesitation, "He's the finest human being it's ever been my privilege to represent."

If ever the quality of mercy were absent in a courtroom, Graser says, it was in Irish's case. Irish, a carpenter with no criminal background who was known as hardworking, honest and devoted to his family, was offered a deal one day—several hours of work in exchange for more money than he had ever made in a year. It was an offer someone in comfortable circumstances might have considered, and Irish was in desperate straits. His wife's cancer had wiped out the family's savings, and he had recently been laid off from his job. The three hours' work was unloading boxes of hashish from a boat. Caught and tried in federal court, Irish was convicted and sentenced to twelve years in prison with no possibility of parole.

If he had been tried in state court, he might have gotten two years' probation. But drug cases are now routinely tried at the federal level, and the punishments are meted out according to mandatory minimum sentencing rules.

If Irish had been convicted of murder, he would be serving only half as long.

The Original Intent of Mandatory Sentencing

According to Stuart Taylor Jr., a writer with the *American Lawyer*, mandatory minimums "may well represent the most complete triumph of political cowardice and public ignorance over common sense and fundamental fairness in the history of our nation's criminal justice system."

Strong words, but Taylor is not alone. Mandatory minimums are increasingly being attacked from the left and the right as frustrating, draconian, unjust, racist and completely ineffective. Opponents maintain that there are detailed federal sentencing guidelines already on the books that should be used instead.

Proponents of mandatory minimums say they relay a message of swift and certain justice and let criminals know they will be dealt with harshly. These supporters decry the effectiveness of the current sentencing guidelines (which have never been fully implemented) and insist on even more minimums.

The two sides have polarized along increasingly inflexible lines, with accusations of unfairness, ignorance, softness on crime and bleeding-heart liberalism emerging as favorite fighting words.

It wasn't supposed to be this way. When mandatory minimum sentencing was first introduced in the Boggs Act of the 1950s, it was intended to end sentencing disparity so that everyone committing the same crime did the same time, regardless of family connections, race or other factors. In the 1970s, mandatory minimums were abolished because of concerns that they were overly harsh and inflexible; then-Rep. George Bush of Texas was among those who praised this return to "more equitable actions by the court" and "fewer disproportionate sentences."

Existing Mandatory Sentencing Laws

But Congress quickly forgot history, and was doomed to repeat it. In 1984, with the advent of the war on drugs, Congress took two mutually contradictory actions. First, it passed the Sentencing Reform Act, the main feature of which was the presidentially appointed U.S. Sentencing Commission, which was supposed to draw up detailed sentencing guidelines for more than 2,000 crimes. Curiously, however, Congress immediately negated the intent of the new law when it passed a large number of mandatory minimum sentences two years later, thus ignoring both the failures of the Boggs Act and the work of the Sentencing Commission, which released the results of its painstaking efforts in 1986.

Those mandatory minimums were followed swiftly by others, buried in the 1986 and 1988 Anti-Drug Abuse Acts. The same era saw passage of the Armed Career Criminal Act; not to be outdone, the Justice Department joined the parade in 1990 with Operation Triggerlock, which encouraged resentencing for earlier crimes.

The dizzying result of all this legislation is a still-dismayed Sentencing Commission and a collection of about sixty statutes for mandatory minimums, only four of which are used with any regularity. These four, dealing with drug- and gun-related offenses, account for more than 90 percent of the mandatory minimum sentences handed out.

Resurrecting Sentence Disparity

Laying aside arguments for and against mandatory minimums, two things are undeniable: mandatory minimum sentencing has led to a huge increase in the federal and state prison populations—the "land of the free" now has an incarceration rate three times higher than those of South Africa or the former Soviet Union—and no one feels any safer.

Critics charge that mandatory minimums have resurrected the very monster they were supposed to slay; sentencing, they say, is now even more confused, and confusing, than it was under previous systems. That's largely because under mandatory minimums, sentences can be modified only by prosecutors—who can do so only in cases in which the defendant can trade valuable information—rather than by judges as in traditional sentencing. In 1991, the Sentencing Commission presented a report to Congress stating that prosecutorial discretion and uneven application of the minimums had led to a marked and clear reintroduction of sentencing disparity.

"Mandatory minimums are to sentencing uniformity what a meat ax is to brain surgery" is the blunt summation offered by Henry Scott Wallace of the National Legal Aid and Defender Association. "Sentencing," Wallace says, "is the art of rationally individualizing a punishment to fit a crime. You have to consider things such as levels of violence or threat of violence, criminal background, mitigating circumstances, quantities (say, of drugs sold or items stolen)—all the things that are routinely weighed for other offenses. Mandatory minimums don't permit any of these individual factors."

This is particularly evident in trials for drug offenses. Since only prosecutors can reduce a mandatory minimum sentence, they often use that reduction as a way of bargaining for important information on other criminals.

The only problem is that low-level offenders, particularly in drug cases, rarely have access to high-level information. In fact, studies show that low-level offenders serve, on the average, 70 percent to 80 percent of their given sentence; mid-level dealers, 62 percent; and high-level kingpins, 60 percent.

There also are anecdotal accounts of defendants bargaining their way into reduced sentences by turning in innocent people.

Nicole Richardson of Mobile, Ala., has firsthand experience of this skewed justice. Her mistake was dating the wrong guy, not unusual for a twenty-year-old. One day an undercover agent asked her where he could buy LSD; she told him that her boyfriend was a dealer. For that level of involvement, she was sentenced to ten years in prison with no possibility of parole. Her boyfriend had some tips on other dealers. He got five years.

"All right, let's accept the premise that we have to give stiff punishments to drug traffickers," Wallace says. "Do we want to then send the message that if you're going to get involved in drugs, you better become a big-time kingpin so you can get a smaller punishment? Is that a useful message to send to society?"

Fifty percent of the cases now in federal courts are for drug offenses. The trend is part of a greater one of federalizing crimes, which is clogging federal courtrooms with cases that used to be handled by the far larger state courts system and is commandeering time and resources from state law enforcement efforts.

Federal vs. State Jurisdiction

Supreme Court Chief Justice William Rehnquist noted that mandatory minimums were fueling the overfederalizing of crimes. At the National Symposium on Drugs and Violence in America, Rehnquist warned that huge amounts of resources will be necessary to run the federal courts "unless we reach a different allocation of jurisdiction that both supports state efforts and preserves federalism. And the federal courts will be changed, perhaps irrevocably, unless the current federalization trends are halted." He also tentatively opposed mandatory minimums, saying they "frustrate the careful calibration of sentences, from one end of the spectrum to the other, which the sentencing guidelines were intended to accomplish."

That's precisely the point, say mandatory-minimum advocates such as Sen. Phil Gramm, a Texas Republican who calls the rules "a massive no-confidence vote by the American people in the discretionary powers of our judges."

That's only partially true. Americans are extremely concerned about violent crime and many agree that justice needs to be swifter and harsher, but most people don't believe in the indiscriminate locking-up of small-time offenders. Regarding the drug war, Bureau of Justice Statistics figures note that 40 percent of Americans would direct the majority of resources to educating the young, 28 percent to working with foreign governments to control the influx of drugs, only 19 percent to arresting drug pushers and 4 percent each to treatment programs and to arresting users. A 1993 poll commissioned by the National Rifle Association found similar results: When people were asked what they thought was the "single most important thing that can be done to help reduce violent crime," the top answer was preventive programs, followed in descending order by stricter prosecution and penalties, the teaching of values, more law enforcement efforts and gun control.

A common thread in arguments made by supporters of mandatory minimums is that people want to see "violent criminals" locked up. The word violent is repeated like a mantra; even when talking about nonviolent offenders, these supporters are fond of using terms such as "deadly," "brutal" and "dangerous" to describe federal inmates.

That confusion between violent and nonviolent offenders is the most frustrating one for those who want to repeal mandatory minimums. These critics repeatedly draw the distinction between violent and nonviolent offenders, but often find their careful delineations overwhelmed by voices warning of city streets filled with marauding murderers if mandatory minimums are abolished.

Not so, respond these critics, who maintain that allowing the sentencing guidelines to work would keep tough sentences in place for tough offenders and still allow for some flexibility. The guidelines, they say, are complete and carefully drawn, and if implemented would result in fairer overall sentencing at both ends of the criminal spectrum. "If we could go back and start over," says Kent Larsen, a spokesman for the Sentencing

Commission, "people would see that these guidelines would really work."

Mandatory minimums, in fact, are often used against nonviolent offenders. A 1992 Sentencing Commission report found that 50 percent of those incarcerated for drug offenses were nonviolent offenders who had no criminal record for 15 years prior to their convictions. These offenders, who have a high rate of rehabilitation when given a chance through alternative sentencing, are serving tougher sentences than the violent criminals that mandatory-minimum advocates rail against. (The average federal sentence for a drug conviction is 6.5 years, nearly twice that for manslaughter or assault.)

In fact, one of the great ironies of mandatory-minimum sentencing is that burglars, rapists and murderers are being released early to make room for people such as Michael Irish and Nicole Richardson. In North Carolina, violent offenders are serving one month for every year of their sentences. The state of Florida repealed its mandatory-minimum policy after finding that violent criminals were serving less than half their sentences so that prisons could accommodate drug offenders. According to Wallace, "Florida is the federal system a few years down the road.". . .

The Price Tag for Mandatory Minimums

Stories about jails and prisons being finishing schools for crime are not new. With mandatory minimums, however, the new twist is a growing problem with prison discipline. Michael Quinlan, director of the Bureau of Prisons under Presidents Reagan and Bush, says of prisoners coming in under mandatory minimums, "The things that matter to other inmates just don't matter to them. You can't get them to behave or cooperate because they know they're not going to get any time off for good behavior, or have to worry about qualifying for parole."

A stint in stir costs around $30,000 a year per inmate. Even opponents of mandatory minimums agree that's not too high a price to keep a truly dangerous person out of society, but they also point out that alternative sentencing, by comparison, costs very little. It almost pays for itself, they note, because nonviolent offenders have a low rate of recidivism and often make a speedy return to respectability, getting jobs, paying taxes and raising families.

Quinlan says: "We also need to think about the costs we're paying for loss of tax revenues from these incarcerated people, and also for increased social services that their families are using. If the offender is a male supporting a family, that family might have to go on welfare, or they might need the help of social workers. They become huge burdens on the state." Adds Bill Maynard, a defense lawyer in El Paso, Texas:

147

"What happens when these people come out of jail? How can they compete in the job market? It's easy to say, 'Well, they should have thought of that before they committed the crime,' but we're the ones who end up paying."

Mandatory Minimums Convey a Message

In practice if not in theory, mandatory minimums convey the message that there is no such thing as rehabilitation. Despite the fact that the majority of Americans believe in the concept of rehabilitation and that rehabilitation for nonviolent offenders is an attainable and inexpensive goal, current drug war policies deny ex-offenders any certainty that their efforts at reentering society will be acknowledged.

A case in point is that of Bill Keagle, one of Maynard's clients. Keagle, who Maynard admits is "no one's idea of an angel," had a criminal record for nonviolent burglaries he committed as a young man. He served six years in prison for those crimes, but came out and "turned his life around," Maynard says. "He got a job and stayed out of trouble. He got married and adopted his wife's two boys, to whom he became extremely attached. It was a complete turnaround—this was a shining example of rehabilitation."

Keagle had a couple of guns that he used for target shooting. When he was laid off from his job, he sold the guns to a pawn shop to pay some bills. What he didn't reckon on was a recently passed federal statute, the Armed Career Criminal Act, which mandates prison time for any ex-felon in possession of firearms who has three prior convictions that involved either violence or drugs. The catch in the law is that violence is defined amorphously, so that even though Keagle never assaulted anyone, never used a gun or any other weapon, his crimes were considered "potentially violent" and therefore qualified for the same punishment. Keagle was turned in to the local agent of the Bureau of Alcohol, Tobacco and Firearms and, like Irish, ended up in a federal court.

If Keagle had been tried in Texas courts, his offense might have netted him two years' probation at most; in some states, where the right to own firearms is eventually reinstated to ex-convicts, not even that. What he got was the federal mandatory minimum: 15 years.

"This law," Maynard says, "was intended for a person who can't obey the law, who's a danger to society. Not for someone like Bill Keagle. The logic here is that you can't ever be rehabilitated, that you're a career criminal for life." He notes that the act makes no allowance for recidivism or recency of crime and that the average murderer serves five or six years. "Where is the justice here? Look, I believe that long prison terms should be used to protect society from a dangerous person, or to punish

148

someone for a particularly evil crime. But Bill Keagle did nothing against the laws of God, nothing that was inherently evil. Let's put it this way: No one in El Paso was locking their doors at night because they were afraid of Bill Keagle.". . .

No one doubts that something needs to be done, both about violent crime and about prison overpopulation. Quinlan predicts that by 1999, the state and federal prison populations will have swelled from the current 740,000. No one, he adds, talks about who will pay. (In a New York Times op-ed piece, Gramm said the cost of incarceration was cheap compared with the "$430,000 a year" cost imposed by "an active street criminal," but that description does not fit most of these federal inmates.)

"We'll be spending more on prisons than on schools," says Wallace. "More than on hospitals, on keeping libraries open. The choice will come down to these versus prisons."

Predicts Maynard, "We're going to have an unbelievably huge, clumsy bureaucracy regulating us. This is the same government that wants to end poverty, create a government in Somalia and reduce pollution. How well do we think they've done at those? And where is the money supposed to come from? All we can see as an outcome of this 'war on crime' is the tremendous suffering and sorrow that it's wrought."

Critics of mandatory minimums echo the same refrains: Let's reserve those costly prison slots for violent, dangerous offenders. Let the sentencing guidelines work.

Supporters of the minimums have their own chorus: Let's show criminals we mean business. Let the mandatory minimums do the dirty work of levying harsh punishment.

Both sides make appeals to emotion—critics to compassion and humanity, supporters to public safety and frustration with the justice system. Neither side predicts any drastic changes anytime soon. Supporters of the minimums have vowed to fight for them at every opportunity, in every crime bill. Even the fiercest opponents of the sentences admit that they have an uphill battle, and that any changes will be in baby steps.

Much of the work for change seems to rest with individual defendants and their attorneys, trying to interject a human element into a harsh policy debate. Nicole Richardson spoke at congressional hearings and has appeared on television to discuss her case. Maynard has asked Clinton and Attorney General Janet Reno to commute Bill Keagle's sentence. And in Portland, Laura Graser steels her voice and vows, "I don't care what it takes. On this one, I'm just not quitting."

Excerpted from "Sentencing Rules That Shackle Justice" by Chi Chi Sileo, *Insight*, December 6, 1993. Reprinted with permission from *Insight*. Copyright 1993 News World Communications, Inc. All rights reserved.

Racially Based Jury Nullification Corrects Inequities in the Criminal Justice System

by Paul Butler

Paul Butler is an associate professor of law at the George Washington University Law School. In the following viewpoint, he contends that black jurors who are chosen for trials involving nonviolent black defendants have a right to exercise jury nullification—the acquittal of guilty defendants by jurors expressing disagreement with the law. The basis for such action, Butler states, lies in the long-standing and inherent inequities in the criminal justice system. He contends that African Americans are better suited than white lawmakers or the white-controlled justice system to determine what conduct should be punished. Race-based jury nullification, says Butler, can restore a measure of fairness to an unfair system.

"Jury nullification affords African Americans the power to determine justice for themselves . . . regardless of whether white people agree or even understand."

In 1990 I was a Special Assistant United States Attorney in the District of Columbia. I prosecuted people accused of misdemeanor crimes, mainly the drug and gun cases that overwhelm the local courts of most American cities. As a federal prosecutor, I represented the United States of America and used that power to put people, mainly African-

American men, in prison. I am also an African-American man. During that time, I made two discoveries that profoundly changed the way I viewed my work as a prosecutor and my responsibilities as a black person.

The first discovery occurred during a training session for new assistants conducted by experienced prosecutors. We rookies were informed that we would lose many of our cases, despite having persuaded a jury beyond a reasonable doubt that the defendant was guilty. We would lose because some black jurors would refuse to convict black defendants who they knew were guilty.

The second discovery was related to the first but was even more unsettling. It occurred during the trial of Marion Barry, then the second-term mayor of the District of Columbia. Barry was being prosecuted by my office for drug possession and perjury. I learned, to my surprise, that some of my fellow African-American prosecutors hoped that the mayor would be acquitted, despite the fact that he was obviously guilty of at least one of the charges—an FBI videotape plainly showed him smoking crack cocaine. These black prosecutors wanted their office to lose its case because they believed that the prosecution of Barry was racist.

There is an increasing perception that some African-American jurors vote to acquit black defendants for racial reasons, sometimes explained as the juror's desire not to send another black man to jail. There is considerable disagreement over whether it is appropriate for a black juror to do so. I now believe that, for pragmatic and political reasons, the black community is better off when some non-violent lawbreakers remain in the community rather than go to prison. The decision as to what kind of conduct by African Americans ought to be punished is better made by African Americans, based on their understanding of the costs and benefits to their community, than by the traditional criminal justice process, which is controlled by white lawmakers and white law enforcers. Legally, African-American jurors who sit in judgment of African-American accused persons have the power to make that decision. Considering the costs of law enforcement to the black community, and the failure of white lawmakers to come up with any solutions to black antisocial conduct other than incarceration, it is, in fact, the moral responsibility of black jurors to emancipate some guilty black outlaws.

Distrusting the System

Why would a black juror vote to let a guilty person go free? Assuming the juror is a rational, self-interested actor, she must believe that she is better off with the defendant out of prison than in prison. But how could any rational person believe that about a criminal?

Imagine a country in which a third of the young male citizens are under the supervision of the criminal justice system—either awaiting trial, in prison, or on probation or parole. Imagine a country in which two-thirds of the men can anticipate being arrested before they reach age thirty. Imagine a country in which there are more young men in prison than in college.

The country imagined above is a police state. When we think of a police state, we think of a society whose fundamental problem lies not with the citizens of the state but rather with the form of government, and with the powerful elites in whose interest the state exists. Similarly, racial critics of American criminal justice locate the problem not with the black prisoners but with the state and its actors and beneficiaries.

The black community also bears very real costs by having so many African Americans, particularly males, incarcerated or otherwise involved in the criminal justice system. These costs are both social and economic, and they include the large percentage of black children who live in female-headed, single-parent households; a perceived dearth of men "eligible" for marriage; the lack of male role models for black children, especially boys; the absence of wealth in the black community; and the large unemployment rate among black men.

According to a *USA Today*/CNN/Gallup poll, 66 percent of blacks believe that the criminal justice system is racist and only 32 percent believe it is not racist. Interestingly, other polls suggest that blacks also tend to be more worried about crime than whites; this seems logical when one considers that blacks are more likely to be victims of crime. This enhanced concern, however, does not appear to translate to black support for tougher enforcement of criminal law. For example, substantially fewer blacks than whites support the death penalty, and many more blacks than whites were concerned with the potential racial consequences of the strict provisions of 1994's crime bill. Along with significant evidence from popular culture, these polls suggest that a substantial portion of the African-American community sympathizes with racial critiques of the criminal justice system.

The Power to Acquit

African-American jurors who endorse these critiques are in a unique position to act on their beliefs when they sit in judgment of a black defendant. As jurors, they have the power to convict the accused person or to set him free. May the responsible exercise of that power include voting to free a black defendant who the juror believes is guilty? The answer is "yes," based on the legal doctrine known as jury nullification.

Jury nullification occurs when a jury acquits a defendant who it believes is guilty of the crime with which he is charged. In finding the defendant not guilty, the jury ignores the facts of the case and/or the judge's instructions regarding the law. Instead, the jury votes its conscience.

The prerogative of juries to nullify has been part of English and American law for centuries. There are well-known cases from the Revolutionary War era when American patriots were charged with political crimes by the British crown and acquitted by American juries. Black slaves who escaped to the North and were prosecuted for violation of the Fugitive Slave Law were freed by Northern juries with abolitionist sentiments. Some Southern juries refused to punish white violence against African Americans, especially black men accused of crimes against white women.

The Supreme Court has officially disapproved of jury nullification but has conceded that it has no power to prohibit jurors from engaging in it; the Bill of Rights does not allow verdicts of acquittal to be reversed, regardless of the reason for the acquittal. Criticism of nullification has centered on its potential for abuse. The criticism suggests that when twelve members of a jury vote their conscience instead of the law, they corrupt the rule of law and undermine the democratic principles that made the law.

There is no question that jury nullification is subversive of the rule of law. Nonetheless, most legal historians agree that it was morally appropriate in the cases of the white American revolutionaries and the runaway slaves. The issue, then, is whether African Americans today have the moral right to engage in this same subversion.

Most moral justifications of the obligation to obey the law are based on theories of "fair play." Citizens benefit from the rule of law; that is why it is just that they are burdened with the requirement to follow it. Yet most blacks are aware of countless historical examples in which African Americans were not afforded the benefit of the rule of law: think, for example, of the existence of slavery in a republic purportedly dedicated to the proposition that all men are created equal, or the law's support of state-sponsored segregation even after the Fourteenth Amendment guaranteed blacks equal protection. That the rule of law ultimately corrected some of the large holes in the American fabric is evidence more of its malleability than its goodness; the rule of law previously had justified the holes.

If the rule of law is a myth, or at least not valid for African Americans, the argument that jury nullification undermines it loses force. The black juror is simply another actor in the system, using her power to fashion a particular outcome. The juror's act of nullification—like the act of the citizen who dials 911 to report Ricky but not Bob, or the police officer who arrests Lisa but not Mary, or the prosecutor who charges Kwame but not Brad, or the judge who finds that Nancy was illegally entrapped but Verna was not—exposes the indeterminacy of law but does not in itself create it.

A similar argument can be made regarding the criticism that jury nullification is anti-democratic. This is precisely why many African Americans endorse it; it is perhaps the only legal power black people have to escape the tyranny of the majority. Black people have had to beg white decision makers for most of the rights they have: the right not to be slaves, the right to vote, the right to attend an integrated school. Now black people are begging white people to preserve programs that help black children to eat and black businesses to survive. Jury nullification affords African Americans the power to determine justice for themselves, in individual cases, regardless of whether white people agree or even understand.

Ethical Nullification

At this point, African Americans should ask themselves whether the operation of the criminal law system in the United States advances the interests of black people. If it does not, the doctrine of jury nullification affords African-American jurors the opportunity to exercise the authority of the law over some African-American criminal defendants. In essence, black people can "opt out" of American criminal law.

How far should they go—completely to anarchy, or is there someplace between here and there that is safer than both? I propose the following: African-American jurors should approach their work cognizant of its political nature and of their prerogative to exercise their power in the best interests of the black community. In every case, the juror should be guided by her view of what is "just." (I have more faith, I should add, in the average black juror's idea of justice than I do in the idea that is embodied in the "rule of law.")

In cases involving violent *malum in se* (inherently bad) crimes, such as murder, rape, and assault, jurors should consider the case strictly on the evidence presented, and if they believe the accused person is guilty, they should so vote. In cases involving non-violent, *malum prohibitum* (legally proscribed) offenses, including "victimless" crimes such as narcotics possession, there should be a presumption in favor of nullification. Finally, for non-violent, *malum in se* crimes, such as theft or perjury, there need be no presumption in favor of nullification, but it ought to be an option the juror considers. A juror might vote for acquittal, for example,

154

when a poor woman steals from Tiffany's but not when the same woman steals from her next-door neighbor.

How would a juror decide individual cases under my proposal? Easy cases would include a defendant who has possessed crack cocaine and an abusive husband who kills his wife. The former should be acquitted and the latter should go to prison.

Difficult scenarios would include the drug dealer who operates in the ghetto and the thief who burglarizes the home of a rich white family. Under my proposal, nullification is presumed in the first case because drug distribution is a non-violent *malum prohibitum* offense. Is nullification morally justifiable here? It depends. There is no question that encouraging people to engage in self-destructive behavior is evil; the question the juror should ask herself is whether the remedy is less evil. (The juror should also remember that the criminal law does not punish those ghetto drug dealers who cause the most injury: liquor store owners.)

As for the burglar who steals from the rich white family, the case is troubling, first of all, because the conduct is so clearly "wrong." Since it is a non-violent *malum in se* crime, there is no presumption in favor of nullification, but it is an option for consideration. Here again, the facts of the case are relevant. For example, if the offense was committed to support a drug habit, I think there is a moral case to be made for nullification, at least until such time as access to drug-rehabilitation services are available to all.

Why would a juror be inclined to follow my proposal? There is no guarantee that she would. But when we perceive that black jurors are already nullifying on the basis of racial critiques (i.e., refusing to send another black man to jail), we recognize that these jurors are willing to use their power in a politically conscious manner. Further, it appears that some black jurors now excuse some conduct—like murder—that they should not excuse. My proposal provides a principled structure for the exercise of the black juror's vote. I am not encouraging anarchy; rather I am reminding black jurors of their privilege to serve a calling higher than law: justice.

I concede that the justice my proposal achieves is rough. It is as susceptible to human foibles as the jury system. But I am sufficiently optimistic that my proposal will be only an intermediate plan, a stopping point between the status quo and real justice. To get to that better, middle ground, I hope that this essay will encourage African Americans to use responsibly the power they already have.

Excerpted and adapted from "Racially Based Jury Nullification: Black Power in the Criminal Justice System" by Paul Butler. Reprinted by permission of The Yale Law Journal Company and Fred B. Rothman and Company from the *Yale Law Journal*, vol. 105 (December 1995), pp. 677–725.

Racially Based Jury Nullification Creates Inequities in the Criminal Justice System

by Karl Zinsmeister and Michael Weiss

Karl Zinsmeister is a DeWitt Wallace Fellow of the American Enterprise Institute and the editor of *American Enterprise*, a bimonthly conservative journal. Michael Weiss is an attorney in Houston, Texas, and a senior fellow at the Texas Public Policy Foundation in Galveston. In the following viewpoint, Zinsmeister and Weiss contend that race-based jury nullification, which occurs when jurors (usually black) assert their disagreement with the law by refusing to convict members of their own race, hurts the minority community most. Rather than correcting possible injustices, they state, jury nullification adds to inequities in the system by denying justice to crime victims and by freeing offenders to commit more crimes in their communities.

"By letting clearly guilty individuals go, jurors are only 'infecting their own neighborhoods with criminals.'"

In 1992, a white congressional aide working for Senator Richard Shelby of Alabama was shot to death in his Capitol Hill home. A few weeks later, a young black man named Edward Evans was arrested for the crime. Two of his friends testified that they saw him shoot the young aide; one said that Evans harbored strong anti-white sentiments and had earlier vowed to kill a white man. Although this and the material evidence presented what seemed to be an overwhelming case against Evans, one African American juror refused to convict. A frustrated jury foreman told the judge that Velma McNeil would simply not give any credence to the prosecution's evidence. A hung jury and mistrial resulted. A *Washington Post* photograph showed McNeil emerging from the courtroom hugging a relative of the accused murderer.

• In 1994, a Towson State college student who became lost in the Dutch Village section of Baltimore was robbed and murdered by Davon Neverdon. After the student willingly handed over his wallet, Neverdon shot him in the face. Prosecutors presented four eyewitnesses who testified they saw Neverdon kill the man. Two other witnesses reported that Neverdon told them afterwards that he committed the murder. The evidence against Neverdon was so strong he bargained for a forty year sentence in exchange for a guilty plea, an offer which was rejected by the prosecution at the request of the victim's family. Yet a jury comprised of eleven African Americans and one Pakistani acquitted Neverdon because of "witness credibility" problems. Before the verdict, the Pakistani juror reported that "race may be playing some part" in the jury's decision.

• In another Baltimore case, a white man was killed when a cinder block was dropped on his head from a third floor balcony of a public housing project. Three witnesses identified the black defendant as the murderer and another testified in court that the defendant had confessed to him. The defendant was acquitted.

• After off-duty black police officer Rudy Thomas was murdered in Brooklyn in 1994, defendant Johnny Williams confessed to the crime on videotape, describing his motive and the murder weapon. Williams's fingerprints were found on the slain officer's motorcycle, and bullets from his gun matched those found in the victim. There were also three eyewitnesses to the crime. "We had enough evidence to supply three or four cases," reports the prosecuting attorney. But the defense claimed, with no evidence, that Williams was beaten by the white detective on the case, and a hung jury resulted. A juror who refused to give in to those favoring acquittal reported the deliberations were "blatantly racial."

• In 1994, a suburban white woman named Rebecca Gordon was driving through Detroit when she was gunned down by a group of blacks in an adjoining car. Defense counsel played the "race card" at the 1995 trial, and the inner city jury refused to convict defendant Brian Marable of murder, turning in a guilty verdict only on the misdemeanor charge of reckless discharge of a firearm.

• Darryl Smith, a black drug dealer in Washington, D.C., tortured eighteen-year-old African American Willie Wilson to death as he begged for mercy in front of witnesses. Despite massive amounts of evidence linking him to the crime, an all-black D.C. jury acquitted Smith in his 1990 murder trial. According to other jurors, forewoman Valerie Blackmon refused to convict because "she didn't want to send any more young black men to jail." After long deliberations, other members of the panel caved in to Blackmon's argument that the "criminal justice system is stacked against blacks" and let Smith off, though most believed that he was guilty. Three weeks after the verdict, a letter from an anonymous juror arrived at D.C. Superior Court expressing regret over the verdict.

• On August 19, 1991, after a traffic accident in which a black child was killed by a car carrying a Jewish leader, a black mob rioted down a street in the Crown Heights section of Brooklyn, shouting "Let's go get the Jews." A Jewish scholar visiting New York named Yankel Rosenbaum was stabbed to death when they encountered him on the street. Within minutes police arrived and apprehended Lemrick Nelson, Jr. at the scene with a bloody knife in his pocket. He was taken to the dying Rosenbaum, who identified Nelson as his attacker. Nelson later admitted the crime to two Brooklyn detectives, and signed a written confession. Prosecutors presented this evidence to a predominantly black jury. They refused to convict Nelson. After the acquittal, jurors celebrated with Nelson at a local restaurant. (Nelson later moved to Georgia and was convicted of slashing a schoolmate.)

Racialized Legal Bias

Clearly, there has been a booming trade in black racism in American courtrooms for some time. Then came the O.J. Simpson verdict. "The jury did not deliberate, it emoted," observed commentator Mona Charen afterwards. "If the prosecution's case was so weak, why did Johnnie Cochran argue in his summation that jurors disregard the evidence? . . . The reaction of so many American blacks to the verdict was unseemly and offensive. . . . One of the jurors, a former member of the Black Panther party, gave the black power salute" to Simpson in court right after the acquittal. "Was the jury fair-minded? Is black America?" asks Charen. "Only a nation of fools would lull itself into believing that this was not a racially motivated and a racist verdict." She warns that even "if Marcia Clark had produced a videotape of the murders in progress, the defense would have argued that the filmmaker was a racist and the jury would have found 'reasonable doubt.'"

Charen's videotape scenario is actually not so far-fetched. Racial legal bias exists not only at the street level among black Americans but also high among today's black leadership. This was clearly illustrated by an article published in December 1995 in the *Yale Law Journal*, and excerpted in the December 1995 *Harper's Magazine*. In it, a black George Washington University law professor and former prosecutor in the U.S. Attorney's office in the District of Columbia named Paul Butler describes how "during the trial of Marion Barry, then the second-term mayor of the District of Columbia, Barry was being prosecuted by my office for drug possession and perjury. I learned, to my surprise, that some of my fellow African American prosecutors hoped that the mayor would be acquitted, despite the fact that he was obviously guilty of at least one of the charges—an FBI videotape plainly showed him smoking crack cocaine. These black prosecutors wanted their office to lose its case because they believed that the prosecution of Barry was racist."

In his *Yale Law Journal* and *Harper's Magazine* articles, Butler makes it clear that racialized justice is not only a thriving inner city practice, but also a theory built on determined black intellectual rationalizations. He himself is a case in point. "During a training session for new assistants conducted by experienced prosecutors," he recalls, "we rookies were informed that we would lose many of our cases, despite having persuaded a jury beyond a reasonable doubt that the defendant was guilty. We would lose because some black jurors would refuse to convict black defendants who they knew were guilty . . . some African American jurors vote to acquit black defendants for racial reasons." Though he was then serving as a prosecutor of drug and gun criminals, Butler himself was soon converted to "the juror's desire not to send another black man to jail." Describing America as "a police state," he currently argues that for "pragmatic and political reasons," black jurors have a "moral responsibility . . . to emancipate some guilty black outlaws."

Noting that polls show 66 percent of blacks believe the U.S. criminal justice system is racist, Butler points out that "African American jurors who endorse these critiques are in a unique position to act on their beliefs when they sit in judgment of a black defendant." Today's African Americans "should ask themselves whether the operation of the criminal law system in the United States advances the interests of black people," and if they believe it does not, he urges, they should "opt out," judging defendants by whatever standards they please rather than by the law. This is known as jury nullification.

Butler presents some specific suggestions as to how black juries might take the law into their own hands. He urges that for crimes like drug dealing, gun possession, theft, and perjury, nullification always ought to be considered. He calls for African Americans to exercise double standards as they see fit: "A juror might vote for acquittal, for example, when a poor woman steals from Tiffany's but not when the same woman steals from her next-door neighbor." Specifically conjuring up a case of a black "thief who burglarizes the home of a rich white family," Butler sees "a moral case to be made for nullification."

Black Jurors Distrust Prosecutors

Certainly big city prosecutors will tell you that they see lots of racialized jury-behavior. Lead prosecutor Marcia Clark told CNN after the Simpson acquittal that "a majority black jury won't bring a conviction in a case like this." She later scurried to retract that "off the record" statement, but other officials are not so shy. Los Angeles County deputy district attorney Bobby Grace states that "growing resentment . . . can affect a jury verdict." Atlanta-area assistant district attorney Leigh Dupre estimates that at least one-fourth of all criminal cases that end in acquittal may involve some form of racial nullification.

Prosecutors agree that urban black jurors have turned extremely skeptical of prosecution witnesses, especially police officers. Brooklyn district attorney Charles Hynes states that "the problem my office faced in court in the Yankel Rosenbaum trial is one that confronts prosecutors in most urban areas today: distrust by inner-city residents of the police officers who are sworn to protect and serve them." Bob Agacinski, deputy chief of the Wayne County prosecutors in Detroit, blames defense counsel for introducing this "racial appeal to juries . . . especially in cases where the witnesses are police officers. Police credibility is easy to attack . . . and juries are buying the argument that the police are looking to lock up any black man. . . . Minor inconsistencies in police testimony become reasonable doubt when the case has racial overtones." Racial pleas are "notoriously overused" by defense counsel, says Agacinski. He estimates that over "50 percent of the cases which go to trial involve some type of racial appeal."

Prosecutors have noted a "more blatant use" of the racial defense since the Simpson trial began. In the summer of 1994, for instance, after an elderly man was beaten to death by a black defendant at a Detroit-area McDonald's, defense attorneys invoked racial sympathies even though the defendant confessed the murder to police officers. They claimed the confession was coerced by the white officers, and the predominantly black jury voted to acquit.

Rogue cops really do exist, as the vile Mark Fuhrman reminded us. But at present, *every* cop is viewed as a rogue by many inner-city jurors. "Police officers now have to prove that race was *not* an issue in an arrest," reports a former prosecutor in the U.S. attorney's office in Washington, D.C. Baltimore assistant state attorney Ahmet Hisim illustrates the problem using a rating scale. In a typical city today, he says, "black jurors will automatically assess at least thirty points out of a hundred against a police officer's credibility, without even hearing any testimony."

Defense counsel are also quick to attack the credibility of non-police prosecution witnesses. A former assistant U.S. attorney in D.C. maintains that "in major metropolitan cities where prosecutors deal with predominantly black juries, defense counsel will put the government on trial because of the kinds of witnesses that the government must use." Often the prosecution has to rely on informants involved in the same kinds of activity as the defendant, and today's suspicious juries leap to discount their testimony. Determined skepticism of this sort can be very difficult to overcome. D.C. Detective Donald Gossage, who worked on the Darryl Smith case, notes that "you don't have your nuns and doctors and lawyers standing on these street corners."

The Outcome of Racialized "Justice"

In addition to prosecutors' estimates like the startling ones above from Detroit's Agacinski and Atlanta's Dupre, there are other small and localized indicators of increased racialism in court. More hung juries are one obvious sign. The black teenager who murdered English tourist Gary Colley at a Florida rest stop, for instance, had to be tried three times before he was convicted because his first two trials ended in hung juries. This despite the fact that he and his three teenage accomplices had more than a hundred arrests amongst them at the time of the murder. In California, there are currently between 10,000 and 11,000 hung juries annually—up to 15 percent of all cases tried. That figure represents a lot of foregone justice, and also a huge public expense, given that the average trial costs taxpayers $10,000 a day, according to the California District Attorney's Association.

Hard nationwide figures on acquittals by race of defendant, victim, and jury are hard to come by. Data from the U.S. Bureau of Justice Statistics do show that in the 75 largest counties in the U.S., rates of felony prosecution and conviction are slightly lower for blacks than whites. In a few jurisdictions where clear statistics are available, the patterns are dramatic. Nationwide, the felony acquittal rate for defendants of all races is only 17 percent, but in the Bronx, where more than eight out of ten jurors are black or Hispanic, 48 percent of all black felony defendants are acquitted. In Washington, D.C., where more than 95 percent of defendants and 70 percent of jurors are black, 29 percent of all felony trials ended in acquittal in 1994. In Wayne County, which includes mostly black Detroit, 30 percent of felony defendants are acquitted.

On the day of the O.J. Simpson acquittal, a veteran New York law enforcement official estimated off-handedly to criminologist John DiIulio that "there's 100,000 O.J.s. We've reached the point where the system is rigged to let murderers, and not just rich ones, escape justice."

What are the ultimate effects of this racialized judgment in U.S. courtrooms? Obviously there is tremendous personal hurt in cases where justice is not done, and the number of such cases is rising. There is also more disrespect for the law, and a lot more crime and society-wide damage done by perpetrators who should be locked up instead of roaming the streets.

Former U.S. attorney Joseph DiGenova argues that advocates of jury nullification on racial grounds are "pushing anarchy." The refusal to convict by black juries is "rampant" and getting worse, he warns, and this is feeding the inner-city crime cycle. DiGenova also notes that "we fought like hell to get blacks into the system as cops and prosecutors and judges, and now these guys are being fiercely ostracized and pressured, and told in their own community that a black person shouldn't work in such a position. Well, who *is* supposed to respond to black criminals? Or are we just supposed to pretend there aren't any black criminals?"

John DiIulio adds that big city prosecutors today view cases where there is a white victim and a black defendant as "no win situations." Recognizing that it will be difficult to get a conviction, prosecutors pull their punches: avoiding the death penalty like the plague even where it is clearly merited (like the Simpson case), avoiding multiple counts and other moves that might give the appearance of piling on, largely letting defense attorneys pick the juries, and trying desperately to plea bargain everything to avoid going to a jury in the first place. The result, DiIulio says, is that "blacks are being substantially and systematically under-prosecuted today, not only in cases of black-on-white crime, but also in cases of black-on-black."

Baltimore prosecutor Hisim advises that it is dangerous for jurors to attempt to "fix the system by being revolutionary." Recognizing that "black jurors seem to be striking back at society," Hisim suggests that they should be educated about the consequences of racially-based nullification, since 90 percent of crime is committed by people living in a juror's own community. The irony is that by letting clearly guilty individuals go, jurors are only "infecting their own neighborhoods with criminals."

From "When Race Trumps Truth in Court" by Karl Zinsmeister and Michael Weiss, *American Enterprise*, January/February 1996. Reprinted by permission of the *American Enterprise*, a Washington, D.C.–based magazine of business, politics, and culture.

CHAPTER 4

Does Racism Stifle Black Progress?

Chapter Preface

It is apparent that blacks in America have progressed since the 1960s. According to a recent survey conducted by the *New York Times*, "The number of black lawyers, doctors and engineers has risen sharply; the earnings of a growing contingent of government workers, pharmacists, mathematicians, designers, engineers and others approaches or even surpasses that of comparable whites, and this group now accounts for a higher proportion of blacks in their chosen professions than their proportion in the general population."

Yet, other statistics reveal that blacks still remain unequal to whites. According to the same survey: "The proportion of poorest blacks has also grown. . . . Blacks, overall, still lag far behind whites in income—earning about $63 for every $100 a white household earns—and they lag even farther behind in accumulated wealth." Blacks also suffer higher rates of imprisonment, illegitimacy, and poor, single-parent households.

The cause of these social and economic discrepancies between blacks and whites leads to much discussion. Are blacks themselves responsible for the lack of progress, or is racism to blame? If blacks themselves are responsible, as Dinesh D'Souza, author of *The End of Racism*, argues, then it is blacks themselves who must change. Gregory Howard Williams, author of *Life on the Color Line*, describes being brought up in the worst kind of segregation and poverty in Virginia in the 1950s, then concludes that his success has more to do with upbringing than society: "I . . . realize that my five degrees and more than 20 years in higher education didn't make me Dean of the Ohio State University College of Law. It was the belief of a woman with an eighth grade education [who raised him] that I deserved a chance, and her willingness to share everything she had to make that a reality."

If, on the other hand, blacks' continual lagging behind whites is society's fault, and racism prevents blacks' attainment of equality, then perhaps government must pursue policies that can enable blacks to achieve an equal piece of the American dream. Douglas S. Massey and Nancy A. Denton argue in *American Apartheid: Segregation and the Making of the Underclass* that persistent segregation is proof that blacks have a more difficult time entering the world of economic opportunity: "It seems to us amazing that people [are] even debating whether race [is] declining in importance when levels of residential segregation [are] so high and so structured along racial lines." The following chapter offers viewpoints from some of the most authoritative authors examining these controversial issues.

White Oppression Is to Blame for Black Inequality

by bell hooks

bell hooks is Distinguished Professor of English at City College in New York. Her books and essays frequently address issues of race and feminism. In the following viewpoint, hooks argues that black men and women can never attain equality and achieve progress as long as equality requires assimilation into a dominant and oppressive white society.

"While it is true that the nature of racist oppression and exploitation has changed . . . white supremacy continues to shape perspectives on reality and to inform the social status of black people."

Black people in the United States share with black people in South Africa and with people of color globally both the pain of white supremacist oppression and exploitation and the pain that comes from resistance and struggle. The first pain wounds us, the second pain helps heal our wounds. It often troubles me that black people in the United States have not risen en masse to declare solidarity with our black sisters and brothers in South Africa. Perhaps one day soon—say, Martin Luther King's birthday—we will enter the streets at a certain hour, wherever we are, to stand for a moment, naming and affirming the primacy of black liberation.

As I write, I try to remember when the word "racism" ceased to be the term which best expressed for me exploitation of black people and other people of color in this society and when I began to understand that the most useful term was "white supremacy." It was certainly a necessary term when confronted with the liberal attitudes of white women active in feminist movement who were unlike their racist ancestors— white women in the early women's rights movement who did not wish to be caught dead in fellowship with black women. In fact, these women often requested and longed for the presence of black women. Yet when present, what we saw was that they wished to exercise control over our bodies and thoughts as their racist ancestors had—that this need to exercise power over us expressed how much they had internalized the values and attitudes of white supremacy.

It may have been this contact or contact with fellow white English professors who want very much to have "a" black person in "their" department as long as that person thinks and acts like them, shares their values and beliefs, is in no way different, that first compelled me to use the term "white supremacy" to identify the ideology that most determines how white people in this society (irrespective of their political leanings to the right or left) perceive and relate to black people and other people of color. It is the very small but highly visible liberal movement away from the perpetuation of overtly racist discrimination, exploitation, and oppression of black people which often masks how all-pervasive white supremacy is in this society, both as ideology and as behavior. When liberal whites fail to understand how they can and/or do embody white supremacist values and beliefs even though they may not embrace racism as prejudice or domination (especially domination that involves coercive control), they cannot recognize the ways their actions support and affirm the very structure of racist domination and oppression that they profess to wish to see eradicated.

Likewise, "white supremacy" is a much more useful term for understanding the complicity of people of color in upholding and maintaining racial hierarchies that do not involve force (i.e., slavery, apartheid) than the term "internalized racism"—a term most often used to suggest that black people have absorbed negative feelings and attitudes about blackness held by white people. The term "white supremacy" enables us to recognize not only that black people are socialized to embody the values and attitudes of white supremacy, but that we can exercise "white supremacist control" over other black people. This is important, for unlike the term "uncle tom," which carried with it the recognition of complicity and internalized racism, a new terminology must accurately name the way we as black people directly exercise power over one another when we perpetuate white supremacist beliefs. Speaking about changing perspectives on black identity, writer Toni Morrison said in a recent interview: "Now people choose their identities. Now people choose to be Black." At this historical moment, when a few black people no longer experience the racial apartheid and brutal racism that still determine the lot of many black people, it is easier for that few to ally themselves politically with the dominant racist white group.

The Dangers of Assimilation

Assimilation is the strategy that has provided social legitimation for this shift in allegiance. It is a strategy deeply rooted in the ideology of white supremacy and its advocates urge black people to negate blackness, to imitate racist white people so as to better absorb their values, their way of life. Ironically, many changes in social policy and social attitudes that were once seen as ways to end racial domination have served to reinforce and perpetuate white supremacy. This is especially true of social policy that has encouraged and promoted racial integration. Given the continued force of racism, racial integration translated into assimilation ultimately serves to reinforce and maintain white supremacy. Without an ongoing active movement to end white supremacy, without ongoing black liberation struggle, no social environment can exist in the United States that truly supports integration. When black people enter social contexts that remain unchanged, unaltered, in no way stripped of the framework of white supremacy, we are pressured to assimilate. We are rewarded for assimilation. Black people working or socializing in predominantly white settings whose very structures are informed by the principles of white supremacy who dare to affirm blackness, love of black culture and identity, do so at great risk. We must continually challenge, protest, resist while working to leave no gaps in our defense that will allow us to be crushed. This is especially true in work settings where we risk being fired or not receiving deserved promotions. Resisting the pressure to assimilate is a part of our struggle to end white supremacy.

When I talk with audiences around the United States about feminist issues of race and gender, my use of the term "white supremacy" always sparks a reaction, usually of a critical or hostile nature. Individual white people and even some nonwhites insist that this is not a white supremacist society, that racism is not nearly the problem it used to be (it is downright frightening to hear people argue vehemently that the problem of racism has been solved), that there has been change. While it is true that the nature of racist oppression and exploitation has changed as slavery has ended and the apartheid structure of Jim Crow has legally changed, white supremacy continues to shape perspectives on reality and to inform the social status of black people and all people of color. Nowhere is this more evident than in university settings. And often it is the liberal folks in those settings who are unwilling to acknowledge this truth.

History from the White Perspective

Recently in a conversation with a white male lawyer at his home where I was a guest, he informed me that someone had commented to him that children are learning very little history these days in school, that the attempt to be all-inclusive, to talk about Native Americans, blacks, women, etc. has led to a fragmented focus on particular representative individuals with no larger historical framework. I responded to this comment by suggesting that it has been easier for white people to practice this inclusion rather than change the larger framework; that it is easier to change the focus from Christopher Columbus, the important white man who "discovered" America, to Sitting Bull or Harriet Tubman, than it is to cease telling a distorted version of U.S. history which upholds white supremacy. Really teaching history in a new way would require abandoning the old myths informed by white supremacy like the notion that Columbus discovered America. It would mean talking about imperialism, colonization, about the Africans who came here before Columbus (see Ivan Van Sertima's *They Came Before Columbus*). It would mean talking about genocide, about the white colonizers' exploitation and betrayal of Native Americans; about ways the legal and governmental structures of this society from the Constitution on supported and upheld slavery, apartheid (see Derrick Bell's *And We Are Not Saved*). This history can be taught only when the perspectives of teachers are no longer shaped by white supremacy. Our conversation is one of many examples that reveal the way black people and white people can socialize in a friendly manner, be racially integrated, while deeply ingrained notions of white supremacy remain intact. Incidents like this make it necessary for concerned folks, for righteous white people, to begin to fully explore the way white supremacy determines how they see the world, even as their actions are not informed by the type of racial prejudice that promotes overt discrimination and separation.

Significantly, "assimilation" was a term that began to be more commonly used after the revolts against white supremacy in the late 1960s and early 1970s. The intense, passionate rebellion against racism and white supremacy of this period was crucial because it created a context for politicization, for education for critical consciousness, one in which black people could begin to confront the extent of our complicity, our internalization of white supremacy, and begin the process of self-recovery and collective renewal. Describing this effort in his work *The Search for a Common Ground*, black theologian Howard Thurman commented:

"Black is Beautiful" became not merely a phrase—it was a

stance, a total attitude, a metaphysics. In very positive and exciting terms it began undermining the idea that had developed over so many years into a central aspect of white mythology: that black is ugly, black is evil, black is demonic. In so doing it fundamentally attacked the front line of the defense of the myth of white supremacy and superiority.

Economic Influences

Clearly, assimilation as a social policy upholding white supremacy was strategically an important counterdefense, one that would serve to deflect the call for radical transformation of black consciousness. Suddenly the terms for success (that is, getting a job, acquiring the means to provide materially for oneself and one's family) were redefined. It was not enough for black people to enter institutions of higher education and acquire the necessary skills to effectively compete for jobs previously occupied solely by whites; the demand was that blacks become "honorary whites," that black people assimilate to succeed.

The force that gave the social policy of assimilation power to influence and change the direction of black liberation struggle was economic. Economic distress created a climate wherein militancy—overt resistance to white supremacy and racism (which included the presentation of self in a manner that suggests black pride)—was no longer deemed a viable survival strategy. Natural hairstyles, African dress, etc. were discarded as signs of militancy that might keep one from getting ahead. A similar regressive, reactionary move was taking place among young white radicals, many of whom had been fiercely engaged in Left politics, who suddenly began to seek reincorporation into the liberal and conservative mainstream. Again the force behind their reentry into the system was economic. On a very basic level, changes in the cost of housing (as in the great apartment one had in 1965 for $100 a month cost $400 by 1975) had a frightening impact on college-educated young people of all ethnicities who thought they were committed to transforming society, but who were unable to face living without choice, without the means to escape, who feared living in poverty. Coupled with economic forces exerting pressure, many radicals despaired of the possibility that this white supremacist capitalist patriarchy could really be changed.

The End of White Radicalism

Tragically, many radical whites who had been allies in the black liberation struggle began to question whether the struggle to end racism was really that significant, or to suggest that the struggle was over, as they moved into their new liberal positions. Radical white youth who had worked in civil rights struggles, protested the war in Vietnam, and even denounced U.S. imperialism could not reconstruct their ties to prevailing systems of domination without creating a new layer of false consciousness—the assertion that racism was no longer pervasive, that race was no longer an important issue. Similarly, critiques of capitalism, especially those that urged individuals to try and live differently within the framework of capitalism, were also relegated to the back burner as people "discovered" that it was important to have class privilege so that one could better help the exploited.

It is no wonder that black radicals met these betrayals with despair and hopelessness. What had all the contemporary struggle to resist racism really achieved? What did it mean to have this period of radical questioning of white supremacy, of black is beautiful, only to witness a few years later the successful mass production by white corporations of hair care products to straighten black hair? What did it mean to witness the assault on black culture by capitalist forces which stress the production on all fronts of an image, a cultural product that can "cross over"— that is, that can speak more directly to the concerns, to the popular imagination of white consumers, while still attracting the dollars of black consumers? And what does it mean in 1987 when television viewers watch a morning talk show on black beauty, where black women suggest that these trends are only related to personal preferences and have no relation to racism; when viewers witness a privileged white male, Phil Donahue, shaking his head and trying to persuade the audience to acknowledge the reality of racism and its impact on black people? Or what does it mean when many black people say that what they like most about the Bill Cosby show is that there is little emphasis on blackness, that they are "just people"? And again to hear reported on national news that little black children prefer playing with white dolls rather than black dolls? All these popular narratives remind us that "we are not yet saved," that white supremacy prevails, that the racist oppression and exploitation which daily assaults the bodies and spirits of black people in South Africa assaults black people here.

The Spirit of Black Militancy

Years ago when I was a high school student experiencing racial desegregation, there was a current of resistance and militancy that was so fierce. It swept over and through our bodies as we—black students—stood, pressed against the red brick walls, watching the National Guard with their guns, waiting for those moments when we would enter, when we would break through racism, waiting for the moments of change—of victory. And now even within myself I find that spirit of militancy growing faint; all too often it is assaulted by feelings of despair and powerlessness. I find that I must work to nourish it, to keep it strong. Feelings of despair and powerlessness are intensified by all the images of black self-hate that indicate that those militant 1960s did not have sustained radical impact—that the politicization and transformation of black consciousness did not become an ongoing revolutionary practice in black life. This causes such frustration and despair because it means that we must return to this basic agenda, that we must renew efforts at politicization, that we must go over old ground. Perhaps what is more disheartening is the fear that the seeds, though planted again, will never survive, will never grow strong. Right now it is anger and rage (see Audre Lorde's "The Uses of Anger" in *Sister Outsider*) at the continued racial genocide that rekindles within me that spirit of militancy.

Like so many radical black folks who work in university settings, I often feel very isolated. Often we work in environments predominantly peopled by white folks (some of whom are well-meaning and concerned) who are not committed to working to end white supremacy, or who are unsure about what that commitment means. Certainly the feminist movement has been one of the places where there has been renewed interest in challenging and resisting racism. There too it has been easier for white women to confront racism as overt exploitation and domination, or as personal prejudice, than to confront the encompassing and profound reality of white supremacy.

What White People Can Do

In talking about race and gender recently, the question most often asked by white women has to do with white women's response to black women or women of color insisting that they are not willing to teach them about their racism—to show the way. They want to know: What should a white person do who is attempting to resist racism? It is problematic to assert that black people and other people of color who are sincerely committed to struggling against white supremacy should be unwilling to help or teach white people. Challenging black folks in the nineteenth century, Frederick Douglass made the crucial point that "power accedes nothing without demand." For the racially oppressed to demand of white people, of black people, of all people that we eradicate white supremacy, that those who benefit materially by exercising white supremacist power, either actively or passively, willingly give up that privilege in response to that demand, and then to refuse to show the way, is to undermine our own cause. We must show the way. There must exist a paradigm, a practical model for social change that includes an understanding of ways to transform consciousness that are linked to efforts to transform structures.

A Need for Continued Change

Fundamentally, it is our collective responsibility as radical black people and people of color, and as white people, to construct models for social change. To abdicate that responsibility, to suggest that change is just something an individual can do on his or her own or in isolation with other racist white people, is utterly misleading. If as a black person I say to a white person who shows a willingness to commit herself or himself to the struggle to end white supremacy that I refuse to affirm or help in that endeavor, it is a gesture that undermines my commitment to that struggle. Many black people have essentially responded in this way because we do not want to do the work for white people, and most importantly we cannot do the work, yet this often seems to be what is asked of us. Rejecting the work does not mean that we cannot and do not show the way by our actions, by the information we share. Those white people who want to continue the dominant-subordinate relationship so endemic to racist exploitation by insisting that we "serve" them—that we do the work of challenging and changing their consciousness—are acting in bad faith. In his work *Pedagogy in Progress: The Letters to Guinea-Bissau*, Paulo Freire reminds us:

> Authentic help means that all who are involved help each other mutually, growing together in the common effort to understand the reality which they seek to transform.

It is our collective responsibility as people of color and as white people who are committed to ending white supremacy to help one another. It is our collective responsibility to educate for critical consciousness. If I commit myself politically to black liberation struggle, to the struggle to end white supremacy, I am not making a commitment to working only for and with black people; I must engage in struggle with all willing comrades to strengthen our awareness and our resistance. (See *The Autobiography of Malcolm X* and *The Last Year of Malcolm X— The Evolution of a Revolutionary* by George Breitman.) Malcolm X is an important role model for those of us who wish to transform our consciousness for he was engaged in ongoing critical self-reflection, in changing both his words and his deeds. In thinking about black response to white people, about what they can do to end racism, I am reminded of that memorable example when Malcolm X expressed regret about an incident with a white female college student who asked him what she could do and he told her: "nothing." He later saw that there was much that she could have done. For each of us, it is work to educate ourselves to understand the nature of white supremacy with a critical consciousness. Black people are not born into this world with innate understanding of racism and white supremacy. (See John Hodge, ed., *Cultural Bases of Racism and Group Oppression*.)

In recent years, particularly among women active in feminist movement, much effort to confront racism has focused on individual prejudice. While it is important that individuals work to transform their consciousness, striving to be antiracist, it is important for us to remember that the struggle to end white supremacy is a struggle to change a system, a structure. Hodge emphasizes in his book "the problem of racism is not prejudice but domination." For our efforts to end white supremacy to be truly effective, individual struggle to change consciousness must be fundamentally linked to collective effort to transform those structures that reinforce and perpetuate white supremacy.

From "Overcoming White Supremacy: A Comment," in *Talking Back: Thinking Feminist, Thinking Black* by bell hooks (Boston: South End Press, 1989). Reprinted by permission of the publisher.

White Oppression Is Not to Blame for Black Inequality

by Glenn C. Loury

Glenn C. Loury is a professor of political economy at Harvard University's Kennedy School of Government in Cambridge, Massachusetts. He writes often on issues relating to race and racism. In the following viewpoint, Loury argues that black achievement is limited not by white oppression but by those who define themselves as oppressed. By defining themselves as such, Loury contends, blacks render themselves helpless.

"The ineluctable truth of the matter is that the most important challenges and opportunities confronting any person arise not from his racial condition but from our common human condition."

As a veteran of the academic culture wars during a period of growing racial conflict in our society, I have often had to confront the problem of balancing my desire to fulfill the expectations of others—both whites and blacks, but, more especially, blacks—with my conviction that one should live with integrity. Sometimes this has led me to act against my initial inclination in ways which would elicit approval from my racial peers. After many years, however, I came to understand that, unless I were willing to risk the derision of the crowd, I would have no chance to discover the most important truths about myself or about life—to define and pursue that which I most value, to make the unique contribution to my family and community as God would have me do. (The stakes are now too high for any of us to do otherwise.)

This small private truth points toward some larger social truths: that the seductive call of the tribe can be a siren's call; that there are no group goals or purposes existing prior to, and independently of, the life plans and the ideals of individual persons; that, unless individualism is truly exalted, multiculturalism descends into crass ethnic cheerleading; that, after all is said and done, race is an epiphenomenon, even here in America, even for the descendants of slaves.

Race talk like this is heresy for those I call racialists. Racialists hold to the doctrine that "authentic" blacks must view themselves as objects of mistreatment by whites and share in a collective consciousness of that mistreatment with other blacks. Believers of this creed have shaped the broad public discussion of racial affairs in America for decades; they have also policed, and therefore stifled, black communal discourse. They have argued, in effect, that the fellow feeling amongst blacks, engendered by our common experience of racism, should serve as the basis for our personal identities. Only if whites fully acknowledge their racist culpability, the racialists insist, can the black condition improve. In this they have been monumentally, tragically wrong. They have sacrificed, on an altar of racial protest, the unlimited potential of countless black lives. These are strong statements, but I regard them as commensurate with the crimes.

The ineluctable truth of the matter is that the most important challenges and opportunities confronting any person arise not from his racial condition but from our common human condition. Group membership alone tells us nothing that is true about how we should live. The social contingencies of race, gender, class, or sexual orientation are the raw materials from which an individual constructs a life. The life project is what brings about the development and expression of an individual's personality. Whatever our race, class, or ethnicity, we must all devise and fulfill a life plan. By facing and solving this problem, we grow as human beings and give meaning and substance to our lives.

Because we share this problem—identical in essentials, different only in details—we can transcend racial difference, gain a genuine mutual understanding of our respective experiences and travails, and empathize with one another. As Sartre might have said, Because we all confront the existential challenge of discovering how to live in "good faith," we are able to share love across the tribal boundaries.

From the Inside Out

Ironically, to the extent that we individual blacks see ourselves primarily through a racial lens, we sacrifice several possibilities for the kind of personal development that would ultimately further our collective racial interests. For, if we continue to labor under a self-definition derived from the outlook of our putative oppressor and confined to the contingent facts of our oppression, we shall never be truly free men and women.

The greatest literature of ethnic writers begins from this truth. In *A Portrait of the Artist as a Young Man*, James Joyce says of Irish nationalism:

> When the soul of a man is born in this country there are nets flung at it to hold it back from flight. You talk to me of nationality, language, religion. I shall try to fly by these nets. . . . Do you know what Ireland is? . . . Ireland is the old sow that eats her farrow.

Just as Irish nationalism stultified Stephen Dedalus of *A Portrait*, so too has the racialist emphasis on a mythic, authentic blackness worked to hold back the souls of young blacks from flight into the open skies of American society.

Toward the end of chapter 16 of *Invisible Man*, Ralph Ellison's hero recalls a lecture on Joyce that he heard while in college at Tuskegee, Alabama, in which the teacher argues:

> [Joyce's] problem, like ours, was not actually one of creating the uncreated conscience of his race, but of creating the uncreated features of his face. Our task is that of making ourselves individuals. . . . We create the race by creating ourselves and then to our great astonishment we will have created a culture. Why waste time creating a conscience for something which doesn't exist? For you see, blood and skin do not think!

This is precisely the point. Ellison understood it. A later generation of black writers have refused to see it: Skin and blood do not think. The "conscience of the race" must be constructed from the inside out, one person at a time. If this is a social truth, it has important consequences for political life and discourse in contemporary America.

My colleague Charles Griswold has nicely captured the impossibility of discourse in a society that is dominated by mutually insulated groups—those who define themselves by race, from the outside in. In a recent essay he writes:

> One frequently hears people declare, with passion: "speaking as an [X] I can inform you that [Y]," where "X" is the name of the relevant group and "Y" stands for some description or evaluation of the condition or beliefs of X. An auditor not in group X cannot speak with any authority about that group; one must

and usually does defer immediately. The moral authority embodied in statements preceded by "Speaking as an [X]" stems in part from an epistemic thesis to the effect that the point of view shared by all members of X is not accessible, or at least not sufficiently accessible, to non-X persons.

Griswold is interested in the paradox of these mutually insulated groups, neither capable of understanding the other, who nevertheless insist upon equal group recognition. This is an apt description of the current state of American pluralism. But we must ask whether recognition can reasonably be demanded when understanding is denied to the outsider? How can genuine respect arise from mutual ignorance? How can the white, who has "no idea of what black people have endured in this country," really honor the accomplishments of blacks who have transcended the barriers of racial constraint? How can a black, who could "never see things the way the white man does," ever hope to persuade the "white man" to meet him halfway on a matter of mutual importance?

It would appear that empathy and persuasion across racial lines are impossible unless an understanding obtains that the conditions and feelings of particular human beings are universally shared. Such an understanding can be had, but only if we look past race to our common humanity. This implies that the problems facing poor, black Americans should not be presented as narrow racial claims but should be conveyed to the rest of the polity in their essential human terms.

From this perspective, the racialist's assertion of epistemic privilege is more than a philosophic stance. In our pluralistic democracy, it leads, as Griswold notes, "to the destruction of any notion of community except as the arena within which war is waged for recognition, and for the political and economic benefits which follow from recognition."

A Politics of Despair

Black-white relations are actually far worse than Charles Griswold's assessment would suggest. Racialists have waged a "war for recognition" under the banner of black victimization for the past 20-some years. This war has now ended with a plaintive demand to be patronized. In a stunning attempt at political jujitsu, the voices of black authenticity insist that the very helplessness of their group gives evidence of whites' culpability, to which the only fit response is the recognition of black claims. This is a politics of despair, especially after the 1994 elections that illustrated that other white responses are possible. The racialist strategy has proved disastrous. . . .

The paradigm of racial accountancy has, of course, spread beyond politics, with deleterious effects. In *The Bell Curve*, Richard Herrnstein and Charles Murray point to a large gap in the average IQ scores between blacks and whites, suggesting that much of this difference is determined by genetic factors. The authors have received perhaps unwarranted criticism for simply stating the fact that, on the average, blacks lag behind whites in cognitive functioning. They certainly deserve criticism for implying, as they do, that we should accommodate ourselves to this difference in mental performance between the races and to the consequent social inequality. Yet Herrnstein and Murray can claim, with cause, that they are merely responding to the *Zeitgeist:* Their psychometrician's brew is expressed in the terms of racial groupings previously anointed by the advocates of social equity. They are saying, in effect, "Counting by race wasn't our idea; but since you've mentioned it, let's look at *all* of the numbers!"

Black American economic and educational achievement in the post-civil-rights era has certainly been ambiguous—great success mixed with shocking failure. The loudest voices among black activists have tried to bluff their way past this ambiguous record by cajoling and chastising anyone who expresses disappointment or dismay. (For instance, on the University of Massachusetts, Amherst, campus, it is now considered a racist act to observe publicly that black basketball players are flunking their academic courses.) These activists treat low black achievement as an automatic indictment of the American social order rather than a revelation of black inadequacies. They are hoist with their own petard by the arguments and data of *The Bell Curve*. Having insisted on the primacy of the racial lens, they must now confront the specter of a racial intelligence accountancy, which offers a rather different explanation for the ambiguous achievements of blacks in the last generation.

The Human Condition

So the question now for blacks, as well as for whites, is whether, given equal opportunity, blacks are capable of gaining equal status. It is a peculiar mind that fails, in light of American history, to fathom how poisonous a question this is for our democracy. Let me state my unequivocal belief that blacks are, indeed, so capable. Still, any such assertion is a hypothesis or an axiom, not a fact. The fact is that we blacks have something to prove, to ourselves and to what W.E.B. Du Bois once called "a world that looks on in amused contempt and pity." This is not fair; it is not right; but it is the way things are.

Some conservatives have signaled their belief that blacks can never pass this test. Some black radicals agree. Increasingly and with greater openness, they argue that blacks cannot make it in "white America" and, so, should stop trying and that blacks should go their own way, burning a few things down in the process. At bottom, these parties share the view that blacks cannot meet the challenge.

Yet the challenge confronting blacks today is not racial at all. It is primarily the human condition, not our racial conditions, with which we must *all* learn to cope. What Paul wrote to the Corinthians many centuries ago remains true: "No temptation has seized you except what is common to man; but God is faithful, He will not allow you to be tempted beyond your ability, but when you are tempted He will provide a way out so that you can bear it." The Greek word for "temptation" here can also be translated as "trial" or "test." If indeed blacks must now endure under the weight of a great human trial, still, God remains faithful. We can either confront and dispel our difficulties or deny and avoid them. That we can and must meet this challenge makes the core of Herrnstein and Murray's race talk spectacularly unhelpful. What they are actually saying is that success is unlikely given blacks' average mental equipment, but never mind, because cognitive ability is not the only currency for measuring human worth. Yet this is where viewing people first as members of racial groups must lead. This is the inevitable fruit of racialism.

Whatever the merits and demerits of IQ tests, the scores need not be bandied about in aggregate terms of race. If low intelligence is a problem, then changing the racial identities of those at the top and bottom of the IQ scale does not solve it. Similarly, the crime problem in our society has nothing to do with the skin colors of the perpetrators and victims. It is a great—if common—moral and political error to advance the view that a person's race is his most important characteristic. Portraying a handful of vicious criminals—who happen to be black, and who prey disproportionately upon other blacks—as themselves victims is an egregious act of racialist propaganda. The result is not to engender sympathy in the minds of whites but instead to foster fear of, and contempt for, the communities from which these criminals have been advertised to have come. Smugly confident of their moral superiority in pursuit of "racial justice" for death-row inmates, the racialists are unable to see how shrill and hysterical their claims sound to the average American.

Toward the "Unum"

How can we begin to overcome the fragmentation of the "unum" that is the result of racialist politics? I propose that we suppress, as much as possible, the explicit use of racial categories in the conduct of public affairs. This will, of course, not erase ethnic identity as an important factor in the society; but a conscious effort to achieve a humanistic, universal public policy and rhetoric would redound to the social, political, and psychological benefit of underprivileged minorities in America. Racialists, of course, will dispute this. Stubborn economic inequality between groups, they will argue, gives the lie to the ideal of "E pluribus unum." But why should we care about group inequality, *per se*? Why not focus on inequality among individual persons, and leave it at that?

The preoccupation with group inequality is usually defended on the grounds that group disparities reveal the oppression of individuals based on their group identity. This rationale is ultimately unconvincing. As Thomas Sowell has shown, the Chinese in Southeast Asia, the Indians in East Africa, and the Jews in Western Europe are groups that, though subjected to oppression, have economically surpassed their oppressors. The lesson of history is not that—absent oppression—all relevant social aggregates must reap roughly equal economic rewards. Indeed, that view ignores the economic relevance of historically determined and culturally reinforced beliefs, values, interests, and attitudes that define ethnic groups. "Historically specific cultures," political theorist Michael Walzer has observed, "necessarily produce historically specific patterns of interest and work."

Nor can we claim that the very existence of distinct beliefs, values, and interests among groups proves oppression. In effect, this is to argue that, but for historical oppression, all groups would be the same along every dimension associated with economic success. Yet, if group differences in beliefs, values, and interests bearing on economic achievement are the fruit of oppression, then so are those differences in group styles celebrated by the cultural pluralists. To put the matter simply by way of a concrete example: If poor academic performance among black students reflects "oppression," then does not outstanding athletic or artistic performance spring from the same source? No. Obviously, the existence of group disparities is not a moral problem *ipso facto*. In any case, to the extent that inequality is a problem, it can be dealt with adequately without invoking group categories. American society has for 30 years pursued government, corporate, and academic policies as if the necessity of using racial categories were a Jeffersonian self-evident truth. The great costs to our sense of national unity arising from this fallacious course are now becoming evident.

Martin Luther King, Jr., is justly famous for his evocation of national unity in his 1963 speech "I Have a Dream," in which he said: "I have a dream that my four little children will one day live in a nation where they will not be judged by the color of their skin, but by the content of their character." Today, it is mainly conservatives who recall King's dream. And to evoke, with any passion, King's color-blind ideal is, in some quarters, to show a limited commitment to racial justice. In the face of formal equality of opportunity, liberals cling to race-conscious public action as the only remedy to the persistence of racial inequality. How deeply ironic that a vigorous defense of the color-blind ideal is regarded by the liberal mind as an attack on blacks. I submit, to the contrary, that establishing the color-blind principle is the only way to secure lasting civic equality for the descendants of slaves.

From "Individualism Before Multiculturalism" by Glenn C. Loury, *Public Interest*, no. 121, Fall 1995, pp. 92–106. Reprinted with permission of the author and the *Public Interest* © 1995 by National Affairs, Inc.

Institutionalized Racism Stymies Black Progress

by Claud Anderson

Claud Anderson is a businessman, educator, political strategist, and researcher. He was appointed by former president Jimmy Carter to serve as assistant secretary in the U.S. Department of Commerce. He is establishing a national research institute called the Harvest Institute, a think tank for social and economic reform of black America. In the following viewpoint, Anderson argues that America's legal and economic systems perpetuate racist attitudes and impede black progress. He contends that blacks cannot achieve economic and political empowerment within this framework.

"The Constitution set the legal, civic and racial tones of the nation and placed numerous impediments and obstacles to black empowerment and self-sufficiency."

The U.S. Constitution has historically been and continues to be an impediment to black political and economic empowerment and self-sufficiency. During the formative years of this nation, the Constitution outright excluded blacks from the privileges of citizenship, the acquisition of wealth and power, and the enjoyment of the fruits of their own labor. Moreover, the Constitution shackled blacks so that members of the majority white society and any other ethnic or racial group could use blacks for socioeconomic gains. The social acceptance and grants of wealth that the government has given to European, Asian, and Hispanic immigrants, but withheld from blacks, left blacks decidedly ill-equipped to compete with the more advantaged groups.

Worse, the Constitution is again being used to block even the slightest effort by blacks to redistribute resources to remedy the wealth and power imbalance between blacks and whites. Conservative forces within the court system and government now seek to maintain the status quo of inequality between blacks and whites by mandating that blacks and whites be treated equally in all future endeavors. Any efforts whatsoever to correct past injustices are found to be unconstitutional forms of reverse discrimination against whites. Thus, equal protection has come to mean the equal treatment of fundamentally unequal groups, which in effect perpetuates the unequal distribution of wealth, power and resources.

White society enjoys a virtual monopoly over wealth, power and governmental and business resources, because to a large degree the Constitution decreed that whites would solely possess those advantages. Equality for blacks, therefore, amounts to anything other than the equal ownership and control of resources and power, because the Constitution set the legal, civic and racial tones of the nation and placed numerous impediments and obstacles to black empowerment and self-sufficiency. The following is an analysis of the obstacles that the Constitution has used to impede black people's progress:

Obstacle #1

Constitutional Racism: Termites in the Foundation—The Constitution has formed the foundation for the subordination and exploitation of black Americans by perpetrating racist attitudes and hurtful behavior toward blacks.

The Constitution espoused values of individual rights, freedom and opportunities, but gave slave holders the legal right to deny blacks their personal freedom to benefit from their own labor. Further, since the framers of the Constitution did not consider blacks full human beings they did not assign them individual rights. Thus, blacks were never really meant to be included in the Constitution at all. Professor Harold Cruse spoke of this tragedy by stating:

> The legal Constitution of American society recognizes the rights, privileges and aspirations of the individual, while America has become a nation dominated by the social powers of various ethnic and religious groups. The reality of the power struggles between competing ethnic or religious groups is that an individual has few rights and opportunities in America that are not backed up by the political and social power of one group or another.[1]

America is, in principle, a majority-rule society. However, in areas of the country where blacks constituted the majority of the population, all

184

manner of legal and illegal means have been used to ensure that they nevertheless cannot wrest control from whites. Whether blacks were the majority populations in Mississippi, Louisiana, South Carolina, or the inner cities of many urban areas, a white minority controlled the halls of government. The framers declared the nation to be a democracy while operating a Southern plutocracy, a government run by a wealthy class of plantation owners.

In 1786, the framers of the Constitution laid the legal foundation for a black-white wealth and power imbalance by: 1) counting blacks as three-fifths of a person; 2) postponing for 20 years the effective date for outlawing the slave trade; and 3) obligating the government to defend fugitive slave laws and to use its forces to suppress black insurrections and violence. The federal government was a co-conspirator in black slavery.

The Constitution placed white wealth interests over black personal rights because the framers were wealthy, conservative white men. More than 31 percent of the delegates to the Philadelphia Convention were slave holders who together owned approximately 1,400 slaves.[2] The framers were idealists, but they were also racist. James Madison and George Washington were two of the larger and more prosperous of all the Constitutional delegates.[3] Their capital investment in slaves would be worth approximately $105 million today. They and their fellow delegates protected their own slave investments and the nation's free labor system. The delegates believed that black slave labor was necessary for the development of the nation and the prosperity of white Europeans in this country. All of the nation's power and wealth were in the hands of white males. Any antislavery sentiments that might have been voiced did not prevail. The well-being of blacks was not a concern.

The framers spoke out against concentrated power in the hands of the British, but ignored the concentration of power within their own developing aristocratic ranks. "The accumulation of all powers in the same hands, whether of one, a few, and whether hereditary, self-appointed, or elective," cautioned James Madison, "may justly be pronounced the very definition of tyranny."[4] If the concentration of power in British hands constituted tyranny, why was that not so when it was concentrated in the hands of white colonialists? Blacks became permanent victims of a tyrannical majority, when their lowly role was inscribed into the founding documents. . . .

Obstacle #2

Racism in the Supreme Court and the Legal System—The Supreme Court has been a major player in the denigration of blacks. It has exercised powers that the Constitution never gave it in order to overrule the U.S. Congress. In the famous 1857 Dred Scott Decision that concluded that blacks had no rights, the Supreme Court made itself coequal to the U.S. Congress and began issuing rulings that declared congressional acts to aid blacks were unconstitutional.

According to the Constitution, courts were supposed to be sanctuaries of judicial objectivity, fairness and justice. It is ironic, then, that for nearly 200 years, only wealthy, white male lawyers served in the high court. And even today, they are the overwhelming dominant class of judges and justices. The judicial system cannot be fair and impartial to all citizens because judges' decisions naturally reflect their experiences and beliefs. How fair and impartial to all is a judicial system that is composed of 99 percent conservative white males? How unbiased are the courts' decisions when the judges are appointed or elected because of their social and political ideologies? . . .

Supreme Court decisions are based on the Constitution. But, since the original intent of the Constitution was to enslave blacks and deny them their humanity, fairness for blacks is impossible. To change conditions and make them sympathetic to black goals of empowerment and wealth would be to drastically change the intent of the framers. If judges rely on original intent, blacks would have no rights.

According to Eric Black, there were serious disagreements among the framers on many issues, but on the specific issue of slavery the framers' original intent was crystal clear: The framers intended to approve and codify the subordination and exploitation of blacks into law.[5] They intended to reward slave holders and give them extra representation and power in Congress. And, they intended to make it unconstitutional for anyone to attempt to harbor or assist a black slave. Seemingly, these intentions were very strong forces underlying the Constitution.

It is likely that blacks would have continued their battle for constitutional rights in the 19th century had they not been discouraged by the Supreme Court's unrelenting pattern of biased interpretations of black people's rights under Emancipation and the 14th Amendment. A critical examination of court rulings and the legal status of black Americans prior to the 1954 Brown decision should make even the heartiest optimist wonder why blacks would try to seek protection from any court, especially the Supreme Court. Over the last century and a half, various court rulings followed a circular course, from indifference to hostility, to benignity. The Supreme Court stood silent while lower courts emasculated the 14th and 15th Amendments. There were few, if any, favorable rulings for blacks during the first 160 years of the Court's existence. . . .

Obstacle #3

Absence of Group Economics and Capitalism—The practice of perceiving and acting on issues and events from a social rather than a capitalistic perspective is a major impediment to black empowerment. An old adage says, "When in Rome, do as the Romans do." Blacks are in America and America is a capitalist nation. Thus, blacks will have to adopt the American capitalistic approach if they are to build their economic strength. The founding fathers intended this nation to be an experiment in capitalism.

Dr. William E.B. Dubois, the preeminent black scholar, once described the concept to a black audience in Atlanta. He said: "Capitalism is like having three ears of corn: You eat one, you sell one, and you save one for seed for next year's planting."[6] Using Dubois' definition as a measuring device, blacks have yet to practice capitalism. Black people are neither producers nor savers. Primarily, blacks are consumers.

Blacks spend 95 percent of their annual disposable income with businesses located within white communities. Of the 5 percent that remains within black communities, another 3 percent is spent with nonblack owned businesses. It is difficult, if not impossible, for black communities to maintain a reasonable quality of life and be economically competitive when only 2 percent of their annual disposable income remains within black communities.[7]

Conditions in black communities are made worse by the fact that too many black business owners believe in developing their business but not the black community. They are shortsighted in valuing temporary business development above long-term community development. *USA Today* reported on April 11, 1994, that of approximately $9 billion that went to black 8(a) businesses from government setaside contracts, nearly all of the black businesses were located in white communities. The tax revenue and jobs from these government contracts went into white rather than black communities, but supporters of the programs explained that they fostered "minority businesses" not community development.

With black consumers and black businesses spending 95 percent of their income in white communities, whites live comfortably off double incomes, reaping 100 percent of their own and 95 percent of blacks' income. Essentially, black consumers and business owners have joined whites in boycotting black communities. Their failure to practice group economics further impoverishes black communities.

Obstacle #4

Pursuing Myths and Elusive Dreams—To achieve economic power, blacks as a group must redesign civil rights traditions. Blacks are out of sync with the times and are still chasing civil rights. The process of rethinking our civil rights tradition begins with reexamining America's race problem from the perspective of black economic and political empowerment. The section below explores myths or dreams that are to their detriment.

Myth No. 1: Integration

Real integration is a dream that will never come true for blacks. Even if it did, it would not change the nature of black life in America. The reality of integration is that the integrating group loses all self-determination, since all plans and goals must be processed through and approved by the dominant society into which the minority group is integrating. Integration is a detriment to blacks, because the larger white society will neither allow blacks to assimilate nor give them assistance to alter the negative marginal conditions in which they must live.

Black businesses and individuals situated in and wholly dependent on the continued acceptance and goodwill of white communities are vulnerable and powerless. They cannot change anything in the white communities or businesses because they are only guests. Integrated blacks' conditions are made more precarious by the reasoning that they have little, if any, support within the white community and they cannot depend upon receiving support from the black community whose powers were weakened by those who abandoned the community to integrate. Similarly, it is difficult for the nonintegrated black masses to identify with the integrated few. Therefore, both the integrated and the nonintegrated are rendered powerless by their social divisions.

Power flows from the group, the trunk of the tree, not in reverse from the individual or limb to the trunk. So, as long as the black masses remain powerless then every black individual remains powerless and vulnerable, even if they or their businesses are "integrated."

The integration process has major political significance in large urban areas where blacks are in control of government apparatus. When blacks are the majority population and are the controllers of government, the last things they should be concerned about are integration and minority development. It is self-destructive to continue to behave as a powerless minority seeking integration when one's group is the dominant majority population.

While urban revitalization plans should be built around economically and politically empowering cities' black masses, black elected officials are reading outdated development strategies that suggest the best way to help blacks is to re-attract whites into the cities. Such development philosophies are racist and shortsighted. It confirms the belief in white superiority and black inferiority, that blacks cannot govern and progress without white involvement. Integration will be a no-win situation for black people until they have sufficient racial power, wealth, competitiveness, and respect. At that point, integration will become just one of a number of options open to them.

Myth No. 2: Equal Opportunity for All

Black America devotes a significant amount of time and energy chasing the myth of equal opportunity, which was the forerunner of the dream of racial integration. Both the myth and the dream are improbables. Inequality of power and wealth will naturally exist, so long as human greed and competition motivate human behavior.

On the other hand, the myth of equality does perform an invaluable service for those who hold a disproportionate share of the wealth, power and material resources. This myth not only keeps blacks distracted from learning how to increase their share, but it keeps blacks believing that at least their children or their children's children will have a fair chance at the brass ring. The greatest service that the myth of equality provides for the dominant power holders is the idea that, if blacks are not successful achieving a fair share of power, wealth, and material resources, it is their own fault.

Integration and equal opportunity are grounded in the belief that dominant white society will voluntarily share power with blacks. Power is rarely shared, especially between competitive groups. Power holders have no desire for equality. James R. Kluegel and Eliot R. Smith, in the research for *Beliefs About Equality*, showed that whites resist changes regarding racial inequalities, because they tend to classify inequalities that relate to the black underclass as "non-issues."[8]

Many whites do not believe that structural limitations impede blacks. Some even believe that, if individuals would coexist with their social peers, and stop trying to integrate, inequality would not be an issue. Everyone would then be in common groupings, they reason. Whites will accept blacks as equals only when blacks have acquired parity of wealth and power. Pursuing the concept of equality rather than the basis of equality—which is wealth and power—is a quagmire that bogs blacks down and wastes their time and efforts.

Conservative logic holds that if all people acknowledge that America is race neutral, then blacks have achieved their long-sought "equality" without whites ever having to redistribute resources and power to blacks. Through the 1980s, conservatives checkmated blacks on preferential policies and quotas by arguing that America is a color-blind society and all governmental policies should be race neutral. The only way

America will ever be color-blind is if everyone literally lost their sight. Conservatives have learned to use black rhetoric against blacks. They argue that any decision that is race conscious violates the 14th Amendment and is therefore unconstitutional. However, without preferential treatment, or affirmative action for blacks, structural racism will continue to advantage whites. This is the way the power holders want it to be. If the white power holders had wanted blacks to have equality, they would not have kept them outside and beneath mainstream society for nearly 400 years. . . .

Obstacle #5

Criminalizing Blacks—The criminalizing of blacks, especially black males, is a major obstacle to black empowerment for at least three reasons: 1) American society has long linked crime to blacks, especially young, black males; 2) blacks have been forced to live in marginal social conditions that produce pathological, survival behavior; and 3) black communities lack an accountability mechanism that could establish, reward, and punish behavior that is detrimental to them. Since the late 1960s, blacks have been so overexposed to black crime within their communities, that they now accept it as normal black behavior.

National public policies and institutions began centuries ago to produce and perpetuate the laws, racial images, and myths that imprisoned blacks within the concepts of crime and violence. For blacks, criminal justice has never been blind. White society criminalized black behavior out of fears and financial self-interest. According to Leonard Curry, the author of *The Free Black In Urban America, 1800-1850*, blacks were arrested for activities that would not have been a crime for whites, such as strolling in certain neighborhoods and looking suspicious. Sometimes blacks were imprisoned for even less specific crimes, such as "violating various city ordinances" and "playing games with whites." In some instances, no crimes were committed. White planters would commit blacks to prison "just for safe keeping." All of these incarcerations showed up in the records as black crimes against society.

An abusive use of the legal system to criminalize blacks primarily occurred in urban areas where the white power structure had fewer options for controlling and using blacks. As far back as 1826, in Massachusetts, free blacks were less than 1 percent of the population, but nearly 17 percent of the prisoners. In Pennsylvania, blacks were 2 percent of the population, but nearly 34 percent of the prisoners; and in New Jersey, blacks were also only 2 percent of the population, but nearly 50 percent of the prisoners.[9] Today, blacks still make up 35 to 50 percent of the state or federal penal total population. Approximately 37 percent of America's black male population is either in jail or on parole or probation. The criminalizing phenomena has destroyed black individuals, families and communities. . . .

The greatest impediment to black empowerment and economic justice has been the Constitution, which institutionalized the relative social and economic status of blacks and whites and codified racism in America. After using the Constitution to expropriate black labor, create a racial ordering of acceptability and foster a wealth and power imbalance between blacks and whites, the government and the court system are now using the Constitution to impede any effort to correct the disparities. The government and the courts now allege that any preferential treatment for blacks would be unconstitutional reverse discrimination. The Constitution ought to be just as supportive or tolerant of affirmative action, setasides and preferential treatment for blacks as it has been for whites. Indeed, in all their wisdom, the drafters of the Constitution had to have known that discrimination against blacks was in fact preferential treatment for whites.

Notes

1. Harold Cruse, *The Crisis of the Negro Intellectual: A Historical Analysis of the Failure of Black Leadership*. New York: Quill Books, 1984, 7–8.
2. John A. Garraty, *The American Nation: A History of the United States to 1817*. 7th ed. New York: HarperCollins 1991, 145.
3. Erick Black, *Our Constitution: The Myth That Binds Us*. Boulder, CO: Westview Press, 1988, 21.
4. James Madison and Jay Hamilton, *The Federalist Papers*, ed. Clinton Rossiter. New York: Mentor Books, 1961, 301.
5. Black, p. 8.
6. Note from the author: W. E. B. Dubois made the remarks in a speech on black business development, in 1915, in Atlanta Georgia.
7. Note from the author: These remarks were taken from a taped interview with Tony Brown, the host of *Black Journal*, in a Black History presentation entitled *Contributions: African-Americans and The American Mosaic*. The taped series was made possible by Philip Morris Companies, Inc., and produced by Radio America. Tony Brown's *Black Journal* is a long-running nationally syndicated television program that addresses black issues.
8. James R. Kleugel and Eliot R. Smith, *Beliefs About Inequality*. New York: Aldine De Gruyter, 1986.
9. Leonard P. Curry, *The Free Black in Urban America, 1800–1850*. (Chicago: The University of Chicago Press, 1981), 136–37.

Excerpted from *Black Labor, White Wealth: The Search for Power and Economic Justice* by Claud Anderson (Edgewood, MD: Duncan & Duncan, 1994); © 1994 by Claud Anderson, Ed. D. Reprinted with permission of the publisher.

Individual Behavior Stymies Black Progress

by Byron M. Roth

Byron M. Roth is a professor of psychology at Dowling College in Oakdale, New York, and has served as academic chair of the college's social science division. In the following viewpoint, Roth argues that individual behaviors and values, particularly among the black underclass, represent the greatest obstacle to black progress. Claims of institutionalized racism, he contends, are not supported by evidence and are contradicted by the large number of blacks who have succeeded.

"Most of the problems blacks face in America today are directly attributable to patterns of behavior that have become common in black underclass communities."

In 1962, the distinguished social scientist Arnold Rose commented on the great strides America had made toward racial equality and racial harmony during the preceding two decades. So great was his optimism that he predicted that over the next three decades racial enmity would decline to "the minor order of Catholic-Protestant" prejudice as it then existed.[1] Rose was not alone; many Americans at the time, perhaps most, shared his optimism.

The history of the past three decades suggests, however, that this earlier view may have been overly optimistic. There can be no doubt that life for large numbers of black Americans has vastly improved since World War II. On the other hand, the widespread deterioration of inner-city black neighborhoods during recent decades has meant that life has grown worse for many blacks. Furthermore, the gradual improvement in race relations in the early days of the civil rights movement seems to have stagnated and been replaced by a growing unease about the future of those relations. On the nation's college campuses and in its largest cities, there are troubling reports of new tensions and animosities between blacks and other groups. Prominent black Americans reflect pessimistically on the pervasiveness of white racism, while civil rights advocates argue for more-strenuous efforts to overcome the effects of that racism. It is my purpose in what follows to examine the sources of this unease and to attempt to discover why progress in civil rights for black Americans does not appear to have been matched, at least in recent years, by equal progress in social harmony. . . .

Correcting Historic Wrongs

It was about fifty years ago that America began the task of correcting the historic wrongs visited on black Americans by pervasive discrimination in the laws and customs of American society that continued long after the shameful chapter of American slavery had been brought to a close. The injustices that blacks suffered were particularly egregious in light of the American attachment to fair play and open opportunity. The enormous contradiction between those values and America's treatment of its black citizens was brought to the fore by the events of World War II. It is noteworthy that the generation that came of age in that terrible period of history was the one that embarked upon the momentous task of dismantling the legal and social apparatus that kept black Americans from achieving their rightful place in American society.

The task seemed relatively straightforward. Black Americans lagged behind white Americans socially and economically because of widespread discrimination and prejudice. If that discrimination and prejudice were eliminated, blacks would, in due course, rise to the same level as whites. As Arnold Rose's comments make clear, the first two decades of those efforts had been remarkably successful. Government-sponsored segregation was largely dismantled, and strenuous educational efforts were undertaken to reduce racial prejudice and discriminatory social customs. By the 1960s, black Americans were indeed moving into the mainstream, albeit slowly but nonetheless steadily.

For many people, the slow and gradual nature of black progress was to be expected due to the fact that blacks had so much to overcome and so far to go. The transformation of a whole race of people from the status of a despised caste in society to that of equal participants could not, in this view, occur overnight. The prejudicial attitudes and discriminatory behaviors that white Americans had acquired over centuries would require time to overcome; in some places this might require the actual passing of one or more generations of people who were too fixed in their ways to adjust to new realities. Blacks too would have to make difficult adjustments. They would have to develop new skills in order to take advantage of new opportunities. They would have to acquire new habits of thought and shed attitudes that centuries of slavery and injustice had imposed. All of these changes would require time, perhaps decades, before they could be thoroughly assimilated by all Americans. The development of a new accommodation between the races, made possible by legal equality, could not, in this view, be imposed by law, but could only evolve naturally over time as new realities took hold. Progress toward racial equality, accordingly, would not be measured in years, but rather in generations, much as had the progress of various immigrant groups who established themselves in America after very humble beginnings. For those who held this view, the removal of legal discrimination was a necessary first step toward eventual social equality, the actual attainment of which would necessarily be halting and gradual, however much one may have wished to speed the process.

"A Dream Deferred"

For others, however, the lumbering pace toward racial equality in the two decades following World War II seemed to promise once again, in Langston Hughes's poignant phrase, "a dream deferred."[2] To people of this view, the real but modest success of government efforts during the previous decades suggested that more-strenuous government efforts could and should be made to bring about equality sooner. How, these people asked, could one ask black Americans to wait generations after all they had suffered at the hands of a cruel and indifferent America? Such people argued for radical change to correct past injustices.

This argument over the pace of progress in the 1960s was won, in large measure, by those who argued for more-radical government action. A wide range of policies were implemented in that decade and since then to eliminate segregation and speed the assimilation of black Americans. Affirmative action guidelines were instituted to assure that blacks were fairly represented in the workplace and in the universities. Compensatory education programs, such as Head Start, were initiated. Educational programs in the schools and in the media were undertaken to stamp out prejudice. A wide range of legal changes were implemented to reduce discrimination in the criminal justice system and in other areas of life.

The more-strenuous efforts undertaken since the 1960s have had decidedly mixed results. On the one hand, blacks have continued in greater numbers to move into the mainstream of middle-class American life. Paralleling this progress, however, has been the growth of an increasingly troubled black underclass and the decay of the central cities where many blacks live. As I will attempt to demonstrate in the pages that follow, it is the growth of the black underclass that represents the greatest impediment to black progress and racial harmony today. . . .

The Black Underclass

A thorough analysis of the social science literature will reveal that most of the problems blacks face in America today are directly attributable to patterns of behavior that have become common in black underclass communities. Underclass neighborhoods are plagued by welfare dependency, crime, illegitimacy, and educational failure, all of which seriously undercut black economic and social advancement, and in addition serve to undermine efforts to facilitate racial integration. The common charge by civil rights advocates that disapproval of underclass behavior patterns is a cover for racist sentiment, a charge often construed as an attempt to justify those behavior patterns, serves mainly to widen the gap between blacks and whites.

The above understanding, of course, runs counter to the common understanding espoused by the media and by government bureaucrats, for whom the problems of black Americans, including the growth of the underclass, are usually explained in terms of an endemic white racism and the discrimination it fosters. In the pages that follow I make the case that the continuing attempt to counter the purported racism of white Americans may be largely counterproductive today and, insofar as it obstructs dealing with the real sources of black difficulties, serves to exacerbate them. Why has the scientific literature of which I speak had so little impact on popular understanding and government policy? . . .

Probably the most important reason: social scientists are acutely sensitive to the possibility that they might contribute to the acceptance of doctrines of racial superiority or inferiority. . . .

The fear of being in league with the devil continues to haunt most thoughtful social scientists and has had a pervasive influence on their contributions to the current civil rights debate. This is especially so with regard to their treatment of alternatives to the prevailing view that black difficulties are rooted in white prejudice and discrimination. The most obvious alternative to that view is the common-sense view that people's failures and successes, including the failures and successes of blacks, are in large measure the result of their own behaviors and values. That is the argument made most notably by the well-known black economist

Thomas Sowell.[3] The problem, however, with accepting this argument is that it opens up the possibility that the differences in behaviors and values between blacks and whites may be related in some more basic way to native differences between the races. In other words, perhaps blacks have educational and economic difficulties because they lack the same level of abilities as whites? Perhaps the higher incidence of violent criminal behavior among blacks is the result of more-fundamental differences in aggressiveness or in impulse control between the races? It is not at all an exaggeration to say that the social science discussion of race relations is conditioned by a desire to avoid even the possibility of lending support to such explanations of black problems.

Even when it is patently clear that a pattern of behavior among blacks is a direct cause of black poverty, as is clear in the case of illegitimacy, social scientists hesitate to emphasize the need to change behavior, and look rather for the causes of that behavior in white discrimination. The very possibility of seeming to buttress doctrines of racial inferiority is, understandably, so abhorrent to the vast majority of academics that any evidence that *seems* to lend any support to such a thesis tends to be dismissed or ignored. The aversion to addressing the negative impact of many black patterns of behavior forces the social sciences into a mental straightjacket, as it were, requiring all black problems to be viewed as rooted in white racism. Research that contradicts the prevailing view is dismissed or, where possible, ignored. When contrary research cannot be dismissed or ignored, it is often rendered impotent by the charge that it was motivated by racist intent. The net result is that the full and damaging consequences of many underclass behaviors for black economic advancement remain poorly understood. . . .

The Prevailing View of White Racism

Consider the following comments on prejudice presented in a popular textbook on social psychology:

> In the United States, racial prejudice against blacks by whites has been a tenacious social problem. It has resulted in an enormous catalog of social ills, ranging from the deterioration and near bankruptcy of large cities, to poverty, shorter life expectancy, high levels of crime and drug abuse, and human misery of all kinds among blacks themselves.[4]

In a similar vein the distinguished black psychologist Kenneth Clark (a past president of the American Psychological Association)—whose research was cited by the Supreme Court in the 1954 school-desegregation decision—gave the following explanation for black-white differences in SAT scores in a 1982 op-ed piece in the *New York Times*:

> Black children are educationally retarded because the public schools they are required to attend are polluted with racism. Their low scores reflect the racial segregation and inferiority of these schools. These children are perceived and treated as if they were uneducable. From the earliest grades they are programmed for failure. Throughout their lives, they are classic examples of the validity of the concept of victimization by self-fulfilling prophecy.[5]

The above statements are fairly representative of the views of social scientists commonly heard in the popular media. Under the prevailing view, white America is endemically racist and racism is the primary cause of the problems that blacks confront. Racism is claimed as the primary, almost exclusive cause of poverty, crime, illegitimacy, drug abuse, and educational failure among blacks. In fact, it is the assumption of widespread racism which is the justification for most of the laws and policies associated with the civil rights movement—laws and policies that a large majority of social scientists support.

But even modest reflection must give one pause. It is simply not reasonable to attribute *all* black problems to the single cause of white racism. In fact, it is almost always the case that complex social phenomena are caused and influenced by a multitude of factors. It is of course true and indisputable that, in the ultimate sense, everything about blacks in America today can be traced to the racism of the white Europeans who enslaved their ancestors. In addition, it is probably true that historical black responses to centuries of abuse have played a prominent, perhaps determinative, role in many of the responses of blacks today. But to say that is by no means to outline in precisely what ways past racist practices shaped the behavior patterns common today. Nor is it clear what impact current white attitudes have upon blacks in the very different circumstances of the late twentieth century. These are questions of great importance for blacks and whites and the future of America, and it is unlikely that the answers to them will be simple. At the very least, we should examine the empirical evidence with great scrutiny before accepting this or that answer as if it were a foregone conclusion.

Historical Racism's Role

For instance, it is a reasonable hypothesis to assert that the educational difficulties blacks face may be due to the fact that historically blacks were denied the fruits of educational success by racist practices. But that is a very different hypothesis from one that suggests that these educational problems are the result of current white racism. Indeed, these hypotheses are radically different and would lead to very different policy prescriptions for improving black educational performance. The historical-racism hypothesis would recommend an effort to change the attitudes of black children about the current opportunities that educational success can provide. The hypothesis that current racism is to blame would suggest attempts to eliminate racism among whites, especially those in the schools. There are, however, many reasons to question the impact of current racism on black children today. It is by no means clear how the racism of some white teachers—I doubt that even the supporters of the white-racism hypothesis would argue that all white teachers are racist—undermines the education of black children in Atlanta, Georgia, where, according to Abigail Thernstrom, "white teachers have almost disappeared from the school system."[6] Even more unclear is how the attitudes of white teachers could have affected children in the earlier segregated schools of the South when virtually all teachers in segregated black schools were themselves black and were given considerable freedom in what and how they taught.[7]

Certainly the segregationist practices in the South of the past may have demoralized black children and interfered with their motivation to learn, but that is very different from arguing that America today denies educated blacks fair opportunities. The latter is merely an assertion and one that runs counter to everyday experience. . . .

Illegitimacy in the black community, to take another example, is a very serious problem. Some 64 percent of all black children are born to unmarried women.[8] It is certainly a reasonable hypothesis to suggest that discrimination against black men leads to unemployment among them and thereby contributes to high rates of unwed motherhood due to the scarcity of men able to support a family. But this hypothesis must also account for the fact that the illegitimacy rate was less than one-third of today's rate in the 1950s when, by all accounts, discrimination against black men was more severe than it is today.[9] The point is that reasonable hypotheses are not the same as sound scientific explanations. In fact, it is not at all clear what factors contribute to high rates of illegitimacy among blacks. It is very clear, however, that so long as the rate of unwed motherhood remains high, so will poverty among black women and children. Policies to improve the economic prospects for blacks would do well to aim at reducing the illegitimacy rate, whatever the ultimate causes. Attributing the problem to white prejudice, even if that were the case, would not solve the problem, since it is unclear how white prejudice could be more effectively dealt with than it is today.

Black Successes Contradict Racism Explanation

A very serious problem with the white-racism explanation is the fact that large numbers of blacks have done very well in recent decades. It is difficult to explain why a pattern of discrimination that is said to be so pervasive has been relatively ineffective in thwarting the ambitions of the many blacks who perform well in school and the many who succeed in highly desirable occupations. The large number of successful blacks argues against the notion that they are merely "tokens" to assuage white guilt. It is interesting that among the 2.4 million blacks who are Catholic (9 percent of all blacks) the high school dropout rate is lower than that of white Americans. Black Catholics are 40 percent more likely to be college graduates than other blacks. In fact, among forty- to fifty-year-olds, more black Catholics (26 percent) have college degrees than do other blacks (15 percent) and more even than whites (24 percent).[10]

Such statistics force us to question the white-discrimination hypothesis, since it is unreasonable to suppose that whites make distinctions about blacks on the basis of religion. Similar questions arise when we are confronted with statistics comparing black Americans of Caribbean descent to those whose ancestors were born in America. Blacks of Caribbean background have higher rates of employment in professional occupations than American-born blacks and higher rates of such employment even than Americans in general.[11]

Further reflection leads to other questions regarding the white-racism hypothesis. How is it possible for racism to be so virulent after all these years of educational and media efforts to reduce it? Have these efforts been ineffective, and if so, why? We have all been witness in recent years to highly publicized incidents of physical assaults on black individuals, and numerous reports of racial incidents on college campuses. Are these incidents newsworthy because they represent only the tip of the iceberg, as it were, or are they newsworthy because they are so atypical in America today? Perhaps the incidents receive the coverage they do because they seem consistent with the prevailing view that racism is widespread among white Americans.

Other Explanations Are Needed

It is important to stress the point that questioning the hypothesis that white racism is the primary source of black problems is not the same as denying the existence of white racism. There can be little doubt that there are people who openly express antagonism to blacks, and probably many others who secretly share their antagonism. But it is simply not clear how many white Americans are avowed racists. Nor is it clear what proportion of racists there are in positions of influence who can in any major way affect what happens to blacks. So long as such questions remain unanswered, it is unwise and perhaps counterproductive to accept many common assertions as to the sources of black difficulties. I do not think it is useful to argue that many blacks fare poorly in school because American education is polluted with racism, when no evidence for such a claim can be brought forward.

On its face such a charge seems extremely dubious in light of the fact that college professors and public school teachers are generally known to be liberal on racial matters. Similar reasoning undermines the frequent claim that a disproportionate number of blacks have criminal records because of the racism endemic to the criminal justice system, when no evidence is brought forward to show that racism is common among judges, lawyers, or police officers. There are, to be sure, anecdotal reports of police misconduct and highly publicized accounts of incidents of police brutality such as the Rodney King beating, but these hardly substitute for sound evidence of widespread racism within the system. If anything, the public outcry against such incidents tends to suggest that such misconduct is, in fact, unrepresentative of the system as a whole. Also questionable is the charge that blacks suffer disproportionate health problems because racism taints American medicine. Doctors and nurses are among the least likely candidates upon whom to pin the label of bigotry.

In other words, the claim that black Americans suffer the problems they do because of the racism of white Americans requires considerable scrutiny before it is accepted as a sound explanation. On its face it seems unreasonable to assume that large numbers of white Americans, including the best educated and most influential, are as bigoted and mean-spirited as were many uneducated whites earlier in the century. If American bigotry is in fact still the primary source of black problems, then the future of black Americans is grim indeed, since it is hard to see how further efforts to eradicate bigotry can be more successful than have been those of the past four decades. Unfortunately, the prevailing orthodoxy, if closely analyzed, leads inexorably to such an unhappy conclusion. Perhaps it is time to cast aside the current view and look for alternative explanations that may produce a more useful and less pessimistic conclusion.

Notes

1. Arnold Rose, "Postscript: Twenty Years Later," in Gunnar Myrdal, with Richard Sterner and Arnold Rose, *An American Dilemma: The Negro Problem and Modern Democracy*, 20th anniversary ed. (New York: Harper & Row, 1962), p. xliv. Rose went on to say: "These changes would not mean that

there would be equality between the races within this time, for the heritage of past discriminations would still operate to give Negroes lower 'life chances.' But the dynamic social forces creating inequality will, I predict, be practically eliminated in three decades."

2. Langston Hughes, *Selected Poems of Langston Hughes* (New York: Alfred A. Knopf, 1959), pp. 252–54.
3. See, for example, Thomas Sowell, *Civil Rights: Rhetoric or Reality?* (New York: William Morrow and Company, 1984).
4. David O. Sears, Letitia Anne Peplau, Jonathan L. Freedman, and Shelley E. Taylor, *Social Psychology*, 6th ed. (Englewood Cliffs, NJ: Prentice Hall, 1988, p. 413
5. *Brown v. Board of Education of Topeka*, 74 S. Ct. 686 (1954); the quoted material is drawn from Kenneth B. Clark, "Blacks' S.A.T. Scores," *New York Times*, October 21, 1982, p. 31.
6. Abigail Thernstrom, "Beyond the Pale," *New Republic*, December 16, 1991, p. 22
7. Myrdal, Sterner, and Rose, *An American Dilemma*, 20th anniversary ed., pp. 800–801.
8. U.S. Bureau of the Census, *Statistical Abstract of the United States 1992*. 112th ed.)Washington, DC), p. 69.
9. U.S. Bureau of the Census, *Statistical Abstract of the United States 1982–83*. 103d ed. (Washington, DC), p. 66.
10. Seymour P. Lachman and Barry A. Kosmin, "Black Catholics Get Ahead," *New York Times*, September 14, 1991, p. 19. Barry Kosmin identified as the director of the City University of New York's survey of religious identification, from which this information was obtained.
11. Sowell, *Civil Rights*, p. 77.

CHAPTER 5

Is Gender Bias Prevalent in American Society?

Chapter Preface

Accusations of gender bias surface in many areas of American life. U.S. Department of Labor statistics show that women who work outside the home earn seventy cents for every dollar men earn. Many people conclude from these figures that American society treats women unfairly. Sylvia Ann Hewlett, vice president for economic studies at the United Nations Association, argues, "Women do encounter discrimination in the workplace." She points out that most top executives in American companies are men and men hold most of the highest paying jobs. Women tend to hold positions in what Hewlett and others call the "pink-collar ghetto"—jobs traditionally held by women, such as teaching, nursing, and clerical work, for which the salaries have remained low. These critics conclude that women's lower earnings are proof of discrimination.

Others disagree that the difference between men's and women's salaries proves discrimination. Yale economics professor Jennifer Roback argues, "Many of the factors that contribute to the earnings gap are the result of personal choices made by women themselves, not decisions thrust on them by bosses." For example, Roback and others state, women take time off to have children and thus do not establish the seniority and experience male employees do. Also, women are more likely than men to choose part-time work because women often need more off-the-job time to care for their children. Roback is one of many who conclude that the difference in men's and women's earnings is not proof of discrimination.

The workplace is not the only source of accusations of gender bias. Some researchers contend that the justice system—particularly in the areas of divorce and family law—routinely demonstrate bias against one gender or the other. The nation's educational system has also been accused of bias, mostly against girls and young women. The authors of the viewpoints in the following chapter debate whether gender bias is a problem in American society, and for whom.

Discrimination Slows the Advancement of Women in the Workplace

by Carol Moseley Braun

Senator Carol Moseley Braun is a Democrat from Illinois. She was elected to Congress in 1992. This viewpoint is an excerpt of a speech she made before Congress on March 30, 1995. In the following viewpoint, Braun contends that an invisible but nevertheless real barrier confronts women and minorities who seek full participation and advancement in the workforce. She contends that this barrier, commonly referred to as a "glass ceiling," is built on a foundation of white male middle managers' prejudices and stereotypes and a lack of follow-through from top corporate executives who have made an initial commitment to diversity and expanded economic opportunity. Braun argues that the glass ceiling hurts all Americans, not just women and minorities, and that the government must actively seek its demise through programs such as affirmative action.

"Our country will fall behind . . . if we do not act aggressively to shatter the glass ceiling."

Affirmative action is about working people, about middle-class families, and about jobs. It is about the basic right of all Americans to have access to education, to have the opportunity to get a good job, to have the opportunity to be promoted when they work hard—to do better than their parents did. It is, quite simply, about ensuring fundamental economic fairness for all our citizens. We have come a long way in ensuring that economic opportunity exists for all Americans; yet much work remains to be done. That is why it would be extremely short-sighted at this point in time for the Senate to retreat on affirmative action. Before we act, we must consider all of the facts. We cannot allow cynical political games to be played with an issue of this much importance. And we cannot allow ourselves to fall prey to attempts to make affirmative action a debate about race. It is not. What affirmative action is really about is fundamental fairness. It is about whether each of us will be allowed to participate fully in society, regardless of our gender or race, or will instead be held back by conditions that have nothing to do with merits, or talents and abilities. It is a debate that lies at the core of our national economic competitiveness.

The Importance of Equal Economic Opportunity

If we consider all the facts, it is abundantly clear that affirmative action is about equal economic opportunity, not just for minorities, but for women as well. It is about providing a chance to compete for those who may still be limited by a glass ceiling or artificial barriers to participation in our economy. In addition, affirmative action is now a business imperative for our country. In spite of the rhetoric and myths surrounding this concept, the truth is that every American stands to benefit when each citizen is given a chance to contribute to the maximum extent of his or her ability. Our workforce is changed. Our country has moved in the direction of making the American dream of opportunity a dream that is open to all Americans. Affirmative action has played a major role in opening up doors and providing opportunity for the millions of people who did not have a chance to participate in the full range of economic activities this country has to offer. And our society has benefitted as a result.

In 1964, when the first Executive Order on affirmative action was issued, there were approximately 74 million working Americans. By last year, that number had grown to just over 123 million. In other words, since 1964, our economy has created 50 million new jobs. Although women and minorities entered the workforce in unprecedented numbers, these new jobs were not created by taking away jobs held by men. Rather, they were created by making use of the talents that a diverse workforce brings to our economy, and using those talents to help create new economic growth and more, new jobs. Affirmative action is not about taking away opportunity but about creating it.

Gains Made by Women

I would like to take a moment to review the experience working women have had with affirmative action. Because many employers made a commitment to fostering diversity, women made significant inroads into professions that had previously been off limits to them. In 1972, women comprised a mere 3 percent of architects. By 1993, that number had climbed to 18.6 percent. In 1972, women were 10 percent of all physicians, but by 1993, that number had grown to 22 percent. In 1972, women made only 4 percent of all lawyers, a number that grew to 23 percent by 1993. This is despite the fact that the Supreme Court, in *Bradwell v. Illinois*, once upheld a decision by my home State to deny an eminently qualified woman, Myra Bradwell, the right to practice law, solely on the basis of her gender.

Women have made equally significant gains in the science fields. In 1972, women comprised a dismal 0.8 percent of all engineers—less than 1 percent! But by 1993, that number had grown to 8.6 percent. In chemistry, women's share of the jobs grew from 10 percent in 1972 to almost 30 percent in 1993. In 1972, there were so few female airline pilots that the Department of Labor did not even bother to keep track. By 1993, women were 4 percent of airline pilots—a gain worth celebrating, although there is clearly still a long way to go. In the advertising profession, women went from 22 percent of the workforce in 1972, to 50 percent in 1993—almost equal their percentage of the population. Women hold 42 percent of teaching positions, compared to 28 percent in 1972.

Even more importantly, a rapidly growing number of women now own their own businesses—they are the bosses! During a recent 5-year period, the number of women-owned businesses increased by 58 percent, four times the rate of growth for all businesses. And during that same period, the revenues for women-owned businesses nearly tripled to over $275 billion. The number of women-owned manufacturing businesses more than doubled in that 5-year period, and the revenues of those businesses increased almost six-fold over those 5 years. I want to underscore here, that the achievements working women have made, would not have occurred without a commitment by employers to seek out, and to foster, diversity. Affirmative action is at the heart of that commitment.

Progress for Black Men Still Lags

When we discuss the progress that women have made, it is also worth pointing out, that African Americans in general, and African American men in particular, have benefitted the least of any group from affirmative action. When you say the words, "affirmative action," many people automatically think of a black man as the beneficiary. Consider this: Median annual earnings for African American men have actually shown little or no improvement over the past two decades compared to white men. In 1975, black men earned 74.3 percent of what white males did. In 1985, that figure was 69.7 percent, a drop of almost 5 points. In 1993 that figure was back up to 74 percent—but still lower than the 1975 average.

In 1979, 99.1 percent of senior level male employees were white, while 0.2 percent were black. In 1989, the figure for white males had declined slightly to 96.9 percent, while blacks' has risen to 0.6 percent—still less than 1 percent. Unfortunately, the lack of progress by black men applies across the board, regardless of qualifications or education level. And the fact remains that, for black men, professional degrees do not necessarily close the earnings gap: African American men with professional degrees earn 79 percent of the amount earned by white males who hold the same degree, and who are in the same job category.

And finally, a *Wall Street Journal* study showed that in the 1990–91 recession, black men were the only group that suffered a net employment loss. They suffered job losses in 36 States, and in 6 of the 9 major industries. They held 59,479 fewer jobs at the end of the recession than they had held at the beginning. I could go on citing statistics. But what these numbers tell us is that, despite the claims of affirmative action opponents, black men are not taking all of the jobs that were formerly held by white men.

This group—black men—is the segment of the population that has faced the most persistent discrimination, that has encountered the toughest problems, and has had the longest road to travel. Without our past efforts to create equal opportunity, black men might be much worse off; at the very least, this is not the time to compound the problem.

The fact remains that, while white men are approximately one-third of the population, they comprise 80 percent of the Congress, hold four-fifths of tenured positions at colleges and universities, constitute 95 percent of Fortune 500 companies' senior managers and 99.9 percent of athletic team owners, and have been 100 percent of U.S. presidents. In addition, an examination of historical unemployment tables debunks the myth that jobs are going to black men at the expense of white males. The fact is that unemployment rates for white males have remained relatively steady, while unemployment rates for black males have increased. In 1972, unemployment among white males was 5.1 percent, compared to 10.4 percent for black males. In 1994, the unemployment level for white males was 5.3 percent, a slight increase of +0.2 percentage points from 1972. In contrast, the 1994 unemployment rate for black males was 11.5 percent, an increase of +1.1 percentage points. Again, in spite of affirmative action, the facts show that white men are not losing jobs to black men.

Affirmative Action Opens Opportunities

I cite the numbers because it is important to debunk the notion that affirmative action is a zero sum game that pits one group of Americans against another, and may be seen as a basis for dividing us to whatever degree is necessary. This is why this debate is so important and why we have to communicate the truth about affirmative action to the people. As my mother used to say, we may be as different as the five fingers are, but we are all parts of one hand. We need each other and the benefits that our diversity provides. To allow affirmative action to be reduced to a them versus us conflict allows a short-sighted political game to obscure our common long-term interests.

The fact is, as Americans, we are all in this together, and we all have a tremendous challenge to face together in this time of change in the world, and in our country. Affirmative action ought to be the focus of our collective efforts to make things better for everyone—it ought to be part of the great debate about the direction we must take—together—to address the critical economic and social issues of our time. If there is any objective that should command complete American consensus, it is ensuring that every American has the chance to succeed—and that, in the final analysis, is what affirmative action is all about. No issue is more critical to our country, and no issue is more critical to me. Nothing makes a bigger difference in a person's life than opening up opportunities. Certainly, nothing has made a bigger difference in my life—and nothing has had a more positive impact on the economic well-being of our nation.

The fact is that the successes in the economy that women and minority men have achieved over these past three decades since the first affirmative action Executive Order by President Johnson have not been due to quotas. The quota debate is fraudulent. It is an attempt to reduce affirmative action to an absurdity that serves only to pander to negative emotions. It is a myth that only those who either do not know or do not care about the truth would even discuss in the context of affirmative action. Quota is often the buzzword of choice used by those who prefer myth to truth, and who want to create fear from insecurity and confusion. When we speak of affirmative action, we are talking about a range of activities calculated to support opportunity and diversity in the workplace and in our economy. We are talking about goals and timetables, not quotas. What goals do is encourage employers to look at their workforce, to consider if women and minorities are under-represented and—if they are—to try and correct the situation. Goals are flexible, temporary, and are instruments of inclusion. There are no legal penalties if employers make good faith efforts, but are unable to comply with their goals or timetables.

Quotas Are Not the Point

The perspective of affirmative action is actually the opposite—the reverse—of the quota perspective. The quota argument suggests that one look at numbers before the fact to limit opportunity for some. Affirmative action, on the other hand, looks at numbers after the fact, to observe the effects of diversity in the workplace. The two concepts are simply incompatible. Affirmative action does not tell employers they have to hire 12.5 women, or 2.5 Native Americans—or that they have to follow any inflexible numeric formula. Instead it provides a bench mark for diversity, a progress report, to help decision-makers and employees identify whether impairments to opportunity have been adequately addressed and removed. In fact, arguably since the 1978 case of *Regents of the University of California v. Bakke*, and definitively since the case of *City of Richmond v. J.A. Croson Co.*, the use of quotas by State and local governments, or educational institutions, has been held by the Supreme Court to violate the equal protection clause of the Constitution. There are exceptions of course, for cases involving prior, positive and systematic discrimination, and the Court has applied slightly different standards to the federal government.

In addition, the Equal Employment Opportunity Commission's guidelines governing voluntary affirmative action programs provide that in order to be valid, voluntary affirmative action programs must comply with a number of guidelines. First, they must be adopted to break down patterns of racial segregation, and to expand employment opportunities to those who have traditionally been barred from certain occupations or positions. In addition, the plans cannot unnecessarily trample the rights of those who were not targeted, that is, non-minorities, or men. Finally, plans can only seek to hire qualified individuals, and they must be flexible. So clearly, if any individual feels they were not hired due to an explicit quota provided for a minority or a woman, they can bring suit for a violation of equal protection.

A Benchmark for Diversity

As a benchmark for diversity, affirmative action must always be fair action. The concept of fairness in education and employment particularly rests on fundamentals relating to merit, to competence, to qualifications. No one benefits, not the community in general, the company, nor the individuals involved, if unqualified people displace qualified ones. But that is not what affirmative action is supposed to do. It is never fair to promote an unqualified individual at the expense of a qualified individual, which is why affirmative action does not require that employers do so. To require that a person be hired or promoted, solely on the basis of their gender or race, not their competence, is exactly the type of discrimination affirmative action seeks to end.

Instead, affirmative action encourages employers or educators to seek out all qualified applicants, regardless of their gender or race. There are a number of workplace practices—word of mouth recruiting, job requirements unrelated to actual duties, et cetera—that can have an effect of limiting a hiring or promotion pool, whether intentional or not. Affirmative action works to ensure this does not occur, by reaching out to qualified minorities.

In addition, affirmative action helps ensure that job requirements fit the job. Under affirmative action, employers are no longer allowed to establish irrelevant criteria that applicants must fulfill before being considered for hiring or promotion—requirements that may work to exclude otherwise qualified individuals.

There have been suggestions that our existing affirmative action programs must be reviewed, and I agree; no program should ever be immune to review. However, a review cannot mean a retreat from the proposition of equal opportunity for all. I am confident that any review of affirmative action will show what the nation's major employers already know: Affirmative action is good for the community, good for companies, good for working people, and good for the country.

The Glass Ceiling Report

I do not think that our current debate over affirmative action could have come at a more ironic time. The Department of Labor just recently issued its fact-finding report on the existence of the "glass ceiling"—those invisible, yet very real barriers that continue to confront women and minorities as they attempt to participate in the workforce. The Glass Ceiling Report reviews in great detail the barriers to participation that fall short of overt exclusion but which still operate to limit the full participation of women and minorities in our economy. It clearly identifies the relevance of diversity in the workplace. Most important, it is a compelling endorsement of the value of affirmative action.

The foundation for the report was a document prepared by the Department of Labor—which helped publicize the glass ceiling phenomenon. As our distinguished majority leader, Senator Robert Dole, stated at that time, the report has confirmed what many of us have suspected all along—the existence of invisible, artificial barriers blocking women and minorities from advancing up the corporate ladder to management and executive level positions. The issue boils down to ensuring equal access and equal opportunity. These principles are fundamental to the establishment of this great nation, and the cornerstone of what other nations and other people consider unique to the U.S.—namely, the possibility for everyone to go as far as their talents and hard work will take them.

Congress created the Glass Ceiling Commission as part of the Civil Rights Act of 1991. The commission, comprised of 21 members, was charged with conducting a study and preparing recommendations on "eliminating artificial barriers to the advancement of women and minorities." The current attack on affirmative action coincides almost exactly with the release of the commission's fact-finding report, entitled "Good for Business: Making Full Use of the Nation's Human Capital." It is also, however, fortuitous, for the commission's report provides those of us in Congress, who will soon be debating the future of affirmative action, with two fundamental truths: the first of these truths is that, though we have come far since Lyndon Johnson issued Executive Order No. 11246, there is still much progress yet to be made. The U.S. still fails to utilize the talents and resources of far too great a percentage of its population in far too many industries. The second truth is that, if progress is not made, it will not be just minorities and women who suffer, but the community as a whole. Affirmative action is about far more than just equal opportunity—it is about our economic prosperity. It is about access to education and jobs for working people, for middle-class families, and for our children. Indeed, a recent *Washington Post* article entitled "Affirmative Action's Corporate Converts," documented this fact. In the article, the chairman of Mobil Corporation, Mr. Lucio A. Noto summed up the view of many employers: "I have never felt a burden from affirmative action, because it is a business imperative for us."

Women and Minorities Are Excluded from Top Management Positions

The overview of the Glass Ceiling Commission's fact-finding report begins: Corporate leaders surveyed, women and minorities who participated in focus groups, researchers, and government officials all agree that a glass ceiling exists, and that it operates substantially to exclude minorities and women from the top levels of management. This statement is underscored by a wealth of detailed factual information, which illustrates this conclusion in no uncertain terms. Take, for example, a survey

211

of senior level managers of Fortune 1000 industrial companies and Fortune 500 service industries, which established that 95 to 97 percent of senior managers—vice-president and above—are white men. And the problems are not limited to the business world. While women hold over 4 in every 10 college teaching jobs—more than 40 percent—they only hold 11 percent of tenured positions.

The Glass Ceiling Commission's report makes it clear what the problem is. It is not a "women's problem." It is not a problem related to any lack of ability on the part of women or minorities. It is a problem going to the heart of the American dream—whether the workforce is for some Americans, or for all Americans. The report concluded, after years of research, that there are two major impediments to full participation by women and minorities. First, the prejudices and stereotypes of many white male middle managers. Second, the need for greater efforts by many corporate CEOs—who have made an initial commitment to diversity and expanded economic opportunity—to fully translate those words into realities.

The subheading on a recent *New York Times* article by reporter Peter T. Kilborn, which detailed the commission's findings, highlighted the problems presented by stereotyping. The heading reads: "Report Finds Prejudices Block Progress of Women and Minorities." And the story goes on to depict the barriers that, unfortunately, still must be overcome by women and minorities seeking to climb the corporate ladder. Kilborn writes:

> In exploring the demography of American upper management, a government commission Wednesday put its official stamp on what many people have suspected all along: Important barriers to the progress of women and minorities are the entrenched stereotypes and prejudices of white men. Women, the report of the Federal Glass Ceiling Commission said, are perceived by white males as not tough and unable or unwilling to relocate. Black men? Undisciplined, always late. Hispanic men are deemed heavy drinkers and drug users who don't want to work—except for Cubans, who are brave exiles from communism. Asians? More equipped for technical than people-oriented work. And, the report said, white males believe that none of these folks play golf. Never mind that women's attendance records are better than men's, discounting maternity leaves; that Hispanic Americans work longer than the non-Hispanic white men putting them down, or that American management is impressed enough by Asian management that it often apes it.

The Glass Ceiling report speaks to some of the reasons for this persistent bias. Too many white male middle managers still allow false myths to obscure their vision. They are still unable to see the benefits of making full use of the talents of women and minorities. The problem we face now—the problem of persistent bias—is different than the blatant, officially sponsored discrimination faced in the 1950s and 1960s, but it is no less real. It is certainly no less harmful to those who are not considered for a job, or a loan, or a government contract. And it is most definitely no less worthy of congressional action than the official discrimination that Congress addressed in the 1960s.

The Glass Ceiling Is Bad for Business

Most of us can remember the time in our country when women who worked outside the home had to face official barriers to their participation in the labor force. Or when black and other minorities were denied employment or other economic opportunity solely because of their color. Legislation such as the Civil Rights Act of 1964, which was designed to provide equality of employment and educational opportunities, or the Civil Rights Act of 1968, which sought to provide fair housing laws, has gone a long way toward striking down those official barriers. But the unofficial ones still remain. It is as though the hurdles have been taken off the track, but the ruts have not yet been removed for women and minorities who seek to participate in the economy of our country. President Johnson made the point eloquently when he issued Executive Order 11246, which requires that all employers with federal contracts in excess of $50,000 file affirmative action plans with the government. Under that order, which is the foundation of affirmative action, the plans must include goals and timetables—not quotas—for the hiring of minorities and women, and employers are required to make good faith efforts to comply with the plans. President Johnson stated when signing the order:

> Freedom is not enough. You do not wipe away the scars of centuries by saying: Now, you are free to go where you want, do as you desire, and choose the leaders you please. You do not take a man who for years has been hobbled by chains, liberate him, bring him to the starting line of a race, saying "you are free to compete with all the others," and still justly believe you have been completely fair, thus it is not enough to open the gates of opportunity . . . we seek not just equality as a right . . . but equality as a fact and as a result.

The progress we have made in opening up opportunity is no cause for resting on our laurels—the end of discrimination did not mean the beginning of inclusion. We still have a long way to go to eliminate the persistent bias which creates barriers to the full participation—and the complete con- tributions—all our people have to give. It stands to reason that, if we cre- ate conditions that allow our nation to tap the talents of 100 percent of our people, we will be better off than if we can only tap the talents of half.

And that is the conclusion of the report just issued by the Glass Ceil- ing Commission, a conclusion which is expressed in the report's title: "good for business—making full use of the nation's full human capital." Simply stated, the conclusion reached was that

> Increasing numbers of corporate leaders recognize that Glass Ceilings and exclusion of members of groups other than white non-Hispanic males are bad for business because of recent dra- matic shifts in three areas that are fundamental to business sur- vival: changes in the demographics of the labor force, changes in the demographics of the national consumer markets, and the rapid globalization of the marketplace.

These shifts—changes in the demographics of the labor force, changes in the demographics of the national consumer markets, and rapid globalization of the marketplace—highlight why a retreat from af- firmative action will hurt us all.

The *Washington Post* article, previously quoted, underscored that point. The article points out that the opinion that affirmative action is a business imperative is

> not a maverick view. At many of the nation's largest corpora- tions, affirmative action is woven into the fabric of the compa- nies. And the diversity that affirmative action regulations has encouraged has become a valuable marketing and recruiting tool, an important edge in fierce global competition.

A 1993 study of Standard and Poor 500 companies showed that firms that succeed in shattering their own glass ceilings racked up stock-market records that were nearly two and one-half times better than otherwise comparable companies.

Ability Should Determine Success

It is often the case that those of us in Congress are called upon to vote on issues with which we have had no personal experience. But the issue of creating opportunity for women and minorities to become full eco- nomic partners in our society is dear to my heart, because as a woman, and a minority, I have seen firsthand the benefits that accrue from cre- ating a climate of opinion that sets the stage for hope and for real opportunity in the areas where potential and talent matter most. I would ask my colleagues to consider the experience of those of us who have had to overcome artificial barriers to achievement. What our experiences illustrate are the basic principles that Congress must consider—and must preserve—as it debates affirmative action.

The first of these principles is that every American must have access to education. The opportunity to attend the University of Illinois, and the University of Chicago Law School, gave me the tools I needed to enter the workforce. The climate created by congressional support for affirmative action encouraged my law school to seek out and embrace diversity. The second basic principle is that every American must have access to good jobs. My first job out of law school was working as an assistant U.S. attorney—a job that would have been virtually impossible for a woman to hold just 20 years earlier. Because of affirmative action, I was given a choice and a chance in the career path.

And the third basic principle, from which there can be no retreat, is that every American must have the opportunity to advance as far in their field as their hard work will take them. As the Glass Ceiling report has shown, getting a job is only half the battle. Just as bias must not be allowed in hiring, it must also not be allowed in promotion, or in access to capital, or policy making, or in any other endeavor that affects the community as a whole. It is not enough that women and minorities are able to enter the workforce; they also have to have the opportunity to succeed based on their ability.

It has been argued by some that in this debate we are focused too much on the past. They say that they were not there when the Constitution was drafted, leaving women and African Americans out of its promise of equal opportunity for all. They did not take any past actions, they did not carry out any past "wrongs," and they should not have to work to correct those wrongs in the present.

But this debate is not about the past. The need for continued action is not just about righting past wrongs—although past wrongs warrant strong actions: nor is it about repaying old debts—although substantial debts are owed to those people and their descendants who were harmed by their past exclusion from full participation in our economy. This debate is about the future, and the expanded economic opportunity that will come if all Americans are allowed to participate in the economy.

The Glass Ceiling Must Be Shattered

What we are debating is whether the majority of America's people—and that is what you get if you count our nation's 51 percent women and 10

215

percent non-white males—will have a shot, a chance to participate on an equal footing in America's economic affairs. Last month, I met with a group of young schoolchildren. I talked with them about the historic nature of the 104th Congress, and how we had come so far in the 75 years the women's suffrage amendment became part of our Constitution. I pointed out to them that there are now eight women in the U.S. Senate. I spoke of this as if it were a great accomplishment. The children looked at me in confusion—one little girl looked at me and said: "Is that all?"

What that young girl was telling us, is that we need to look at the whole picture. And when we do, we know without a doubt that much work remains to be done.

Majority leader Dole stated, when he authored the legislation creating the Glass Ceiling Commission, "Whatever the reasons behind the glass ceiling, it is time we stopped throwing rhetorical rocks and hit the glass ceiling with enough force that it is shattered." That recipe for action made sense then, and, with the issuance of the commission's report, it makes even more sense now. International competition is becoming tougher and tougher. We cannot succeed by bailing out of the competition, or by wasting the talents of half our citizenry. But that is what will happen—our country will fall behind—if we do not act aggressively to shatter the glass ceiling. If we do not make full use of the education and the skills of women and minorities, they are hurt as individuals, but we are hurt as a nation as well.

In 1992, approximately 590,000 women and 163,000 minority students graduated from college. Are we really prepared to say to them, "Sorry, you're not allowed to compete." As parents, we all have hopes and dreams for our children. Are we really prepared to say to our daughters, "Sorry, but you're not allowed to compete. Work hard, but you will still get paid less than the men working next to you, and you should not expect to be promoted." Are we really prepared as a matter of national policy to diminish their expectations that way? Are we really prepared to permit restrictions on their potential and their opportunities to continue for even one more day if there is anything we can do about it?

The answer should be obvious. There can be no retreat from the fundamental goals of affirmative action. There can be no compromise with the objective of ensuring full economic opportunity for every American.

Affirmative action has helped every American, not just women and minorities. Although opponents suggest that affirmative action is about creating race and gender preference, in fact, the opposite is true. It is about ending preferences based on prejudice and stereotype. It is about opening up our economy so that it works for all, and not just some. I hope that my remarks here today will sound the alarm bell not just for minorities, but also for women across the nation. In the 1940s, when the men of America went off to Europe and Asia to fight World War II, women entered the workforce in record numbers. "Rosie the Riveter" provided the essential support needed back home to keep America's factories running—both to fuel the war effort, and to sustain the domestic economy. During the war, women were hailed as heroes. But when the war was over, women were told that their services were no longer needed. Well, I have news for those who would seek to roll back the gains women have made under affirmative action. This is not 1945. We will not go back—nor can the country afford for us to go back.

There are those who fear the loss of preferences created over time—the 100 percent set-asides of the past—which limited competition from the vast pool of talent women and minorities constitute. To them I say, it is counterproductive to handicap the competition, you lose, they lose, we as a nation all lose. Instead of being seduced by fear, be inspired by the hope of our founders that if in equality of opportunity lay the key to prosperity, the quality of life for all Americans would be lifted up.

There can be no retreat from our purpose, no compromise from our objective—expanding economic opportunity, taking advantage of our diversity, moving the U.S. ever closer to the day when the eloquent vision set out in our Declaration of Independence becomes a reality for every American. Abraham Lincoln, in his 1862 message to Congress, spoke words that resonate and reflect the seriousness of this debate:

> Fellow citizens, we cannot escape history. We of this Congress and this administration will remember in spite of ourselves. No personal significance or insignificance can spare one or another of us. The fiery trial through which we pass will light us down, in honor or dishonor, to the latest generation. We—even we here—hold the power and bear the responsibility. In giving freedom to the slave, we assure freedom to the free—honorable alike in what we give and what we preserve. We shall nobly save or meanly lose the last, best hope of Earth. Other means may succeed: this could not fail. The way is plain, peaceful, generous, just—a way which, if followed, the world will forever applaud, and God must forever bless.

Affirmative action is a quintessential American challenge. I hope this Congress will prove worthy of it.

Excerpted from a speech of Carol Moseley Braun delivered before Congress, March 30, 1995.

Personal Choices Slow the Advancement of Women in the Workplace

by Michael Lynch and Katherine Post

Michael Lynch is the Washington, D.C., Bureau Chief for *REASON* magazine. Katherine Post is a public policy fellow at the Pacific Research Institute in Washington, D.C. In the following viewpoint, Lynch and Post contend that discrimination is not the cause of the differences in wages and management opportunities for men and women. The causes, they contend, can be found instead in the educational and career choices made by women. Overall, the authors state, women prefer careers in lower paying professions (such as teaching) that allow them to spend more time with family. Additionally, the authors contend, new research suggests that young women who are preparing themselves for top corporate positions are reaching those positions and achieving salaries comparable to their male counterparts' without need of or help from sex-based government preference programs.

"Like the wage gap, the glass ceiling, at its core, reflects a choice gap, an age gap, and an aspirations gap."

We recently completed a study in which we . . . compiled relevant data from the Census Bureau and the Bureau of Labor Statistics. Our findings, which are consistent with those of other scholars, are (1) the wage gap has been closing in recent years, and that, when the data are controlled for relevant variables, it virtually disappears; and (2) the so-called glass ceiling is more a product of relative ages and qualifications of men and women than of explicit discrimination. In general, we found that women's current economic position relative to men is more a product of individual choices than of third-party discrimination.

Is There Really a Wage Gap?

In the 1960s, feminist activists donned "59 cents" buttons to decry the fact that women, on average, earned 59 cents for every dollar a man earned. They maintained that this was hard proof of "gender" discrimination. By 1995, however, women were earning 74 cents for every dollar earned by a man; but preference advocates still called for government involvement in the economy to redress gender discrimination.

The wage-gap figure has proved to be a powerful political tool, though it is less useful as a measure of discrimination. As a statistical aggregate, the wage gap is only an amalgamation of all of the wages paid to women divided by all of the wages paid to men. To infer discrimination from such an aggregate, one must assume that the factors that determine wages—such as education level and concentration, field of work, and continuous time in the workforce—are constant across the sexes. As it happens, such an assumption is highly suspect. In fact, even when a particular wage-gap figure is advertised as having been corrected for such factors, this is usually only partially true.

For example, it is true that women earn less than men at every level of education achieved. In 1994, among those who held bachelor's degrees, women earned 76 cents on the male dollar. This ratio increased to 79 cents for those with master's degrees and to 85 cents for those with doctorates. The implication that is usually drawn is that, since the data is controlled for education, the remaining disparity proves that women continue to face discrimination in compensation levels. This level of aggregation, however, fails to account both for the fields in which men and women hold degrees and for the actual fields in which the graduates find employment. Residual differences in earnings are best explained by variations in choices of educational and career fields, not discrimination.

In 1992, more than one-third of the bachelor's degrees earned by women were in communications, education, English literature, the health professions, and the visual and performing arts. Of the bachelor's degrees earned by men in 1992, only 17 percent were in these fields. In the same year, 26 percent of men who earned bachelor's degrees did so in business, compared to 20 percent of women. Thirteen percent of men's bachelor's degrees were earned in engineering, compared to 2 percent of women's.

The contrast becomes more striking when we move from bachelor's to advanced degrees (master's and doctorates). While one out of four women who earned Ph.D.'s did so in education—a field in which an individual with an advanced degree earns, on average, a mean monthly income of $3,048—one out of five men who earned doctorates did so in engineering, a field in which an individual with an advanced degree, on average, earns a mean monthly income of $4,049.

In 1992, the last year for which published data are available, women earned 75 percent of the advanced degrees conferred in education, 70 percent of the advanced degrees conferred in public administration, 65 percent of the advanced degrees conferred in English literature, and 63 percent of the advanced degrees conferred in ethnic and cultural studies. In this same year, by contrast, men earned 86 percent of the advanced degrees conferred in engineering, 75 percent of the advanced degrees conferred in physical sciences and science technologies, 65 percent of the advanced degrees conferred in business management and administrative services, and 60 percent of advanced degrees conferred in mathematics.

Furthermore, it must be emphasized that these figures are for one year and do not represent the total labor pool. The wage-gap figures, however, are based on the total pool. Since women have increased their representation in such fields as business and engineering in recent years, these 1992 figures overstate the proportion of women qualified to work in these fields.

Thus if we examine cumulative figures, we find even more pronounced differences. As of 1990, more than one in four women who held a bachelor's degree or higher earned that degree in education, while less than one in ten men who held a bachelor's degree or higher earned that degree in education. By this same year, nearly one in four men who held a bachelor's degree or higher earned that degree in business management and nearly one in six men held a degree in engineering. By contrast, less than one in eight women who held a degree in 1990 earned that degree in business management and less than 2 in 100 in engineering. As to be expected, these different concentrations hold major implications for earnings. Regardless of the sex of its holder, the market demand dictates that a degree in engineering is worth more than a degree in education.

Market Discrimination or Personal Choice?

Many feminists interpret the above data as precisely the problem: Women's work is undervalued relative to men's. The truth is that all professions have costs and benefits that are both monetary and non-monetary. While investment bankers make more money than school teachers, teachers derive non-monetary benefits—e.g., long summer breaks—which are not available on Wall Street. It must also be noted that it is entirely consistent with economic theory for wages to drop in an industry in which a significant number of women enter. If women suddenly enter a field previously dominated by men, and if there is not a reduction in male participation in the field, overall labor supply will increase, thus exerting downward pressure on wages.

There are also psychological reasons why women have historically tended to concentrate in certain fields. For example, the preponderance of evidence suggests that women, on average, have a stronger preference for children than do men. It is this difference, concludes Stanford economist Victor R. Fuchs, which contributes to women's economic disadvantages. While this claim continues to be debated, a myriad of both statistical and anecdotal evidence supports it. In 1995, the Whirlpool Foundation, in conjunction with the Families and Work Institute, sponsored a poll conducted by Louis Harris and Associates, Inc. The results were published as a study entitled "Women: The New Providers." Some of this study's findings indicate that women, more so than men, define success in terms of home and family. "The New Providers" found that "family remains at the core of what's important for women, whether they work inside or outside the home." Only 15 percent of the women polled would work full time if they didn't feel they had to financially, while more than twice that of men would.

Expectations about the future also shape the fields women enter. June O'Neill, the current director of the Congressional Budget Office, has pointed out that, as recently as the late 1960s, less than 30 percent of the women in the National Longitudinal Survey of Youth expected to be working at age 35, even though more than 70 percent actually were. As a result, it made little sense for women of this generation to spend time and resources acquiring skills that they didn't expect to use. Moreover, it made sense for those women, who expected to spend time outside of the workforce raising a family, to specialize in flexible fields, such as teaching. Thus rational self-interest, not discrimination, appears to account for women's occupational clustering.

Fewer Hours, Less Pay

In addition to the fact that men and women vary in the fields in which they specialize, they also differ in the amount of time they devote to paid work. The accumulated evidence shows that, even as the gap between labor-force participation rates of men and women closes, men consistently work more hours than women.

A 1992 Census study on the relationship between education level and earnings found that, at every level of education, men have more months with work activity than women. A 1984 Census study found that, while only 1.6 percent of a man's work years were spent away from work, 14.7 percent of a woman's work years were spent away from work—an eightfold difference. This prompted the U.S. Department of Labor (DOL) to conclude that "women spend significantly more time away from work and are apparently unable to build the seniority that men achieve." In addition, the DOL noted that the turnover rates are higher for women than for men.

With less seniority, it is hardly surprising that women's earnings are, on average, lower than men's. A 1990 National Bureau of Economic Research working paper found "a very strong connection between job seniority and wages in the typical employment relationship: other things held constant, 10 years of job seniority raises the wage of the typical worker by over 25 percent." In addition, women who work still put in less time than men. DOL data show that, in 1994, 55 percent of women worked 40 or more hours a week compared to 75 percent of men. While 16 percent of men worked 55 or more hours a week that same year, only 6 percent of women did. Again, it is reasonable to expect that someone who works 55-hour weeks will earn more, over time, than someone who works 40 hours, regardless of whether they are male or female. While it is simply common sense to conclude that those who work more produce more and, as a result, earn more, these inconvenient facts are often ignored.

Same Work, Same Pay

The pay gap between men and women virtually disappears when age, educational attainment, and continuous time spent in the workforce are factored in as wage determinants. In fact, this is neither a new phenomenon nor a product of preference programs. Economist Thomas Sowell has shown that, as early as 1971, never-married women in their thirties who had worked continuously earned slightly higher incomes than men of the same description. In the academic world, single women who earned Ph.D.'s in the 1930s became full professors by the 1950s at slightly higher rates than their male counterparts. In addition, never-married academic women earned slightly more money in some years than men of the same description.

Similarly, June O'Neill has found that women between the ages of 27 and 33 who had never had a child earned nearly 98 percent as much as men in this same demographic. In another study, O'Neill and Solomon Polachek found that the gap in earnings between men and women with Ph.D.'s in economics was a mere 5 percent.

A less scientific but more comprehensive salary survey by *Working Woman* magazine in February 1996 indicates a shrinking wage gap as well.

Compiling data on 950 positions in 38 industries, the *Working Woman* survey found that, on average, women in the study earned 85 percent to 95 percent of what men in similar positions earned. While there were some fields in which women earned much less than men, there were other fields, such as university administrators, in which they earned more. In fact, while pay for males has dropped 11 percent since 1974, the average female worker's pay has increased by 6.1 percent. For women in high-powered jobs, pay levels have shot up 16.4 percent. This is consistent with data from a 1992 study by Korn/Ferry International, which found that women had reached the base salary of $100,000 at a younger age than the men polled in their 1989 survey. More than 50 percent of women were already earning $100,000 by the time they reached 40, while at that age, only 31 percent of men were earning at least $100,000.

An Unbreakable Glass Ceiling?

In March 1995, the Federal Glass Ceiling Commission released its report on the status of diversity in corporate America, *Good for Business: Making Full Use of the Nation's Human Capital.* The central point of the report is that only 5 percent of senior managers at Fortune 1000 companies are women. Like the wage gap, this has become a rallying cry for advocates of preference programs for women. It suffers, however, from many of the same defects as the wage-gap theory.

Like the wage gap, the glass ceiling, at its core, reflects a choice gap, an age gap, and an aspirations gap. A typical corporate career lasts 40 to 45 years, which spans two generations. The people who run today's largest corporations were in their twenties in the 1960s. But, as we mentioned earlier, the National Longitudinal Survey shows that, as late as the 1960s, only 30 percent of women expected to be working at age 35. Since most women didn't expect even to be working at 35, it is doubtful that many of them prepared to be CEOs at 55. Indeed, both educational and professional data bear this out.

The National Longitudinal Survey finds that today most women expect to work outside of the home. As a result, they are preparing to be professionals. The most popular major for women today is business, which accounted for 20 percent of the bachelor's degrees awarded to women in 1992. Moreover, women of late have been filling the professional schools. In little more than two decades, women have increased their share of M.B.A.'s, M.D.'s, and J.D.'s by more than 400 percent. The percent of M.B.A.'s earned by women increased from 3.6 percent in 1970 to 35.6 percent in 1993. Over this same period, the percent of M.D.'s earned by women jumped from 8.4 percent to 37.7 percent, and women increased their share of law degrees from 5.4 percent to 42.5 percent. These women will be the CEOs, chief surgeons, and law partners of tomorrow, if they so desire.

This suggests that women are on the cusp of even greater representation at the senior-most levels of our country's major corporations. The 1992 Korn/Ferry survey found that the average age of senior corporate women was 44. Twenty-one percent of the women were under 40, and a mere 1.6 percent were over 60. This compares to an average age in their 1989 predominantly male survey of 52. Of the men, only 1.4 percent were under 40, and 15.9 percent were over 60. This study did find a wage gap: The women in 1992 earned two-thirds of what the men in 1989 did. This might be partially explained by the relative youth of the women and by the fact that, on average, they had been with the same firms six fewer years than the men.

This study also found that corporations are competing for top-level women. Women reached the $100,000 base salary earlier than the men, and, on average, women in the top positions were less likely to have either an undergraduate degree (90.4 percent for women compared to 96.9 percent of men) or a graduate degree (51.9 percent for women and 62.6 percent for men). In contrast to the Glass Ceiling Report, this study found that, from 1982 to 1992, the number of women holding the title of Executive Vice President more than doubled, from 4 percent to 9 percent, and that women increased their presence at the Senior Vice President level from 13 percent to 23 percent.

The coming years will thus find women reaching the top in virtually every area of American life, and without the aid of preference programs. But it would be a mistake to conclude that this will produce statistical parity. Professional women and men do not all hold the same aspirations. While the Korn/Ferry survey found that women expected to be part of their company's senior management team for the year 2000 at higher rates than men, far fewer aspired to be CEOs (14.1 percent of women compared to 44.6 percent of men). This, when coupled with plans for early retirement (76.5 percent of women wish to retire before age 65 while only 30.4 percent of men do), suggests that there may be an aspirations gap between the sexes. It is this choice gap, not discrimination, that will slow the onset of statistical parity.

Women Entrepreneurs

Another problem with the glass-ceiling theory is that, by focusing on only the largest companies, it misses much of the economy. Consistent with their educational and career choices, women have made major gains in the broader economy in recent years. In 1984, women held 33.6 percent of the managerial and executive positions in America's companies and accounted for nearly one out of two professionals (48.5 percent), according to the DOL. A decade later, women held 48.1 percent of managerial/executive positions and accounted for more than one-half (52.8 percent) of people employed in professional occupations.

More significantly, the glass-ceiling statistics neglect women's economic advances as private entrepreneurs. A study by Dun & Bradstreet Information Services found that there were 7.7 million women-owned businesses in the United States in 1994. Far from small drops in the economic bucket, these businesses generated $1.4 trillion in sales. Showing employment growth rates 118 percent higher than the economy as a whole between 1991 and 1994, these businesses employ 35 percent more people than the Fortune 500 employ worldwide. Nor are these businesses concentrated in sectors categorized as "pink collar." In the 1980s, women moved into agriculture, communications, transportation, and manufacturing. Between 1991 and 1994, the number of women-owned construction companies increased by 19.2 percent, and the number of women-owned manufacturing firms increased by 13.4 percent.

The Dun & Bradstreet findings have been recently replicated by a study from the Interagency Committee on Women's Business Enterprise, which was created by President Clinton in 1995. Using Census data from 1987 to 1992, the report shows that, in 1992, women-owned businesses represented one-third of all domestic firms operating in the United States and 40 percent of all retail and service firms. The report notes that, from 1987 to 1992, the number of women-owned firms grew by 43 percent, almost double the rate of growth for all firms. During this same period, employment by women-owned firms increased 100 percent, compared to 38 percent for all firms.

The advocates of sex-based preferences argue in part that affirmative action is necessary to overcome discrimination and to ensure the economic progress that women are due. In fact, as we have shown, women have made a great deal of economic progress over the last several decades, to the point that qualified women who do the same work as similarly qualified men receive the same pay as men (and sometimes more). The differences that now exist are the result of individual choices, not of third-party discrimination. That is good news, and it is a shame that it will be obscured by the political head-counting that will undoubtedly occur in the debates that lie ahead.

From "What Glass Ceiling?" by Michael Lynch and Katherine Post, *Public Interest*, no. 124, Summer 1996, pp. 27–36. Reprinted by permission of the authors and the *Public Interest*; © 1996 by National Affairs, Inc.

Gender Bias Cheats Girls Out of a Quality Education

by Myra and David Sadker

Myra and David Sadker are professors in the School of Education at the American University in Washington, D.C. Their research on gender bias in the schools is included in a 1992 report, compiled by the Wellesley College Center for Research on Women, entitled "How Schools Short-change Girls." In the following viewpoint, the Sadkers contend that gender bias is a pervasive, though often unintentional, force in American schools. They argue that teachers devote more time, attention, and energy to boys than girls and that curriculum and textbooks essentially ignore women's contribution to society. This uneven treatment, the authors state, "extinguishes learning and shatters self-esteem," leaving young girls at a huge disadvantage as they reach adulthood.

"Until educational sexism is eradicated, more than half of our children will be shortchanged and their gifts lost to society."

Sitting in the same classroom, reading the same textbook, listening to the same teacher, boys and girls receive very different educations. From grade school through graduate school female students are more likely to be invisible members of classrooms. Teachers interact with males more frequently, ask them better questions, and give them more precise and helpful feedback. Over the course of years the uneven distribution of teacher time, energy, attention, and talent, with boys getting the lion's share, takes its toll on girls. Since gender bias is not a noisy problem, most people are unaware of the secret sexist lessons and the quiet losses they engender.

Girls are the majority of our nation's schoolchildren, yet they are second-class educational citizens. The problems they face—loss of self-esteem, decline in achievement, and elimination of career options—are at the heart of the educational process. Until educational sexism is eradicated, more than half our children will be shortchanged and their gifts lost to society.

Award-winning author Susan Faludi discovered that backlash "is most powerful when it goes private, when it lodges inside a woman's mind and turns her vision inward, until she imagines the pressure is all in her head, until she begins to enforce the backlash too—on herself."[1] Psychological backlash internalized by adult women is a frightening concept, but what is even more terrifying is a curriculum of sexist school lessons becoming secret mind games played against female children, our daughters, tomorrow's women.

Teacher-Student Interaction Is Key

After almost two decades of research grants and thousands of hours of classroom observation, we remain amazed at the stubborn persistence of these hidden sexist lessons. When we began our investigation of gender bias, we looked first in the classrooms of one of Washington, D.C.'s elite and expensive private schools. Uncertain of exactly what to look for, we wrote nothing down; we just observed. The classroom was a whirlwind of activity, so fast paced we could easily miss the quick but vital phrase or gesture, the insidious incident, the tiny inequity that held a world of meaning. As we watched, we had to push ourselves beyond the blind spots of socialization and gradually focus on the nature of the interaction between teacher and student. On the second day we saw our first example of sexism, a quick, jarring flash within the hectic pace of the school day:

Two second graders are kneeling beside a large box. They whisper excitedly to each other as they pull out wooden blocks, colored balls, counting sticks. So absorbed are these two small children in examining and sorting the materials, they are visibly startled by the teacher's impatient voice as she hovers over them. "Ann! Julia! Get your cotton-pickin' hands out of the math box. Move over so the boys can get in there and do their work."

Isolated here on the page of a book, this incident is not difficult to interpret. It becomes even more disturbing if you think of it with the teacher making a racial distinction. Picture Ann and Julia as African-American children moved away so white children can gain access to the math materials. If Ann and Julia's parents had observed this exchange, they might justifiably wonder whether their tuition dollars were well spent. But few parents actually watch teachers in action, and fewer still have learned to interpret the meaning behind fast-paced classroom events.

The incident unsettles, but it must be considered within the context of numerous interactions this harried teacher had that day. While she talked to the two girls, she was also keeping a wary eye on fourteen other active children. Unless you actually shadowed the teacher, stood right next to her as we did, you might not have seen or heard the event. After all, it lasted only a few seconds.

It took us almost a year to develop an observation system that would register the hundreds of daily classroom interactions, teasing out the gender bias embedded in them. Trained raters coded classrooms in math, reading, English, and social studies. They observed students from different racial and ethnic backgrounds. They saw lessons taught by women and by men, by teachers of different races. In short, they analyzed America's classrooms. By the end of the year we had thousands of observation sheets, and after another year of statistical analysis, we discovered a syntax of sexism so elusive that most teachers and students were completely unaware of its influence. . . .[2]

Sexism Can Be Subtle

Subtle sexism is visible to only the most astute readers of *Among Schoolchildren*, Tracy Kidder's chronicle of real-life educator Chris Zajac. A thirty-four-year-old teacher in Mt. Holyoke, Massachusetts, Mrs. Zajac is a no-nonsense veteran of the classroom. She does not allow her fifth-grade students to misbehave, forget to do their homework, or give up without trying their hardest. Underlying her strict exterior is a woman who cares about schoolchildren. Our students admired her dedication and respected her as a good human being, and it took several readings and discussions before they discovered her inadvertent gender bias. Then came the questions: Does Mrs. Zajac work harder teaching boys than girls? Does she know there is sex bias in her classroom?

These questions probably do not occur to most readers of *Among Schoolchildren* and might jolt both Chris Zajac and the author who so meticulously described the classroom. Here's how Tracy Kidder begins the story of a year in the life of this New England teacher:

> Mrs. Zajac wasn't born yesterday. She knows you didn't do your best work on this paper, Clarence. Don't you remember Mrs. Zajac saying that if you didn't do your best, she'd make you do it over? As for you, Claude, God forbid that you should ever

need brain surgery. But Mrs. Zajac hopes that if you do, the doctor won't open up your head and walk off saying he's almost done, as you said when Mrs. Zajac asked you for your penmanship, which, by the way, looks like who did it and ran. Felipe, the reason you have hiccups is, your mouth is always open and the wind rushes in. You're in fifth grade now. So, Felipe, put a lock on it. Zip it up. Then go get a drink of water. Mrs. Zajac means business, Robert. The sooner you realize she never said everybody in the room has to do the work except for Robert, the sooner you'll get along with her. And . . . Clarence. Mrs. Zajac knows you didn't try. You don't just hand in junk to Mrs. Zajac. She's been teaching an awful lot of years. She didn't fall off the turnip cart yesterday. She told you she was an old-lady teacher.[3]

Swiftly, adroitly, Kidder introduces the main characters in the classroom—Clarence, Claude, Felipe, Robert, and back to Clarence, the boy in whom Mrs. Zajac invests most. But where are the girls?

As our students analyzed the book and actually examined whom Mrs. Zajac was speaking to, they saw that page after page she spent time with the boys—disciplining them, struggling to help them understand, teaching them with all the energy and talent she could muster. In contrast, the pages that showed Mrs. Zajac working with girls were few and far between.

When we ask teachers at our workshops why they spend more time helping boys, they say, "Because boys need it more" or "Boys have trouble reading, writing, doing math. They can't even sit still. They need me more." In *Among Schoolchildren*, Chris Zajac feels that way, too. Kidder describes how she allows boys to take her over because she thinks they need her.

So teachers of good intention, such as Chris Zajac, respond to boys and teach them more actively, but their time and attention are not limitless. While the teachers are spending time with boys, the girls are being ignored and shortchanged. The only girl clearly realized in *Among Schoolchildren* is Judith, a child who is so alert that she has a vast English vocabulary even though her parents speak only Spanish. But while Judith is a girl of brilliant potential, she rarely reaps the benefit of Mrs. Zajac's active teaching attention. In fact, rather than trouble her teacher and claim time and attention for herself, Judith helps Mrs. Zajac, freeing her to work with the more demanding boys. Mrs. Zajac knows she isn't giving this talented girl what she needs and deserves: "If only I had more time," she thinks as she looks at Judith.

On a field trip to Old Sturbridge Village, the children have segregated themselves by sex on the bus, with the boys claiming the back. In a moment of quiet reflection, Chris realizes that in her classroom "the boys rarely give her a chance to spend much time with her girls." She changes her seat, joins the girls, and sings jump rope songs with them for the remainder of the trip.[4]

But her time spent with the girls is short-lived—the length of the day-long field trip—and her recognition of the gender gap in time and attention is brief: a paragraph-long flash of understanding in a book of more than three hundred pages. On the whole, Chris Zajac does not invest her talent in girls. But nurturing children is not unlike tending a garden: Neglect, even when benign, is withering; time and attention bear fruit. Mrs. Zajac and other caring teachers across the country are unaware of the full impact of uneven treatment. They do not realize the high academic and emotional price many girls pay for being too good.

Inequity Seen Through a Magnifying Glass

Drawn from years of research, the episodes that follow demonstrate the sexist lessons taught daily in America's classrooms.[5] Pulled out of the numerous incidents in a school day, these inequities become enlarged, as if observed through a magnifying glass, so we can see clearly how they extinguish learning and shatter self-esteem. Imagine yourself in a sixth-grade science class like the one we observed in Maryland.

The teacher is writing a list of inventors and their discoveries on the board:

Elias Howe	sewing machine
Robert Fulton	steamboat
Thomas A. Edison	lightbulb
James Otis	elevator
Alexander Graham Bell	telephone
Cyrus McCormick	reaper
Eli Whitney	cotton gin
Orville and Wilbur Wright	airplane

A girl raises her hand and asks, "It looks like all the inventors were men. Didn't women invent anything?" The teacher does not add any female inventors to the list, nor does he discuss new scholarship recognizing the involvement of women in inventions such as the cotton gin. He does not explain how hard it was in times past for women to obtain patents in their own names, and therefore we may never know how many female inventors are excluded from the pages of our history books. Instead he

230

grins, winks, and says, "Sweetheart, don't worry about it. It's the same with famous writers and painters. It's the man's job to create things and the woman's job to look beautiful so she can inspire him." Several boys laugh. A few clown around by flexing their muscles as they exclaim, "Yes!" One girl rolls her eyes toward the ceiling and shakes her head in disgust. The incident lasts less than a minute, and the discussion of male inventors continues.

We sometimes ask our students at the American University to list twenty famous women from American history. There are only a few restrictions. They cannot include figures from sports or entertainment. Presidents' wives are not allowed unless they are clearly famous in their own right. Most students cannot do it. The seeds of their ignorance were sown in their earliest years of schooling.

In the 1970s, analyses of best-selling history books showed a biological oddity, a nation with only founding fathers.[6] More space was given to the six-shooter than to the women's suffrage movement. In fact, the typical history text gave only two sentences to enfranchising half the population. Science texts continued the picture of a one-gender world, with the exception of Marie Curie who was permitted to stand behind her husband and peer over his shoulder as he looked into a microscope. Today's history and science texts are better—but not much[7]. . . .

When girls do not see themselves in the pages of textbooks, when teachers do not point out or confront the omissions, our daughters learn that to be female is to be an absent partner in the development of our nation. And when teachers add their stereotypes to the curriculum bias in books, the message becomes even more damaging. . . .

Role-Playing Can Show Bias

Women who have spent years learning the lessons of silence in elementary, secondary, and college classrooms have trouble regaining their voices. In our workshops we often set up a role play to demonstrate classroom sex bias. Four volunteers, two women and two men, are asked to pretend to be students in a middle school social studies lesson. They have no script; their only direction is to take a piece of paper with them as David, playing the part of the social studies teacher, ushers them to four chairs in front of the room. He tells the audience that he will condense all the research on sexism in the classroom into a ten-minute lesson, so the bias will look blatant, even overwhelming. The job of the parents and teachers in the audience is to detect the different forms of egregious sexism. He begins the lesson.

"Today we're going to discuss the chapter in your book, 'The Gathering Clouds of War,' about the American Revolution. But first I'd like you to take out your homework so I can check it." David walks over to Sarah, the first student in the line of four. (In real life she is an English teacher at the local high school.)

"Let's see your paper, Sarah." He pauses to look it over. "Questions three and seven are not correct." Sarah looks concerned.

David moves to Peggy (who is a communications professor at a state college). "Oh, Peggy, Peggy, Peggy!" She looks up as everyone stares. David holds up Peggy's paper. "Would you all look at this. It is sooo neat. You print just like a typewriter. This is the kind of paper I like to put on the bulletin board for open school night." Peggy looks down, smiles, blushes, looks up wide-eyed, and bats her eyelashes. She is not faking or exaggerating these behaviors. Before our eyes she has returned to childhood as the stereotypical good girl with pretty penmanship. The lessons have been well learned.

Next David stops by Tony (who is a vocational education teacher) and looks at the blank paper he is holding. "Tony, you've missed questions three, seven, and eleven. I think you would do better on your assignments if you used the bold headings to guide your reading. I know you can get this if you try harder." Tony nods earnestly as David moves to Roy. Sarah, who missed questions three and seven, looks perplexed.

David scans Roy's paper and hands it back. "Roy, where's your homework?"

Roy (a college physics teacher) stammers, "Here it is," and again offers the blank paper that served as homework for the others in the role play.

"Roy, that's not your history homework. That's science." Roy still looks puzzled. "Trust me, Roy," David says. "No matter what you come up with, it won't be history homework. Now, where is it?"

"The dog ate it," Roy mutters, getting the picture and falling into the bad boy role.

Next David discusses revolutionary battles, military tactics, and male leaders—George Washington, John and Samuel Adams, Paul Revere, Benjamin Franklin, Thomas Jefferson, and more. He calls on Roy and Tony more than twenty times each. When they don't know the answer, he probes, jokes, challenges, offers hints. He calls on Sarah only twice. She misses both her questions because David gives her less than half a second to speak. After effusively praising Peggy's pretty paper, David never calls on her again. As the lesson progresses, Sarah's face takes on a sad, almost vacant expression. Peggy keeps on smiling.

When the scene of blatant sexism is over, many in the audience want to know how the two women felt.

"That was me all through school," Peggy blurts out. "I did very well. My work was neat. I was always prepared. I would have had the right answer if someone had called on me. But they never did."

"Why did you watch the two males get all the attention?" we ask. "If you weren't called on, why didn't you call out?"

"I tried. I just couldn't do it."

"Why? You weren't wearing a muzzle. The men were calling out."

"I know. I felt terrible. It reminded me of all those years in school when I wanted to say something but couldn't."

"What about you, Sarah?" we ask. "Why didn't you just shout out an answer?"

"It never occurred to me to do it," Sarah says, then pauses. "No, that's not true. I thought about it, but I didn't want to be out there where I might get laughed at or ridiculed."

Ignored and Harassed

David has taught this role play class hundreds and hundreds of times in workshops in big cities and small towns all across the United States. Each time he demonstrates sex bias by blatantly and offensively ignoring female students, and almost always the adult women, put back into the role of twelve-year-olds, sit and say nothing; once again they become the nice girls watching the boys in action. Inside they may feel sad or furious or relieved, but like Sarah and Peggy, they remain silent.

When women try to get into classroom interaction, they rarely act directly. Instead they doodle, write letters, pass notes, and wait for the teacher to notice them. In a California workshop one parent who was playing the part of a student developed an elaborate pantomime. She reached into her large purse, pulled out a file, and began to do her nails. When that failed to attract David's attention, she brought out a brush, makeup, and a mirror. But David continued to ignore her, talking only with the two males.

"I was so mad I wanted to hit you," the woman fumed at the end of the role play when she was invited to express her feelings.

"What did you do to show your anger?" David asked.

"I didn't do anything." Then she paused, realizing the passive-aggressive but ultimately powerless strategy she had pursued. "No, I did do something—my nails," she said sadly.

After hundreds of these role plays, we are still astonished at how quickly the veneer of adulthood melts away. Grown women and men replay behavior they learned as children at school. The role plays are always revealing—funny, sad, and sometimes they even have a troubling twist.

At a workshop for college students at a large university in the Midwest, one of the young women ignored in the role play did not exhibit the usual behavior of silence or passive hostility. Instead, in the middle of the workshop in front of her classmates, she began to sob. She explained later in private that as one of only a few girls in the university's agricultural program, she had been either ignored or harassed. That week in an overenrolled course an instructor had announced, "There are too many students in this class. Everyone with ovaries—out!"

"What did you do?"

"What could I do? I left. Later I told my adviser about it. He was sympathetic but said if there was no room, I should consider another major."

Silent Losses

Each time a girl opens a book and reads a womanless history, she learns she is worth less. Each time the teacher passes over a girl to elicit the ideas and opinions of boys, that girl is conditioned to be silent and to defer. As teachers use their expertise to question, praise, probe, clarify, and correct boys, they help these male students sharpen ideas, refine their thinking, gain their voice, and achieve more. When female students are offered the leftovers of teacher time and attention morsels of amorphous feedback, they achieve less.

Then girls and women learn to speak softly or not at all; to submerge honest feelings, withhold opinions, and defer to boys; to avoid math and science as male domains; to value neatness and quiet more than assertiveness and creativity; to emphasize appearance and hide intelligence. Through this curriculum in sexism they are turned into educational spectators instead of players; but education is not a spectator sport.

When blatantly sexual or sexist remarks become an accepted part of classroom conversation, female students are degraded. Sexual harassment in business and the military now causes shock waves and legal suits. Sexual harassment in schools is dismissed as normal and unavoidable "boys will be boys" behavior; but by being targeted, girls are being intimidated and caused to feel like members of an inferior class.

Like a thief in school, sexist lessons subvert education, twisting it into a system of socialization that robs potential. Consider this record of silent, devastating losses.[8]

- In the early grades girls are ahead of or equal to boys on almost every standardized measure of achievement and psychological well-being. By the time they graduate from high school or college, they have fallen back. Girls enter school ahead but leave behind.[9]

234

- In high school, girls score lower on the SAT and ACT tests, which are critical for college admission. The greatest gender gap is in the crucial areas of science and math.
- Girls score far lower on College Board Achievement tests, which are required by most of the highly selective colleges.
- Boys are much more likely to be awarded state and national college scholarships.
- The gap does not narrow in college. Women score lower on all sections of the Graduate Record Exam, which is necessary to enter many graduate programs.
- Women also trail on most tests needed to enter professional schools: the GMAT for business school, the LSAT for law school, and the MCAT for medical school.
- From elementary school through higher education, female students receive less active instruction, both in the quantity and in the quality of teacher time and attention.[10]

In addition to the loss of academic achievement, girls suffer other difficulties:

- Eating disorders among girls in middle and secondary schools and in college are rampant and increasing.[11]
- Incidents of school-based sexual harassment are now reported with alarming frequency.[12]
- One in ten teenage girls becomes pregnant each year. Unlike boys, when girls drop out, they usually stay out.[13]
- As girls go through school, their self-esteem plummets, and the danger of depression increases.[14]
- Economic penalties follow women after graduation. Careers that have a high percentage of female workers, such as teaching and nursing, are poorly paid. And even when women work in the same jobs as men, they earn less money. Most of America's poor live in households that are headed by women.

If the cure for cancer is forming in the mind of one of our daughters, it is less likely to become a reality than if it is forming in the mind of one of our sons. Until this changes, everybody loses.

Notes

1. Faludi, Susan. *Backlash: The Undeclared War Against American Women.* New York: Crown, 1991, p. xxii.
2. Our first study, which analyzed gender bias in elementary and secondary classrooms, lasted more than three years and was funded by the National Institute of Education. The report submitted to the government was Sadker, Myra, and David Sadker, *Year 3: Final Report: Promoting Effectiveness in*

235

Classroom Instruction. Washington, DC: National Institute of Education, 1984.

  Sadker, Myra, and David Sadker. "Sexism in the Schoolroom of the Eighties," *Psychology Today* (March 1985), pp. 54–57.

  Sadker, Myra, and David Sadker. "Sexism in the Classroom: From Grade School to Graduate School," *Phi Delta Kappan* 67:7 (March 1986), pp. 512–15.

  We also reported this study as one of the contributing authors to Wellesley College Center for Research on Women. *How Schools Shortchange Girls: The AAUW Report*. Washington, DC: American Association of University Women Educational Foundation, 1992.

3. Kidder, Tracy. *Among Schoolchildren*. Boston: Houghton Mifflin, 1989, p. 3.

4. Kidder, *Among Schoolchildren*, p. 262.

5. These episodes are drawn primarily from our three-year study of sex bias in elementary and secondary classrooms. They are also taken from classroom observations conducted as we supervised student teachers at the American University and as we consulted with schools around the country and assessed their classrooms for gender bias.

6. Trecker, Janice Law. "Women in U.S. History High School Textbooks," *Social Education* 35 (1971), pp. 249–60.

7. Weitzman, Lenore, and Diane Rizzo. *Biased Textbooks: Images of Males and Females in Elementary School Textbooks*. Washington, DC: Resource Center on Sex Roles in Education, 1976.

  Saario, Terry, Carol Jacklin, and Carol Tittle. "Sex Role Stereotyping in the Public Schools," *Harvard Educational Review* 43, pp. 386–416.

  Women on Words and Images. *Dick and Jane as Victims: Sex Stereotyping in Children's Readers*. Princeton, NJ: Carolingian Press, 1972.

8. Sadker, Myra, David Sadker, and Susan Klein. "The Issue of Gender in Elementary and Secondary Education." In Grant, Gerald (ed.), *Review of Research in Education*, vol. 17. Washington, DC: American Educational Research Association, 1991.

  Wellesley College Center for Research on Women, *How Schools Shortchange Girls: The AAUW Report*.

9. Data documenting the loss of academic achievement were obtained from reports, tables, news releases, and studies issued by test publishers. The Educational Testing Service in Princeton, New Jersey, provided several reports and statistics related to the Preliminary Scholastic Aptitude Test, the Scholastic Aptitude Test, the Achievement tests, the Graduate Record Exam, and the Graduate Management Admissions Test. While the Graduate Record Exam data were from 1987–1988 (the most recently published), all other data reflected 1991 and 1992 test administrations. The American College Testing Program data were derived from a variety of profile and normative reports for 1990 and 1991 issued by American College Testing in Iowa City, Iowa.

  Professional organizations and schools often contract with testing services to develop and administer their admissions tests. For example, the Medical College Admission Test (MCAT) is developed by ACT in Iowa City. For each of these admission tests the professional association responsible was contacted first, and it provided the requisite information. These organizations included the Association of American Medical Colleges, the Graduate Management Admissions Council, and the Law School Data Assembly Service.

10. Sadker and Sadker, *Year3: Final Report.*

   Sadker and Sadker, *Final Report: Project Effect.*

11. Nagel, K.L., and Karen H. Jones. "Sociological Factors in the Development of Eating Disorders," *Adolescence* 27 (Spring 1992), pp. 107–13.

   Wiseman, Claire, James Gray, James Mosimann, and Anthony Ahrens. "Cultural Expectations of Thinness in Women: An Update," *International Journal of Eating Disorders* 11: 1 (1992), pp. 85–89.

   Button, Eric. "Self-Esteem in Girls Aged 11–12: Baseline Findings from a Planned Prospective Study of Vulnerability to Eating Disorders," *Journal of Adolescence* 13 (December 7, 1990), pp. 407–13.

12. Hughes, Jean O'Gorman, and Bernice Sandler. *Peer Harassment: Hassles for Women on Campus.* Washington, DC: Project on the Status and Education of Women, Association of American Colleges, 1988.

   Stein, Nan. "Sexual Harassment in Schools," *The School Administrator* (January 1993), pp. 14–21.

13. Earle, Janice. *Counselor/Advocates: Keeping Pregnant and Parenting Teens in School.* Alexandria, VA: National Association of State Boards of Education, 1990.

14. A vast body of research documents girls' declining self-esteem at adolescence:

   Allgood-Merten, Betty, Peter Lewinsohn, and Hyman Hops. "Sex Differences and Adolescent Depression," *Journal of Abnormal Psychology* 99:1 (February 1990), pp. 55–63.

   Brutsaert, Herman. "Changing Sources of Self-Esteem Among Girls and Boys in Secondary Schools," *Urban Education* 24:4 (January 1990), pp. 432–39.

   Kelly, Kevin, and LaVerne Jordan. "Effects of Academic Achievement and Gender on Academic and Social Self-Concept: A Replication Study," *Journal of Counseling and Development* 69 (November-December 1990), pp. 173–77.

   Widaman, Keith, et al. "Differences in Adolescents' Self-Concept as a Function of Academic Level, Ethnicity, and Gender," *American Journal of Mental Retardation* 96:4 (1992), pp. 387–404.

   Williams, Sheila, and Rob McGee. "Adolescents' Self-Perceptions of Their Strengths," *Journal of Youths and Adolescence* 20:3 (June 1991), pp. 325–37.

Evidence Does Not Support Claims of Gender Bias in Education

by Christina Hoff Sommers

Christina Hoff Sommers is an associate professor of philosophy at Clark University in Worcester, Massachusetts. She specializes in contemporary moral theory. In the following viewpoint, Sommers argues that research purporting to prove gender bias in American schools is seriously flawed. She specifically takes issue with the work of gender bias researchers Myra and David Sadker and with a 1992 report, compiled by the Wellesley College Center for Research on Women, entitled "How Schools Short-change Girls." Sommers contends that the Wellesley Report "illegitimately bolsters" its point by omitting all comparisons of boys and girls in areas where boys have difficulty. Additionally, she contends that the Sadkers' research methods are biased and that their conclusions ignore evidence that boys, not girls, have an overall academic deficit. Sommers concludes that such studies, being used to provoke congressional action, do a disservice to the nation's schoolchildren.

"What is highly questionable is the value and integrity of the research and the way the advocates have deployed the 'findings' to activate the United States Congress."

The American Association of University Women had every reason to be gratified and exhilarated by the public success of [its 1991] self-esteem report. It had "proved" that American girls "do not believe in themselves." The association moved quickly to commission a second study. This new study would show *how* schoolgirls are being undermined and point to remedies. Its advent was announced by Sharon Schuster: "The survey and the roundtable are just the first steps in AAUW's effort to stimulate a national discussion on how our schools—and our entire society—can encourage girls to believe in themselves. . . . We have awarded a grant to the Wellesley College Center for Research on Women to review the growing body of research on how girls learn."[1]

The Wellesley Report was completed in 1992, a year after the self-esteem report was released. Not surprisingly, it appeared to dramatically reinforce the tragic tidings of the earlier report. The AAUW had called the self-esteem study "Shortchanging Girls, Shortchanging America"; they called the Wellesley Report "How Schools Shortchange Girls."

The Media Seizes on the Gender Bias Issue

The AAUW distributed the findings in attractive little booklets and pamphlets, providing all interested parties, especially journalists, with convenient summaries and highlights that could serve as the basis for their stories. Writing the foreword for the new report, Alice McKee, president of the AAUW Educational Foundation, repeated and reinforced the theme of the AAUW's first study: "The wealth of statistical evidence must convince even the most skeptical that gender bias in our schools is shortchanging girls—and compromising our country. . . . The evidence is in, and the picture is clear: shortchanging girls—the women of tomorrow—shortchanges America."[2]

The Wellesley revelations turned out to be even more newsworthy than the Greenberg-Lake poll on self-esteem, generating more than fourteen hundred stories by journalists and newscasters. The *San Francisco Chronicle* reported the "Dreadful Waste of Female Talent."[3] "Powerful Impact of Bias Against Girls," cried the *Los Angeles Times*.[4] *Time* magazine informed its readers that "the latest research finds that the gender gap goes well beyond boys' persistent edge in math and science."[5] The *Boston Globe* emphasized the distress of girls: "From the very first days in school American girls face a drum-fire of gender bias, ranging from sexual harassment to discrimination in the curriculum to lack of attention from teachers, according to a survey released today in Washington."[6] The *New York Times* weighed in with "Bias Against Girls Is Found Rife in Schools, with Lasting Damage."[7]

The AAUW was quick to seize on the largesse provided by a cooperative and trusting press. Most of the press stories cited above were reprinted in brochures showing how "AAUW is making headlines." The whole of *Time* magazine's adulatory article became part of the AAUW's promotional packet.

Once again, the release of a sensational AAUW study was the occasion for a gathering of notables who would be influential in the association's "call for action" on the federal level. In April 1992, the Council on Foundations, an umbrella organization of leaders of the most powerful philanthropic organizations in America, met at the Fountainbleau Hilton Resort in Miami. One of the most popular events, entitled "How Schools Shortchange Girls," included a wine and cheese party and a talk by Susan Bailey, principal author of the AAUW-Wellesley report. Guests received handsomely produced information kits presenting the AAUW findings and hailing their significance. The day before Susan Faludi had delivered a keynote address on "the undeclared war against American women."

The Gender Equity in Education Bill

The next step was already in the works. The $360 million "Gender Equity in Education" bill was introduced in Congress in April of 1993 by the bipartisan Congressional Caucus for Women's Issues.[8] Among the bill's sponsors were Patricia Schroeder, Olympia Snowe, Susan Molinari, Patsy Mink, Connie Morella, Nita Lowey, Dale Kildee, Lynn Woolsey, Cardiss Collins, Jolene Unsoeld, and Louise Slaughter. The Gender Equity in Education Act (H.R. 1793) would establish a permanent and well-funded gender equity bureaucracy. It calls for an Office of Women's Equity within the Department of Education, charged with "promoting and coordinating women's equity policies, programs, activities and initiatives in all federal education programs and offices."

Politically, a bill calling for gender equity would seem to have clear sailing apart from any merits it might or might not have. On the one hand, it offered some members of Congress a welcome opportunity to show they were sensitive to women's issues. On the other hand, the dangers of challenging the AAUW or the Wellesley College Center for Research on Women were obvious.

Congresswoman Patricia Schroeder cited the Wellesley Report in introducing the bill. For her, the report was an unquestioned source of truth: our nation's girls are being systematically undermined, and Congress must act. In September of 1993, Senators Edward Kennedy, Tom Harkin, Carol Moseley-Braun, Paul Simon, and Barbara Mikulski introduced a Senate version of the Gender Equity in Education Act. Referring to the Wellesley Report, Senator Kennedy said: [It] "refutes the common assumption that boys and girls are treated equally in our educational system. Clearly they are not."[9]

Walteen Grady Truely, President and CEO, Women and Foundations/Corporate Philanthropy, which had sponsored Susan Bailey and Susan Faludi in Miami, appeared before the congressional subcommittee to argue for the Gender Equity in Education Act. She pointed out that "girls' self-esteem plummets between pre-adolescence and the 10th grade."[10] Like Pat Schroeder, Senator Kennedy, and others, Ms. Truely appears to have relied in part on the AAUW brochures.

Everyone expects the bill to pass. The National Council for Research on Women reported the AAUW's success as an inspiring example of how women's research can lead directly to congressional action:

> Last year a report by the American Association of University Women (AAUW) documented serious inequities in education for girls and women. As a result of that work, an omnibus package of legislation, the Gender Equity in Education Act (H.R. 1793), was recently introduced in the House of Representatives. . . . The introduction of H.R. 1793 is a milestone for demonstrating valuable linkages between feminist research and policy in investigating gender discrimination in education.[11]

That the linkages are of value to those doing the research is unquestionable. What is highly questionable is the value and integrity of the research and the way the advocates have deployed the "findings" to activate the United States Congress.

Boys Are Worse Off Than Girls

Are girls really being insidiously damaged by our school systems? That question actually remains to be investigated. Everyone knows we need to improve our schools, but are the girls worse off than the boys? If one does insist on focusing on who is worse off, then it doesn't take long to see that, educationally speaking, boys are the weaker gender. Consider that today 55 percent of college students are female. In 1971, women received 43 percent of the bachelor's degrees, 40 percent of the master's degrees and 14 percent of the doctorates. By 1989 the figures grew to 52 percent for B.A.'s, 52 percent for M.A.'s, and 36 percent for doctoral degrees. Women are still behind men in earning doctorates, but according to the U.S. Department of Education, the number of doctorates awarded to women has increased by 185 percent since 1971.[12]

The Wellesley study gives a lot of attention to how girls are behind in math and science, though the math and science test differentials are small compared to large differentials favoring girls in reading and writing. On the National Assessment of Education Progress Tests (NAEP), administered to seventeen-year-olds in 1990, males outperformed females by three points in math and eleven points in science. The girls outperformed boys by thirteen points in reading and twenty-four points in writing.[13]

Girls outnumber boys in all extracurricular activities except sports and hobby clubs. Almost twice as many girls as boys participate in student government, band and orchestra, and drama or service clubs. More girls work on the school newspapers and yearbooks. More are members of honor and service societies.[14] Boys far outnumber girls in sports, but that gap is narrowing each year. In 1972, only 4 percent of girls were in high school athletic programs. By 1987 the figure was up to 26 percent, more than a sixfold increase.[15]

On the purely academic front, progress continues apace. The UCLA Higher Education Research Institute's annual survey of college freshmen shows more women (66 percent) than men (63 percent) planning to pursue advanced degrees.[16] The UCLA data show a tripling in the percentage of women aiming for higher degrees in less than twenty-five years. As the institute's director, Alexander Astin, notes, "To close such a wide gap in the relatively short span of two decades is truly remarkable." David Merkowitz of the American Council on Education agrees: "If you want a long-term indicator of major social change, this is one." But indicators that girls are doing well are not the stuff of the Wellesley Report.

The report illegitimately bolsters its "shortchanged girls" thesis by omitting all comparisons of boys and girls in areas where boys are clearly in trouble. In a study of self-reports by high school seniors, the U.S. Department of Education found that more boys than girls cut classes, fail to do homework assignments, had disciplinary problems, had been suspended, and had been in trouble with the police.[17] Studying transcripts of 1982 high school graduates, the Department of Education found girls outperforming boys in *all* subjects, from math to English to science.[18] It also learned that in all racial and ethnic groups, "females were generally more likely than males to report their parents wanted them to attend college."[19]

The Wellesley researchers looked at girls' better grades in math and science classes and concluded that the standardized tests must be biased. Girls get better grades, but boys are doing better on the tests. But their conclusion would have had more credibility had they also considered the possibility that there could be a grading bias against boys.

According to the 1992 *Digest of Educational Statistics*, more boys drop out. Between 1980 and 1982, 19 percent of males and 15 percent of females between the tenth and twelfth grade dropped out of school. Boys are more likely to be robbed, threatened, and attacked in and out of school. Just about every pathology—including alcoholism and drug abuse—hits boys harder.[20] According to the Wellesley Report, "adolescent girls are four to five times more likely than boys to attempt suicide."[21] It mentions parenthetically that more boys actually die. It does not say that *five* times as many boys as girls actually succeed in killing themselves. For boys fifteen to twenty-four the figure is 21.9 per 100,000; for girls it is 4.2 per 100,000. The adult suicide rate is not very different. In the United States in 1990, 24,724 men and 6,182 women committed suicide.[22] What would the Wellesley investigators and other advocates have made of these statistics were the numbers reversed?

Teacher Inattention

The tribulations of schoolboys are not an urgent concern of the leadership of the AAUW; its interest is in studies that uncover bias against girls and women. For details on how American girls are suffering from inequitable treatment in the nation's classrooms, the Wellesley investigators relied heavily on the expertise of Myra and David Sadker of the American University School of Education, who had already found just the kind of thing the AAUW was concerned about: "In a study conducted by Myra and David Sadker, boys in elementary and middle school called out answers eight times more often than girls. When boys called out, teachers listened. But when girls called out, they were told to 'raise your hand if you want to speak.'"[23] The telling difference in "callouts" has become a favorite with those who seek to show how girls are being cheated. Pat Schroeder faithfully echoed the claim in introducing the Gender Equity in Education Act: "Teachers are more likely to call on boys and to give them constructive feedback. When boys call out answers, teachers tend to listen to their comments. But girls who call out their answers are reprimanded and told to raise their hands."[24]

The Sadkers have been observing teachers in the classroom for more than two decades, gathering their data on gender bias. Convinced that "America's schools cheat girls," as the subtitle of their new book, *Failing at Fairness*, claims, they have devised strategies for ridding teachers (a majority of whom happen to be women) of their unconscious gender bias that the Sadkers feel is at the root of the problem. The Sadkers' latest book describes their work as the "backbone" of the Wellesley Report, and they are among the report's chief authors. Certainly their work provided key support for the report's claim that "whether one looks at preschool classrooms or university lecture halls, at female teachers or male teachers, research spanning the past twenty years consistently reveals that males receive more teacher attention than do females."[25]

Teachers tend not to be surprised to hear that boys in their classes may be getting more attention—boys tend to be rowdier in the classrooms and to require more supervision. But is that a sign or form of discrimination? Despite their decades of attention to the problem, the Sadkers supply us with no plausible evidence that girls are losing out because teachers are less attentive to them. Instead, they argue that it stands to reason: "The most valuable resource in a classroom is the teacher's attention. If the teacher is giving more of that valuable resource to one group, it should come as no surprise that group shows greater educational gains."[26]

As we have seen, however, the evidence suggests that it is boys who are suffering an overall academic deficit. Boys do perform slightly better on standardized math tests, but even that gap is small, and closing. In the 1991 International Assessment of Educational Progress (IAEP), the Educational Testing Service found that on a scale of 100, thirteen-year-old American girls average 1 point below boys. And this slight gap is altogether negligible in comparison with the gap that separates American students from their foreign counterparts. Taiwanese and Korean girls are more than 16 points ahead of American boys on this same test.[27]

In addition to measuring abilities, the Educational Testing Service asked students around the world whether or not they thought math was "for boys and girls equally." In most countries, including the United States, almost all students agreed it was. The exceptions were Korea, Taiwan, and Jordan. In Korea, 27 percent said that math was more for boys; for Taiwan and Jordan, the figure was 15 percent. "Interestingly," the report notes, "the three countries that were more likely to view mathematics as gender linked . . . did not exhibit significant differences in performance by gender."[28] And girls in two of those countries—Korea and Taiwan—outperformed American boys.

From the IAEP at least, it appears that gender-linked attitudes about math are not strongly correlated to performance. The Educational Testing Service did find one key variable positively related with achievement throughout the world: the amount of time students spent on their math homework—irrespective of gender.

Despite this, the Wellesley Report sticks to its guns. Tackling the gender problem is the first priority in making America educationally strong for the global economy of the future.

In any case, gender inequity in the form of teacher inattention to girls is what the Sadkers' research is all about, and many of the Wellesley conclusions stand or fall with their expertise and probity. . . .

Observer Bias

What had the Sadkers found? They and their assistants visited hundreds of elementary classrooms and observed the teachers' interactions with students. They identified four types of teacher comments: praise ("Good answer"), acceptance ("Okay"), remediation ("Give it another try; think a little harder this time"), and criticism ("Wrong"). They determined that fewer than 5 percent of teachers' interactions constituted criticism. Praise accounted for about 11 percent of interaction; 33 percent was remediation. The remainder (approximately 51–56 percent) was bland acceptance.[29] Although boys and girls got close to the same amount of bland acceptance ("Okay"), boys got a larger share of the other categories. The exact number is difficult to determine from the data. In their many published articles, the Sadkers generally do not specify the actual size of the difference, but instead make claims about discrepancies without specifying them: "Girls received less than their share in all categories."[30]

In the kind of observations the Sadkers and their researchers made, the chances of observer bias in selecting the data are extraordinarily high. It is all too easy to "find" just what one believes is there. As I have noted, the Wellesley Report relies strongly on research by the Sadkers that purportedly found boys calling out eight times more often than girls, with boys being respectfully attended to, while the relatively few girls who called out were told to "please raise your hands if you want to speak." Professor Jere Brophy of Michigan State, who is perhaps the most prominent scholar working in the area of classroom interaction, is suspicious of the Sadkers' findings on call-outs. "It is too extreme," he says. "It all depends on the neighborhood, the level of the class, and the teacher. Many teachers simply do not allow call-outs." I asked him about the Sadkers' claim that boys get more careful and thoughtful teacher comments. According to Brophy, any differences that are showing up are negligibly slight. Did he see a link between the ways teachers interact with boys and girls and their overall achievement? "No, and that is why I have never tried to make that much of the sex difference findings."

Questionable Research

For details of the Sadkers' findings, the Wellesley Report refers to research reported in a 1981 volume of a journal called *The Pointer*.[31] *The Pointer* is now defunct, but when I finally got to read the article I was surprised to see that what it said about classroom discipline in particular was not, in my view, at all indicative of bias against girls. This portion of the *Pointer* article focuses not on "call-outs," but on how teachers reprimand boys and girls differently, emphasizing that boys are disciplined more than girls. Here is what the Sadkers and their coauthor, Dawn Thomas, found:

> Boys, particularly low-achieving boys, receive eight to ten times as many reprimands as do their female classmates. . . . When

both girls and boys are misbehaving equally, boys still receive more frequent discipline. Research shows that when teachers are faced with disruptive behavior from both boys and girls, they are over three times as likely to reprimand the boys than the girls. Also, boys are more likely to get reprimanded in a harsh and public manner and to receive heavy penalties; girls are more likely to get reprimanded in a softer, private manner and to receive lighter penalties.[32]

The article says nothing at all about "call-outs," and nothing about girls being told to raise their hands if they want to speak. Yet it is cited as the source for the Report's oft-repeated claims about this matter. Thinking that I must be in error, I looked at a 1991 article in the *Review of Research in Education* by the Sadkers themselves, in which they, too, cite the research reported in the *Pointer* article:

> D. Sadker, Sadker, and Thomas (1981) reported that boys were eight times more likely than girls to call out in elementary- and middle-school classrooms. When boys called out, the teacher's most frequent response was to accept the call-out and continue with the class. When girls called out, a much rarer phenomenon, the teacher's most typical response was to remediate or correct the inappropriate behavior with comments such as "in this class, we raise our hands."[33]

But the Sadkers are misquoting themselves; *The Pointer* contains no such findings. Support for the Sadkers' claim about "call-outs" may well exist. But putting aside both the Wellesley Report and the Sadkers' apparent error in citing the *Pointer* article for support, one can note that the claim about "call-outs" keeps the drums of outrage beating and gives fuel to the notion that American girls "spend years learning the lessons of silence in elementary, secondary, and college classrooms," after which they find it difficult or impossible to "regain their voices."[34]

Suppose, indeed, that teachers do call on boys more often. There is no clear evidence that girls lose because of that. Girls are getting the better grades, they like school better, they drop out less, and more of them go to college. If teacher attention were crudely to be correlated with student achievement, we would be led to the perverse conclusion that more attention causes poorer performance.

In any case, I could find no study showing a direct relation between teacher and student interaction and student output. . . .

Oddly enough, the authors of the Wellesley Report do mention, almost as an aside, that "new evidence indicates that it is too soon to state a definitive connection between a specific teacher behavior and a particular student outcome."[35] The report does not say what this new evidence is and never mentions it again. Nor are we told why the existence of such evidence does not vitiate the report's sensational conclusion that gender bias favoring boys is rife and its correction a matter of national urgency. To put it mildly, the literature on the subject of classroom bias seems confusing and not a little confused.

A Troubling Lack of Skepticism

The advocacy research on classroom bias would not matter much were it not for the lack of skepticism on the part of legislators who now see gender equity in the classroom as a critical national issue. The testimony of Anne Bryant, the executive director of the AAUW, before Congress in April 1993 in favor of the Gender Equity in Education Act is typical of what it has heard:

> Myra and David Sadker of the American University and other researchers have extensively documented gender bias in teacher-student interactions. . . . Teachers tend to give girls less attention, with some studies showing teachers directing 80 percent of all their questions to boys.[36]

In her presentation, Ms. Bryant indicated that the AAUW had worked with the Congressional Caucus on Women's Issues to develop the bill and vowed that "we will continue to work with you as the omnibus educational equity package moves through Congress."[37]

It was a close relationship. The wording of the bill echoed that of the AAUW brochure:

> Research reveals that, at all classroom levels, girls receive different treatment from teachers than do boys. . . . To address this problem, this legislation would create programs to provide teacher training in identifying and eliminating inequitable practices in the classroom.[38]

Members of Congress have competent and intelligent staffs who are accustomed to checking up on all kinds of claims made by special interest groups. One hopes they will look into the data behind the AAUW and Wellesley brochures before voting millions of dollars for the Gender Equity Act and reaping us the bitter fruits of the AAUW's irresponsible and divisive initiative. . . .

Gaps in Math and Science

The Wellesley Report is correct when it points out that American girls are trailing boys in math and science. The gap is small but real, and the report

247

is right to suggest that schools must make every effort to "dispel myths about math and science as 'inappropriate' fields for women."[39] Unfortunately, that sound suggestion is accompanied by more than twenty questionable and distressing recommendations that would, if acted upon, create a nightmarish "gender equity" bureaucracy with plenty of time and money on its hands—just the sort of recommendation anyone who cares about the well-being of American schools should fear and loathe: "The U.S. Department of Education's Office of Educational Research and Improvement (OERI) should establish an advisory panel of gender equity experts to work with OERI to develop a research and dissemination agenda to foster gender-equitable education in the nation's classrooms."[40]

Who would be training the gender experts? Who would monitor the nation's schools on how well they conform to the ideals of a correct sexual politics? More generally, who would benefit most from the millions being requested for the Gender Equity in Education Act? Would it not be those who insist that gender equity is our foremost educational problem? Our system cannot handle much more pressure from these muddled but determined women with their multistage theories and their metaphors about windows, mirrors, and voices, their workshops, and above all their constant alarms about the state of male-female relations in American society.

Which leads us back to what is most wrongheaded about the Wellesley Report: its exploitation of America's very real problem as a nation educationally at risk. Despite its suggestion that solving the "problem of gender equity" will somehow help us to bridge the gap between American children and the educationally superior children of other countries—what the education researcher Harold Stevenson aptly calls the "learning gap"—the report never says how. The reason for the omission is obvious: the authors have no plausible solution to offer. . . .

Will Gender Bias Studies Further Weaken Schools?

Feminism is not well served by biased studies or by media that tolerate and help to promote them. Had journalists, politicians, and education leaders been doing a proper job of checking sources, looking at the original data, and seeking dissenting opinions from scholars, had they not put their faith in glossy brochures and press releases, the alarming findings on self-esteem, gender bias in the classroom, and harassment in the hallways would not be automatically credited. In a soundly critical climate, the federal government would not be on the verge of pouring tens of millions of dollars into projects that will enrich the gender-bias industry and further weaken our schools.

Notes

1. "A Call to Action: Shortchanging Girls, Shortchanging America" (Washington, D.C.: American Association of University Women, 1991), p. 5.
2. *The AAUW Report: How Schools Shortchange Girls* (commonly referred to as the "Wellesley Report") (Washington, D.C.: AAUW Educational Foundation, 1992), p. vi. I am referring to the second AAUW study as the Wellesley Report to distinguish it from the first AAUW study on self-esteem.
3. *San Francisco Chronicle*, February 13, 1992, p. A22.
4. *Los Angeles Times*, February 22, 1992, p. B6.
5. Richard N. Ostling, "Is School Unfair to Girls?" *Time*, February 24, 1992, p. 62.
6. *Boston Globe*, February 2, 1992.
7. *New York Times*, February 12, 1992.
8. The Gender Equity in Education Act (H.R. 1793) is made up of nine separate bills. Two of them seem reasonable and free of gender feminist ideology (a child abuse prevention program and a nutrition and family counseling program). But the other seven appear to be based on questionable gender feminist advocacy research.
9. *Boston Globe*, September 16, 1993, p. 5.
10. Executive summary, "Testimony before the House Subcommittee on Elementary, Secondary, and Vocational Education," April 21, 1993, p. 5.
11. *Women's Research Network News* (New York: National Council for Research on Women, 1993), p. 11.
12. *The Condition of Education* (Washington, D.C.: National Center for Education Statistics, U.S. Department of Education, 1991), p. 44.
13. *The Condition of Education*, 1992, pp. 42–49.
14. *Digest of Education Statistics* (Washington, D.C.: U.S. Department of Education, 1992), p. 136.
15. Wellesley Report, p. 45.
16. *Boston Globe*, January 24, 1994. The UCLA Center does a yearly study of the attitudes and goals of college freshmen. The 1993 results are based on a survey of approximately 250,000 students from 475 colleges and universities.
17. *The Condition of Education*, 1985, p. 66.
18. Ibid., pp. 50, 52.
19. Ibid., p. 206.
20. *Digest of Education Statistics* (Washington, D.C.: National Center for Education Statistics, U.S. Department of Education, 1992), p. 137.
21. Wellesley Report, p. 79.
22. *Monthly Vital Statistics Report*, "Advance Report of Final Mortality Statistics, 1990" (Washington, D.C.: U.S. Department of Health and Human Services, January 1993), p. 27.
23. The quote is from an AAUW brochure called "Executive Summary: How Schools Shortchange Girls," p. 2; the information is taken from the Wellesley Report, p. 68.
24. Testimony of Rep. Patricia Schroeder on the Gender Equity in Education Act before the House Education and Labor Committee Subcommittee on Elementary, Secondary, and Vocational Education, April 21, 1993.
25. Wellesley Report, p. 68.
26. Myra Sadker and David Sadker, "Sexism in the Classroom: From Grade

School to Graduate School," *Phi Delta Kappan*, March 1986, p. 514.

27. International Assessment of Educational Progress (IAEP), (Princeton, N.J.: Educational Testing Service, 1992), p. 145. The underperformance of American boys vis à vis foreign girls is consistent with the 1988 IAEP, which showed the Korean girls similarly outperforming American boys, IAEP (Princeton, N.J.: Educational Testing Service 1989), figure 1.3.
28. IAEP, 1992, p. 21.
29. David Sadker and Myra Sadker, "Is the O.K. Classroom O.K.?" *Phi Delta Kappan*, January 1985, p. 360.
30. Ibid., p. 361.
31. Wellesley Report, p. 68, and *Review of Research in Education* 17 (1991): 297–98.
32. David Sadker, Myra Sadker, and Dawn Thomas, "Sex Equity and Special Education," *The Pointer* 26, no. 1 (1981): 36.
33. Myra Sadker, David Sadker, and Susan Klein, "The Issue of Gender in Elementary and Secondary Education" in ed. Gerald Grant, *Review of Research in Education* 17 (1991): 297–98.
34. Myra Sadker and David Sadker, *Failing at Fairness: How America's Schools Cheat Girls* (New York: Scribners, 1994), p. 10.
35. Wellesley Report, p. 70.
36. Testimony submitted to the House Subcommittee on Elementary, Secondary, and Vocational Education, April 21, 1993, by Anne L. Bryant, p. 2.
37. Ibid, p. 2.
38. From summary of Gender Equity in Education Act (H.R. 1793) distributed by the Congressional Caucus on Women's Issues (1993).
39. Wellesley Report, p. 86.
40. Ibid., p. 87.

The Divorce Courts Are Biased Against Women

by Karen Winner

Karen Winner is a journalist and former policy analyst and investigative writer for the New York City Department of Consumer Affairs. In the following viewpoint, Winner contends that lawyers, judges and even the laws that guide divorce proceedings discriminate against women. Many women, she argues, are coerced into giving up custody, property, and other rights as a result of economic and emotional assaults by their own lawyers. Judges also exhibit bias against divorcing women despite growing awareness of the problem, Winner states. Equally troubling, she contends, are laws that promised women more economic equality in divorce. Far from righting inequities, she states, these laws have been the "springboard" for even greater calamities and abuses.

"Judicial discrimination against divorcing women in all areas—custody, property rights, and alimony—is rampant."

Each year more than one million marriages in the United States are dissolved in divorce court. Before these legal proceedings start, the husband and wife share one standard of living in their single household. Something strange happens, however, by the time the divorce decree is issued: the division of the household income between the two parties no longer remains equitable and the new arrangement is lopsided, almost always against women. These facts are startling to researchers because our country's divorce laws—known as equitable distribution and community property laws—were intentionally designed to financially protect women and children in divorce. Yet newly divorced women find

251

that their standard of living has plummeted, on the average, by 30 percent, and mothers' and children's available income has fallen as much as 37 percent. Meanwhile, the standard of living for their ex-husbands has risen from 10 to 15 percent.[1] Why is it that divorcing women overwhelmingly face economic hardship after being processed through the legal system, while divorcing men prosper?

To understand this puzzling question I turned to a seemingly obvious place to look for answers: in the lawyer suites and courtrooms where women go for their divorces. Lawyers and judges control the main events in the legal process of divorce and determine what is in the woman's final divorce decree. I have found that while their behavior as advice-givers and decision-makers crucially affects the outcomes of women's lives after divorce, they are often strongly influenced by factors other than the woman's needs.

What emerges from my research is that the present divorce court system is, in fact, a very lucrative industry run by lawyers and judges. This industry is buoyed by a fee-for-profit system benefiting lawyers and judges, often at the expense and welfare of clients. My findings show that practices specific to the divorce industry, and some others attributed to the legal profession as a whole, are cause for deep concern to divorcing women as well as for public officials. These findings are based on interviews with ethicists, jurists, lawyers, academicians, women's rights activists, and victims, as well as a review of divorce industry trade literature and court and government records.

Justice Is for Sale

To begin to understand the divorce industry and its hold over families in divorce, it is important to recognize that lawyers are in a different position from other professionals. What differentiates lawyers is that they exclusively control the public's access to the judicial branch of our government. For all practical purposes, a person cannot gain access to the court if she or he does not have enough money to afford a lawyer. The well-worn phrase that justice is for sale is as true in divorce as in other fields of law. Only the well-off can comfortably afford divorce lawyers; the rest have trouble getting through the courtroom door.[2] In civil court, lawyers aren't usually appointed, so the only way to obtain legal representation is to hire a lawyer. Services like Legal Aid, meant to provide a safety net for poor people, are so typically understaffed that in some places, such as New York City, long waiting lists cause them to shut the door on divorcing people trying to get help. There aren't enough pro bono lawyers, but with those who do there are problems too.[3] Technically speaking, anyone can represent herself, but she will be no match for an experienced lawyer.

We might expect poor and working-class women to have difficulty finding affordable, competent representation, but as these pages will reveal, well-off women who are at the end of their marriages may also find it hard to gain access to the court. That's because women, even professional, affluent women, typically don't control the family assets. Consequently, they often find themselves in the peculiar position of being cash-poor at the end of their marriages and at the beginning of the divorce process. This has a most dire consequence: If a divorcing woman can't afford a lawyer, she's left without representation or protection in a situation that will totally affect her life. There is no ceiling to lawyers' fees, but these women's resources (personal life savings, parental loans, etc.) are finite. That's just the beginning of an explanation of how formerly wealthy women find themselves impoverished through the process of divorce. Even worse, whether a woman can afford to hire a lawyer or not at the outset, all divorcing women stand an equal chance of being priced out of their lawyer. . . .

Injury piles on injury for those women thrust into divorce involuntarily. Not only may divorce be imposed on women by their husbands, but the legal apparatus and industry that are divorce court may force these women to face involuntary economic sanctions as well. The penalties start with the imposed high cost of having to hire a lawyer and culminate with having to abide by financial settlements in which the women's needs may not have been represented at all. The sad truth is that lawyers in the industry of divorce court use the woman's divorce as an opportunity to enrich themselves at her expense.

Economic and Emotional Assaults on Women

Several practices that are standard industry-wide enhance the lawyer's profit potential:

- Lawyers in most states are not required to provide clients with itemized bills, which makes it nearly impossible for the clients to know what they are paying for.[4] Even when the bills are itemized, it does not preclude common abuses such as fee padding.
- Lawyers are permitted to hold their clients' files hostage if the clients refuse to pay, which can make it extremely difficult for clients to pursue their divorces. There is an ethical prohibition against retaining the documents in the file if damaging to the client's case, but this ethical code is poorly enforced.
- The legal establishment allows a judicial-selection process heavily tainted by politics.

- The legal establishment allows a judicial-selection process that does not screen applicants for psychological suitability for the job.
- Lawyers are allowed to use children as bargaining chips in the divorce to force mothers into giving up financial rights in return for gaining custody.
- Lawyers are allowed to charge legal fees that exceed the amount of the marital estates.
- Lawyers in many states are allowed to force the sale of the family home in compensation for legal fees even if this leaves family members homeless.[5]

As a result of these practices, women are subject to any number of economic and emotional assaults by their own attorneys, who may well collude with their husbands' attorneys to manipulate a settlement favorable to the lawyers. Vulnerable spouses are overcharged, coerced into trading off property rights for the right to keep custody of their children, and manipulated in various ways into conceding their rights.

Legalities Take Precedence over Fairness

Some of these practices . . . are unethical, others clearly illegal. There are also those vast, murky, gray areas that allow ethics and common decency to be evaded. On one hand, there are so many ethics rules, so many of them ill-defined and cast along such narrow technical lines, that what clearly seems like morally indefensible behavior to the layperson turns into a debate between lawyers over legal technicalities. Lawyers rest their argument on what's legal rather than what's right or wrong, unfair or equitable. For example, in a contemporary case, a matrimonial lawyer not only properly advised his affluent client that it was perfectly legal not to pay sufficient alimony if the judge agreed and ordered a low award, but then, when the client decided to adopt this option, the lawyer agreed to take the case. All the while, the lawyer knew that without sufficient alimony the woman would lose all financial security and become destitute. Contrast this to what Abraham Lincoln told a prospective client whose legal claim to $600 meant bankrupting a widow and impoverishing her six children. "Some things that are right legally are not right morally," Lincoln said, refusing to take the case, and adding: "I advise a sprightly, energetic man like you to try your hand at making six hundred dollars in some other way."[6] While appealing to common decency might sound naive or even laughable in these cynical times, Abraham Lincoln knew there was a court of higher justice, by which civilization need abide.

The situation for legal consumers in divorce is that the foxes are guarding the courthouse. Self-regulation of the legal profession by lawyers only adds to the problems for women. The present disciplinary system is seriously deficient. With a few very recent exceptions, consumer safeguards have been sorely lacking. . . .

A One-Sided System

The one-sided features of the divorce court system extend all the way up to the highest court in the land. Equal protection under the law is supposed to be guaranteed for all. But when a divorcing woman's civil rights are violated by a judge, she has little chance to redress these wrongs in the federal courts, where violations of Constitutional rights are normally addressed. The reason is that federal courts have ruled—with few exceptions—that family issues belong solely in the lower state courts. In theory, individuals can have their Constitutional rights addressed in federal court, but as Lynn Hecht Schafran, director of the Legal Defense and Education Fund at the National Organization for Women (NOW), points out: "Realistically, you can't [get into federal court]. I suppose in some dream world you could. . . . But the federal courts absolutely do not want any part at all, under any circumstances, of anything having to do with domestic relations. So it is extremely difficult."[7]

Schafran's view is supported by case law precedent and, more recently, a 1992 U.S. Supreme Court decision in the case of *Ankenbrandt v. Richards*. In that case, the Supreme Court addressed this issue very plainly when the majority accepted the existence of a "domestic relations exception" barring spouses in divorce from federal court and held that this exception applies to cases "involving divorce, alimony and child custody."[8]

Even more recently, a 1994 law passed by Congress to curb domestic violence includes a provision to protect the civil rights of victims of gender-motivated violence, but the act specifically forbids civil rights violations in domestic relations cases from being heard in federal court. Under Subtitle C—Civil Rights for Women, the provision reads: "Neither section 1367 of title 28, United States Code, nor subsection (c) of this section shall be construed, by reason of a claim arising under such subsection, to confer on the courts of the United States jurisdiction over any State law claim seeking the establishment of a divorce, alimony, equitable distribution of marital property or child custody decree."[9]

Constitutional Rights Are Not Guaranteed

Because of these rulings, Constitutional rights are not guaranteed. For example, when a state court or state agency wrongfully removes a child from its parents, this is considered a violation of a parent's Constitutional rights. The U.S. Supreme Court has ruled on this matter, in the case of *Santosky v. Kramer* (New York, 1982), that the state courts "can't terminate rights without clear and convincing evidence. . . ." But when mothers try to use this ruling or other similar rulings to get into federal court, they may be turned away. As child rights activist Michelle Etlin explained: "I know of more than a dozen cases where the mothers suing for civil right violations perpetrated on them were kicked out of the federal courts in anywhere from fifteen minutes to two years, on the stated basis that domestic relations cases are not entitled to federal jurisdiction—even though the cases that sought federal jurisdiction were based on *Santosky v. Kramer* and *Duchesne v. Sugarman.*"[10]

Without adequate consumer safeguards in place to curb the divorce industry and its culture, or the ability to address grievances in federal court, the most vulnerable are the first to get hurt. These are financially dependent spouses, predominantly women in long-term marriages who are uprooted by divorce, and mothers with children. These two groups are literally at the mercy of lawyers and the courts.

Each year a huge number of women are potentially affected by the present crisis: between one third and one half of all civil litigation in this nation involves family law issues. Divorce, child support enforcement, and domestic violence make up the bulk of these court cases, in which the woman must seek legal representation or go through legal proceedings to have her rights defended. . . .

The Extent of Abuse Is Unknown

The exact extent of lawyer and court-related abuse remains unknown. It is hard to quantify for a few major reasons. The divorce industry has not been examined until very recently, and there are only a few reports and government hearings dealing specifically with the ethics and practices of lawyers in family law. In fact, the first-ever report on this topic was one I wrote for the New York City Department of Consumer Affairs in 1992: *Women in Divorce: Lawyers, Ethics, Fees, and Fairness.* It dealt specifically with the mistreatment of women by their divorce lawyers.

The extent of the problem is also difficult to gauge because the abuse is often hidden, taking place quietly, routinely, and out of public view, without the input or awareness of citizens. Each woman who goes through divorce court tends to think her own experience, however painful or outrageous, is an isolated one, and she has no way of knowing otherwise. The environment that allows for abuses is so dominated by the foxes that the consumer who presses forward with her own complaint is doing far more than arguing the facts of her case. She is taking on the entire system. Consumers who attempt to draw public attention to the abuses in their own cases face the very real possibility of retribution from the court.

While numerical data on how lawyers treat women is lacking, plenty of evidence has been amassed that shows that the crisis for divorcing women is real and that indicates why women rather than men are disproportionately affected by divorce court abuse. We know, for example, that judicial discrimination against women is a major nationwide phenomenon. As of 1993, 38 states and the District of Columbia had gender bias task forces. Over 30 of these were appointed by the states' chief justices. These reports cumulatively show that judicial discrimination against divorcing women in all areas—custody, property rights, and alimony—is rampant. Although the state judiciaries recognize the prejudice against women, there is no overall indication that divorcing women are treated any better now than when the reports were written, or that judges have changed their attitudes. Lynn Hecht Schafran, the lawyer who is credited with having designed the studies, sounded doubtful in 1994, when she was asked if the system was making progress in addressing judicial discrimination against divorcing women. In 1996, Schafran sounded a little more optimistic: "I think there have been some changes but not enough—and every litigant is still subject to the vagaries of the judge before whom she finds herself." And as revealing as they are, these reports oddly do not raise the larger question of why judges are not held accountable when they violate their own laws.

The System Blocks Exposure

Of course, not all judges are unfair. There are some judges who feel tremendous compassion toward the women and children who are suffering from mistreatment by officials in our judicial system. But even judges can be blocked and suppressed from exposing perceived wrongs, because they are up against the same system too. Kentucky Court of Appeals Judge Michael O. McDonald, now retired, is a hero to some women's advocates. He was one of the judges who reviewed a 1992 decision by a lower trial court judge who ordered the placement of a seven-year-old boy into permanent custody with his father—a lawyer—whom the boy accused of sexually molesting him (and whose claims were backed up by medical reports that showed anal scarring). Judge McDonald said in a telephone interview that he was shocked at all the irregularities he saw in the way the lower court judge handled the case, and sought to overturn the decision. ". . . The deck was stacked against her [the mother]. In a pre-

257

vious finding the judge said she was not believable. Then why was he hearing the case? He had already made up his mind." Judge McDonald wrote the dissenting opinion in the case, showing that the lower court judge was biased, but McDonald said he could not get the other two judges to go along with him. And so the lower court judge's order stood. Judge McDonald said he was further stymied when the other two judges would not even let him publish his dissent, which was highly critical of the lower court judge's actions. "When you see this stuff firsthand it makes you sick," Judge McDonald noted, adding that this case only helped to increase his motivation to retire in 1995.

Despite local variations in divorce laws, accounts of abuse permeate all local judicial systems and nearly all states. There is a familiar theme of intimidation and coercion running through these accounts, regardless of the client's resources or how much the attorney has already made for him- or herself on the client's case. . . .

New Laws Add to Inequities

Ironically, new laws that promised women more economic equality in divorce were the springboard for calamities and abuses. The new no-fault, equitable distribution, and gender-neutral custody laws created in the 1970s had the reverse of their intended effect: the more "equality" women got, the less they received from the courts.[11] The inequities that were banished on paper were guaranteed to be continued through judicially prejudiced rulings. The new laws also opened the door to financial exploitation and mistreatment of women by their own lawyers and the judges. Lawyers' fees, for example—as opposed to the needs of the clients—became a very important factor in determining the outcomes of cases. . . .

I hope that by exposing the illegitimate, inhumane legal practices in divorce court, I will help people understand that this is not just a "women's issue." This [information] is also for men who just want divorces and don't want their wives and children to be deliberately harmed by the proceedings.

From a broader perspective, the mounting danger is to our democratic processes, in which large segments of our population are routinely discriminated against and deprived of their liberties and rights in high-stakes cases involving their children, home, and property.

Notes

1. "Family Disruption and Economic Hardship: The Short-Run Picture for Children," survey of Income & Program Participation, U.S. Bureau of the

Census, March 1991, P-70, No. 23. Greg J. Duncan and Saul D. Hoffman, "What are the Economic Consequences of Divorce?," *Demography* 25, no. 4 (Nov. 1988): 641. The 30 percent income drop cited for women is a conservative figure, and other respected researchers have found an even greater magnitude in the drop of income for divorced women. Arizona State University Professor Sanford Braver, for example, studied the psychological effects of economic hardship on mothers after divorce. Professor Braver found in a random-sample study that the mothers' income dropped 42 percent after separation and divorce. (See "Economic Hardship and Psychological Distress in Custodial Mothers" by Sanford Braver et al, *Journal of Divorce* 12[4], 1989, page 19.)

2. Philip Stern in his book *Lawyers on Trial*, published in 1980, described an American legal scene in which only the top strata of society could afford lawyer fees. His comment "justice is for sale" is still apt twenty-six years later.

3. "Fee-For-All: Savvy Lawyers Find Way to Make Millions: Win Pro Bono Cases" by Amy Stevens, *Wall Street Journal*, November 29, 1995, pages Al and A6.

4. A few states technically require itemized billing, but these rules are typically not enforced unless the client brings another suit in court.

5. A notable and recent exception to this practice is New York.

6. *The Wit and Wisdom of Abraham Lincoln: An A–Z Compendium of Quotes from the Most Eloquent of American Presidents*, edited by Alex Ayves, New York: Penguin, 1992, page 113.

7. Telephone interviews, February 12, 1994 and January 19, 1996. Schafran is head of the National Judicial Education Program to Promote Equality for Women and Men in the Courts. This ambitious national educational program for judges, started more than a decade ago, was designed to eliminate judicial bias against women.

8. 60 U.S. L.W. 4532 (June 15, 1992). While the court unanimously ruled that two children could bring a federal lawsuit against their father, the majority accepted the existence of a "domestic relations exception" and held that it only applies to cases involving divorce, alimony, or child custody. For more on this entire subject, see "'Naturally' Without Gender: Women, Jurisdiction, and the Federal Courts" by Judith Resnik. *New York University Law Review* 66(1682), December 1991.

9. Public Law 103-322, Sept. 13, 1994. 42 USC 13981.

10. Duchesne v. Sugarman 566 F2d 817 (2d Cir. 1977). Santosky v. Kramer 455 U.S. 745 (1982).

11. The unanticipated consequences of the new laws were first documented by Lenore Weitzman, a sociologist, whose 1985 book, *The Divorce Revolution*, studied the California matrimonial courts.

Excerpted from the Introduction to *Divorced from Justice* by Karen Winner. Copyright © 1996 by Karen Winner. Reprinted by permission of HarperCollins Publishers, Inc.

The Divorce Courts Are Biased Against Men

by Jeffery M. Leving with Kenneth A. Dachman

Jeffery M. Leving is a lawyer who specializes in fathers' rights. He speaks frequently about laws that affect men and their children. Kenneth A. Dachman is a doctor of psychology and author of numerous books. In the following viewpoint, Leving and Dachman argue that the courts routinely discriminate against men in divorce and custody cases despite prohibitions against gender bias. This discrimination, they contend, stems from ingrained and outdated ideas about men, women, and parenting. One such idea, the authors state, is the belief that femininity and parental ability are naturally intertwined. Another is that men are incapable of providing competent, attentive child care. Leving and Dachman contend that attitudes such as these pervade the family court system and directly influence rulings that favor women over men and harm relationships between fathers and their children.

"The pure, clear equity promised by family law statutes filters through a thick labyrinth of deep-seated and widely held prejudices."

The tender years doctrine was banished from domestic relations law long ago, but, as I see it, the notion that a mother is a child's "real" parent remains alive and kicking in this judge's mind. Most states now have laws specifically excluding even the suggestion that a parent's gender will be given any weight in custody, support, or access decisions. It doesn't seem to matter. The pure, clear equity promised by family law statutes filters through a thick labyrinth of deep-seated and widely held prejudices before delivery of real-life "justice" occurs. Often enough to trigger valid outrage, certain family court decisions plainly indicate that the influences of outdated cultural stereotypes and social presumptions can overwhelm reasonable and gender-neutral application of the law—and, in some cases, defy simple common sense.

A number of studies have found that although fathers are generally granted statutory equality by domestic relations law, they do not always receive fair treatment from family courts. Legislative inquiries in several states throughout the 1990s overwhelmingly support the conclusion of the Colorado Supreme Court Task Force on Gender Bias. This task force examined hundreds of family court rulings and found "a clear preference for the mother." In fact, the study team wrote, a mother had to be "nearly dysfunctional" not to win custody of her children.

The Mythological Maternal Instinct

The foundation of the pro-female bias that permeates too many domestic relations courtrooms is part myth, part social history. . . .

The belief that women are blessed with a "maternal instinct" is still widely held and rarely questioned—despite the fact that no scientist has ever been able to confirm its existence. A century of reverence for the traditional roles and trappings of motherhood have become embedded in our culture, continuing to influence judges, lawyers, and the general public long after women's roles in the family, and in society, have changed dramatically.

A brief return to a time when the tender years doctrine governed custody decisions provides disturbing but useful insights into the size and strength of the maternal preference.

Remember, the tender years presumption—a concept formally incorporated into family law in 1839—*required* that custody of young children be presumptively awarded to their mothers. Only a mother, the law stated, was capable of providing the nurturance and love children needed. The doctrine, although purged from most states' custody laws in the 1970s, lives on in the minds of many family court judges. But courts today must disguise their preference for mothers; they can't blatantly ignore the law's demand for gender equity. Current decisions are careful to cite some element of the child's best interests when a mother wins custody.

When adherence to the tender years doctrine *was* legal, judges freely expressed their respect and admiration for motherhood. A Wisconsin court declared that "nothing can be an adequate substitute for mother love . . . a nurture that only a mother can give because in her alone is service expressed in terms of love." In Washington State, a family court judge found "mother love" to be a "dominant trait in even the weakest of women, surpassing the paternal affection for the common offspring." The same judge suggested: "A child needs a mother's care much more than a father's." In Iowa, motherhood was described as "God's own institution for the rearing and upbringing of the child." A North Dakota court decided that no judiciary should ever "rend the most sacred ties of nature which bind a mother to her children."

Since most states have outlawed gender bias in custody cases, eloquent essays on the celestial nature of motherhood no longer clutter family court transcripts. That doesn't mean, however, that pro-female bias has been eliminated. . . .

The Pro-Female Bias Is Strong

In most jurisdictions across the United States, a predisposition favoring mothers in custody issues exists quietly, an integral element of business as usual. Raw numbers demonstrate the depth and breadth of the judicial prejudice facing fathers expecting equal treatment from family courts: Mothers win 85 percent of all custody disputes.

A strong pro-female bias is also evident in the courts' allocation of support obligations. A noncustodial father is almost always ordered to pay child support; judges rarely ask a noncustodial mother to contribute to the economic support of her children. A recent week in domestic relations court offers examples of this distorted principle in action.

On Tuesday of this sample week, a family court judge ordered a father to pay his former spouse child support in the amount of $1,200 a month—about half the father's income. Three days later, in the same courtroom, the same judge ruled that a noncustodial mother was not required to pay child support, even though she owned and operated a successful business.

Another clear indicator of the overpowering influence of gender discrimination in family court policies can be seen by examining the system's enforcement practices. Courts typically deal swiftly and harshly with fathers who violate orders and decrees. In many jurisdictions, a father who returns his child two hours late after visitation will often have his visitation rights suspended or revoked. And, of course, most family court judges deal swiftly and harshly with fathers who fail to meet their child support obligations. Wage garnishment, seizure of assets, criminal prosecution, and jail time are freely and frequently employed to enforce support orders.

A mother needing help to collect child support can rely on an extensive enforcement structure built and operated at taxpayer expense. On the other side of the aisle, a father seeking a court's help in protecting or preserving his parental rights too often spends a lot of money and a lot of time securing the judicial equivalent of a smile and a shrug. . . .

The Ultimate Old Wives' Tale

The ingrained presumption that femininity and parental ability are "naturally" intertwined is a hardy, durable myth, apparently immune to the forces of science, social reality, political pressure, and public opinion.

Numerous studies of single-parent households have reached similar conclusions: There is no correlation between gender and child-rearing competence. While several differences in parenting styles were noted by researchers, both mothers and fathers were found to be equally capable as caregivers. (Parental competence, in all the studies cited, was measured through comprehensive evaluation of children's behavior, attitudes, school performance, and social skills.)

The results of these academic investigations are validated every day, in homes all over the country. Mothers and fathers are sharing child-care duties, often not because they want to but mainly because that's the way it has to be. That reality leads us to the aspect of the bias evident in many family courts that fathers, their attorneys, and social scientists find most unbelievable: Many judges continue to decide children's fates based on narrow, sexist stereotypes. . . .

In most homes today, mothers and fathers share child-care duties and the daily labors necessary to operate a family (cooking, cleaning, shopping, feeding and bathing the kids, helping with homework, and so forth). With both parents working in so many modern families, child rearing often involves day care, baby-sitters, or an infinite array of creative scheduling choices. Both mothers and fathers have become, in the words of one pediatric psychologist, "executive parents"—more parental care managers than direct caregivers. In other words, families today are a lot like small businesses, with dads, moms, relatives, and hired help doing whatever must be done, with little regard for titles or status.

Over the past thirty years, women have made remarkable progress in areas of society that had been dominated by men for centuries. The women's movement was responsible for much of this advancement, and it was feminists who first pointed out that traditional gender roles were oppressive and demeaning to both men and women. Interestingly, only half of feminism's message has made a meaningful impression on our collective consciousness. Women are now viewed as being capable of success in the workplace. Men, however, are not yet seen as being capable of providing competent, attentive child care— at least not in the eyes of many family court judges.

In a recent *USA Today* poll, 88 percent of the eleven thousand Americans surveyed believed that mothers and fathers should share equally in all child-rearing activities. Because local judiciaries usually are in tune with prevailing public opinion, many political experts find the invincibility of the maternal presumption in family law to be remarkable. As one veteran analyst commented, "Walking into some of these courtrooms is like traveling back in time."

A Lack of Respect for Fatherhood

Years of experience and research have convinced me that to understand the gender bias condoned by many family courts, we must recognize the interaction of all elements of the phenomenon. An inappropriate reverence for a long extinct ideal of motherhood is certainly one important piece of the puzzle. The belief that fathers can't handle the rigors of child care is another. The conviction that children need a father's money much more than the father himself also plays a part. The final key might be the perception—widely held within the judiciary and shared by many "civilians"—that fathers don't really want, or need, parental rights or responsibilities.

Society's lack of respect for fatherhood and the inaccurate assumption that fathers are not truly interested in parenting combine to perpetuate a comfortable rationalization, a judicial delusion that plays out something like this: Mothers and children need each other. Fathers and children don't, or at least not as much. Accept that dubious premise and gender bias, although illegal and unfair, doesn't seem all that harmful. It's not like real bigotry. There's no violence, no blatant oppression. No one is lynching anyone; no flaming crosses are showing up on fathers' lawns. . . .

A Wider View of the Effects of Bias

There is no question that the intense suffering and toxic trauma inflicted on fathers and children by judicial bias and incompetence is serious, widespread, and shameful. For an evaluation of the cumulative, long-term consequences of family court failures, however, we must step away from the personal chaos for a moment. By broadening our perspective, we can see how our court system's inequities and deficiencies affect our society, and our nation's future.

No other country in the world has a higher divorce rate than the United States. Over the past decade, an average of one million divorces have occurred each year, involving 1.2 million children annually.

According to the Census Bureau, 18 million U.S. children now live in single-parent homes. Only 3.5 percent of these kids live with their dads. Unless my calculator is broken, that means we have 17.4 million children growing up fatherless.

Admittedly, in accordance with visitation agreements, some of these kids do see their fathers from time to time. . . . The average visitation order gives a father fifty days a year with his children. Because 20 percent of custodial mothers see no value in maintaining the father-child relationship, visitation interference is common. That fifty-day allotment quickly evaporates. Only one in six divorced fathers sees his children once a week or more. Almost 40 percent of children who live with their mothers haven't seen their fathers in at least a year. The bottom line is, fathers are vanishing from the social landscape, and, as the following facts compiled by the National Fatherhood Initiative demonstrate, father absence has dramatic and extremely serious effects on us all:

- Seventy-two percent of all teenaged murderers grew up without fathers.
- Sixty percent of rapists were raised in fatherless homes.
- Seventy percent of the kids now incarcerated in juvenile corrections facilities grew up in a single-parent environment.
- Fatherless children are twice as likely to drop out of school as their classmates who live with two parents.
- Fatherless children are eleven times more likely than are children from intact families to exhibit violent behavior.
- Children whose fathers are absent consistently score lower than the norm in reading and math tests.
- Three of four teen suicides occur in single-parent families.
- Children who live apart from their fathers experience more accidents and a higher rate of chronic asthma, headaches, and speech defects.
- Eighty percent of the adolescents in psychiatric hospitals come from fatherless homes.
- Compared to girls raised in homes where both parents are present, the daughters of single parents are 164 percent more likely to become pregnant before marriage, 53 percent more likely to marry as teenagers, and 92 percent more likely to dissolve their own marriages.
- A growing body of evidence establishes a high correlation between fatherlessness and violence among young men (especially violence against women).
- The absence of a biological father increases by 900 percent a daughter's vulnerability to rape and sexual abuse (often these assaults are committed by stepfathers or the boyfriends of custodial mothers).

A Destructive Trend

In the opinion of social critic David Blankenhorn, author of *Fatherless America*, "Fatherlessness is the most destructive trend of our generation." Vice President Al Gore concurred, declaring in a recent speech that "absent fathers are behind most social woes."

Knowledgeable social scientists have linked fatherlessness to a wide range of social nightmares and developmental deficiencies. Among these problems, judging by the results of numerous studies, are substantial increases in juvenile crime, drug and alcohol abuse, teenage pregnancy, promiscuity, truancy, and vandalism. Strong connections have also been established between a father's absence and a child's likelihood of becoming a dropout, jobless, a suicide victim, or a target of sexual abuse. A study of state prison populations found that only 41 percent of the inmates grew up with two parents. FBI statistics indicate that a missing father is a more reliable predictor of criminal activity than race, environment, or poverty.

U.S. News & World Report recently described the frightening reality faced daily by residents of fatherless city neighborhoods this way: "There are places in America where fathers—usually the best hope to socialize boys—are so rare that bedlam engulfs the community. Teachers, ministers, cops and other substitute authority figures fight losing battles in these places to present role models to pre-teen and teenage boys. The result is often an astonishing level of violence and incomprehensible incidents of brutality."

Two years ago, the National Center for Health Statistics reported that a child living with a divorced mother is almost twice as likely as a child living with both parents to repeat a grade of school, contract anemia, and suffer from intestinal distress, bed-wetting, and stuttering.

Several psychologists have documented the developmental difficulties endured by fatherless children. Low self-esteem, poor school performance, hyperactivity, lack of discipline, rejection of authority, depression, withdrawal, and several degrees of paranoia were among the disorders identified. As a group, these emotional and behavioral symptoms form what one researcher calls "the adolescent reactive adjustment syndrome." For years after childhood, hundreds of thousands of the fatherless continue to encounter educational, career, and relationship failures far more often than their peers from intact families.

The Economics of Father Absence

About half the fatherless families in the United States live below the poverty line. Children of these families are five times more likely to grow up poor than children who live with both parents. Children who are raised by a father and a mother usually climb higher on the socio-economic ladder than their parents did; fatherless children generally slip lower on the scale.

The evil monster responsible for this deplorable psychosocial devastation is, in the eyes of the public, the deadbeat dad. Hated by all good Americans, this selfish weasel is arrogantly avoiding his legal and moral obligations to his children. Slipping, sliding, dodging, and hiding, the villainous scoundrel thumbs his nose at the formidable enforcement arsenal aligned against him.

"Get tougher on the bastards," the public demands.

Harsh no-nonsense legislation becomes even more punitive. Local law-enforcement officials form special task forces. The hammer comes down.

The cumulative costs of our decade-long war on deadbeat dads are staggering; yet there has been no measurable reduction in child support delinquencies.

Why not?

For openers, more than half of the delinquent fathers are dead, or in prison, or disabled, or seriously ill, or unemployed. Of the delinquent dads who do have jobs, 52 percent earn less than $6,200 a year (not enough to support one person).

Spending taxpayer money and government manpower trying to force men to ante up cash they simply don't have is ludicrous. An infinitely more productive use of public resources would target fathers able to pay child support but unwilling to do so *because they have been excluded from the lives of their children.* Reconnecting these fathers with their kids would reduce our alleged "child support crisis" to a nonissue.

Census Bureau data indicate that more than 90 percent of fathers with joint custody pay child support on time and in full. So do 80 percent of fathers who are satisfied with their visitation arrangements. On the other side of the coin, so to speak, we find that over 50 percent of fathers whose involvement with their children is minimal or nonexistent do not meet their child support obligations. I think it's safe to say that a clear pattern of cause and effect is apparent here.

A father's refusal to live up to his child support responsibilities cannot be defended, condoned, or rationalized. In many cases, however, a father's emotions, and not his character, rule his actions.

Many estranged fathers believe that withholding of child support is the only weapon they have to counteract the banishment, visitation obstruction, harassment, and alienation suffered at the hands of former spouses. Unable to obtain relief for legitimate grievances from biased or uncaring family courts, these fathers, essentially, are trying to use support funds to buy parenting time. It's a desperate measure by desperate men.

Other noncustodial fathers, frustrated and defeated by vindictive ex-wives and a useless judicial system, simply drift away from their children, overwhelmed by intolerable feelings of anger, failure, hatred, and loss. They stop paying child support because their children, their children's mothers, and the courts have stripped them of fatherhood. They retaliate by refusing to acknowledge the obligations of fatherhood. It's illegal, and morally wrong, but as one fathers' rights advocate explained, "To a father denied the sight of his daughter's piano recital, or his son's jump shot at the buzzer, child support is the modern equivalent of taxation without representation."

Our legal system's definition of "support," it seems to me, must be expanded—to include the love, nurturance, discipline, guidance, and companionship a child needs from both parents. Financial support is only one contribution parents can make to a child's well-being, and, it turns out, the money is not nearly as important as we've been led to believe. In academics and in tests of social competence, children from low-income two-parent families consistently outperform kids from wealthy single-parent homes. A recent study of 273,000 children identified thirty requirements vital to a child's successful growth and development. Financial support didn't make the cut. Parental availability, approachability, communicativeness, and involvement were at the top of the list. Please note that all these qualities rely on frequent parent-child interaction. Apparently, the most valuable support a parent can provide isn't payable in cash. . . .

Change Is Slow

Change is coming slowly, but it is coming. The antiquated cultural myths that cling to the walls in many family courts won't fade away completely until the judiciary becomes younger or more closely attuned to modern family life. Meanwhile, fathers seeking equitable treatment must assume that the playing field is not yet completely level and act accordingly. . . .

Preserving fatherhood after divorce should not be such a challenge, but it is. Fathers must recognize that asserting their parental rights will require substantial reserves of self-control, patience, resolve, tenacity, and flexibility. Hardship, frustration, and stress must be endured because, as we've seen, the stakes are high. The lives, and futures, of millions of children are at risk, and so is the basic fabric of our society.

Excerpted from chapter 2 of *Fathers' Rights* by Jeffery M. Leving and Kenneth A. Dachman. Copyright © 1997 by Jeffery M. Leving and Kenneth A. Dachman. Reprinted by permission of BasicBooks, a division of HarperCollins Publishers, Inc.

CHAPTER 6

Does Society Discriminate Against the Elderly?

Chapter Preface

While traveling from Connecticut to New York City one day, author Ram Dass (Sanskrit for "servant of God"), a former Harvard University professor, was offered the choice of a "regular" or a half-fare "senior citizen" train ticket. He recalled:

> I realized then, "I am a senior citizen." I had never put those words together. I started feeling how society defines me as old. Being a senior citizen is not necessarily a bargain. Our society is so youth-oriented it treats older people as "less than."

Pat Moore took an extreme step to experience such treatment firsthand. Disguised as a poor eighty-five-year-old woman in New York City, the twenty-five-year-old encountered condescension, impatience, hostility, and was even brutally mugged. According to Moore, "Young people tend to focus on what they see as the disadvantages of being older, believing that above all else, to be old is to be ugly."

Ram Dass and authors such as Betty Friedan and Gail Sheehy, have worked to combat the perception of elderly persons as incompetent or obsolete "geezers." In the words of Friedan, "We have to break through that mystique of age as only decline and deterioration, as a problem for society."

Senior citizen advocates contend that negative images of the elderly pervade American society. Such images have poisoned the atmosphere in the workplace, they argue, where many older workers say age bias has cost them jobs. Likewise, many senior citizens view calls for age-based health care rationing as one more example of bias against America's elderly population.

Senior advocates argue that senior citizens are crucial for maintaining the strength of communities and civic life. Others worry that efforts to meet the demands of today's elderly population, especially in the area of medical and social entitlements, threaten the nation's ability to meet its commitments to later generations. Society's disparate views toward discriminatory inequities and the elderly are explored in this chapter.

Society Favors the Young at the Expense of the Elderly

by Nancy J. Osgood

Nancy J. Osgood is a professor of gerontology and sociology at Virginia Commonwealth University/Medical College of Richmond, Virginia. In the following viewpoint, Osgood argues that American society glorifies youthfulness while at the same time viewing the elderly as a burden. She contends that rampant ageism—prejudice against and stereotyping of the elderly—and an atmosphere of narcissism are to blame for these attitudes. As a result, Osgood states, older persons are scapegoated and are imbued with a sense of helplessness and powerlessness.

"In America today our core attitude about older people is that they are useless people whose lives are over."

On June 4, 1990, fifty-four-year-old Janet Adkins ended her life lying on a cot in the back of a Volkswagen van parked in a Michigan suburb. Aided by a retired pathologist, Dr. Jack Kevorkian, Adkins was hooked up to his homemade "suicide machine." She had a needle inserted in her arm, which first started saline flowing and, then, when she pressed the button on the macabre death machine, sent first a sedative and then deadly potassium chloride flowing into her veins.

An active woman with loving children and grandchildren, Adkins had flown two thousand miles from her Oregon home to Michigan to seek Kevorkian's assistance in ending her life when she was diagnosed with Alzheimer's disease. Adkins was an active member of the Hemlock Society, an organization that supports legalizing assisted suicide in America. She made a deliberate decision to end her life rather than face the mental decline associated with senile dementia.[1] Kevorkian, a long-time proponent of physician-assisted suicide, took that opportunity to use his suicide machine as a way of making a public statement to the medical community and the larger society that suicide is acceptable and that doctors should be willing to assist those who choose to die. . . .

Older Adults—Victims of Ageism and a Burden on Society

The fact that we have created a society that is so harsh to its old that ever-increasing numbers are choosing suicide as a solution to their problems is a sad commentary on America. To argue for the right to suicide and assisted suicide for older persons is a symbol of our devaluation of old age and our own ageism and fear of aging. This position endorses the belief that the answer to the problems of old age is suicide. Moreover, it may in fact be setting up conditions that rob older people of their right to live. Older people, living in a suicide-permissive society characterized by ageism, may come to see themselves as a burden on their families or on society and feel it is incumbent on them to take their own lives. Others may be pressured into suicide by uncaring or greedy family members. Those who need expensive medical technology to live may be denied help and die. The right to die then becomes not a right at all but rather an obligation. We may create a climate in which suicide is viewed as a rational choice. In a society that devalues old age and old people, in which older adults are seen as "expendable" and as an economic burden on younger members, older people may come to feel it is their social duty to kill themselves. As in more primitive societies in earlier historical periods, the old in America may be sacrificed for the good of the society.

The position that suicide and assisted suicide should be available for older people is not new, nor is it unique to America. Pliny the Elder considered the existence of poisonous herbs proof of a kindly providence because it allowed people to die painlessly and quickly and thus avoid the pain and sickness of old age. Zeno, the founder of Stoic philosophy, similarly advocated suicide to avoid the pain and sickness of late life; at age ninety-eight, when he fell down and pulled his toe out of joint, he hanged himself. Socrates, who drank hemlock at seventy, also cited old age as one reason for taking his own life. In primitive societies, it was conventional, and occasionally obligatory, for old people to commit suicide or to be assisted in dying if, because of infirmity, they had become a burden on their society. The ancient Scythians regarded suicide as the greatest honor when they became too old for the nomadic life. They had themselves buried alive as soon as age or sickness troubled them.[2]. . .

In America today our core attitude about older people is that they are useless people whose lives are over. In an attempt to discover what it is like to be old in America, a young industrial designer assumed the appearance and character of an eighty-five-year-old woman. In 1979 Pat Moore, author of the book *Disguised*, began a three-year journey into the world of the old in America.[3] With the help of a makeup artist, Moore learned to apply heavy prosthetic makeup to add decades to her twenty-six-year-old face. She bought jowls, crow's feet, under-eye bags, and extra neck skin. A white wig covered her hair. To complete the look, she wore a pair of heavy orthopedic shoes, used white gloves to hide her young hands, walked with a cane, wore a pair of spectacles to hide her youthful eyes, and stained and discolored her youthful white teeth with a special crayon. As she wandered disguised through city streets all over the United States, Moore was routinely ignored, treated rudely and crudely, and nearly beaten to death. Many people totally ignored her as if she did not exist. Others assumed she was hard of hearing and shouted at her or pushed in front of her to get on a bus or to get ahead in the grocery line. She was intentionally shortchanged when buying items at the store, an easy trick because one-dollar and ten-dollar bills look and feel the same to those with dimmed vision. Worst of all, some teenagers took pleasure in bashing her.

Moore's social experiment dramatically illustrates the ageism that exists in our society. Ageism, a term coined by Robert Butler in 1968,[4] is similar to racism and sexism. He defined ageism as "a deep and profound prejudice against the elderly and a systematic stereotyping of and discrimination against people because they are old."[5] In other words, ageism means "not wanting to have all those old people around." It results in a deep hatred of and aversion toward people who are old simply because they are old. Like racism and sexism, ageism is a form of prejudice and discrimination against one group in the society—in this case, the old.

Individualism

The ideological changes that occurred between 1780 and 1820, when the French and American Revolutions occurred, had a profound effect on the nature of age relations and the cultural value system in America. The emphasis on freedom and equality resulted in an individual achievement orientation, which has dominated our society for the last 170 years. It places a high value on activity, personal productivity through work, materialism, success, individual achievement, independence, and self-sufficiency. Older adults, who are no longer able to produce due to physical and mental changes or to social policies that remove them from gainful employment (such as retirement), are at a distinct disadvantage in a society dominated by such a value orientation. Demographics had a major impact on how we view and treat older people today. In 1810 the median age in America began to rise, resulting in larger numbers of people over age fifty in the population. Since the mid-1800s the number of older people in the U.S. population and the average life expectancy have increased greatly. As more people live longer, intergenerational competition for jobs and economic resources increases. Perceived economic scarcity is a factor in ageism.

Our ideas about age are inherited from the classical Greeks, who viewed aging as an unmitigated misfortune and terrible tragedy. The Greeks believed "those whom the gods love die young." Youth was the only period of life of true happiness. During the heroic age, manhood was measured by the standard of physical prowess. Old age robbed the person of such prowess and the ability to fight like a valiant warrior and robbed males of sexual powers. Early Greek and Roman writings were filled with images glorifying youth and beauty and denigrating old age, which was associated with the loss of youth and beauty. *Oedipus Rex*, written in the middle of the fifth century, depicted old age as a time of decline in physical and mental functioning. The image of the strong, young man also dominated Greek art and sculpture from the fifth through seventh centuries B.C. The love of youth is evident in the statues of young men and women of the Archaic period, the Parthenon frieze, and the well-known statue of the discus thrower that accentuates the strong, young, muscular physique of an athlete at the peak of his physical powers. Except in the Hellenistic period (323–27 B.C.), Greek sculptors never portrayed older figures.

America is also a country in which youth and beauty are highly valued. The glorification of youth and development of the youth cult in America began in the nineteenth century and grew rapidly in the twentieth, and it now flourishes in our present atmosphere of narcissism. Youth is associated with vitality, activity, and freshness. To be young is to be fully alive, exciting, attractive, healthy, and vigorous. Old age, on the other hand, is associated with decline, disease, disability, and death rather than wisdom, inner peace, and other positive qualities.

Ageism in Society

Psychological factors influence ageism in our culture. The youth cult grows out of a profound fear of growing old. Through the ages, few fears have cut as deeply into the human soul as the fear of aging. Americans especially have a stark terror of growing old. Old age is associated with loss of independence, physical disease, mental decline, loss of youthful vitality and beauty, and finally death, and old people are reminders of our own mortality. Because many people have limited contact with healthy, vibrant old people and lack accurate knowledge about the aging process, their fear escalates.

Ageism is manifested through stereotypes and myths about old people and aging. In medical circles older patients are stereotyped as "crocks" or "vegetables." Other common terms for older people are *old fuddy duddy*, *little old lady*, and *dirty old man*. Old people are thought of as being fit for little else but sitting idly in a rocking-chair. Older women are referred to as *old witch*, *old bag*, and *old biddy*. Old men are stereotyped as *old geezers*, *old goats*, and *old codgers*. Common stereotypes of aging view the old as out to pasture, over the hill, and all washed up.

In American culture, several mechanisms perpetuate and communicate ageist images, stereotypes, and myths: common aphorisms, literature, the media, and humor. Aphorisms about aging and older people permeate American culture. Some of the most common include: "You can't trust anyone over forty"; "You're only as old as you feel"; and "Age before beauty." These common sayings convey the idea that age is something to be denied or feared and allude to imagined losses accompanying the aging process.

The Western heritage in literature is replete with negative images of old age, beginning with medieval works. The foolish lust of older women is described in the works of Chaucer and Boccaccio. The physical ugliness and disgusting behavior of the old were frequently highlighted in fairy tales such as "Hansel and Gretel" and "Snow White," where old women are portrayed as wicked witches. The emptiness of old age is a major theme in American literature. In the poem "Gerontion," T.S. Eliot provides a description of the empty misery of an old man, "a dry brain in a dry season."[6] In his works Eliot describes old age as an empty wasteland.

In every culture humor conveys attitudes about the aged. In our own society these attitudes are expressed through jokes, cartoons, comic strips, and birthday cards. Predominant themes include the decline of physical appearance, lessening of sexual ability, decline in mental and physical abilities, loss of attractiveness, and denial of aging. The old become the brunt of many negative and cruel jokes.

The Effects of Ageism

Ageism has many negative effects on older people in America. As they come to see themselves as old, with all of the negative connotations surrounding the status of the old in American culture, many feel they are abnormal, deviant, or marginal members of the culture. As Pat Moore described the feeling in *Disguised*, they feel like an uninvited, unwelcome guest at the family reunion.[7] To use sociologist Erving Goffman's term, they feel they have a "spoiled identity."[8] As a result many disengage from participation in civic, social, and other groups and become isolated. Ageism contributes to a sense of helplessness and powerlessness among older adults. If they accept the negative stereotypes and myths about old people, they may come to see themselves in negative terms. They believe they can no longer effectively live life and influence people and their environment.

Ageism results in the use of older adults as scapegoats for all of the social, political, and economic problems of the day. Arguments go something like this: The reason the federal deficit is so large is that we pay too much money out in Medicare and Social Security payments to those aged sixty-five and older. The reason the health care industry is in such a mess is that sick old people are draining all the health care resources. By categorizing the old negatively, younger members of society can see the old as different, deviant, not quite as good as the young, and possibly even as less than human. Ageism makes it easier for society to ignore the old and to shirk its economic and social responsibility to older citizens. Ageism blinds us to the many problems older men and women face and keeps older people from receiving the social, economic, and spiritual services they need and deserve. It facilitates control of younger people in power over older people by rationalizing their subordination, exploitation, and devalued status. By labeling the old as different or abnormal, it is easier for other members of the society to deny older citizens access to health care and societal resources and thus retain for the young power, status, wealth, and authority.

Euthanasia and Suicide

In a book chapter entitled "Rational Suicide Among the Elderly," Derek Humphry contends that old age is "sufficient cause to give up" even without unbearable suffering.[9] He sees suicide as a "preemptive alternative to growing old."[10] Mary Barrington, past president of the London-based Voluntary Euthanasia Society, in her "Apologia for Suicide" argues that a disabled older individual in poor health and in need of constant care and attention may feel a burden to the younger person(s) who must provide that care.[11] This situation may be such that the young person is in "bondage" whether willingly or unwillingly. The older person may want to "release" the young person but has no real choice but to continue to live on. There is a strong implication in her writing that the older person who is a burden to the younger people should (has an obligation to) release younger family members from the burden of caring for her by opting for suicide. Stating the same position in even stronger terms, Dr. Glanville Williams argues for the elimination of "the senile" elderly.[12] He writes:

> A decision concerning the senile may have to be taken within the next twenty years. The number of old people are [sic] increasing by leaps and bounds. Pneumonia, 'the old man's friend,' is now checked by antibiotics. The effects of hardship, exposure, starvation and accident are now minimized. Where is this leading us? . . . What of the drooling, helpless, disoriented old man or the doubly incontinent old woman lying log-like in bed? Is it here that the real need for euthanasia exists?[13]

. . . As the aging population continues to expand rapidly and we as a nation continue to spend more dollars on health care costs and advanced medical technology, which are disproportionately utilized by older persons, the need for budget cutting, health care rationing, and redistribution of health and other resources becomes more pressing. Older adults are viewed as an emotional and financial burden to be borne by the younger members of society. Cries for rational suicide, the right to die, and legalized assisted suicide grow louder. It seems easier to eliminate the problem of too many expensive old people to care for, or to encourage the problem to eliminate itself through sanctions encouraging suicide, rather than to face hard moral choices about our financial spending as individuals and as a society and our appropriate obligations to our older members, who have created and improved the society we now live in.

Notes

1. Lisa Belkin, *Doctor Tells of First Death Using His Suicide Device*, N.Y. Times, June 6, 1990, at A1.
2. ALFRED ALVAREZ, THE SAVAGE GOD: THE STUDY OF SUICIDE 53–54 (1972).
3. PAT MOORE, DISGUISED (1979).
4. ROBERT N. BUTLER, WHY SURVIVE? GROWING OLD IN AMERICA 14 (1968).
5. *Id.*
6. T.S. Eliot, *Gerontion, in* A CASEBOOK ON GERONTION 3 (E. San Juan, Jr. ed., 1970).

7. MOORE, *supra* note 13, at 39.
8. ERVING GOFFMAN, ASYLUMS 355 (1963).
9. Derek Humphry, *Rational Suicide Among the Elderly, in* SUICIDE AND THE OLDER ADULT 125 (Antoon A. Leenaars et al. eds., 1992).
10. *Id.*
11. Mary Barrington, *Apologia for Suicide, in* EUTHANASIA AND THE RIGHT TO DIE 152 (A.B. Downing ed., 1969).
12. GLANVILLE WILLIAMS, THE SANCTITY OF LIFE AND THE CRIMINAL LAW (1957).
13. *Id.* at 112.

Excerpted from "Assisted Suicide and Older People—a Deadly Combination: Ethical Problems in Permitting Assisted Suicide" by Nancy J. Osgood. Reprinted by permission of the publisher and author from *Issues in Law and Medicine*, vol. 10, no. 4, Spring 1995. Copyright © 1995 by the National Legal Center for the Medically Dependent & Disabled, Inc. (Original footnotes have been renumbered and set as endnotes.)

Society Favors the Elderly at the Expense of the Young

by Rob Nelson and Jon Cowan

Rob Nelson and Jon Cowan are cofounders of *Lead . . . or Leave*, a non-partisan organization aimed at increasing the political clout of Americans born after 1960, commonly referred to as Generations X and Y. In the following viewpoint, Nelson and Cowan contend that American public policy pits seniors against struggling young families and young singles. To this point in time, the authors argue, economic and political policy decisions have generally favored the elderly and soon-to-be elderly in the areas of health care, entitlements, tax breaks and tax cuts, and spending priorities. The authors predict intergenerational warfare between younger Americans, particularly those in their twenties and thirties, and older Americans if public policy continues in this direction.

"If elderly boomers want the same kinds of benefits as today's seniors . . . that means higher and higher taxes on our generation and the generations that follow us."

January 1, 2011. Mark it down on your calendar. It will be the turning point, a watershed for America. Either we will have prepared ourselves for this moment, or we will have ignored the warning signs and moved toward a generational schism.

It's the year when the first of the baby boomers begin retiring, turning 65, all 56 million of them. From Woodstock to nursing homes. From LSD to CAT scans.

Advances in medical technology will help them to live healthier and longer, but will also place an unbearable strain on our economy and social welfare systems.

279

As they retire, as they begin their massive migration to second homes in Florida, condominiums in Vail, and modest retirement communities across America, a half-century of economic infrastructure could come tumbling down on the heads of the generation that follows.

If it collapses, the thunderclap will echo across the trading floors of the world's financial centers, through the sacred institutions of political power in America, and into the homes of millions of unsuspecting baby busters. The shock wave could blast people from their homes, rapidly plummet millions into poverty, and threaten the economic security and financial stability of our entire nation.

Those born after 1960 will face an ugly choice:

Surrender their future to the generation that preceded them—or fight for their lives.

A Clash Between the Generations

A quiet crisis is brewing today in America.

It gets little notice in the media and is rarely discussed around the dinner table, but it will radically change all of our lives. That crisis is the baby boomers' retirement early next century.

For as the baby boomers (Americans born in the post–World War II boom between 1946 and 1960) age, their economic interests will directly clash with those of our generation and the generation behind us— their kids and grandkids.

As they grow gray, boomers will step right into the shoes of today's seniors, demanding more and more attention be paid to the largest conglomeration of elders America has ever seen: over 50 million highly organized boomer seniors demanding extensive health care and retirement services from the government.

If elderly boomers want the same kinds of benefits as today's seniors (and most likely they will), that means higher and higher taxes on our generation and the generations that follow us.

And if today's politics are any indication, the boomers will have more than enough political power to win what they want—whatever the cost to those who come behind them.

With over 34 million members, the American Association of Retired Persons is already considered the most powerful lobby in the country— able to scare politicians of both parties into supporting virtually any policy it wants. The boomers' retirement will nearly double that power.

In addition, retired boomers will be better educated than today's seniors (the number of senior citizens with high school diplomas will double by 2020), which has historically meant a higher voting rate. They will be more affluent as well.

As a group of demographic experts warns in *Lifetrends*, the baby boomers, in an effort to get age-related benefits from the government, could "come on like a political juggernaut in the twenty-first century, ramming their pet programs through . . . Congress."

The problem: Who will pay for them?

The Source of a Generational Schism

Strapped by a $6 trillion (or much larger) debt and an ever-widening social gap, Washington will not be able to continue borrowing to finance the boomer retirement without dramatically raising our taxes.

The U.S. Office of Management and Budget found that by the end of fiscal year 1991, the baby boomers had been promised $14 trillion more in federal benefits than they contributed in payroll taxes.

That's where the generational conflict will occur: Seniors expecting their benefit checks will be pitted against young families and struggling workers who will already be paying steep taxes and who won't want to pay more.

Everyone will be deserving—but only some of us will be able to get a bigger slice of a rapidly shrinking pie. So Washington will have to make a harsh choice:

- Sharply boost taxes for everyone under age 65 (the Social Security Administration projects that the cost of Social Security and Medicare could rise to between 38 and 53 percent of payroll in 2040);

- Slash spending on all other government programs to keep pumping money to seniors; or

- Cut benefits to baby boomers who've been paying into Social Security since their early 20s and are counting on their U.S. government retirement check.

In simplest terms, it comes down to this: Our generation, and to a larger extent the younger generations behind us, will be forced to take another blow to our already declining living standards or cut off a deserving but unaffordable senior population. We will in effect have to choose between providing for our parents or our kids.

Heading Toward a Conflict

No one wants to face this kind of intergenerational tension. It runs completely against the grain of family ties and social responsibility. As activists, neither of us has ever advocated starting a generational political war, and we have argued against those who do.

But unless America dramatically shifts our budget priorities over the next 10 to 15 years to create new policies that are fair to all generations, we will confront an unprecedented budget battle between the baby boomers and everyone born after 1960.

The signs pointing to such a battle are numerical, not rhetorical; they grow out of the economic and social trends. . . . They are based on reliable demographic and economic forecasts, not on radical projections.

Three main trends drive us toward a generational conflict:

- As the baby boomers reach age 65, America will have the largest senior (and retirement) population in its history;

- At the same time, the ratio of workers supporting those retirees will be shrinking, with record numbers of illiterate and poorly trained adults inflicting a drag on the economy;

- As the financial costs of caring for the elderly spiral out of control, we will be forced to cut or shut down senior programs like Social Security and Medicare (as well as many other government services that benefit Americans of all ages), or else raise taxes dramatically.

The genesis of potential generational conflict is that simple. As Wall Street banker Pete Peterson says, "When [our kids] understand the size of the bad check we are passing them, they could, amid ugly generational conflict, simply decide not to honor it at all."

If pushed to the edge economically, younger Americans, particularly people in their 20s and early 30s, would be the principal activists in this battle, taking to the streets and ballot boxes to demand immediate redress of their equity grievances. And the highly organized senior lobbies would hit back twice as hard.

Whether the youth of the 21st century will succeed in mobilizing enough political support to maintain generational equity is uncertain. But an economic battle between generations would be dangerously disruptive to America's social order and its economic stability. . . .

Let's take a closer look at the three trends that are leading America toward intergenerational chaos.

Rising Senior Population

Around 2010, tens of millions of baby boomers will be stepping off the employment treadmill and into their retirement slippers. Once in retirement, they will make up the largest block of elderly that America has ever seen—roughly 20 percent of our nation's population by the year 2030.

To put that in perspective, in 1950, 8 percent of the population was made up of senior citizens. Today the number is 13 percent. California has a projected 69 percent increase in elderly population by 2010—and that's *before* the baby boom retirement.

The number of people over 85 (who are four times more likely than younger seniors to require expensive long-term care) is going to triple or quadruple by 2030. Never before will America have aged so rapidly, and with such startling implications for our national budget and economic priorities.

Fewer Workers

If the only issue were the skyrocketing number of seniors, perhaps we'd be able to survive their massive retirement. But the ratio of workers to retirees is shrinking rapidly—and that's where the trouble lies.

Between 2010 and 2025, the number of working-age Americans (people 15–65) will increase by only 4.5 percent—or 9 million—while the elderly population (people 65 and over) is expected to grow by 22 million, a 55 percent increase. In the bigger picture, over the next 50 years America's elderly population will grow by 135 percent while our working-age population will grow by only 35 percent.

In 1900, workers outnumbered the elderly by a margin of 15 to 1, so there were more than enough workers whether families were supporting seniors at home, or whether the government was providing a benefit check.

By 1980, however, the margin had shrunk to just under six workers for every retiree. By 2010 it will be down to five to one; and by 2030, there will be only three workers for every senior, hardly a ratio that is sustainable over the long run.

An Explosion in Federal Benefit Programs

In 1966, at the height of the Great Society, President Lyndon Johnson strong-armed Congress into passing a new tax on workers.

The tax was intended to finance a new health care program for the elderly called Medicare. Medicare was one of a series of government programs—like Social Security, farm aid, veterans' pensions—that were intended to provide a social safety net, lifting millions of Americans out of poverty.

These programs, called entitlements, now account for the fastest-growing portion of the federal budget. And unlike other items on the federal budget, entitlements aren't funded by annual government allocations. If you qualify, you get them. It's automatic. . . .

According to the Urban Institute, almost all retirees since 1940, whatever their income or family status, have received (or will receive) more than they paid into Social Security.

Why? Because politicians swayed by powerful lobbies keep handing out more benefits than we can afford—and sticking the tab on their Congressional Express charge card (to be paid off down the line by all of us and our kids, tomorrow's workers). . . .

The Social Security and Medicare boards of trustees have already warned that the Medicare trust fund will go bankrupt within the decade, or earlier. At that point, the government will have to raise our taxes dramatically to cover the benefit demand—or stop paying benefits to retirees.

We can close our eyes to the problem, or we can attempt to deal with it today, in a way that is fair to all generations and that protects those most in need of the government's helping hand. The costs of avoidance are frighteningly high for all of us.

The Coming Generational Backlash

If America does not begin to plan for demographic shifts ahead, a backlash against the elderly might be unavoidable, where reasonable but difficult demands for change from younger workers could mean moving retired boomers closer to the edges of poverty.

Flashpoints in a boomer-buster conflict might include

- rationing of health care to the elderly;

- shutting off the entitlement spigot, even to the poor;

- eliminating all tax breaks that benefit older Americans;

- shifting unprecedented amounts of federal funding into schools and training and away from all senior programs; and

- massive political pressure for a steep payroll-tax cut.

Before we're driven to this point, we need to take strict measures now. Health care rationing, for example, sounds draconian from today's vantage point, but it will be inevitable tomorrow without a dramatic restructuring of our economic priorities.

According to the Congressional Budget Office, health care costs will account for 18 percent of the U.S. economy by the year 2000, three times as much as in 1960.

With the very old as the fastest-growing segment of the country, experts estimate that a new 220-bed nursing home will have to open every day between 1987 and the year 2000 just to keep even with the demand—and this is long before the arrival of the baby boomers.

The cost of helping to defray the health care expenses of the growing retiree population will soon be enough to bankrupt many companies.

How will a company like the Bethlehem Steel Corporation—which has 21,000 working employees and 70,000 retirees—get by?

Instead of paying the higher taxes needed to finance the retirement health care of the baby boomers, younger workers would be forced to either form their own health care cooperatives (excluding seniors) or push the government to ration health care based on life expectancy.

Given the burst in the number of elderly, and the rising costs of their care, we must all face one tough question: Unless current trends are reversed, will we be able to take care of all our elderly—and still have the resources to defend America, invest in our children and our companies, and provide a reasonable living standard for coming generations?

Unless our economy grows at a record-setting pace, the answer must be *no*. Because of the confluence of the three trends we looked at in the first part of the [viewpoint], the benefit package for America's seniors could eat up as much as 63 percent of the total federal budget by 2025.

Add in interest on the debt and national security, and that kind of spending doesn't leave much for anyone else.

From "The Baby Boom Backlash," in *Revolution X* by Rob Nelson and Jon Cowan. Copyright © 1994 by Rob Nelson and Jon Cowan. Used by permission of Viking Penguin, a division of Penguin Books USA, Inc.

Age-Based Health Care Rationing Demonstrates Respect for the Elderly

by Daniel Callahan

Daniel Callahan is president of the Hastings Center, a nonpartisan research organization that examines ethical issues in medicine and the life sciences. His other books include *Setting Limits: Medical Goals in an Aging Society*. In the following viewpoint, Callahan contends that old age has been robbed of its meaning and social significance by medical efforts to prolong life. Those efforts, he argues, treat aging as something to be overcome rather than as a natural part of the life cycle. In his view, the latter would allow society to consider the forms and amount of health care most appropriate for different stages of life while at the same time restoring dignity to the aging process.

"To treat aging as if it is tantamount to a disease to be overcome is to open the way to an unlimited and insupportable claim on health care resources."

Aging poses a peculiar puzzle for medicine. As a biological reality, aging is an inherent part of organic life, affecting humans no less than animals, plants, and microorganisms. It is in that sense beyond the realm of medicine, a permanent backdrop to all of life. But aging is also ordinarily accompanied by disease, bodily decline, and disability. It is thus well within the realm of medicine, whose historical mission has been the cure of disease and the relief of pain, each much desired by those who grow old.

Yet is it necessarily true that aging as an inherent part of life is "beyond the realm of medicine"? If genetic engineering, or other scientific advances, could fundamentally change the phenomenon of aging—extending life significantly, for instance, to forestall the sicknesses of age—would it not then come within the traditional sphere of medicine? Why should medicine not attempt to manipulate the biology of aging rather than, as it now does, only the deadly and unpleasant clinical and psychological manifestations of that biological process? Should we go so far as to make the moral judgment that aging is in and of itself humanly unacceptable, a worthy candidate for scientific intervention, and even for eradication if we are clever enough?

Acceptance of Aging

There is, to be sure, a classical compromise response to these questions, first mentioned by the French philosopher Condorcet two hundred years ago and pursued most recently by Dr. James Fries: accept aging as a biological given but work medically to reduce the illness and disability associated with it. That heuristic ideal, the "compression of morbidity," seems the perfect answer; and it might be, in the best of all possible worlds. Unhappily, nature has not nicely played its assigned part, and so far, there is little evidence that any such thing is happening to any significant degree.

It has been little noted, moreover, that for the compression of morbidity to actually work, we would also have to forswear intensive medical intervention at the end of life. Yet might it not happen that many of those who lived so nicely and well until eighty-five would be unwilling to let go—just *because* they had lived so well—thereby setting the stage for a resumption of the now familiar technological battle against death? Another possibility presents itself also: if we do not achieve a compression of morbidity and lengthening life spans bring instead an increased burden of illness and disability, will we not then feel compelled to intervene more decisively in the biology of aging to combat that trend? Put another way, could it already be the case that we have come so far along the road in the extension of life, and so far along the road in the accumulation of the chronic and degenerative diseases of aging, that only some radical science can save us?

I want to suggest with these troubling questions just how difficult it will be to come up with good answers, but also just how portentous any set of answers is likely to be. At the least, with a growing proportion and number of elderly in every society, there is a critical policy issue at stake. To treat aging *as if* it is tantamount to a disease to be overcome is to open the way to an unlimited and insupportable claim on health care resources. If the diseases associated with aging bring about pain and suffering, as they do, then this is the basis for a time-honored claim to throw at them the same kind of research and resources as we throw at them at other stages of life. There are many who make exactly that claim, in the name of equality and age-blind social policy. If, in contrast, we want to pursue the idea of building policy on the basis of some kind of reasonable natural or cultural limits to such unlimited claims, we are open to the charge of ageism and to that of turning our back on medical advances that could improve the life of the elderly.

The Relationship Between Medicine and Aging

There is no easy way out of these dilemmas of policy, but it might help if we can sensibly frame the right questions to pursue about two principal ingredients of the dilemma: the nature of medicine as a practice and an institution, and of aging as a problem of biology and human meaning. Let me propose two broad questions we might begin with, each bearing on the other:

What understanding of the nature and goals of medicine is most likely to be helpful to the aging and aged in the future?

What understanding of the meaning of old age is most likely to foster the most helpful kind of medicine?

Of course what I mean to suggest by these two questions taken together is that there is, and must be, a reciprocal relationship between medicine and aging. On the one hand, the biological and technological possibilities of altering the aging process will shape our ideas and expectations about aging. On the other hand, what we want aging to be will help shape the research and clinical agendas of medicine. We cannot, in short, any longer think about human aging purely as an independent biological phenomenon (though on occasion it is worth trying to do just that). Human aging is, we now know, plastic to some as yet unknown degree and open to scientific change. We no less know that cultural attitudes and practices affecting our conceptions of the social and individual meaning of aging are open to change as well.

Aging is as good a place as any to observe the social consequences of medical progress, most notably the historical move from palliation to cure as a principal goal of medicine; and then from a narrow definition of health, focused on the body, to a broad definition, centering on the entire well-being of people; and from there to a static, nature-bound picture of the possibilities of living a life to a more open, wish-driven picture where nothing seems utterly impossible. What that process shows is not just medicine changing but, simultaneously, the culture with which it interacts. In the case of our culture, medicine is drawn to the promotion of autonomy and scientific innovation, the fashioning of an old age of one's choosing with whatever technology lies at hand, not bound by previous biological or historical models. The ideology of the anti-ageism campaign of recent decades is in part deeply rooted in individualism, celebrating the diversity and heterogeneity of the old—not what they share, the fact that they are at the end, not the beginning, of their lives. . . .

I want to suggest another cut at the issues. . . . Two different models of the goals of medicine and the response to aging can be discerned, not formally articulated perhaps but nonetheless implicit in some familiar ways of discussing the problem. I will call one of these models progressive incrementalism and the other life cycle traditionalism.

Progressive Incrementalism

By the term "progressive incrementalism" I mean an approach to aging that is dedicated to unlimited progress in the long run but cultivates small, incremental steps in the short run. Average life expectancy can be increased to an unknown extent, but for the time being it is sufficient to add additional years slowly. And if a full compression of morbidity is not yet on the horizon, there is no reason we can't do something about osteoporosis, Alzheimer's disease, and arthritis in the reasonably near future. More generally, progressive incrementalism is sustained by the belief that medicine has no final inherent teleological goal for the elderly and that it can and ought to go as far as we want it to go. There are no intrinsic biological limits—or at least we will not know them unless we keep pushing the present limits, which always seem to give way—and there are no necessary moral limits, assuming we use ordinary common sense and sociomedical prudence along the way. There is no reason we should not seek both to extend average life expectancy indefinitely and to aim for a compression of morbidity along the way.

There is a social dimension to this incrementalism. It is, first of all, thought dangerous to think of the elderly in the aggregate as a discrete group or to think of individual elderly in general terms. Here the individualism of anti-ageism comes to the fore, arguing that for policy purposes age is no more relevant than height, eye color, or ethnicity. Just as medicine should have unlimited horizons in treating the elderly, so our culture should focus on the possibilities of individual development in the elderly, shorn of stereotypes or fixed boundaries. We need not worry about intergenerational strife because we will all pass through each stage of life: the sensible young will not see themselves in competition with the needy old but will see in the old their own future lives.

Progressive incrementalism, in short, combines a view of medicine and its possibilities with a view of aging and its possibilities. They work together, each stimulating the other: medical progress provokes new visions of what old age could be, and what people hope for from old age is an impetus to medicine to provide it.

Life Cycle Traditionalism

An alternative view I call life cycle traditionalism. It is traditional in that it does not entertain unlimited progress as a goal of medicine or a goal of aging. It is based on the biological rhythm of the life cycle as a way of providing a biological boundary to medical aspiration. This view looks to find a decent harmony between the present biological reality of the life cycle as an important characteristic of all living organisms—even if the length of that cycle varies—and the feasible, affordable goals of medicine. This view need not deny that considerable future progress in longevity is possible. What it does deny is that such progress will be of great human benefit, even if it may satisfy the wishes of some individuals. Neither does it deny the value of aiming for a compression of morbidity, even though it holds that there is nothing in nature, or the evidence to date, to suggest that compression will easily be obtained. It would, however, point out that if longevity and a compression of morbidity are sought simultaneously, the outcomes of the former may continually undermine the achievement of the latter.

The goals of medicine that lie behind life cycle traditionalism are to help people remain in good health within the boundaries of a finite life span and to help them cope well with the poor health they may have. It is thus a more modest view of medicine's appropriate goals, aiming to restore and maintain health rather than substantially improve the human condition. At the same time, it does not treat aging as a disaster to be overcome but a condition to be alleviated and ameliorated. Even though individual elderly people will differ in their physical and mental condition, they share the common trait of being elderly, that is, proportionately much closer to the end of their life cycle than to its beginning or middle; and as a consequence they are more subject to illness and death than younger people. Old age combines a biological stage in life and a social status in society, and it is not inappropriate that they be understood as intertwined. The same is true of every other age-group.

For policy purposes, the group characteristics of the elderly are as important as their individual variations. Those characteristics legitimate age-based entitlement and welfare programs as well as social policies designed

290

to help the elderly maintain social respect. They could also be used to sanction a limit to those entitlements in the face of resource scarcity. The campaign against stereotyping the old as demented, frail, and burdensome is legitimate and needed. But there is a difference between a stereotype and a valid policy generalization. All elderly are not demented or frail. Yet it is a valid generalization to say that the elderly are a greater risk for dementia and frailty than young people—and thus to devise special policies to help the elderly, based on those generalizations.

Setting a Course for the Future

The two contrasting models I have offered differ both in their interpretation of the proper goal of medicine and in the meaning of old age. Progressive incrementalism has soaked up the optimism and ambition of modern science, its sense of wonder and hope in the face of a sometimes hostile nature. The nature that brings human beings down at the end of their lives can be changed. For its part, the meaning of old age is no less malleable, and medical progress can, together with enlightened social policy, change that meaning. Progressive incrementalism is of course the dominant ethos in scientific medicine more generally and not limited to the elderly. It implies an effort to overcome all biological barriers, from the beginning of life to its end; and it has no general goal, simply that of moving as far as is possible, wherever "far" might take us. Yet it is precisely this feature of progressive incrementalism that makes it so corrosive of meaning, so unable to offer a set of medical goals that will help make more sense of the place of aging in human life. It leaves that search for meaning up to individuals but manages nicely to simultaneously undercut that search by holding out a wide-open frontier of transformed aging, asking us, in effect, not to settle for aging as we know it—even while the aging we do know offers no radical transformation, only perhaps now a delay in the onset of the worst feature of growing old until a little later in the life cycle.

Life cycle traditionalism is skeptical of that pattern, noting in particular the difficulty that science is actually having in sundering the connection between getting old and getting sick, in overcoming the sheer stubbornness of those chronic and degenerative conditions that mark our modernized old age; and it sees no special reason to indulge the dream of a transformed old age. It notes as well a certain perversity about the progress we have actually witnessed: there has not been a heightened or rejuvenated appreciation of the social role of the elderly because of their longer lives and larger number. Instead, because of a pervasive ambivalence about whether old age is to be fought, rejected, and resisted, or graciously accepted and embraced, old age has been robbed of any substantive meaning it might have once had as an honored stage in an inevitable life cycle. Apart from ideological commitments, no one really knows now what to make of old age.

Age Is a Pertinent Social Category

My own bias is that the life cycle perspective remains the most promising way of making medical and human sense of our aging. That perspective has three distinct assets. The first is that it remains the most compatible medically with the results to date of efforts to overcome the disabilities of old age, still more hope than reality. While much enthusiasm has been invested in the dream of a compression of morbidity prior to death, the evidence of movement in that direction is scanty indeed. So far, the longer life that is the fruit of the great gain in longevity over the past century has shown an increased, not decreased, burden of sickness and disability; those over eighty-five are particularly burdened (even if many do quite well). A life cycle perspective assumes, or should reasonably assume, that old age will see a physical decline prior to death and that up to 50 percent of those over eighty-five will likely suffer some degree of dementia. There is as yet no good reason to assume this general situation can soon, if ever, be overcome; and a life cycle perspective is useful in countering the endemic optimism of progressive incrementalism.

The second asset of life cycle incrementalism is that it offers a better framework than progressive incrementalism for individuals to come to terms with their aging, not holding out the expectation that the vigor of youth or healthy middle age will be indefinitely sustained—and thus not engaging in that most subtle but devastating disparagement of old age that the scientific fantasies inevitably feed, seeing it as nothing more than a condition to be overcome. While the campaign against ageism has been necessary and important, it has had, I believe, an untoward, unexpected consequence. By its stress on the individuality and heterogeneity of the elderly, it seems to have sought to make light of the fact that the old, however much they may differ from each other, are still old, that is, closer to the end of their life than to the beginning. Progressive incrementalism nurtures the ambition to pacify aging, to break the hold of the life cycle. An important, harmful consequence of the hope thus engendered is to create a profound uncertainty about whether aging is to be gracefully accepted or vigorously fought. Life cycle traditionalism pushes us toward acceptance; and acceptance makes the inevitability of aging more tolerable than that of a fight which must end in defeat.

The third asset of the life cycle perspective is that it enhances the possibility of devising an equitable health care policy—by recognizing the relevance of age as a pertinent social category, by resisting the notion that the diseases of aging are just one more biological accident to be conquered with better medicine, and by accepting the possibility that an excessive individualism in thinking about the elderly could run roughshod over the needs of the young. Progressive incrementalism, by contrast, has shown itself unwilling to see age as policy-relevant; it has altogether resisted that way of thinking about health policy and the equitable allocation of resources. But life cycle traditionalism accepts aging as a permanent human reality and sees no reason why that fact should not have a place in thinking about resource allocation. It helps set the stage for trying to discover the forms and amount of health care most appropriate at different stages of life, working from there to devise an equitable, age-relevant policy.

Confusion and Aimlessness

These three assets of the life cycle approach help us to better understand as well what appropriate goals medicine should have in caring for the elderly. The goal of medicine in the face of biological aging should be, above all, the targeting of those physical and mental conditions that tend to rob old age of human meaning and social significance. Medicine cannot create that meaning, which must come from individual reflection and social policy and practices. But it can enhance the background physical and mental conditions necessary to make that task a little easier. Yet it can only do so if it strenuously resists that most powerful of all medical temptations, that of seeing a direct and invariable correlation between medical progress and human happiness, of conflating the quest for meaning and the quest for health. They do not go hand in hand.

Yet, having expressed my own bias, I confess that I do not believe there is a decisive argument to be made for either the incrementalist or the traditionalist approach. The former appeals to our modern love of progress and open possibilities, while the latter can appeal to a sense of human finitude and a certain skepticism that the solution to aging as a human phenomenon of body and spirit lies in scientific advancement. This is a long-standing struggle, which would not have lasted so long were there not strength in both perspectives. Moreover, if it is reasonable to believe that there will always be a dialectical relationship between the medical possibilities of changing and manipulating the process of aging and our social ideals about old age, then there is little reason to expect that either will, or could, remain static: one or the other will change, thus shifting the equation over time.

Can there, then, be a long-term solution to the problem of human aging, or are we fated to have time-bound solutions, reflecting the medical knowledge of the scientific moment and the social ideals (and ideas) of the historical moment? Our solutions will have to be time-bound, but that does not mean we cannot have some permanent values that will help us better make sense of and manage the inevitable medical and social shifts that will occur. Three such values seem imperative and realizable. The first is that of intergenerational reciprocity, the mutual obligation of the young and old toward the welfare of each other. The second is that of the centrality of the problem of meaning to devising our ideals of old age, that of meaning as a value and a social aspiration. These two values—reciprocity and meaning—are long-standing and familiar, even if the subject of debate. The third value I would propose is less familiar: the value of moderate and modest and reasonably clear medical goals for the care of the elderly. The present situation, where there no longer seem to be such goals, at least at the research level, offers simply confusion and aimlessness, a progressive incrementalism that is going somewhere, but no one can say where. Life cycle traditionalism, for all of its problems, does offer a direction, one that is not beguiled by the promise that old age will just get better and better. That is something to hold on to.

From "Aging and the Life Cycle: A Moral Norm?" by Daniel Callahan, in *A World Growing Old: The Coming Health Care Challenges*, edited by Daniel Callahan, Ruud H.J. ter Meulen, and Eva Topinková (Washington, DC: Georgetown University Press, 1995). Copyright © 1995 by Georgetown University Press. Reprinted by permission of the publisher.

Age-Based Health Care Rationing Is Unethical and Unjust

by Nancy S. Jecker and Robert A. Pearlman

Nancy S. Jecker is an associate professor in the Department of Medical History and Ethics at the University of Washington School of Medicine. Robert A. Pearlman is an associate professor of medicine and health services at the University of Washington Division of Gerontology and Geriatric Medicine. In the following viewpoint, Jecker and Pearlman state that health care rationing in some form is unavoidable but that age is not an ethically sound basis for limiting care. They argue that discrimination on the basis of age may denigrate the value and worth of individuals. They propose standards other than age for limiting health care. In particular, they suggest medical benefit as a standard, that is, allocating health care resources to those who stand to benefit the most.

"The commonly held stereotype that older people have no role to play in the social system becomes self-justifying; it is a basis for denying older persons opportunities to . . . make productive contributions."

The proposal to ration medical care by age has taken center stage in present debates. This should come as no surprise in light of the phenomenon of an aging society. Since 1900 there has been an eightfold increase in the number of Americans over the age of sixty-five and almost a tripling of their proportion in the population. Those over the age of eighty-five, the fastest growing age group in the country, are twenty-one times as numerous as in 1900.[1] The elderly are also the heaviest users of health services. Persons sixty-five and over, 12 percent of the population, account for one-third of the country's total personal health care expenditures (exclusive of research costs).[2] Of course, the fact that the ranks of older Americans are swelling and the cost of their care is disproportionately high does not suffice to make limiting health care to the elderly rational or just; it merely focuses attention on this group and makes them an obvious target.

Many arguments can be marshalled both for and against rationing based on age. Arguments favoring an age criterion can be usefully grouped into three categories: productivity arguments, person-centered arguments, and equality arguments.[3]

Productivity Arguments

Productivity arguments advise us to maximize achievement of some end or goal. One such approach puts a premium on efficient output and measures the worth of individuals in terms of their productive work or contribution to the social order.[4] Older individuals generally contribute in fewer areas and function less efficiently where they do contribute. For example, older people generally cease professional work and take leave of active participation in other social roles, such as parenting. According to this argument, then, in order to maximize public welfare, scarce medical resources should be aimed at prolonging the life for the young, who are relatively more productive and efficient in their contribution to society.

Another kind of productivity argument takes reducing health expenditures as its goal and justifies denial of care to the elderly as the most effective means to achieve this. This argument highlights the fact that the financial savings that could be achieved if the elderly were excluded, not only from life-extending care but from various other forms of care as well, is disproportionately high, owing to the fact that the elderly as a group are much more frequent utilizers of health services than are other age groups. For example, as Kilner notes, if only those over fifty-five years of age were excluded from treatment for renal disease in the United States, 45 percent of the costs of the renal-disease program would be saved. In other areas, such as intensive care, a tremendous financial gain could be realized by excluding the elderly.

A final version of the productivity approach invokes as a goal maximizing return on life-years saved. One way of spelling this out is that the young have, on average, many more years ahead to live than older people do. Therefore, life-extending technology applied to the young will yield, on average, a greater return on investment, where return on investment is measured in terms of life-years saved. Even supposing an old and a young person have the same number of years remaining, still the quality-adjusted value of future life-years is generally higher for the younger person. For example, younger years typically include a lower incidence of disease and disability, which have a negative impact on quality of life.[5]

Not Ethically Defensible

It is a credit to each of these utilitarian-style arguments that they proffer an objective scale by which to gauge the relative value of distributing goods to different age groups. The issue before us, however, is not to furnish an empirical argument but to furnish an ethically defensible one. Measured in these terms, the foregoing arguments encounter formidable obstacles. First, both the functionally-based argument and the argument based on maximizing life-years or quality-adjusted life-years oversimplify the ways in which we actually value persons. We value persons, not merely as means to productive or efficient output, but as ends in themselves. We view older and younger persons as possessing equal worth and dignity, despite discrepancies in their efficiency and productive contribution. For instance, in our society murderers are not punished less for killing sixty-five-year-olds than for killing twenty-five-year-olds.[6] We believe that people of all ages possess an underlying equality of value.

Second, the argument based on maximizing quality-adjusted life-years is difficult to sustain because methods for rating life quality are notoriously controversial.[7] For example, large discrepancies have been found between the life-quality ratings that the general population assigns to various diseases and disabilities and the ratings assigned by persons who actually experience these conditions. Dialysis patients, for example, rank quality of life with dialysis much higher than nondialysis patients do.[8] This suggests that the population at large may be prone to underestimate the quality of life associated with diseases and disabilities. If so, we can expect to find the quality-adjusted value of life in old age to be underestimated as well.

Third, even if the social worth of persons is simply a function of their productive contribution, many older people could be far more productive than they are now if social barriers were removed. As Spitter points out, many older persons who seek and are capable of carrying out vocational or artistic tasks are treated with patronizing amusement, indifference, or neglect. The commonly held stereotype that older people have no role to play in the social system becomes self-justifying; it is a basis for denying older persons opportunities to continue to make productive contributions.

Finally, the productivity argument that appeals to the principle that excluding older persons produces disproportionate savings is satisfying only if one assumes that greater return on monetary investment is the most appropriate measure of whether medical treatment is ethically warranted. An alternative approach asserts that the aim of medicine should be not to maximize returns on investments but, rather, to compensate for the deficiencies of opportunity and happiness wrought by disease and disability. If these deficiencies fail disproportionately to a certain group then it is ethically legitimate for medicine to serve that group disproportionately, rather than to underserve it as rationing by old age implies.

Productivity arguments generally can be faulted on various other grounds: (1) in the process of identifying and promoting maximization of some end, they unacceptably demean people;[9] and (2) since the elderly are not a monolithic group, but an extremely heterogeneous one, it is unfair to discriminate against some older people on the grounds that their group as a whole is not a productive investment.[10]

Person-Centered Arguments

If these objections to productivity arguments are convincing, we should then explore alternative justifications for rationing by age. Use of an age criterion has been championed recently on person-oriented grounds by philosophers such as Daniel Callahan,[11] Harry Moody,[12] and Norman Daniels.[13] Holders of person-oriented views claim to respect individuals for their own sake, regardless of the goods they produce. For example, Daniel Callahan maintains that denial of health care to elderly persons is consistent with respect for the elderly. This is because, in old age, death is often not an evil to the one whose death it is. According to Callahan, death is tolerable once a "natural lifespan" has been reached, provided that an individual has discharged filial duties and that his or her dying process does not involve tormenting or degrading pain. In situations where death is tolerable, it is tolerable as well to allow death to happen, for example, by withholding government-financed life-extending care.

Harry Moody advances a similar person-oriented argument. He reasons that if we were forced to choose between living in (1) medical institutions that provide excellent palliative and other sorts of care aimed at improving life quality, but provide no life-extending care, and (2) medical institutions that afford mediocre palliative care and mediocre life-extending care, the former would have distinct appeal for older persons. In other words, from the perspective of older people themselves, the opportunity to optimize life quality is often esteemed more than the opportunity to lengthen life. If so, then barring the elderly from life-extending care in order to make possible a better quality of life does not display a lack of respect. Even if the cost of optimizing quality of life in old age is a shorter life, this cost is one older people themselves would be willing to bear. To illustrate this point, Moody asks us to imagine a large and well-endowed volunteer nursing home, spectacularly equipped with all the medical equipment and staff support that could be imagined, but the nursing home lacks basic equipment of an intensive care unit. In this situation, failure to provide intensive care reflects a rational decision to spend finite resources enhancing the quality of life for the residents (most in their eighties), rather than providing life-saving technologies to extend life during a medical crisis.

Finally, Norman Daniels also focuses on respect for individual old people who may be denied beneficial care. He holds that if individuals view their lives as a whole (from a "life-time" perspective), rather than from a particular moment in time (a "time-slice" perspective), they would sometimes prefer distributing life-extending medical resources to earlier, rather than later, years. This would be so, for example, whenever increasing one's odds of living beyond normal life expectancy results in diminishing one's chance of ever reaching normal life expectancy.

Sound Basis for Rationing by Age Is Absent

Person-oriented arguments offer the clear advantage of exhibiting respect for individuals. But this approach still fails to provide a sound basis for rationing by age. In the first place, as Churchill points out, these arguments routinely presuppose a larger health care system that is cohesive, just, and meets broader social needs of the elderly. For example, as Daniels himself notes, the justification for age-based rationing works only on the contrary-to-fact assumption that individuals live the duration of their lives under a closed health care system (and a system to which a fair share of public funds has been allocated). Only then will it make sense to say that taking life-extending resources away from older age groups results in individuals having access to more life-sustaining services in younger life. If individuals move from one health system to another, say, from a state or federal insurance plan to a health maintenance organization, then the disadvantages they experience at one point will not be offset by advantages at some other point. Similarly, Callahan's and Moody's arguments support an age-based criterion for life-extending care only on the assumption that older people who forego life-extending care will gain more appropriate services, such as better rehabilitative and chronic care. But policies explicitly linking these trade-offs are not presently forthcoming; thus the elderly would be foolish to agree to such sacrifices at the present time.

Additional objections to person-centered arguments include the following. First, Callahan's argument fails to distinguish between rights, on the one hand, and best interests, on the other hand. Even supposing we accept Callahan's view that death in old age is sometimes tolerable, this does not suffice to establish that allowing death to happen is consistent with respecting an older person's rights. It merely shows that letting death occur may be consistent with promoting a person's best interest.[14] Second, Callahan's argument also can be faulted on the grounds that attainment of a natural lifespan is not itself a sufficient condition for the disenfranchisement of older persons from life-extending care; other considerations emerge as ethically important.[15] For example, if an older person chooses to continue living or personally experiences life as worth continuing, disenfranchising that person from the means to extend life would be objectionable.[16] Third, Daniels's argument can be faulted on the ground that it presupposes controversial definitions of health and disease, and these definitions skew the resulting account.[17]

Equality Arguments

A final set of arguments supporting rationing of medical services based on age appeals to the principle of equality. The thrust of this approach is that ageism is not objectionable in the way it is usually thought to be. Unlike sexism or racism, differential treatment by age is compatible with treating individuals equally. For example, as Daniels notes, "If we treat the young one way and the old another, then over time, each person is treated both ways. The advantages (or disadvantages) of consistent differential treatment by age equalize over time." But although differential treatment by age does not imply unequal treatment between persons over a lifetime, equality arguments are no more convincing than productivity or person-oriented arguments. Even if the opportunities that different ages have to gain health care services are consistently age based, this will not always serve to equalize the actual benefits individuals enjoy. First, a young person with a serious disease may have already received a great deal of medical care, while a relatively healthy older person may have received very little. It would not be accurate to say, in this particular case, that the younger party has not been given as great a chance to live as the older person.[18] Second, men and women do not enjoy equality of opportunity under age-based rationing, because women reach older stages of life with greater frequency, anticipate more years of life ahead when they reach old age, and rely to a greater extent on public insurance to cover their health care costs.[19]

Arguments Against Rationing Based on Age

Despite the fact that unstinting support for age-based rationing is forthcoming in many quarters, the various arguments on behalf of such a policy are encumbered by serious objections. Countering these arguments, however, represents only the barest beginnings of a sustained argument against such a basis for rationing. Three positive arguments are put forth to show that rationing by age is not an ethical option. These arguments appeal to disproportionate need, invoke special duties, and make the charge of invidious discrimination.

Needs-Based Arguments

First, needs-based arguments underscore the fact that geriatric patients experience a greater incidence of disease and disability than do those in other age groups. Needs give rise to duties, in this case, because the vast majority of old people do not possess the financial wherewithal to meet the increasingly high costs of basic medical services. A growing number of elderly people rely heavily on government programs, such as Medicare. The crux of a needs-based approach is to establish that society is obligated to meet the essential needs of citizens if these needs would otherwise go unmet.

One way of establishing this is to invoke the ethical perspective outlined by Rawls.[20] According to this perspective, just principles are those that would be chosen by individuals in an "original position." In this position, rational agents make choices without knowledge of such things as their gender, class position, social status, natural assets or liabilities, intelligence, rational plan of life, or the particular circumstances of their society. Presumably, in an original position persons are additionally ignorant of their present age, and so they are unsure how the advantages and disadvantages of principles affect their age group. From this perspective, it could be argued, individuals would be concerned to guarantee, as far as possible, that the essential needs of persons of all ages are met. For to the extent that essential needs are left unmet, persons are prevented from carrying out the particular plan they have set for each stage of life. Thus, persons in the original position would prefer to ration whatever constitutes more extravagant, higher cost care with respect to a given society in order to underwrite a decent minimum of care and meet the essential needs of citizens.

Arguments Appealing to Special Duties

A second argument opposing rationing based on age invokes the idea of special duties. In one account, described by Kilner,[21] special duties to provide medical care to older persons derive from the relationship of the older individual to the community:

> Whereas the utilitarian view . . . conceives of the social good atomistically in terms of individual (mainly job-related) contributions summed over the breadth of society . . . this view presupposes a social network of interpersonal relations within which one becomes more and more an essential part the older one becomes. The more personally interwoven a person becomes with others through time, the greater the damage done to the social fabric when that person is torn away by death.

So, for example, if one cannot avoid choosing between saving the lives of two individuals, an older person should be saved before a neonate because the former has more social responsibility and is more deeply integrated and finely fastened within a network of social relationships.

One difficulty with this view is that it appears to depend on the idea that interpersonal relationships are sustained throughout old age. It could be contended, however, that as one moves further into old age the relationships one forged earlier are increasingly severed: spouses and friends die, work associates retire and go their separate ways, and offspring mature and refocus energy toward new family members they wed and parent. But, in response to this, it could be held that even if relational ties are cut or recede in significance in extreme old age, still the depth and character of past participation should be respected. Such respecting calls for refusing to neglect or disown those who at one time occupied a significant place in the social web.

Another way of mounting an argument for special duties to older persons appeals to the fact that the elderly as a group have made past contributions to the social good that entitle them to present acknowledgment. Jonsen elucidates such an argument in the following way.[22] He begins with the premise that the process of having lived through a history, regardless of how calamitous or satisfying it was, is itself an achievement. The second premise asserts that should the society in which that personal history has been lived refuse to acknowledge it in an effective way, resentment—experienced as injustice or the feeling that one is not given adequate recognition—will be generated in those who have lived those histories. The touchstone of the argument is stated in the next premise: this experience of injustice is not a mere epiphenomenon; it reflects a genuine right to acknowledgment. The argument supporting this last premise states that the elderly themselves, as members of society even though not necessarily as individuals, have participated in the creation of social goods. The present state of science, technology, medicine, and culture are the results of their having lived communally through their histories. The conclusion of the argument maintains that effective recognition of the elderly's contribution makes imperative the application of science, technology, medicine, and culture to benefit the elderly.

As it stands, the ability of Jonsen's argument to establish the relative priority of health needs for older persons is unclear. It would seem that the entitlement for the elderly that this argument generates is a prima facie entitlement only: older persons, no matter how old, are prima facie entitled to health care along with everyone else. This would seem to follow from the fact that Jonsen's argument offers a counterpart to the utilitarian position discussed earlier, that is, the view that the young have priority because of potential future contributions. The counterpart to this argument makes evident that older persons as a group are on roughly equal footing in respect to social contribution, because their past contributions offset their lack of future ones. Also, not rewarding the elderly for their past contributions may discourage younger members from making their own contributions.

Arguments Charging Invidious Discrimination

A final sort of defense of the principle that we ought to include, rather than exclude, older groups makes much of the idea that rationing by age represents invidious discrimination. The guiding theme of this view is that discrimination based on age is invidious either because it is buttressed by negative attitudes toward older persons or because it will inevitably engender such attitudes. According to the former account,[23] rationing based on age is supported by nefarious cultural prejudices against older persons. For example, it is unusual to watch an hour of television, without noting offers for products designed to rid our bodies of the signs of aging. The message such sentiments convey is clear: old age is synonymous with ugliness. This attitude allows us to develop the belief that older people, as a group, are different; next, we consider them not equal; finally, we think of them merely as objects to be passed over. Clearly, if these emerge as the underlying reasons why age-based rationing is heralded, rationing based on age should be vigorously opposed, and ageism replaced with an attitude of proper respect.

The second version of an anti-ageist view holds that even if rationing of health care based on age is justified on other, more cogent, grounds, instituting it as a widespread policy would impart a dangerous message. It would be interpreted by many as signaling that older persons are less worthy human beings and so can be legitimately disenfranchised from other essential goods, such as housing and food. In other words, age-based rationing of medical care would constitute a first step down a slippery slope of age-based exclusion in many areas of life. It would also strengthen negative attitudes already present toward personal aging: aging panics people, is experienced as calamitous, and so on. By contrast, enfranchising older persons in the area of health care would impress on people the importance of according respect to all persons, regardless of their age. It would thus foster positive virtues, instill a sense of responsibility for aging parents, and encourage personal celebration of the ripening of human life, as well as its birth and beginning.

In summary, there are many reasons for continuing to include older persons, including the extreme old, within the rubric of publicly financed health care, whether life-extending or palliative. To the extent that scarcity forces rationing, older persons should not be excluded because they are old.

Notes

1. C. Mills, "The Graying of America," *QQ: Report from the Institute for Philosophy & Public Policy*, vol. 8 (1987), pp. 12–15.
2. U.S. Senate Special Committee on Aging, *Aging, America: Trends and Projections* (Washington, D.C.: Public Health Service, Department of Health and Human Services, 1985–86).
3. J. Kilner, "Age as a Basis for Allocating Lifesaving Medical Resources: An Ethical Analysis," *Journal of Health Politics, Policy and Law*, vol. 13 (1988), pp. 405–23.
4. M. Spitter, "Growing Older in America: Can We Restore the Dignity of Age?" in *Bioethics and Human Rights*, ed. E. Bandman and B. Bandman (Boston: Little, Brown and Co., 1978), pp. 191–96.
5. J. Avron, "Benefit and Cost Analysis in Geriatric Care: Turning Age Discrimination into Health Policy," *New England Journal of Medicine*, vol. 310 (1984), pp. 1294–1301.
6. N. Bell, "Ethical Considerations in the Allocation of Scarce Medical Resources," (Ph.D. diss., University of North Carolina at Chapel Hill, 1978).
7. Spitter, "Growing Older in America," pp. 191–96.
8. D.L. Sackett and G.W. Torrance, "The Utility of Different Health States as Perceived by the General Public," *Journal of Chronic Diseases and Therapeutics Research*, vol. 31 (1978), pp. 697–704.
9. Kilner, "Age as a Basis for Allocating Resources," pp. 405–23.
10. Kilner, "Age as a Basis for Allocating Resources," pp. 405–23.
11. D. Callahan, *Setting Limits: Medical Goals in an Aging Society* (New York: Simon and Schuster, 1987).
12. H. Moody, "Is It Right to Allocate Health Care Resources on Grounds of Age?" in *Bioethics and Human Rights*, ed. E. Bandman and B. Bandman (Boston: Little, Brown and Co., 1978), pp. 197–201.
13. N. Daniels, *Am I My Parents' Keeper? An Essay on Justice Between the Young and the Old* (New York: Oxford University Press, 1988).

14. N.S. Jecker, "Should We Ration Health Care?" *Journal of Medical Humanities*, vol. 10 (1989), pp. 77–90.

15. N.S. Jecker, "Disenfranchising the Elderly from Life-Extending Care," *Public Affairs Quarterly*, vol. 2, no. 3 (July 1988), p. 51.

16. N.S. Jecker, "Excluding the Elderly: A Reply to Callahan," *QQ: Report from the Institute for Philosophy & Public Policy*, vol. 8 (1987), pp. 12–15.

17. N.S. Jecker, "Towards a Theory of Age Group Justice," *Journal of Medicine and Philosophy*, vol. 14 (1989), pp. 655–76.

18. Kilner, "Age as a Basis for Allocating Resources," pp. 405–23.

19. N.S. Jecker, "Age-Based Rationing and Women," *Journal of the American Medical Association*, vol. 266 (1991), pp. 3012–15.

20. J. Rawls, *A Theory of Justice* (Cambridge: Harvard University Press, 1971).

21. Kilner, "Age as a Basis for Allocating Resources," pp. 405–23.

22. A. Jonsen, "Resentment and the Rights of the Elderly," in *Aging and Ethics: Philosophical Problems in Gerontology*, ed. N.S. Jecker (Totowa, N.J.: Humana Press, 1991), pp. 341–52.

23. P. Brickner, "Older People, Issues and Problems from a Medical Viewpoint," in *Bioethics and Human Rights*, ed. E. Bandman and B. Bandman (Boston: Little, Brown and Co., 1978), pp. 191–96.

Workplace Bias Hurts Older Workers

by Esther B. Fein

Workers over age fifty-five have increasing difficulty gaining jobs and acceptance among America's employers, Esther B. Fein contends in the following viewpoint. According to experts and displaced workers interviewed by Fein, employers are disregarding the proven abilities of older workers and discriminating against them simply because of their age. Fein is a reporter for the *New York Times*.

"Employers continue to view age not in terms of experience or stability but as deterioration and staleness."

Despite a decade-long push by private and government organizations to market older people as reliable and mature workers, advocates for people 55 and older say their efforts have largely failed. They say that employers continue to view age not in terms of experience or stability but as deterioration and staleness.

People who have worked to promote the older labor force say that 10 years ago they were confident that, through intensive public relations and educational efforts, American businesses would recognize and harness what they argued are the skills of older workers. Although it is impossible to tally how much money went toward that end, people who work in the field estimated that tens of millions of dollars were spent nationwide on studies, job fairs, seminars for executives and advertising.

Libby Mandel is 69 years old and has been looking for a job for two years. She has taken advantage of many of these programs, going to computer classes, resume writing workshops and job fairs, and thrusting herself forward as an experienced secretary who had, for 25 years, skill-fully handled the paper, telephone and student traffic at Seward Park High School in Manhattan.

"These senior programs were all supposed to show people that age doesn't matter," said Mrs. Mandel, in a voice more resigned than hope-ful. "But it does. It still does. It's like a handicap. Really."

Anger and Frustration

Now people running these programs, as well as older workers them-selves, say they are frustrated and angry at how little headway they have made in changing attitudes and hiring practices.

To be sure, all agree, the recession has not helped. But in many cases, they say, the burden of age in the job market is as profound as those of race and gender.

The Federal Age Discrimination in Employment Act, which was en-acted in 1967 and amended several times since, prohibits any form of discrimination in the workplace due to a person's age. The law now eliminates mandatory retirement ages for all but very select positions, including top-level executives.

Employers may not ask a job applicant's age or consider it when mak-ing a hiring decision, except where it is a so-called "bona fide occupa-tional qualification." An example of that would be a job like construction, where physical strength is an issue, but even then a fit and robust older worker would be protected. The fact that a job is entry-level or that a company envisions training someone for a long-term ca-reer track would be irrelevant to the law.

But it is too often relevant to employers, complain advocates for older workers, although proving age discrimination in employment is very difficult.

People like Mrs. Mandel who have journeyed futilely about the job market say that they can actually feel themselves dissolve from vital in-dividuals into antique stereotypes as they sit before interviewers who, careful not to run afoul of discrimination laws, try surreptitiously to find out applicants' ages and couch their biases in the most deferential terms.

"When I look at myself, I see a funny person basically, a helper; I'm enthusiastic," Mrs. Mandel said. "But when I talk to these recruiters or go on interviews, I know what they see is an old lady. They don't have to see my date of birth. They see the gray hair, they see the wrinkles, and they think, 'Old.'"

Dire Statistics

The job market, while showing some recent signs of recovery, is still a grim odyssey for most unemployed people, but it is particularly so for older people. Statistically, the situation for older workers in the New York region is significantly worse than the country as a whole. Nationwide in 1992, about 738,000 people age 55 and older were unemployed and actively looking for jobs, a rise of about 51 percent in five years, according to the Bureau of Labor Statistics. In the New York area, those ranks swelled nearly $2^1/_2$ times in the same period—from 28,000 to 67,000—due, in large measure, to the corporate reorganization that took place here in the 1980's and the subsequent recession.

Still, the jobless rate for older workers—4.8 percent in the United States and 6.8 percent in the New York region in 1992—is lower than that of the general work force. But experts say those figures reflect the stability of workers who have had steady jobs and have not been forced back into the marketplace. The numbers also don't reflect older workers who, put off by dismal prospects, have stopped looking for jobs.

Weeding Out Older Workers

There are, to be sure, some companies that have responded and have reached out to aging workers. But experts say that the "untapped resource," as one report referred to workers 55 years and older, remains largely that—untapped.

"I wish I could say that because of all these case studies, companies are running out in droves to hire older workers," said Michael Barth, a labor economist and senior vice president for ICF, a Washington consulting firm that specializes in labor market studies. "But if anything, they are finding more ways to get rid of them and the reason is because there is a lot of pure bias, of behaving toward older workers totally in the context of their age, not their ability."

People 55 and older are increasingly looking for jobs for many reasons. People are living longer and healthier and have a desire and ability to keep active professionally for longer.

In addition, in a period of massive corporate layoffs and downsizing, older workers are frequently induced into taking early retirement, afraid that if they don't accept severance packages one year, they will be let go without any safety net the following year. But the money is usually not enough for them to live on, considering average life expectancy and a troubled economy.

Studies Offer Praise

A variety of studies—some of which surveyed human resources executives at hundreds of firms, others of which focused on particular companies—have found that workers age 55 and older are more reliable, have lower rates of absenteeism, higher productivity and were just as easy to retrain as their younger colleagues.

But the prejudices against older workers are so ingrained, people who have studied the issue say, they defy logic and hard data.

"In the beginning, I was more optimistic that if we corrected the stereotype, if we could document productivity, that it would help change attitudes," said Karen Davis, the executive vice president of the Commonwealth Fund, a private foundation based in New York that recently completed a five-year, $4 million study of workers over 55. "I really thought the reports would have had more of a positive impact. But we are running against the economic trends and some deep-rooted bias. I still think it may turn around, but it's clearly going to be an uphill struggle to make it happen."

At a . . . job fair for older workers at the Roosevelt Hotel in Manhattan—promisingly named "Ability is Ageless"—participants walked from booth to booth, leaving their resumes with recruiters and commiserating with each other about the indignities of job-hunting at their age.

New Yorkers Handle the Age Question

"I'm ashamed to admit it, but I dye my hair, like a lady, to give myself a more youthful appearance," said one man, a 62-year-old former salesman from Flushing who declined to give his name. "And I wear bright ties. They should think I'm with it, and not stuffy." He fingered a yellow swath of silk with aqua crests and sighed, "So far, it hasn't helped."

Similar laments are repeated at job fairs in other cities and at workshops and training programs designed to make aging workers more competitive. At AgeWorks, a 16-week skills-improvement course run by the New York City Department for the Aging, several women compared euphemisms for "you're too old" that they had encountered in their job quests.

"They say that you're overqualified, even if you're willing to take a lower-level job," said Sara Lerner, a former bookkeeper from Riverdale, who, like many people interviewed, would give her name, but not her age.

"That's the main one they use," said Karen Halpern, who was given early retirement recently from her job at I.B.M.

"There's also, 'I'd love to hire you, but you just won't fit in,'" said Helen Miller, of Ridgewood, Queens, who was candid about her 66 years and is looking for clerical work. "They also get around asking you your age by asking what year you graduated, or asking to see your driver's license."

If they do get hired, many older workers find that it is for a job that is far lower in pay and stature than their previous position.

For 25 years, Cecil Frazier was a chef at the Gloucester House, a pricey midtown restaurant where he was known for his lobster bisque. Now he grills burgers and fries chicken for a T.G.I. Friday's restaurant in Manhattan, and in spite of that drop in status, he is grateful.

Most of the people he worked with before the Gloucester House closed in 1992 are still looking for work, their years of experience proving no lure to potential employers. "They're working 20 years and more and can't get no jobs," said Mr. Frazier, who is 60 and searched nearly a year before finding work. "But the younger guys, now they got the jobs. They've got no experience, but they got the jobs."

Signs of Change?

There are some in the field who say they are optimistic that the trend is beginning to turn. But those voices are all but drowned out by the once hopeful—and now befuddled—advocates in the field, who say they are at a loss trying to figure out how to translate their information into jobs.

In a [1993] study . . . the American Association of Retired Persons and the Society for Human Resource Management surveyed about 1,000 managers in a range of businesses and found that even though "workers over the age of 50 are admired for their skills and their work habits" they are nonetheless "underutilized and undervalued."

"Everybody saw them as reliable, like a Saint Bernard," said Dr. Martin Sicker, director of Work Force Programs for A.A.R.P. "They love them, but they won't hire them and we really couldn't get at why. None of the negative stereotypes show up in the answers, but even positive stereotypes cause pigeonholing.

"They use words like 'mature' and 'dependable' but they don't look at individual skills and characters. They lump older workers together in a way that they don't younger ones, and any buzz words set off alarms for me. It does just come down to 'ageism' and we haven't found a way to crack it."

From "For Older Job Seekers a Sad Refrain: 'I'd Love to Hire You, but You Just Won't Fit In'" by Esther B. Fein, *New York Times*, January 4, 1994. Copyright © 1994 by The New York Times Company. Reprinted by permission.

Laws Aimed at Redressing Workplace Bias Harm Older Workers

by Richard A. Posner

The Age Discrimination in Employment Act was a response to a largely nonexistent problem and on balance probably hurts elderly workers more than it helps them, Richard A. Posner contends in the following viewpoint. Posner argues that employers are reluctant to hire older workers because, under the law, they have more legal rights against their employers than younger workers have. He also states that the law discourages keeping older workers who voluntarily accept lower pay to compensate for age-related decreases in productivity. Posner is chief judge of the U.S. Court of Appeals for the Seventh Circuit and senior lecturer at the University of Chicago Law School.

"The age discrimination law adds to the cost of employing older workers, and hence to the reluctance of employers to employ them."

Even before the enactment of ERISA made it more likely that an employer would resort to the threat of discharge (a threat that to be credible would have to be carried out from time to time) in order to discipline its employees, Congress had made it more difficult to fire older employees by enacting the Age Discrimination in Employment Act in 1967.[1] The Act, as subsequently amended, forbids employers to discriminate on grounds of age against any employee aged 40 or over. Originally the protected class was 40 to 65, so mandatory retirement at age 65 was permitted. The lid was raised to 70 in 1978 and removed altogether in 1986. Mandatory retirement at any age, along with any other measures retail or wholesale by which an employer treats an employee worse because of age, is, with a few exceptions, now forbidden. I argue that the age discrimination law is largely ineffectual but that to the extent it is effective it has a perverse impact both on the welfare of the elderly and on the equality of income and wealth across the entire population. The age discrimination law is at once inefficient, regressive, and harmful to the elderly.

An Unlikely Scenario

The justification offered for the law was that people over 40 are subject to a form of prejudice, "ageism," that is analogous to racism and sexism. After putting to one side the use of the word as a synonym for anything that disadvantages an older worker[2] (so presbyopia would be "ageist"), we can posit two kinds of ageism, only one plausible. The implausible is a systematic undervaluation, motivated by ignorance, viciousness, or irrationality, of the value of older people in the work place. This is sometimes referred to as "animus discrimination." I do not deny that there is resentment and disdain of older people in our society, or widespread misunderstandings, some disadvantageous to the old. . . .

But the present viewpoint is about the work place. Even apart from competitive pressures for rational behavior, which are considerable in private markets, the people who make employment policies for corporate and other employers and most of those who carry out those policies by making decisions about hiring or firing specific workers are at least 40 years old and often much older. It is as if the vast majority of persons who established employment policies and who made employment decisions were black, federal legislation mandated huge transfer payments from whites to blacks, and blacks occupied most high political offices in the nation. It would be mad in those circumstances to think the nation needed a law that would protect blacks from discrimination in employment. Employers—who have a direct financial stake in correctly evaluating the abilities of their employees and who for the most part are not young themselves—are unlikely to harbor either serious misconceptions about the vocational capacities of the old (so it is odd that employment should be the main area in which age discrimination is forbidden) or a generalized antipathy toward old people.

To put the point differently, the kind of "we-they" thinking that fosters racial, ethnic, and sexual discrimination is unlikely to play a large role in the treatment of the elderly worker.[3] Not because a young person will (in all likelihood) someday be old; to put too much weight on the continuity

312

of personal identity would slight the multiple-selves issue. But because the people who do the hiring and firing are generally as old as the people they hire and fire and are therefore unlikely to mistake those people's vocational abilities. One should not be surprised at how slight and equivocal the evidence that employers misconceive the ability of older workers is. Such workers do have trouble finding new jobs at high wages. But this is because the wages in their old jobs will have reflected firm-specific human capital that disappeared when they left and that they cannot readily replace because of the cost of learning new skills, and also because the proximity of these workers to (voluntary) retirement reduces the expected return from investing in learning new skills.[4]. . .

Statistical Discrimination

The form of ageism (if it should be called that) that is more plausible and better substantiated than animus discrimination against the old consists of attributing to all people of a particular age the characteristics of the average person of that age. It is an example of what economists call statistical discrimination and noneconomists "stereotyping": the failure or refusal, normally motivated by the costs of information, to distinguish a particular member of a group from the average member. Age, like sex, is one of the first facts that we notice about a person and use to "place" him or her. We do this because we operate with a strong, though often an unconscious, presumption, echoing the rigid age grading that structures activities and occupations in many primitive societies, that particular attitudes, behaviors, and positions in life go with particular ages. . . .

Age grading illustrates how statistical discrimination can sometimes operate in favor of, rather than against, a particular group, here by ascription of the maturity, wisdom, and disinterest possessed by some old people to all or most of them. Another circumstance that has favored the old is that few people understand selection bias. People generalize from the impressive performance of octogenarian judges that octogenarians have unsuspected capabilities; but the advanced age at which most judges are appointed operates to draw judges from an unrepresentative segment of the aging population. If the elderly benefit from statistical discrimination as well as being hurt by it, maybe they would enjoy an undue advantage over other groups if the law succeeded in eradicating statistical discrimination against, as distinct from statistical discrimination in favor of, the elderly. I would not put too much weight on this factor, however. For reasons stated earlier, I would expect *employers* to have a generally clear-headed notion of the characteristics of the average worker in the different age groups and not be fooled by selection bias. . . .

The Effects of Age Discrimination Law on Workers

The previous section questioned the need for a law against discrimination on grounds of age. But we have the law, and we must now consider more carefully its probable effects both on elderly workers and on the rest of society. The first thing to note is the misfit between the scope of the Act and the concerns of the elderly. The prohibition against mandatory retirement is clearly related to those concerns, since mandatory retirement before 65 was rare. But the Act's general prohibition against age discrimination kicks in when a worker turns 40. I have done a study of court cases under the Act, and only 10 percent of the plaintiffs in my sample of cases, including those plaintiffs who challenged mandatory retirement, are 65 or older—a smaller percentage than the percentage of elderly people in the U.S. population as a whole. The main reason is plain enough; most people who are 65 or older are voluntarily retired, so are not protected by the Age Discrimination in *Employment* Act. Yet the Act was "sold" by means of emotional rhetoric concerning the plight of the elderly, in 1967 still viewed as a disadvantaged segment of American society, even though the Act seems to have been designed and to be administered in the interest primarily of nonelderly workers. It is unlikely that an age discrimination statute so configured would benefit the elderly much, and we are about to see that it may harm them.

Of course, since an elderly person's income is apt to depend significantly on his income when he was in his prime working years, a statute that increased the incomes of workers in those years could be thought to be benefiting the elderly. But even if we disregard the multiple-selves problem (the benefited elderly self may not be the same person as the younger self who receives benefits under the age discrimination law), we shall see that, ex ante, the beneficiaries of the law probably bear the costs of it as well, and therefore do not, on average anyway, obtain a net benefit from it.

We know that, wholly apart from any laws, employers are reluctant to hire older workers. The cost of training an older worker is higher than that of training a younger one because of the age-related decline of fluid intelligence, while the expected return to the investment in training is lower because the older worker has a shorter working life expectancy.[5] The age discrimination law adds to the costs of employing older workers, and hence to the reluctance of employers to employ them, by giving them more legal rights against their employer than younger workers have. By thus reducing the hiring prospects of older people, the Act perversely impairs the incentive of the exceptional old to invest in their human capital, by reducing the expected return to such an investment. . . .

The Effects on the Economy

I have emphasized the extent to which the goals, at least the ostensible goals, of the Age Discrimination in Employment Act appear to have been subverted as a result of rational profit-maximizing conduct by employers. But it would be a mistake to conclude that the Act's effect on the economy has been negligible (although probably it has been small), even if costs of litigation and of legal counseling are ignored. The transition costs, both the costs of gearing up for compliance with the new law and the costs of revising the terms of employment in order to reestablish the employer's desired age profile, should not be ignored just because they are transitional.[6] They can, however, be minimized by advance notice of the law. Congress wisely gave universities eight years' notice of the abolition of mandatory retirement at fixed ages, though the universities were . . . insufficiently wise to take advantage of this breathing space.

It is possible that the Act, rather than raising the average retirement age—a stated objective, motivated by the hope of reducing the cost of the social security program—has, by encouraging offers of early retirement some of which are accepted by employees whom the employer does not want to lose, reduced the average retirement age, inducing an inefficient substitution of leisure for work. Although evidence . . . casts doubt on that particular suggestion, the Act has undoubtedly caused other labor-market distortions, as we have seen, including discouraging the hiring of elderly workers. Another way in which the Act may have hurt elderly workers is by discouraging contracts in which a worker agrees to work for a reduced wage, because of his diminished capacity, in lieu of being discharged. Such contracts would not be common even if there were no law against age discrimination, because of the fixed costs of employment and other considerations. . . . Still, there might be some. The age discrimination law does not forbid such contracts, but it makes them unattractive to employers. It is much easier to escape liability by discharging a worker whose productivity has diminished because of his age than by attempting to justify paying a lower wage to the elder of two workers who have the same job. . . .

Neither Victims nor Parasites

There are polar positions on the situation of elderly people in the United States of today. One is that they are—or would be, were it not for extensive government transfer and regulatory programs—an oppressed class no different from blacks or women or homosexuals; are or would be, that is, victims of a pervasive "ageism" just as vicious and irrational as racism, sex-

315

ism, or homophobia are thought to be; victims of false stereotypes concerning the mental and physical capacities of elderly people that make them despised by the young and by themselves and that exclude them from the work place. The opposite position is that the elderly are pampered parasites, denying the reality of aging, selfishly employing their disproportionate political power to siphon the wealth of the country into the support of their ever more clamorous demands for generous pensions and extravagant medical care, dooming the country to gerontocratic stagnation and mediocrity.[7] The discussion . . . suggests that neither extreme position is tenable. The evidence that there really is a process called aging that takes its toll of everyone, albeit at different rates, generating palpable and often occupationally relevant physical and mental differences between older and younger persons, is more compelling than any evidence thus far advanced to demonstrate occupationally relevant differences in the fundamental capacities of men and women, whites and blacks, or persons who differ in their sexual orientation. . . .

Yet it is probably true that old people in the United States of the present day do not command the respect and affection they once did. The fact that they are materially and in point of health better off on average than they ever were has its underside: they are less appealing objects of charity and solicitude. Stated otherwise and more positively, loss of popularity is the price that elderly Americans pay, probably willingly in most cases, for the dramatic increase in their prosperity and political influence. Demographic changes—a falling birth rate and a falling death rate, the latter due to the higher incomes of the old but above all to the advance of medical technology—have greatly increased both the relative and the absolute size of the elderly population. They are less scarce, so less valued. Most important perhaps are social changes, including mass education and the increasing rapidity of social, economic, and technological change—the increasing dynamism of American society—that have reduced the social value of the memories, wisdom, and experience of the elderly. . . .

Misguided Policies

Even if the direst predictions about the effects of our old-age laws on the economy are unfounded, as I believe they are, all is not right with our policies toward the aged. Among many examples, the federal pension law (ERISA) appears to have been a response to largely nonexistent problems and its costs of administration, though modest in the overall scheme of things, appear to buy no benefits. The Age Discrimination in Employment Act is a particularly misbegotten venture in tilting at the windmills of ageism, and not only because most elderly people are retired and therefore are outside the scope of the Act. The Act may have few long-term effects of any sort. Its commands are readily avoidable, probably at modest long-run cost, by offers of early retirement (which are self-financing in the sense that, like other fringe benefits, they are ultimately paid for by the workers themselves in the form of lower wages); by avoidance, at what appears to be only a slight legal risk, of hiring elderly workers; and by matching (as through a carefully designed reduction in force) the termination of unwanted older workers with the termination of some young ones in whose firm-specific human capital the employer has not yet invested heavily. This means that the Act does little good for the aged (and some harm to them) and little harm to the rest of the population.

Notes

1. 29 U.S.C. §§ 623 *et seq.* For contrasting evaluations, both emphasizing the economics of the statute, see Richard A. Epstein, *Forbidden Grounds: The Case against Employment Discrimination Laws*, ch. 21 (1992), and Stewart J. Schwab, "Life-Cycle Justice: Accommodating Just Cause and Employment at Will," 92 *Michigan Law Review* 8 (1993). Many states have their own laws forbidding age discrimination in employment, and there are other federal statutes forbidding age discrimination, such as the Age Discrimination Act, 42 U.S.C. §§ 6101 *et seq.*, but I shall ignore these other laws.
2. The sense in which it is used in William Graebner, *A History of Retirement: The Meaning and Function of an American Institution, 1885–1978*, ch. 2 (1980).
3. Cf. John Hart Ely, *Democracy and Distrust: A Theory of Judicial Review* (1980).
4. Dian E. Herz and Philip L. Rones, "Institutional Barriers to Employment of Older Workers," 112 *Monthly Labor Review*, April 1989, pp. 14, 20.
5. For empirical evidence of employers' reluctance to hire older workers, see Robert M. Hutchens, "Do Job Opportunities Decline with Age?" 42 *Industrial and Labor Relations Review* 89 (1988). Although health costs are also higher for older workers, it is not a violation of the age discrimination law for the employer to take these costs into account in designing a wage-benefits package for his employees.
6. Louis Kaplow, though highly critical of transitional relief (including delayed implementation), acknowledges that it may be efficient when adjustment costs are high. Kaplow, "An Economic Analysis of Legal Transitions," 99 *Harvard Law Review* 509, 591 n. 251, 592 n. 254 (1986).
7. For responsible statements of the respective polar positions, compare Howard Eglit, "Health Care Allocation for the Elderly: Age Discrimination by Another Name?" 26 *Houston Law Review* 813 (1989), with Jan Ellen Rein, "Preserving Dignity and Self-Determination of the Elderly in the Face of Competing Interests and Grim Alternatives: A Proposal for Statutory Refocus and Reform," 60 *George Washington Law Review* 1818 (1992).

CHAPTER 7

Are Poor and Minority Communities Victims of Environmental Racism?

Chapter Preface

Altgeld Gardens is an African-American community in the south side of Chicago. Built atop a nineteenth-century landfill and surrounded by eleven polluting facilities, ranging from sewage treatment plants to incinerators and oil refineries, Altgeld Gardens is considered by some to be a classic example of what has been termed "environmental racism"—the siting of a disproportionate number of the nation's industrial and waste facilities in or near minority residential areas. "Cancer Alley" is another often-cited example: Lining an eighty-mile strip of the lower Mississippi River are the more than one hundred oil refineries and petrochemical plants that have so polluted the environment that several of the local communities of color—many of them historic—are being abandoned. According to the U.S. Environmental Protection Agency (EPA), an "unusually high incidence of cancer, asthma, hypertension, strokes, and other illnesses" plague the citizens who remain in the region.

Those who see in these beleaguered areas the work of environmental racism assert that communities of color are unfairly targeted as sites for polluting facilities because, unlike white neighborhoods, they lack the political representation and economic resources necessary to oppose powerful corporations. Beginning in the 1980s, members of several minority and poor communities began organizing to fight against what they perceived as environmental racism in their neighborhoods and nationwide. In 1989 residents of Cancer Alley organized the first Great Louisiana Toxic March to bring attention to their living conditions. Two years later three hundred delegates from grassroots environmental justice groups across the United States—including an Altgeld Gardens representative—convened the First National People of Color Environmental Leadership Summit in Washington, D.C., where they networked and drafted a manifesto. By this time, the environmental justice

319

movement had been reinforced academically with the publication of several demographic studies asserting not only the existence of environmental racism but also the federal government's complicity, through inaction, in that racism.

Others contend, however, that market forces, not racist practices, may determine the siting of polluting facilities. "Environmental hazards are likely to be placed in any community that . . . is willing to accept risks because they create jobs or generate taxes," New York Law School professor David Schoenbrod explains. Moreover, Schoenbrod asserts, in many cases—such as Altgeld Gardens, which was built atop a landfill— "the environmental hazards did not come to minority neighborhoods, but rather the minority populations came to the hazards."

Whether race-based inequality, market forces, or other factors determine the location of polluting industries is debated by the authors in the following chapter.

Racist Attitudes Guide Environmental Decision Making

by Bill Lawson

Bill Lawson heads the Department of Philosophy at the University of Delaware. He writes often on social and political philosophy and on African American issues. In the following viewpoint, Lawson contends that policy makers and others have negative views of poor urban blacks and that these views influence environmental decisions. Environmental justice cannot be achieved, he contends, until the needs of poor urban blacks are considered equally with the needs of others.

"Being black, poor, and living in the city can seem, in the mind of many persons, a relevant difference for disparate treatment."

Until recently, so-called classic environmentalists have given scant attention to the problems of the cities. Dale Jamieson notes this slight in 1984 and starts his insightful paper "The City Around Us" by stating, "It may seem odd to many people that a book devoted to environmental ethics includes an essay on the city. We often speak of the environment as if it is everywhere except where we live. The environment is Yellowstone, Estes Park, Cape Hatteras, and other vacation spots."[1] According to Jamieson, the environment in which most of us spend most of our time is the urban environment, and any deep understanding of our relationship to the environment cannot ignore this fact.[2]

Cities, Jamieson argues, are an important part of our American heritage and thus are worth preserving. His main point is that cities contain

321

certain cultural landmarks that we should preserve. Jamieson gives an argument based on what he takes to be common wisdom why environmentalists should be concerned with preserving cities. Interestingly enough, Jamieson said nothing about the plight of poor people living in cities, what saving the urban landmarks would mean to them, or what viewing cities as landmarks would mean to urban residents.

While Jamieson was timely in his concerns, I want to raise what I take to be a concern for anyone working on the issue of environmental ethics. I contend that environmentalists have not given due consideration to negative attitudes about cities and how these attitudes influence their environmental policies. I also want to contend that there are negative racial sentiments about black Americans. When negative attitudes about cities combine with certain racial attitudes, there is an adverse impact on the lives of the poor black people who live in cities. That is, if it is true that the overall conception of cities by most Americans is negative, environmentalists must consider what happens when those attitudes combine with negative views of racial groups who live there.

If these two attitudes do influence our conceptions of urban areas and African Americans, then theories of environmental justice, and indeed theories of justice overall, must take into account how theories of justice are applied.[3] There is now little disagreement that urban areas in the United States populated by racial minorities have been low on the environmental protection pecking order. Environmental pollution in large metropolitan areas has affected these areas adversely. Why is there more pollution in these areas? Though this question is complex, I want to suggest that negative conceptions of urban life and African Americans have to be factored into the answer. . . .

Cities as Sociological Entities

We can view cities in many ways. We will note only two here: cities as geographical entities and cities as sociological entities. Cities are of course located somewhere. They exist in a physical space. There are often physical attributes connected with cities. The views of San Francisco Bay and the New York skyline are only two examples. On the sociological side, cities have symbolic meaning. We often understand cities and our experience of them vicariously through the interpretations of symbolic representations.

Complex social interactions build upon these interpretations. In the United States, conceptions of race often color our interpretations of events, persons, and places. We often understand the meaning or nature of a place by reference to the race of the persons living there.

Michael Omi and Howard Winant discuss the connection between views of racial groups and our understanding of the social world.[4] They use the term *racialization* to signify the extension of racial meaning to a previously racially unclassified relationship, social practice, or group.[5] Cities, accordingly, should be to some extent race-neutral places, since members of various racial groups live in them.

However, racialization is the manner in which conceptions of racial standing enter into our understanding of social contexts and experiences. Thus, our understanding of certain social practices and experiences carries the various meanings associated with racial connotations at that time.[6]

The concept of race is an organizing principle of social relations that provides a description, a classification of racial phenomena in the United States, and also explains the continuity of these phenomena.[7]

In the United States, the category of "white" took on class meaning that early European immigrants readily bought into and supported. As chattel slavery evolved into the social fabric of America, Africans whose identity was Ibo, Yoruba, Fulani, and so on, were rendered black. Similarly, all Europeans were classified as white. These racial categories carried class distinctions. These racial distinctions were to transcend the ending of slavery and impact on the formation of the working class. Omi and Winant note that

> the very political organization of the working class was in important ways a racial project. The legacy of racial conflicts and arrangements shaped the definition of interests and in turn led to the consolidation of institutional patterns (e.g., segregated Unions, dual labor markets, exclusionary legislation) which perpetuated the color line within the working class.[8]

The Irish on the West Coast, for example, engaged in vicious anti-Chinese race-baiting and committed many pogrom-type assaults on Chinese in the course of consolidating the trade union movement in California.[9]

The development of both labor union policy and public policy involved notions of race. Labor unions refused to admit blacks as members and many skilled trades were nearly all white. In the public housing arena, politicians reinforced the notions of race as a defining factor in the life of a community. Politicians and realtors tightly enforced the laws and legal restrictions that prevented blacks from buying homes outside certain areas, producing the metropolitan color line. Such policies show the extent that the policy makers understand the negative meaning of race in our conceptions of both living and work space.

Racial Influences

Thus, race is a fundamental organizing principle. The notion of race often works on two levels. It forms our conception of personal identity. Racial understanding informs the way we understand ourselves and interact with others, structuring our practical activity—in work and family. This understanding extends to our cultural practices. Historically, laws restricting interracial marriages can be seen as a way to structure racial standing in the United States, that is, to prevent the races from mixing.[10]

As citizens and as thinkers (or "philosophers") our attitudes are shaped by racial meanings and racial awareness.[11] For example, opinion poll after poll shows that blacks think O.J. Simpson is innocent, while most whites think that he is guilty.[12] Race also shapes our understanding of collective enterprises such as economic, political, and cultural structures. An example of how racial understanding can shape our understanding of a cultural artifact can be seen with the phrase "urban contemporary music." This type of music is readily identified with cities and blacks. Rap music and jazz are often cited as "black music."

Race also influences our understanding of how people fare in life. The current welfare debate has racial overtones. It is being claimed that poor black mothers are failing to do what is "socially correct" to provide for their children. These women, it is argued, have failed to play the social responsibility game as do poor white mothers. While there are more single white females with children on welfare, the face of poverty in the United States is a poor, inner-city, unmarried black woman with children.

In this regard, policy makers organize their understanding of certain events around their views about the race of the persons involved. Our racial views influence our conceptions of events and carry public policy implications that are often not fully or readily appreciated. What happens when cities are seen as predominately populated by blacks? How do views about the behavior of blacks affect our views of cities? How are public policies formulated with racialized conceptions of cities? Have ethicists taken into account the impact of race on their theories of justice in general and of environmental justice in particular? These are important philosophical and public policy questions.

My claim is not that environmentalists are racists. Rather distributive justice requires treating equals equally and treating differently those who have relevant differences. If our culture influences us to perceive race and place negatively, these attributes will be considered relevant differences. These differences are factored into policy considerations. Environmentalists often fail to appreciate the manner in which conceptions of racial and spatial difference may hinder *just* urban environmental policies.

Racialization and the Cities

Claiming that a large number of blacks populate some American cities seems uncontroversial. The African American populations in Philadelphia, New York, Baltimore, Chicago, and Atlanta bear out this claim. However, because of the large black population these cities are often viewed as unsafe. These cities are seen as populated by welfare cheats and urban thugs, where many think that crime and mayhem are rampant.[13] Would you want to live in such a place? For most whites and many blacks the answer is no!

There is a tendency to view some cities as black enclaves. Suburbs are more likely than not viewed as white enclaves. In this way, urban and suburban space has become racialized. For many persons their understanding of the patterns of behavior associated with a racial group is connected with the space, giving meaning to the differences in lifestyles and standards of living based on a racial criterion.[14]

Racialization and Environmental Justice

As Peter Wenz correctly notes, environmental justice features those concerns within the environmental movement directed toward achieving equity and a fair sharing of environmental burdens and benefits.[15] Environmental burdens would include exposure to hazardous materials and toxic wastes, pollution, health hazards, and resource depletion. Environmental benefits would include, but not be limited to, a safe living space, a safe workplace, clean water and air, and the political power to influence environmental decisions.

When cities are seen as black homelands, urban residents claim that policy makers minimize the impact of dumping and other hazardous forms of pollution. Charles Lee, writing in the *Earth Island Journal*, notes "People of color live in communities not only targeted for the disposal of environmental toxins and hazardous waste but in fact live in fully disposable communities to be thrown away when the population they hold have outlived their usefulness."[16]

Obviously we do not store waste in areas where there are people like us; in this case white upper- and middle-class people are the people whom environmentalists must protect. Dumping waste in white neighborhoods would not be the moral thing to do. Environmentalists, it is claimed, often do not give the same moral weight to dumping waste in poor black urban areas.

People sometimes ask the question: "Why should we care what happens to cities?" The blacks have taken them over. The main goal for many whites has been to keep blacks out of white space. Justice has come to mean protecting white space and not hurting white people. This attitude is in some sense the colonial model of urban planning. Why not put waste dumps in poor black neighborhoods? We are not hurting anyone by dumping here. If we (the colonialists) put housing and parks in these native neighborhoods, they will only destroy them. The natives are different, morally and physically.

When we identify a group negatively, its members are unlike us and often not deserving of the same treatment or respect. Accordingly, racial and spatial difference marks important differences that must be given weight in our moral deliberations. That is, we treat all equals the same unless there are some relevant differences that would warrant different treatment. Being black, poor, and living in the city can seem, in the mind of many persons, a relevant difference for disparate treatment.

Environmentalists have a natural conception of pollution as a negative norm. If a place is thought to be already polluted by racial identifiers, we need to contain the pollution by keeping it in that area. If the environment of blacks is negative, it does not seem likely that their environmental interests will be given full consideration. Persons in power will continue to consider the burden of environmental polices using a cost/benefit analysis. Greater weight will be given to those policies that hurt whites the least. Because whites are wealthier, hurting them is usually a greater financial burden.

Environmentalists, in trying to do what is best for all, will have a slanted view of all, if they have not examined and considered their views about race and space in environmental policy. To this end the places where blacks live must be seen as places to protect environmentally, and blacks as persons must have a right to share in the benefits of environmental policies without undue burdens.

For some persons race-based policies connect the environmental justice movement to social justice. As Charles Lee notes, "Environmental issues afford us the opportunity to address many of the critical issues of the decade, including unemployment, community and urban development, energy and defense policy, resource exploitation, public health, and self determination."[17]

Environmental Justice and Race

While blacks often view the rush to dump as a continuation of the social injustices of the past, environmentalists want it known that environmentalism is compatible with social justice and by its very nature must include the cities. I agree that environmentalism is compatible with social justice. We should remember, however, that the claim is not that environmentalism is incompatible with social justice. What I am claiming is that environmentalists often fail to appreciate the manner in which racial categories impinge on their understanding of space. Do environmentalists connect any negative attributes associated with the group to the space? Clearly for many Americans, some cities are black homelands and cities as sources of pollution may reinforce negative images of blacks, for example, "Filthydelphia."[18]

Finally, it might be that liberal theories of distributive justice cannot adequately address the problem of racism in the distribution of social goods. Iris Young notes there is often a failure to appreciate that policies of distribution have a historical context and that this history often shapes views about who gets what and why.[19] Ideas of distributive justice cannot be separated from the institutional context that helps frame them.

People who write about justice in the distributive paradigm claim to be blocking out all the irrelevant differences that would cause a maldistribution of goods and benefits. On a theoretical level this claim works well, yet if my contentions about race and place are correct, attitudes about racialized space have to be addressed. We know that even behind the "veil of ignorance" persons must consider where they will be living. These persons will be thinking of living somewhere. How do these persons conceive of this space? Is it a city or suburb? What is life like in this space?

Clearly, we have viewed racialized black space as a negative living habitat. This raises questions about the notion of the common good.

Some Final Thoughts

The notion of environmental justice is about place. Many environmentalists have a romanticized vision of place, a heightened concern for animals, and yet a seemingly perverse disdain for certain humans and their habitat. Environmentalism has been narrow concerning space. Many people have thought, until very recently, that the greatest concern of environmentalists was for those places with much water and trees. Environmentalists view this space as the wilderness that has to be protected. Urban areas have to be contained and/or the "urban wilderness" renewed.

Most environmentalists do not perceive themselves as having negative racial attitudes. These environmentalists think that their interests align with blacks' around the issue of what is best for the overall environment. Many environmentalists are concerned with local issues, for example, pollution in the Delaware River, and so on. The stock phrase is "Act locally, think globally." Nevertheless, it must be admitted that few people can think globally. So far, the only truly "global" issues, that is, human induced influences that could affect the entire globe, are climate change and ozone depletion. It is very uncertain if climate change, or global warming, is occurring. All other environmental issues are local. Most environmental issues are local, and local interest and bias influence policy decisions. When environmental issues are local, they often do not allow for the interests of blacks.

Is the failure to consider the interests of poor urban blacks just an example of benign neglect? Is this neglect vicious? Clearly persons who are concerned with both the environment and social justice must realize that an ad hoc urban policy will not adequately address the problem of cities, and will consequently hurt the goals of the environmental movement. That is, if environmentalists are truly concerned with protecting urban resources, then protecting and respecting the places where poor people live must be a part of their environmental mandate. It is in this way urban areas can prosper. Thus environmentalists must address the question of what urban living means and what cities mean in the environmental movement.

Environmentalists cannot have the position that cities are sometimes a pleasant place to visit but they would not want to live there and in fact think that no one should live in cities. There is also a perception that many in the classical environmental movement think that urban residents, particularly blacks, deserve their plight. If African Americans were concerned about their welfare, they would not live in the city. This view is, of course, incompatible with the environmentalist's claims of concern for social justice and environmental protection, because environmentalists do not want cities dismantled and urban residents scattered into the pristine wilderness.

Environmentalists have often claimed that urban residents have not taken steps to ensure that they have protected their living space. This view assumes that it is the responsibility of each group to protect its space and that failure to protect one's space is one's own fault. This view takes social responsibility off the government and puts the weight solely on those groups that are usually unable to muster local or national support for their environmental interests. It also places the weight for urban environmental programs on the residents of urban America. If environmentalists take either of these positions, it signals a break between environmental issues and social concerns of justice.

Anyone concerned with the environment has a personal stake in the city. Cities are home to millions of United States residents and as such deserve the interest of those persons concerned with the environment. Many of these urban residents are pushing for a balance between their social justice interests and environmental interests. If the environmental movement is to succeed, it has to take the social justice interests of urban residents to heart. Social and political justice is a necessary condition for environmental justice. Yet, when we conceive of a space racially, attitudes about race may end up overriding theories of justice and fair social practice.[20] Environmentalists must be involved in urban planning with those persons most affected by urban pollution, poor persons of color. To paraphrase Karen Warren, "Any environmental ethic must be an urban ethic."[21]

Notes

1. Dale Jamieson, "The City Around Us," in *Earthbound*, ed. by Tom Regan (Philadelphia: Temple University Press, 1984), 30.
2. Ibid.
3. David Goldberg, "'Polluting the Body Politic': Race and Urban Location," *Racist Culture* (Oxford: Blackwell, 1993), 185–205.
4. Michael Omi and Howard Winant, *Racial Formation in the United States* (New York: Routledge, 1986), 64.
5. Omi and Winant, 64.
6. Omi and Winant, 64.
7. Omi and Winant, 68.
8. Omi and Winant, 65.
9. Omi and Winant, 65.
10. See, for example, James Kenneth Lay, "Sexual Racism: A Legacy of Slavery," *National Black Law Journal* 13, no. 1–2 (Spring 1993): 165–83; and Ellis Cose, "Caught between Two Worlds: Why Simpson Can't Overcome the Barrier of Race," *Newsweek* 124 (11 July 1993): 28.
11. Omi and Winant, 67.
12. Andrew Blum, "Poll: More Lawyers See O.J. Walking: 70 Percent Now Say Simpson Will Go Free. Most Say Race Is a Factor," *National Law Journal* 17, no. 26 (27 February 1995): 1.
13. Joseph Sullivan, "Fearful Urban Neighbors Tell Bradley about Crime; Mugging Draws Senator to a Living Room," *New York Times* 143 (19 February 1994): 24L.
14. Howard McGary, "The Black Underclass and the Question of Values," in *The Underclass Question*, ed. by Bill E. Lawson (Philadelphia: Temple University Press, 1992).
15. Peter S. Wenz, *Environmental Justice* (Albany: State University of New York Press, 1988).
16. Charles Lee, "Urban Environmental Justice," *Earth Island Journal* (Spring 1993): 41.
17. Lee, 40.
18. I learned the term *Filthydelphia* from my colleague Nancy McCagney, who is involved with local environmental groups.
19. Iris Young, *Justice and the Politics of Difference* (Princeton: Princeton University Press, 1990).
20. While I have focused on views of the cities and race, environmentalist Robert D. Bullard writes that wherever blacks or other persons of color live,

there is a flagrant disregard for the effects of environmental pollution in their neighborhoods. There is ample evidence to suggest a correlation between race and where pollutants are dumped or stored. For example, the 1983 GAO study found a strong relationship between the location of off-site hazardous waste landfills and the race and socioeconomic status of the surrounding communities. The study identified four off-site hazardous waste landfills in eight states (Alabama, Florida, Georgia, Kentucky, Mississippi, North Carolina, South Carolina, and Tennessee) that constitute the EPA's Region IV.

African Americans made up the majority of the population in three of the four communities where off-site hazardous waste landfills were located. In 1983, African Americans were clearly overrepresented in communities with waste sites, since they made up only about one-fifth of the region's population, yet African American communities contained three-fourths of the off-site landfills. These ecological imbalances had not been reversed a decade later. In 1992, African Americans constituted about one-fifth of the population of Region IV. However, the two operating off-site hazardous waste landfills in the region were located in zip code regions where African Americans made up the majority of the population. See, for example, Benjamin A. Goldman, *The Truth about Where You Live: An Atlas for Action on Toxins and Mortality* (New York: Random House, 1991).

21. I want to thank Jim Anderson, Peter Wenz, Laura Westra, Bernard Boxhill, Laurence Kalkstein, Nancy McCagney, William Lance Lawson, and the Geography Department at the University of Delaware for their comments on this topic.

Excerpted from "Living for the City: Urban United States and Environmental Justice" by Bill Lawson, in *Faces of Environmental Racism: Confronting Issues of Global Justice*, edited by Laura Westra and Peter Wenz (Lanham, MD: Rowman & Littlefield, 1995). Reprinted by permission of the publisher.

Market Forces May Guide Environmental Decision Making

by Vicki Been

Vicki Been is associate professor of law at New York University School of Law. In the following viewpoint, she argues that market forces, rather than racism or classism, may explain the large number of waste facilities located in poor and minority communities. Been's research suggests that poor people of color, who are often relegated to less desirable neighborhoods because of housing discrimination and low incomes, may have been drawn to these neighborhoods only after the waste facilities drove down housing prices.

"The research fails to prove . . . that the disproportionate burden poor and minority communities now bear . . . is the result of racism and classism in the siting process."

T he environmental justice movement contends that people of color and the poor are exposed to greater environmental risks than are whites and wealthier individuals. The movement charges that this disparity is due in part to racism and classism in the siting of environmental risks, the promulgation of environmental laws and regulations, the enforcement of environmental laws, and the attention given to the cleanup of polluted areas.[1] To support the first charge—that the siting of waste dumps, polluting factories, and other locally undesirable land uses (LU-LUs) had been racist and classist—advocates for environmental justice have cited more than a dozen studies analyzing the relationship between neighborhoods' socioeconomic characteristics and the number of LULUs they host. The studies demonstrate that those neighborhoods in which LULUs are located have, on average, a higher percentage of racial minorities and are poorer than non-host communities.[2]

That research does not, however, establish that the host communities were disproportionately minority or poor at the time the sites were selected. Most of the studies compare the *current* socioeconomic characteristics of communities that host various LULUs to those of communities that do not host such LULUs. This approach leaves open the possibility that the sites for LULUs were chosen fairly,[3] but that subsequent events produced the current disproportion in the distribution of LULUs. In other words, the research fails to prove environmental justice advocates' claim that the disproportionate burden poor and minority communities now bear in hosting LULUs is the result of racism and classism in the *siting process* itself.[4]

In addition, the research fails to explore an alternative or additional explanation for the proven demographics of communities and the likelihood that they host LULUs.[5] Regardless of whether the LULUs originally were sited fairly, it could well be that neighborhoods surrounding LULUs became poorer and became home to a greater percentage of people of color over the years following the sitings. Such factors as poverty, housing discrimination, and the location of jobs, transportation, and other public services may have led the poor and racial minorities to "come to the nuisance"—to move to neighborhoods that host LULUs—because those neighborhoods offered the cheapest available housing. Despite the plausibility of that scenario, none of the existing research on environmental justice has examined how the siting of undesirable land uses has subsequently affected the socioeconomic characteristics of host communities.[6] Because the research fails to prove that the siting process causes any of the disproportionate burden the poor and minorities now bear, and because the research has ignored the possibility that market dynamics may have played some role in the distribution of that burden, policymakers now have no way of knowing whether the siting process is "broke" and needs fixing.[7] Nor can they know whether even an ideal siting system that ensured a perfectly fair initial distribution of LULUs would result in any long-term benefit to the poor or to people of color.

Exploring the Gaps

This viewpoint begins to address both of these gaps in the research. Part I of this viewpoint explains how market dynamics may affect the demographics of the communities hosting LULUs. It then demonstrates why an empirical understanding of the role market dynamics play in the distribution is necessary both to focus discussion about the fairness of the existing distribution of LULUs and to fashion an effective remedy for any unfairness in that distribution.

Part II surveys the existing research and explains why it is insufficient to determine whether the siting process placed LULUs in neighborhoods that were disproportionately minority or poor at the time the facility was opened, whether the siting of the facility subsequently drove host neighborhoods to become home to a larger percentage of people of color or the poor than other communities, or whether both of these phenomena contributed to the current distribution of LULUs.

Part III undertakes empirical research to study the roles that initial siting decisions and market dynamics play in the distribution of LULUs. The research extends two of the studies most often cited as proof of environmental racism—the General Accounting Office's *Siting of Hazardous Waste Landfills and Their Correlation with Racial and Economic Status of Surrounding Communities*[8] and Robert Bullard's *Solid Waste Sites and the Black Houston Community*[9]—by analyzing data about the demographic characteristics of host neighborhoods in those studies at the time the siting decisions were made, then tracing demographic changes in the neighborhoods after the siting.

The larger of the two extended studies indicates that market dynamics may play a significant role in creating the disparity between the racial composition of host communities and that of non-host communities.[10] In that sample, LULUs initially were sited somewhat disproportionately in poor communities and communities of color.[11] After the sitings, the levels of poverty and percentages of African-Americans in the host neighborhoods increased, and the property values in these neighborhoods declined. Accordingly, the study suggests that while siting decisions do disproportionately affect minorities and the poor, market dynamics also play a very significant role in creating the uneven distribution of the burdens LULUs impose. Even if siting processes can be improved, therefore, market forces are likely to create a pattern in which LULUs become surrounded by people of color or the poor, and consequently come to impose a disproportionate burden upon those groups. The smaller study, on the other hand, finds a correlation between neighborhood demographics and initial siting decisions, but finds no evidence that market dynamics are leading the poor or people of color to "come to the nuisance."

Like the original studies, the extensions involve samples too small to establish conclusively the cause of disproportionate siting. The extensions are valuable nonetheless because they reveal the gaps in the existing research, improve upon the methodology of the research, and demonstrate that further study of the demographics of host communities at the time their LULUs were sited is likely to produce helpful information about the causes of, and potential solutions for, environmental injustice.[12]

I. Market Dynamics and the Distribution of LULUs

The residential housing market in the United States is extremely dynamic. Every year, approximately 17% to 20% of U.S. households move to a new home.[13] Some of those people stay within the same neighborhood, but many move to different neighborhoods in the same city, or to different cities.[14] Some people decide to move, at least in part, because they are dissatisfied with the quality of their current neighborhoods.[15] Once a household decides to move, its choice of a new neighborhood usually depends somewhat on the cost of housing and the characteristics of the neighborhood.[16] Those two factors are interrelated because the quality of the neighborhood affects the price of housing.[17]

The siting of a LULU can influence the characteristics of the surrounding neighborhood in two ways. First, an undesirable land use may cause those who can afford to move to become dissatisfied and leave the neighborhood.[18] Second, by making the neighborhood less desirable, the LULU may decrease the value of the neighborhood's property,[19] making the housing more available to lower income households and less attractive to higher income households.[20] The end result of both influences is likely to be that the neighborhood becomes poorer than it was before the siting of the LULU.

The neighborhood also is likely to become home to more people of color. Racial discrimination in the sale and rental of housing relegates people of color (especially African-Americans) to the least desirable neighborhoods, regardless of their income level.[21] Moreover, once a neighborhood becomes a community of color, racial discrimination in the promulgation and enforcement of zoning and environmental protection laws,[22] the provision of municipal services,[23] and the lending practices of banks[24] may cause neighborhood quality to decline further.[25] That additional decline, in turn, will induce those who can leave the neighborhood—the least poor and those least subject to discrimination—to do so.

The dynamics of the housing market therefore are likely to cause the poor and people of color to move to or remain in the neighborhoods in which LULUs are located, regardless of the demographics of the communities when the LULUs were first sited. As long as the market allows the existing distribution of wealth to allocate goods and services, it would be surprising indeed if, over the long run, LULUs did not impose a disproportionate burden upon the poor. And as long as the market discriminates on the basis of race, it would be remarkable if LULUs did not eventually impose a disproportionate burden upon people of color.

Justice or Injustice

By failing to address how LULUs have affected the demographics of their host communities, the current research has ignored the possibility that the correlation between the location of LULUs and the socioeconomic characteristics of neighborhoods may be a function of aspects of our free market system other than, or in addition to, the siting process. It is crucial to examine that possibility. Both the justice of the distribution of LULUs and the remedy for any injustice may differ if market dynamics play a significant role in the distribution.

If the siting process is primarily responsible for the correlation between the location of LULUs and the demographics of host neighborhoods, the process may be unjust under current constitutional doctrine, at least as to people of color. Siting processes that result in the selection of host neighborhoods that are disproportionately poor (but not disproportionately composed of people of color) would not be unconstitutional because the Supreme Court has been reluctant to recognize poverty as a suspect classification.[26] A siting process motivated by racial prejudice, however, would be unconstitutional.[27] A process that disproportionately affects people of color[28] also would be unfair under some statutory schemes and some constitutional theories of discrimination.[29]

On the other hand, if the disproportionate distribution of LULUs results from market forces which drive the poor, regardless of their race,[30] to live in neighborhoods that offer cheaper housing because they host LULUs, then the fairness of the distribution becomes a question about the fairness of our market economy. Some might argue that the disproportionate burden is part and parcel of a free market economy that is, overall, fairer than alternative schemes, and that the costs of regulating the market to reduce the disproportionate burden outweigh the benefits of doing so. Others might argue that those moving to a host neighborhood are compensated through the market for the disproportionate burden they bear by lower housing costs, and therefore that the situation is just. Similarly, some might contend that while the poor suffer lower quality neighborhoods, they also suffer lower quality food, housing, and medical care, and that the systemic problem of poverty is better addressed through income redistribution programs than through changes in siting processes.

Even if decisionmakers were to agree that it is unfair to allow post-siting market dynamics to create disproportionate environmental risk for the poor or minorities, the remedy for that injustice would have to be much

335

more fundamental than the remedy for unjust siting *decisions*. Indeed, if market forces are the primary cause of the correlation between the presence of LULUs and the current socioeconomic characteristics of a neighborhood, even a siting process radically revised to ensure that LULUs are distributed equally among all neighborhoods may have only a short-term effect.[31] The areas surrounding LULUs distributed equitably will become less desirable neighborhoods, and thus may soon be left to people of color or the poor, recreating the pattern of inequitable siting. Accordingly, if a disproportionate burden results from or is exacerbated by market dynamics, an effective remedy might require such reforms as stricter enforcement of laws against housing discrimination, more serious efforts to achieve residential integration, changes in the processes of siting low and moderate income housing, changes in programs designed to aid the poor in securing decent housing, greater regulatory protection for those neighborhoods that are chosen to host LULUs, and changes in production and consumption processes to reduce the number of LULUs needed.

Information about the role market dynamics play in the distribution of LULUs would promote a better understanding of the nature of the problem of environmental injustice and help point the way to appropriate solutions for the problem. Nonetheless, market dynamics have been largely ignored by the current research on environmental justice.

II. The Evidence of Disproportionate Siting

Several recent studies have attempted to assess whether locally undesirable land uses are disproportionately located[32] in neighborhoods that are populated by more people of color or are more poor than is normal. The most important of the studies was published in 1987 by the United Church of Christ Commission for Racial Justice (CRJ).[33] The CRJ conducted a cross-sectional study of the racial and socioeconomic characteristics of residents of the zip code areas surrounding 415 commercial hazardous waste facilities[34] and compared those characteristics to those of zip code areas which did not have such facilities.[35] The study revealed a correlation between the number of commercial hazardous waste facilities[36] in an area and the percentage of the "nonwhite" population in the area.[37] Areas that had one operating commercial hazardous waste facility, other than a landfill, had about twice as many people of color as a percentage of the population as those that had no such facility.[38] Areas that had more than one operating facility, or had one of the five largest landfills, had more than three times the percentage of minority residents as areas that had no such facilities.[39]

Several regional and local studies buttress the findings of the nationwide CRJ study.[40] The most frequently cited of those studies, which is often credited for first giving the issue of environmental justice visibility, was conducted by the United States General Accounting Office (GAO). The GAO examined the racial and socioeconomic characteristics of the communities surrounding four hazardous waste landfills in the eight southeastern states that make up EPA's Region IV.[41] The sites studied include some of the largest landfills in the United States. . . .

[The GAO found that] three of the four communities where such landfills were sited were majority African-American in 1980; African-Americans made up 52%, 66%, and 90% of the population in those three communities.[42] In contrast, African-Americans made up between 22% and 30% of the host states' populations.[43] The host communities were all disproportionately poor, with between 26% and 42% of the population living below the poverty level.[44] In comparison, the host states' poverty rates ranged from 14% to 19%.[45]

Another frequently cited local study was conducted by sociologist Robert Bullard[46] and formed important parts of his books, *Invisible Houston*[47] and *Dumping in Dixie*.[48] Professor Bullard found that although African-Americans made up only 28% of the Houston population in 1980, six of Houston's eight incinerators and mini-incinerators and fifteen of seventeen landfills were located in predominantly African-American neighborhoods.[49]

With one exception, described below, none of the existing studies addressed the question of which came first—the people of color and the poor, or the LULU.[50] As noted by the CRJ, the studies "were not designed to show cause and effect,"[51] but only to explore the relationship between the current distribution of LULUs and host communities' demographics. The evidence of disproportionate siting is thus incomplete: it does not establish that *the siting process* had a disproportionate effect upon minorities or the poor.

Studies Differ

Professor James T. Hamilton of Duke University has performed the only research to date that has addressed the "which came first" question. Professor Hamilton recently examined how the planned capacity changes for hazardous waste processing facilities in 1987 correlated with the political power (measured by voter registration) of the facilities' host counties as of the 1980 census.[52] In the course of his study, Professor Hamilton also examined correlations between planned capacity changes and county demographics. Because Professor Hamilton's analysis examined decisions about whether to expand or contract facilities that were made five or six years after the census from which data on the county's socioeconomic characteristics were derived, and because decisions to expand or contract capacity share some of the same characteristics as initial siting decisions,[53] his analysis is probative of whether there is a correlation between siting decisions and the characteristics of affected communities near the time of those decisions. Professor Hamilton concluded that when other factors were controlled, the race and income of the county at the time of the expansion decisions were not significant predictors of expansion plans.[54] Race was a statistically significant determinant of the facilities' plans to reduce capacity, however; as the percentage of a county's minority population increased, it was less likely that the facility planned to reduce its capacity.[55]

In addition, Professor Hamilton compared 1970 census data regarding the counties in which surveyed facilities were sited in the 1970's and early 1980's to census data for all counties in the United States. Professor Hamilton found that both race and median household income were statistically significant predictors of sitings during the 1970's and early 1980's.[56] Professor Hamilton's study has several limitations: the sample did not include facilities that went out of business before the 1987 survey;[57] the data examined was for entire counties rather than the tracts or county subdivisions in which the facility was actually located;[58] and the 1970 census data was used even for siting decisions made in the early 1980's.[59] The study nevertheless provides important evidence that the siting process itself has had a disproportionate effect on low income communities and communities of color. Professor Hamilton did not examine whether the socioeconomic characteristics of host communities changed once the facilities were sited, however, so his study does not provide any evidence about the role that market dynamics may play in the distribution of LULUs.

In summary, with the exception of Professor Hamilton's study, the existing research fails to focus on the characteristics of communities at the time LULUs were sited, and therefore cannot establish whether the correlation between a neighborhood's current demographics and the number of LULUs it hosts was caused by the siting process. None of the existing research examines how market dynamics affected the socioeconomic characteristics of host neighborhoods. The literature therefore sheds little light on whether the current distribution of LULUs resulted from siting processes that had a disproportionate effect upon minorities and the poor, or from market dynamics, or both.

III. The Effects of Siting Practices and Market Dynamics

To begin to fill the gaps in the literature, this Part expands the GAO and Bullard studies described above. First, it adds to those studies data regarding the socioeconomic characteristics of the host communities at the time the siting decisions were made. Second, it traces changes in the demographics of the host communities since the sitings took place.

The GAO Study

Of the four hazardous waste landfills studied by the GAO, one became operational in 1972, two in 1977, and one in 1979.[60] The process of choosing a site, applying for the necessary permits, and constructing the landfill typically takes at least several years, so it is likely that the sites for the three landfills that became operational in 1972 and 1977 were chosen in the early or mid-1970's.[61] One would therefore learn more about whether those siting choices had a disproportionate effect on the poor or people of color by examining the socioeconomic characteristics of those three communities in 1970, rather than 1980.[62]

The 1970 data for those three sites and the 1980 data for the remaining site reveal that all of the host communities were disproportionately populated by African-Americans at the time of the sitings. The percentage of the host communities' populations that was African-American ranged from 1.6 times to 3.3 times that of the host states' populations.[63] Accordingly, demographic data from the time of the siting supports the inference that the siting process was flawed in a way that caused siting choices to have a disproportionate effect upon people of color.

Conversely, the data provide no support for the theory that market dynamics will cause host neighborhoods to become increasingly populated by people of color. In each of the four communities the GAO studied, the siting of the landfill was followed by a decrease in the percentage of the community that was African-American. While the change was insignificant in two of the host communities, the African-American percentage of the population in two of the host communities declined precipitously. The area surrounding the Industrial Chemical Facility in Chester County, South Carolina, had a 35.8% decrease in the percentage of its population that was African-American between 1970 and 1990. Similarly, the area surrounding the SCA Services facility in Sumter County, South Carolina, had a 32.3% decrease between 1970 and 1990. By contrast, South Carolina as a whole had a 2.3% decrease between 1970 and 1990.

The substantial decrease in the percentage of African-American residents in these communities contradicts the theory that a landfill changes the demographics of neighboring areas by making them less attractive places to live, thereby decreasing property values and rents, and attracting people who are unable to afford other neighborhoods, or who are excluded from other neighborhoods by racial discrimination.[64] The theory is further undermined by the remaining evidence. The relative poverty[65] and relative median family income of the host counties changed only marginally[66] between 1970 and 1990.[67] Further, the relative median housing value changed only slightly between 1970 and 1990, and, in two of the four host communities, the relative median housing value increased. If the market dynamics theory were correct, the data should show decreases in relative median family income and relative median housing values and increases in relative poverty over the decades after the siting.

In sum, an examination of the characteristics of the host communities at issue in the GAO study at the time the facilities were sited shows that the host communities were home to a considerably larger percentage of African-Americans and were somewhat poorer than other communities within the host states. The analysis therefore suggests that the siting process had a disproportionate effect on the poor and people of color. At the same time, the analysis provides no support for the theory that the location of LULUs in poor or minority communities is a result of the dynamics of the housing market.

The Bullard Study

The second part of this study uses a subgroup of the sites that were the subject of Professor Bullard's 1983 study of the location of incinerators and landfills in Houston. Professor Bullard's study concluded that twenty-one of Houston's twenty-five incinerators, mini-incinerators, and landfills were located in predominantly African-American neighborhoods.[68]

The extension of Professor Bullard's study presented here eliminates data about Houston's unpermitted municipal landfills and incinerators from the sample. Those landfills and incinerators were sited as long ago as 1920, and all had ceased to operate by the 1970's. Because census tracts were quite large during the early decades of the century, it is impossible to evaluate in any meaningful way the racial and class characteristics of communities chosen to host LULUs that long ago. In addition, the revision collapses the categories that Professor Bullard differentiated as "Browning Ferris Industries Landfill Sites" and "Texas Department of Health Permitted Municipal Landfill Sites"[69] because three of the landfills fall into both categories, and were essentially "double-counted" in Professor Bullard's study.[70] To avoid double-counting, the revision also combines what Professor Bullard lists separately as the American Refuse Systems and Browning Ferris Industries sites, because those sites are in fact the same landfill.[71] Of what Professor Bullard lists as twenty-five sites, then, the revision looks at three mini-incinerators and seven landfills.

There is another important difference between the extension and

Professor Bullard's original analysis. While Professor Bullard's published accounts of his study do not explain his methodology, Professor Bullard has explained in correspondence that his study did not use census tracts as its unit of analysis, but instead used "neighborhoods."[72] In contrast, this extension examines census tract data. Professor Bullard's published accounts of his study do not provide information about how he defined the neighborhoods surrounding the sites, and it therefore is impossible to replicate his analysis on a neighborhood basis.

In addition, there are significant advantages to using census tracts rather than smaller "neighborhoods" as the unit of analysis for examining the distribution of undesirable land uses.[73] The advantage of neighborhood units of analysis, such as blocks or block groups, is that such data are less likely to hide differences in the population within the unit.[74] The disadvantages of such small units of analysis, however, are substantial. Although a facility may have its most immediate impact on the few blocks immediately contiguous to the facility, there is substantial reason to doubt that the impact stops there.[75] In addition, data often are not available for finer units of analysis, because where a block is so small that the confidentiality of the census survey respondents would be compromised by release of the data, the Census Bureau suppresses the data.[76] Blocks vary greatly in area and density, so comparisons based on block and block group data will be misleading unless adjusted for differences in the size of the population.[77] Finally, block groups change in configuration over time, so problems occur in comparing data across decades.[78]

Census tracts, on the other hand, are structured to be relatively permanent.[79] They are supposed to have between 2500 and 8000 people each, so they can be compared without adjustments for area or density.[80] Tracts comprehensively cover almost all metropolitan populations.[81] When formed, census tracts are supposed to be as homogenous as possible.[82] Because of these advantages, census tracts often are used as the unit of analysis in studying a "neighborhood."[83] Indeed, almost all of the literature on the siting of undesirable land uses described in Part II uses census tracts or larger census units as the unit of analysis; none uses blocks or block grouping.[84]

A Disproportionate Burden

Of the ten sites used in the revision, all the mini-incinerators and four of the landfills were sited in the early 1970's, so 1970 census data is most relevant for those sites. Two adjacent landfills were sited in the early and mid-1950's; for those sites, 1960 data was also analyzed (the tract in which the landfills were located was so large in 1950 that the 1950 data is not comparable to the later data). The remaining landfill was permitted in 1978; because that siting decision was most likely made after 1975, the 1980 census data is most relevant for that site.

[Census data] reveal that, of the seven landfills sited between 1953 and 1978, four host neighborhoods had about the same or a lower percentage of African-Americans in their populations than Houston as a whole, while three had percentages above Houston's. Of the mini-incinerators sited in 1972, one was sited in an almost all-white neighborhood, and the other two were sited in neighborhoods with substantially more African-Americans as a percentage of their populations than Houston as a whole. Accordingly, three of the seven landfills and two of the three mini-incinerators (or half of all the facilities) were sited in areas that were disproportionately African-American at the time of the siting. About one-quarter of Houston's population was African-American during the relevant decades. Thus, the fact that one-half the sites were in neighborhoods that had more African-Americans as a percentage of their population than did Houston as a whole indicates that the siting process had some disproportionate effect.[85]

Analysis of the neighborhoods' demographics in the decades after the LULUs were sited, however, reveals that the siting process was not the sole cause of the disproportionate burden that African-American communities now bear. The number of African-Americans as a percentage of the population increased between 1970 and 1980 in all the neighborhoods surrounding the landfills. That increase was by as much as 223%, compared to a 7% increase in the African-American population of Houston as a whole. As a result, by the 1980 census, four of the seven neighborhoods hosting landfills and two of three neighborhoods hosting mini-incinerators had a greater percentage of African-Americans in their populations than Houston as a whole.

This trend continued between 1980 and 1990. In all but one neighborhood, the percentage of African-Americans continued to increase, even though the percentage of African-Americans in Houston as a whole stayed constant. The increases were less dramatic than the changes between 1970 and 1980, with all but two of the neighborhoods increasing by less than 10%. The end result, however, was that by the 1990 census, all of the neighborhoods hosting landfills had become home to a disproportionate percentage of African-Americans.

Examination of the host neighborhoods' economic characteristics reveals a similar pattern. Only two of the seven areas hosting landfills and one of the three areas hosting mini-incinerators had poverty rates significantly higher than Harris County's [Houston] at the time their facilities were sited.[86] The percentage of the host neighborhoods' populations with income under the poverty level increased between 1970 and 1980, how-

342

ever, in all but two of the host neighborhoods, even though Harris County's poverty rate dropped. Between 1980 and 1990, four of the seven neighborhoods hosting landfills had increases in their poverty rates that were significantly higher than the increases in poverty suffered by Harris County. As a result, by the time of the 1990 census, five of the seven areas hosting landfills and two of the three areas hosting mini-incinerators had become significantly poorer than Harris County.

Median family incomes in all but one of the neighborhoods surrounding landfills also lost ground relative to Harris County between 1970 and 1980, and further worsened between 1980 and 1990. In addition, all but one of the host communities where landfills[87] were sited before 1972 suffered marked declines in their housing values relative to Harris County over the decades following the sitings.[88]

In sum, examining the data for the census closest to the date of each siting decision shows that the siting process had a disproportionate effect upon African-Americans. In addition, such an analysis provides considerable support for the theory that market dynamics contribute to the disproportionate burden LULUs impose upon people of color and the poor. As the argument that LULUs change a neighborhood's demographics by driving down property values would predict, the data reveal that the homes surrounding the landfill sites in most of the host neighborhoods became less valuable properties relative to other areas of Harris County after the landfills were sited, and the host communities became increasingly populated by African-Americans and increasingly poor.

Which Came First?

The extensions of the GAO and Bullard studies, as well as Professor Hamilton's study of facilities' expansion and reduction plans, show the effect of using demographic data from the census closest to the actual siting or capacity change decision (rather than the latest census data). Tracing changes in the demographics from this baseline reveals a significant difference in the evidence the studies provide regarding the burden LULUs impose on minorities and the poor. These studies suggest that the siting process bears some responsibility for the disproportionate burden waste facilities now impose upon the poor and people of color.[89] The extension of the GAO study suggests that market dynamics play no role in the distribution of the burden. The extension of the Bullard study, on the other hand, suggests that market dynamics do play a significant role in that distribution.

The different results obtained by the two extensions may be attributable to the generally slower rate of residential mobility in rural areas, such as those hosting the GAO sites, versus urban areas, such as those hosting the Houston sites.[90] The difference also may be attributable to the size and nature of the facilities studied in the two extensions. The sites studied in the GAO report are quite large, and provide a substantial number of jobs to residents of the host counties.[91] Persons moving to the area to take those jobs may have displaced the African-Americans who previously lived in the community. The sites at issue in Professor Bullard's study, on the other hand, were unlikely to have created many new jobs, and those jobs that were created would have been much less likely than the jobs at the GAO sites to induce people to move nearby in order to take them.

Significant evidence suggests that LULUs are disproportionately located in neighborhoods that are now home to more of the nation's people of color and poor than other neighborhoods. Efforts to address that disparity are hampered, however, by the lack of data about which came first—the people of color and poor or the LULU. If the neighborhoods were disproportionately populated by people of color or the poor at the time the siting decisions were made, a reasonable inference can be drawn that the siting process had a disproportionate effect upon the poor and people of color. In that case, changes in the siting process may be required.

On the other hand, if, after the LULU was built, the neighborhoods in which LULUs were sited became increasingly poor, or became home to an increasing percentage of people of color, the cure for the problem of disproportionate siting is likely to be much more complicated and difficult. The distribution of LULUs would then look more like a confluence of the forces of housing discrimination, poverty, and free market economics. Remedies would have to take those forces into account.

The preliminary evidence derived from this extension of two of the leading studies of environmental justice, along with the evidence offered by Professor Hamilton's study of capacity expansion plans, shows that research examining the socioeconomic characteristics of host neighborhoods at the time they were selected, then tracing changes in those characteristics following the siting, would go a long way toward answering the question of which came first—the LULU or its minority or poor neighbors. Until that research is complete, proposed "solutions" to the problem of disproportionate siting run a substantial risk of missing the mark.

Notes

1. *See, e.g.,* ROBERT D. BULLARD, DUMPING IN DIXIE: RACE, CLASS, AND ENVIRONMENTAL QUALITY 1-6 (1990); Robert D. Bullard, *The Threat of Environmental Racism,* 7 NAT. RESOURCES & ENV'T 23 (1993); Luke W.Cole, *Empowerment as the Key to Environmental Protection: The Need for Environmental Poverty Law,* 19 ECOLOGY L.Q.

619, 629-30 (1992); Karl Grossman, *Environmental Justice*, E MAG., May-June 1992, at 29,31.

2. *See infra* text accompanying notes 32-59. The literature seems to assume that a siting pattern is disproportionate whenever the percentage of people of color in a host community is higher than the percentage of people of color in the nation's population or in the population of non-host communities. This measure of proportionality is simplistic. First, it ignores the density of population within a neighborhood. *Cf.* Michael Greenberg, *Proving Environmental Inequity in Siting Locally Unwanted Land Uses*, 4 RISK: ISSUES IN HEALTH & SAFETY 235, 244-49 (1993) (showing how use of statistics weighted by population of communities studied affects analysis of inequity). Assume, for example, that a siting decisonmaker is faced with two communities, one of which has 5000 people, 12% of whom are people of color, while the other has 1000 people, 20% of whom are people of color. Assume also that the percentage of people of color in the nation is 12%. Under the measure of proportionality generally used in the literature, the LULU would be disproportionately sited if it were placed in the second community, even though that choice would expose fewer people of color to the LULU than would the other site. A better measure of proportionality would take into account the number of people affected by a siting, rather than just focusing on the percentage of the affected population that is composed of people of color. *Cf.* UNITED CHURCH OF CHRIST COMM'N FOR RACIAL JUSTICE, TOXIC WASTES AND RACE IN THE UNITED STATES 53 (1987) [hereinafter CRJ REPORT] (finding that the percentage of people of color living in communities with uncontrolled toxic waste sites—56.32%—was only slightly higher than the percentage of whites living in such communities—53.60%). Second, this measure of proportionality can be misleading if studies do not provide information about how far the distribution of the population within the host neighborhoods deviates from the national distribution. By describing a community as "minority" or "poor" whenever the percentage of people of color or poor in the community exceeds that of the population as a whole, a study using this measure of proportionality could classify a LULU as disproportionately sited even if it is located in a predominantly white neighborhood in which the population variance from the national distribution is statistically insignificant. *Compare* CRJ, *supra*, at 41 (providing information about degree of variance between the distribution of the population in host and non-host communities) *with* the studies discussed *infra* text accompanying notes 41-49 (failing to provide such information).

3. What it means to site LULUs "fairly" is a complex and controversial issue. For a full discussion of that issue, see Vicki Been, *What's Fairness Got To Do with It? Environmental Justice and the Siting of Locally Undesirable Land Uses*, 78 CORNELL L. REV. 1001 (1993). For the purposes of this discussion, a "fair" siting will be considered one that has no disproportionate effect upon the poor or upon people of color.

4. Both of the leading studies of siting disparities recognize that analysis of the current demographics of host communities does not establish that discrimination in the siting process caused any of the disproportionate burden those communities now bear. *See* U.S. GEN. ACCOUNTING OFFICE, GAO/RCED-83-168, SITING OF HAZARDOUS WASTE LANDFILLS AND THEIR CORRELATION WITH RACIAL AND ECONOMIC STATUS OF SURROUNDING COMMUNITIES 3 (1983) [hereinafter GAO REPORT]; CRJ REPORT, *supra* note 2, at 11. For discussions of how existing studies fail to prove causation, see Been, *supra* note 3, at 1016-18; Michael B. Gerrard, *Fear and Loathing in the Siting of Hazardous and Radioactive Waste Facilities: A Comprehensive Approach to a Misperceived Crisis*, 68 TUL. L. REV. (forthcoming 1994) (manuscript at 125, 132, on file with author); James T. Hamilton, *Politics and Social Costs: Estimating the impact of Collective Action on Hazardous Waste Facilities*, 24 RAND J. ECON. 101, 110 (1993); Richard J. Lazarus, *Pursuing "Environmental Justice": The Distributional Effects of Environmental Protection*, 87 NW. U. L. REV. 787, 802 n.56 (1993). *Cf.* Bean v. Southwestern Waste Management Corp., 482 F. Supp. 673, 677 (S. D. Tex. 1979) (holding that to establish a pattern or practice of discriminatory siting, data must show demographics of host communities "on the day that the sites opened"), *aff'd* 782 F.2d 1038 (5th Cir. 1986).

5. While this Article focuses on market dynamics as an alternative explanation for the correlation, other potential explanations should be explored as well. For example, siting decisionmakers may seek to distribute sites fairly but face constraints imposed by regulations over which they have no control, such as zoning regulations. Those zoning regulations may underprotect the interests of the poor or people of color. *See* Jon C. Dubin, *From Junkyards to Gentrification: Explicating a Right to Protective Zoning in*

Low-Income Communities of Color, 77 MINN. L. REV. 739 (1993); Yale Rabin, *Expulsive Zoning: The Inequitable Legacy of* Euclid, in ZONING AND THE AMERICAN DREAM 101 (Charles M. Haar & Jerold S. Kayden eds., 1989).

6. A few studies, ignored by the environmental justice literature, have examined the effects various land uses have had on neighboring property values, turnover within a neighborhood, and the socioeconomic characteristics of the neighborhood. *See, e.g.*, MENTAL HEALTH LAW PROJECT, THE EFFECTS OF GROUP HOMES ON NEIGHBORING PROPERTY; AN ANNOTATED BIBLIOGRAPHY 1-15 (1988) (surveying the literature on the effects community residential facilities have on property values and neighborhood turnover); U.S. GEN. ACCOUNTING OFFICE, GAO/HRD-83-14, AN ANALYSIS OF ZONING AND OTHER PROBLEMS AFFECTING THE ESTABLISHMENT OF GROUP HOMES FOR THE MENTALLY DISABLED app. III at 62 (1983) (reporting results of survey of turnover and demographic change in neighborhoods hosting group homes); Diana A. Arens, *What Do the Neighbors Think Now? Community Residences on Long Island, New York*, 29 COMMUNITY MENTAL HEALTH J. 235 (1993) (finding that group homes for mentally ill adults have no adverse effects on property values); Michael Dear, *Impact of Mental Health Facilities on Property Values*, 13 COMMUNITY MENTAL HEALTH J. 150 (1977) (discussing housing turnover and property values following opening of group homes). Those studies, however, do not focus on how market dynamics affect the distribution of group homes.

7. Nevertheless, Congress is now considering several bills intended to "correct" the siting process. *See, e.g.*, Environmental Justice Act of 1992, H.R. 2105, 103d Cong., 1st Sess. (1993); Environmental Equal Rights Act of 1993, H.R. 1924, 103d Cong., 1st Sess. (1993); S. 533, 103d Cong., 1st Sess. (1993). State legislatures are considering similar proposals. *See, e.g.*, Cal. A.B. 2212, 1993-94 Reg. Sess. (1993); N.Y. S.B. 5742, 1993-94 Reg. Sess. (1993).

8. GAO REPORT, *supra* note 4.

9. Robert D. Bullard, *Solid Waste Sites and the Black Houston Community*, 53 SOC. INQUIRY 273 (1983) [hereinafter Bullard, *Solid Waste*].

10. *See infra* text accompanying notes 85-88.

11. The sitings had a disproportionate effect in that host neighborhoods had a higher percentage of African-Americans and the poor than non-host neighborhoods. For criticism of that measure of proportionality, see *supra* note 2.

12. On basis of the research reported here, the author has received an exploratory research grant from the U.S Environmental Protection Agency (EPA) to pursue further research on the role market dynamics play in the distribution of the burdens LULUs impose. That study will analyze the socioeconomic characteristics of neighborhoods hosting various LULUs as of the census closest to the date of the relevant siting decision. The study will then trace changes in the neighborhoods' demographic characteristics after the LULUs were constructed. The study will focus on those communities that host hazardous waste treatment, disposal, and storage facilities regulated under the Resource Conservation and Recovery Act, 42 U.S.C. §§ 6901-6987 (1988), as well as those that host the toxic waste sites included on the EPA's National Priorities List for cleanup under the Comprehensive Environmental Response, Compensation, and Liability Act, 42 U.S.C. §§ 9601-9675 (1988).

13. BUREAU OF THE CENSUS, U.S. DEP'T OF COMMERCE, CURRENT POPULATION REPORTS, SERIES P-20 NO. 463, GEOGRAPHICAL MOBILITY: MARCH 1990 TO MARCH 1991 VIII (1992) [hereinafter GEOGRAPHICAL MOBILITY]. The figures given are for the period between 1970 and 1991. *Id*. In the Houston area, which is the subject of one of the extended studies reported in Part III, *infra*, only 45% of the population five years old or older lived in 1990 in the same house they had lived in five years earlier. BUREAU OF THE CENSUS, U.S. DEP'T OF COMMERCE, 1990 CPH-3-176B, 1990 CENSUS OF POPULATION AND HOUSING, POPULATION AND HOUSING CHARACTERISTICS FOR CENSUS TRACTS AND BLOCK NUMBERING AREAS, HOUSTON-GALVESTON-BRAZORIA, TX CMSA (PART) 87 (1993).

14. Between 1970 and 1991, for example, between 6.0% and 6.7% of the population moved each year from the county in which they had been residing. GEOGRAPHICAL MOBILITY, *supra* note 13, at VIII. During the five-year period between 1975 and 1980, 21% of all persons 15 years and over moved between counties, between states, or from abroad. BUREAU OF THE CENSUS, U.S. DEP'T OF COMMERCE, PC 80-2-2A, 1980 CENSUS OF THE POPULATION, GEOGRAPHICAL MOBILITY FOR STATES AND THE NATION 65 (1984).

15. *See, e.g.*, ALDEN SPEARE, JR. ET AL., RESIDENTIAL MOBILITY, MIGRATION, AND MET-

346

ROPOLITAN CHANGE 235-36 (1975); Thomas P. Boehm & Keith R. Ihlanfeldt, *Residential Mobility and Neighborhood Quality*, 26 J. REGIONAL SCI. 411, 419 (1986); John M. Quigley & Daniel H. Weinberg, *Intra-Urban Residential Mobility: A Review and Synthesis*, 2 INT'L REGIONAL SCI. REV. 41, 55-56 (1977) (reviewing the literature). Of course, the location of jobs, the size and composition of the family, and ties to family and friends often are the primary factors in a household's decision to move. *See* Quigley & Weinberg, *supra*, at 49-55.

16. *See, e.g.*, SPEARE ET AL., *supra* note 15, at 236-37; David P. Varady, *Influences on the City-Suburban Choice: A Study of Cincinnati Homebuyers*, 56 J. AM. PLAN. ASS'N 22, 26 (1990).

17. *See, e.g.*, Maureen L. Cropper & Wallace E. Oates, *Environmental Economics: A Survey*, 30 J. ECON. LIT. 675, 706-08, 717-18 (1992) (surveying the literature); A. Myrick Freeman III, *The Hedonic Price Approach to Measuring Demand for Neighborhood Characteristics, in* THE ECONOMICS OF NEIGHBORHOOD 191-92 (David Segal ed., 1979) (reviewing the literature).

18. *See, e.g.*, Mark Baldassare et al., *Urban Service and Environmental Stressor: The Impact of the Bay Area Rapid Transit System (BART) on Residential Mobility*, 11 ENV'T & BEHAV. 435, 441-42 (1979); Quigley & Weinberg, *supra* note 15, at 55-56.

19. The data regarding the impact LULUs have on neighboring property values are inconclusive. Most studies show that hazardous waste sites have a statistically significant adverse impact on the value of surrounding properties. *See* Been, *supra* note 3, at nn. 109-10 (reviewing the literature). For studies not included in that review, see M. Greenberg & Hughes, *The Impact of Hazardous Waste Superfund Sites on the Value of Houses sold in New Jersey*, 26 ANNALS REGIONAL SCI. 147 (1992); Robert Mendelson, et al., *Measuring Hazardous Waste Damages with Panel Models*, 22 J. ENVTL. ECON. & MGMT. 259 (1992). Studies of the effect solid waste landfills and incinerators have on neighboring property values have reached contradictory conclusions, with slightly more than half showing no effect. Chris Zeiss, *Municipal Solid Waste Incinerator Impacts on Residential Property Values and Sales in Host Communities*, 20 J. ENVTL. SYS. 229, 238-39 (1990-91) (reviewing the literature). Social services LULUs, such as group homes, generally have been shown to have no detrimental impact on neighboring property values. *See* Been *supra* note 3, at 1022-23 & nn. 113-15 (surveying the literature); *see also* sources cited *supra* note 6.

20. To the extent that people choose to stay in a neighborhood, or to move to a different neighborhood, in order to live among others who have similar socioeconomic characteristics, neighborhoods that become poorer because a LULU has decreased property values will begin a spiral in which "households move in response to the changed character of the neighbors[,] . . . the individual decisions of all who move [further] change the character of their neighborhood," more people then leave, and so on. *See* John M. Quigley, *Local Residential Mobility and Local Government Policy, in* RESIDENTIAL MOBILITY AND PUBLIC POLICY 39, 45 (W.A.V. Clark & Eric G. Moore eds., 1980) . For evidence that people's decision to move and their choice of neighborhood is influenced by their desire to be near others who are "like me," *see* William M. Dobriner, *Class in Suburbia* 64-67 (1963); Andrew Reschovsky, *Residential Choice and the Local Public Sector: An Alternative Test of the "Tiebout Hypothesis,"* 6 J. URB. ECON. 501, 512 (1979).

21. For discussions of the continuing prevalence of racial discrimination in the housing market, *see, e.g.*, PETER MIESZKOWSKI, STUDIES OF PREJUDICE AND DISCRIMINATION IN URBAN HOUSING MARKETS (1980); John O. Calmore, *To Make Wrong Right: The Necessary and Proper Aspirations of Fair Housing, in* THE STATE OF BLACK AMERICA 1989, at 77, 90-95 (Janet Dewart ed., 1989); Dubin, *supra* note 5, at 741 & n. 7, 776 & n. 165. For descriptions of how African-American households are disproportionately located in the poorest of all neighborhoods, *see, e.g.*, Paul A. Jargowsky & Mary J. Bane, *Ghetto Poverty in the United States, 1970-1980, in* THE URBAN UNDERCLASS 235, 252 (Christopher Jencks, & Paul E. Peterson eds., 1991); Richard P. Nathan & Charles F. Adams, Jr., *Four Perspectives on Urban Hardship*, 104 POL. SCI. Q. 483, 504 (1989).

22. For discussions of discrimination in the promulgation and enforcement of zoning laws, *see* Dubin, *supra* note 5; Rabin *supra* note 5. For discussions of discrimination in the enforcement of environmental protection laws, *see* Marianne Lavelle & Marcia Coyle, *Unequal Protection: The Racial Divide in Environmental Law*, NAT'L L. J., Sept. 21, 1992, at S2 (finding that "penalties against pollution law violators in minority areas are lower than those imposed for violations in largely white areas, . . . the gov-

ernment takes longer to address hazards in minority communities, and it accepts solutions less stringent than those recommended by the scientific community"); Rae Zimmerman, *Social Equity and Environmental Risk*, 13 RISK ANALYSIS: INT'L J. 649, 660-64, (1993) (finding that the higher the percentage of African-Americans in community, the less likely it was that hazardous waste sites in community had progressed to "Record of Decision" stage of cleanup, especially when community was also relatively poor; but finding that difference was primarily a function of how long site had been listed on National Priorities List). *But see* John A. Hird, *Environmental Policy and Equity: The Case of Superfund*, 12 J. POL'Y ANALYSIS & MGMT. 323, 337 (1993) (finding no relationship between pace at which sites are cleaned up and host county's socioeconomic characteristics).

23. For discussions of discrimination in the provision of municipal services, *see, e.g.*, CHARLES M. HAAR & DANIEL W. FESSLER, THE WRONG SIDE OF THE TRACKS 38-41 (1986); EQUITY IN THE CITY (P.N. Troy ed., 1981); ROBERT L. LINEBERRY, EQUALITY AND URBAN POLICY (1977); Kenneth W. Bond, *Toward Equal Delivery of Municipal Services in the Central Cities*, 4 FORDHAM URB. L. J. 263 (1976); Robert L. Graham & Jason H. Kravitt, *The Evolution of Equal Protection—Education, Municipal Services and Wealth*, 7 HARV. C.R.-C.L. L. REV. 103, 111, 154-68 (1972); Robert P. Inman & Daniel L. Rubinfeld, *The Judicial Pursuit of Local Fiscal Equity*, 92 HARV. L. REV. 1662, 1697-1701 (1979); Peter A. Lupsha & William J. Siembieda, *The Poverty of Public Services In the Land of Plenty*, in THE RISE OF THE SUNBELT CITIES 169, 183 (David C. Perry & Alfred J. Watkins eds., 1977); Gershon M. Ratner, *Inter-Neighborhood Denials of Equal Protection in the Provision of Municipal Services*, 4 HAR. C.R.-C.L. L. REV. 1 (1968); Carl S. Shoup, *Rules for Distributing a Free Government Service Among Areas of a City*, 42 NAT'L TAX J. 103, 110 (1989); Frederick T. Goldberg, Note, *Equalization of Municipal Services: The Economics of* Serrano *and* Shaw, 82 YALE L. J. 89 (1972); Note, *The Right to Adequate Municipal Services: Thoughts and Proposals*, 44 N.Y.U. L. REV. 753 (1969); Clayton P. Gillette, *Equality and Variety in the Delivery of Municipal Services*, 100 HARV. L. REV. 946 (1987) (book review).

24. For discussion of the evidence of discrimination in mortgage lending, *see e.g.*, Glen B. Canner & Delores S. Smith, *Expanded HMDA Data on Residential Lending: One Year Later*, 78 FED. RESERVE BULL. 801 (1992); Glen B. Canner & Delores S. Smith, *Home Mortgage Disclosure Act: Expanded Data on Residential Lending*, 77 FED. RESERVE BULL. 859 (1991).

25. For a summary of the literature about the downward spiral that may result from declines in neighborhood quality, and increases in the concentration of poverty that may be associated with such declines, see Michael H. Schill, *Deconcentrating the Inner City Poor*, 67 CHI.-KENT L. REV. 795, 804-07 (1991).

26. San Antonio Indep. Sch. Dist. v. Rodriguez , 411 U.S. 1 (1973). Under various theories of fairness, e.g., John Rawls' Difference Principle, however, such discrimination against the poor would be unfair and would justify changes in the siting process. JOHN RAWLS, A THEORY OF JUSTICE 75-83 (1971).

27. Village of Arlington Heights v. Metropolitan Hous. Dev. Corp., 429 U.S. 252 (1977).

28. Because discrimination against the poor is not unconstitutional, whereas discrimination against people of color is, a claim of racial discrimination might need to separate out the disparate effect that a siting process has upon people of color because of their race from the effect it has upon the people of color because of their poverty.

29. Evidence that the siting process had a disproportionate effect upon people of color does not prove that siting officials intentionally targeted people of color to host the LULUs. Instead, it may be that siting officials chose sites on the basis of land prices, proximity to sources, or any number of other nondiscriminitory factors, but that the use of those factors unintentionally resulted in a siting pattern that disproportionately affected people of color. Nevertheless, evidence of disproportionate effect, if accompanied by other indicia of racial animus, may be probative of discriminatory intent. *See* Village of Arlington Heights v. Metropolitan Hous. Dev. Corp., 429 U.S. 252, 265-66 (1977); *see also* R.I.S.E. v. Kay, 768 F. Supp. 1144, 1149 (E.D. Va. 1991); East Bibb Twiggs Neighborhood Ass'n v. Macon-Bibb County Planning & Zoning Comm'n, 706 F. Supp. 880, 884 (M.D. Ga. 1989), *aff'd*, 896 F.2d 1264 (11th Cir. 989); Bean v. Southwestern Waste Management Corp., 482 F. Supp. 673, 678 (S.D. Tex. 1979), *aff'd*, 782 F.2d 1038 (5th Cir. 1986). Under some statutory schemes, the disproportionate effect of a siting could be considered a disparate impact and be actionable even without a finding of discriminatory intent. *See, e.g.*, Huntington Branch, NAACP v. Town of Huntington, 844 F.2d 926, 936-37 (2d Cir. 1988), *aff'd*,

488 U.S. 15 (1988) (The Fair Housing Act, 42 U.S.C. §§ 3601-19, requires only a finding of disparate impact); NAACP v. Medical center, Inc., 657 F.2d 1322, 1328-31 (3d Cir. 1981) (Title VI of the Civil Rights Act of 1964, 42 U.S.C. § 2000d, requires only a finding of disparate impact, at least where regulations implementing the statute specify a disparate impact standard). In addition, under some theories of discrimination, at least some forms of disparate impact should be actionable. See, e.g., LAURENCE H. TRIBE, AMERICAN CONSTITUTIONAL LAW § 16-21, at 1514-21 (2d ed. 1988); Paul Brest, *The Supreme Court, 1975 Term—Foreword: In Defense of the Antidiscrimination Principle*, 90 HARV. L. REV. 1, 22-53 (1976); Theodore Eisenberg, *Disproportionate Impact and Illicit Motive: Theories of Constitutional Adjudication*, 52 N.Y.U. L. REV. 36, 422-83 (1977); Owen M. Fiss, *Groups and the Equal Protection Clause*, 5 PHIL & PUB. AFF. 107, 141-46, 157-60 (1976); Owen M. Fiss, *A Theory of Fair Employment Laws*, 38 U. CHI. L. REV. 235, 244-65 (1971). To avoid the implication that a finding of disproportionate effect necessarily leads to a finding of an illegal disparate impact, I refer to any disparity in the impact of siting decisions as "disproportionate effect."

30. If the market forces at issue are based upon discrimination, i.e., if host neighborhoods became predominantly minority after the LULU was sited because racial discrimination in the housing market relegated people of color to those neighborhoods, siting practices might have to change to account for persistent discrimination in the housing market. *Cf.* United States v. Yonkers Bd. of Educ., 624 F. Supp. 1276, 1531-37 (S.D.N.Y. 1985) (noting that existence of housing discrimination may be relevant to determination of liability for segregation of schools).

31. For discussion of whether proposals to make the siting process fairer might be appropriate even if market dynamics might soon undermine the fairness of the distribution, *see* Been, *supra* note 3, at 1018-24.

32. The studies discussed in this Article focus on the location of LULUs. Other studies show that the poor and people of color bear a disproportionate share of the general burdens of pollution and of the costs of cleaning up pollution, but do not specifically address the burden of hosting polluting LULUs. For reviews of that literature, see Cole, *supra* note 1, at 622-27 & nn.8-18; Maureen L. Cropper & Wallace E. Oates, *Environmental Economics: A Survey*, 30 J. ECON. LITERATURE 675, 727-28 (1992). Lazarus, *supra* note 4, at 796-801; Paul Mohai & Bunyan Bryant, *Environmental Injustice: Weighing Race and Class as Factors in the Distribution of Environmental Hazards*, 63 U. COLO. L. REV. 921, 925-27 (1992). Studies also show that environmental laws are enforced less vigorously in poor and minority communities. See Lavelle & Coyle, *supra* note 22; Zimmerman, *supra* note 22; *see also* Lazarus, *supra* note 4, at 818-19 & nn.125-33 (surveying the literature); *Cf.* CLEAN SITES, HAZARDOUS WASTE SITES AND THE RURAL POOR: A PRELIMINARY ASSESSMENT 50-51 (1990) (finding that hazardous waste sites in rural poor counties were more likely to have been cleaned up than in other counties, without addressing the racial characteristics of the counties). *But see* Hird, *supra* note 22, at 337 (finding no relationship between the pace at which sites are cleaned up and the host county's socioeconomic characteristics).

33. CRJ REPORT, *supra* note 2.

34. The 415 facilities comprised all of the facilities in the contiguous United States that could be identified through the Environmental Protection Agency's Hazardous Waste Data Management System (HWDMS). *Id.* at 10, 65. The HWDMS was an early version of the Resource Conservation and Recovery Information System.

35. The study also examined the demographics of communities that contained uncontrolled hazardous waste sites that the Environmental Protection Agency has identified as posing a potential threat to the environment and to public health and has listed in the Comprehensive Environmental Response, Compensation, and Liability System (CERCLIS). CRJ REPORT, *supra* note 2, at 3-4, 53. The study found that 57% of all African-Americans and Latinos live in communities hosting such facilities, while 54% of all whites live in such communities. *Id.* at 53; *see also* Zimmerman, *supra* note 22, at 657 (finding that African-Americans are about 50% more likely to live in a community with a CERCLIS site deemed sufficiently hazardous to be placed on the National Priorities List).

36. Commercial hazardous waste facilities are public or private facilities that accept hazardous waste from third parties for a fee for the purpose of treating, storing or disposing of the waste. CRJ REPORT, *supra* note 2, at 65.

37. The CRJ REPORT considered a correlation to be significant at the 90% confidence level. Accordingly, there is a 1 in 10 probability that some of the findings of the study were chance occurrences. *Id.* at 11. For criticisms of the methodology of the CRJ, see

Lazarus, *supra* note 4, at 802 n.56.
38. CRJ REPORT, *supra* note 2, at 13, 41-44.
39. *Id.*
40. In addition to the studies discussed in the text, see LAURETTA M. BURKE, ENVIRON-
MENTAL EQUITY IN LOS ANGELES (National Center for Geographic Information and
Analysis Technical Report 93-6,1993) (in Los Angeles, the poorer the area and the
higher the percentage of minorities in the population, the greater the number of polluting facilities in the area); CITIZENS FOR A BETTER ENVIRONMENT, RICHMOND AT
RISK: COMMUNITY DEMOGRAPHICS AND TOXIC HAZARDS FROM INDUSTRIAL POL-
LUTERS 2 121-22 (1989) (residents of Richmond, California census tracts closest to
polluting industrial facilities are disproportionately people of color and the poor);
PAT COSTNER & JOE THORNTON, PLAYING WITH FIRE: HAZARDOUS WASTE INCIN-
ERATION 48-49 (1990) (minority percentage of population in communities hosting or
proposed to host hazardous waste incinerators was 89% and 60% higher, respec-
tively, than the national average); BENJAMIN A. GOLDMAN, THE TRUTH ABOUT
WHERE YOU LIVE 282-83 (1991) (in those counties that rank the worst on various
measures of the presence of toxic substances, the percentage of the population that is
minority is more than twice that of the average for other counties); JAY M. GOULD,
QUALITY OF LIFE IN AMERICAN NEIGHBORHOODS: LEVELS OF AFFLUENCE, TOXIC
WASTE, AND CANCER MORTALITY IN RESIDENTIAL ZIP CODE AREAS 21-24 (1986)
(finding that communities with the highest incomes have the lowest amount of toxic
waste generated); MICHAEL R. GREENBERG & RICHARD F. ANDERSON, HAZARDOUS
WASTE SITES: THE CREDIBILITY GAP (1984) (study of New Jersey's 567 communities
indicated that communities with the greatest number of hazardous waste sites tend to
have more poor, elderly, young, and African-American residents than other communities); E.B. Attah, *Demographics and Siting Issues in EPA Region IV, in* PROCEEDINGS
OF THE CLARK ATLANTA UNIVERSITY AND ENVIRONMENTAL PROTECTION AGENCY
REGION IB CONFERENCE ON ENVIRONMENTAL EQUITY 3-4 (Bob Holmes ed., 1992)
(study of CERCLIS sites in 8 southeastern states revealed that number of sites per
census tract increases as the percentage of the tract's population that is minority increases); Greenberg, *supra* note 2, at 241-43, 244-46 (finding that large waste-to-
energy facilities (WTEFs) in towns of at least 100,000 residents were located in
towns that were poorer and had more minorities as a percentage of the population
than the "service area" of the facility, and that when population data was weighted to
take into account the fact that people of color tend to be located in cities, the percentage of the population comprised of African-Americans was 65% higher in cities
that hosted WTEFs than in the United States as a whole); Kusum Ketkar, *Hazardous
Waste Sites and Property Values in the State of New Jersey*, 24 APPLIED ECON. 647, 653
(1992) (analysis of 62 municipalities in seven urban counties in New Jersey "implies
that the municipalities that have high property tax rates and a greater proportion of
minorities also have a larger number of [hazardous waste] sites," without separating
the effect of race from the effect of high property tax rates); Mohai & Bryant, *supra*
note 32, at 5 (finding that people of color in Detroit were almost four times more
likely than whites to live within one mile of a waste facility); Harvey L. White, *Hazardous Waste Incineration and Minority Communities, in* RACE AND THE INCIDENCE OF
ENVIRONMENTAL HAZARDS: A TIME FOR DISCOURSE 126, 132 (Bunyan Bryant &
Paul Mohai eds., 1992) [hereinafter INCIDENCE] (in Baton Rouge area, minority
communities had average of one hazardous waste incineration facility per 7349 residents, while white communities had only one site per 31,100 residents); Jane Kay,
Minorities Bear Brunt of Pollution, S.F. EXAMINER, Apr. 7, 1991, at A1, A12 (Los Angeles County zip code area with largest amount of waste discharge is predominantly
African-American and Latino); Dennis Pfaff, *Pollution and the Poor*, DETROIT NEWS,
Nov. 26, 1989, at A1 (41 of Detroit's top air polluters, 25 of the 33 sites most conta-
minated with toxic chemicals, and four of five licensed hazardous waste treatment and
storage facilities are located in neighborhoods with average per capita incomes of less
than $10,000 per year); Kevin L. Brown, Environmental Discrimination: Myth or
Reality 17-18 (Mar. 29, 1991) (unpublished manuscript, on file with author) (random
sample of predominantly minority census tracts in St. Louis had 47% more chemical
emissions than comparable sample of predominantly white census tracts). For comprehensive discussions of the existing research, see Been, *supra* note 3, at 1009-15;
Cole, *supra* note 1, at 622-23 nn.8-9, 625 n.17; Lazarus, *supra* note 4, at 801-06.
41. GAO REPORT, *supra* note 4.
42. GAO REPORT, *supra* note 4, at 4. The landfill in Warren County, North Carolina is

sited in an area that was 66% African-American and is within four miles of an area that was 47% American Indian. *Id.* at app. I, 7.

43. *Id.* at app. I, 1, 5, 7.
44. *Id.* at 4.
45. *Id.* at app. I, 1, 5, 7.
46. Bullard, *Solid Waste, supra* note 9.
47. ROBERT D. BULLARD, INVISIBLE HOUSTON 60-75 (1987).
48. BULLARD, *supra* note 1.
49. Bullard, *Solid Waste, supra* note 9, at 279-83. Tables 1 and 2 of *Solid Waste* List five incinerators and three mini-incinerators, and describe four of the incinerators and two of the mini-incinerators as located in African-American neighborhoods. Tables 3, 5, and 6 list five "City of Houston Municipal Landfill Sites," six "Texas Department of Health Permitted Municipal Landfills Sites," and six "Browning Ferris Industries Landfill Sites," for a total of 17 landfills. Of those, all but two are described as located in African-American neighborhoods. Although Professor Bullard does not total the numbers from the different tables, the "bottom line" to be drawn from his study is that six of the eight incinerators and mini-incinerators, and 15 of the 17 landfills, or 21 of 25 sites, are in African-American neighborhoods. Of the four sites that were in non-African-American neighborhoods, Bullard's study showed that two were located in a neighborhood that was undergoing transition from a white to an African-American community (the two landfills actually are the same site, *see infra* text accompanying note 70), and one was located in a Hispanic neighborhood. Only one of the sites was adjacent to a predominantly white community. Bullard, *Solid Waste, supra* note 9, at 279-83.

50. In correspondence with the author, Professor Bullard states that his study was based on host neighborhood demographics as of the census closest to the year that the site was opened. Letter from Robert D. Bullard to Vicki Been (Mar. 18, 1993) (on file with author). None of his published accounts of the study specify the date of the data use. In the first published account, Professor Bullard's list of references includes a citation only to 1980 Census Bureau data. Bullard, *Solid Waste, supra* note 9, at 288. Neither of the later books drawing on that study includes any citation to specific census data. Professor Bullard originally prepared his research to present in Bean v. Southwestern Waste Management Corp., 482 F. Supp. 673 (S.D. Tex. 1979), *aff'd*, 782 F.2d 1039 (5th Cir. 1986). Professor Bullard's testimony in that litigation refers to an exhibit in which he presented data about the racial composition of host census tracts in 1970, 1975, and 1979. Transcript of Proceedings, Nov. 27, 1979, at 345, Bean v. Southwestern Waste Management Corp., 482 F. Supp. 673 (S.D. Tex 1979) (Civ. No. H-79-2215), *aff'd*, 782 F.2d 1039 (5th Cir. 1986) [hereinafter Bean Transcript]. At other points in the testimony, Professor Bullard presents analyses that were based solely on 1979 data. *Id.* at 351. Efforts to verify which of the various analyses that Professor Bullard presented in the litigation formed the basis for the conclusions reported in *Solid Waste* have been unsuccessful. Professor Bullard responded to the author's request for his original data by referring her to the litigation files. The clerk of the court in which the litigation was filed has destroyed the court's copy of all exhibits, however, and the defendants and their lawyers no longer have copies in their files. Telephone Interview with Boone Vastine, Attorney with Browning Ferris Industries (Sept. 2, 1993). In any event, Professor Bullard's *Solid Waste* study does not remedy the gaps in the evidence identified earlier in the Article, *see supra* text accompanying notes 3-7, because it does not focus on the question of how the waste facilities affected the demographics of the surrounding neighborhoods.

51. Although both the CRJ and the GAO studies admit that they do not show cause and effect, CRJ REPORT, *supra* note 2, at 11, GAO REPORT, *supra* note 4, at 3, many discussions of the evidence make causal assertions. Indeed, some environmental justice advocates claim that the evidence supports the charge that siting choices are intentionally discriminatory. Grossman, *supra* note 1, at 31 (quoting Rev. Benjamin Chavis, then Executive Director of Commission for Racial Justice, and one of founders of environmental justice movement, as alleging that developers and siting officials "deliberate[ly] target[ ] . . . people of color communities for toxic waste facilities"); *see also Have Minorities Benefited . . . ? A Forum*, 18 EPA J., Mar.-Apr. 1992, at 32, 36 (comments of Beverly Wright) ("[F]ederal, state, and local agencies and industries . . . target [low income] communities for the siting of undesirable 'but necessary' polluting facilities.").

52. Hamilton, *supra* note 4, at 106-20.

53. Expansion decisions are much less controversial than initial siting decisions, but nevertheless generate opposition. The decision to expand capacity involves some of the same factors as the initial siting decision, such as the site's proximity to potential customers. Accordingly, to the extent that any disproportionate effect arising from siting decisions can be traced to siters' propensity to take the "path of least resistance," or to consider such factors as proximity to potential customers, expansion decisions should also have a disproportionate effect.

54. Hamilton, *supra* note 4, at 116-18.

55. *Id.* at 120.

56. *Id.* at 120-22.

57. *Id.* at 121.

58. Other studies have used county-level data as well. *See, e.g.*, Hird, *supra* note 22. For a full discussion of the appropriate level of data aggregation, see *infra* text accompanying notes 73-84.

59. For a discussion of the problem of correlating siting dates and the decennial censuses, see *infra* note 62.

60. The GAO gives the dates repeated in the text as the dates on which the landfills were "established." The GAO never defined what it meant by "established," but conversations with regulators indicate that the sites began to operate as offsite disposal facilities in those years. Telephone Interview with Willie Morgan, Environmental Engineer, Hazardous Waste Section, South Carolina Department of Health and Environmental Control (June 26, 1992); Telephone Interview with Allan Tinsley, Section Manager, Compliance and Monitoring, Division of Compliance, Monitoring, and Enforcement, South Carolina Department of Health and Environmental Control (June 30, 1992); Telephone Interview with Gary Alberg, Permitting Engineer, Solid Waste Division, North Carolina Department of Environment Health and Natural Resources (June 17, 1992); Telephone Interview with Tracey Williams, Environmental Engineer, Alabama Department of Environmental Protection (June 29 & 30, 1992).

61. *See, e.g.*, Charles J. McDermott, *Environmental Equity: A Waste Manager's Perspective*, LAND USE F., Winter 1993, at 12, 14-15 (describing siting process for Chemical Waste facility in Sumter County, Alabama as beginning in 1974).

62. It would be preferable, of course, to use data from 1975 for the facilities opening in 1977. Data are unavailable for intervals between the 1970 and 1980 censuses, however, so the correlation between the siting date and the census data is less than ideal. The 1970 data are more appropriate than 1980 data for the analysis of sites opened in 1977, however, because the siting decisionmakers were likely to have had only the 1970 data at the time they made their siting decisions.

63. For criticism of the measure of disproportion implicit in the GAO and Bullard studies (and followed by the extensions of those studies reported here), see *supra* note 2.

64. Several explanations might be offered for the decrease in the percentage of the host communities' African-American population. The waste facilities may have brought jobs to the communities. Attracted by those jobs, whites may have immigrated to the area, displacing African-Americans. Alternatively, the waste facilities, or land uses they spawned (such as housing for their workers) may have displaced African-American housing and thereby driven African-Americans from the neighborhood. *See* Dubin, *supra* note 5, at 794-97 (discussing various forms of discriminatory zoning); Rabin, *supra* note 5, at 107-18 (examples of expulsive zoning). To assess which of these (or other) factors might account for the changes in the communities' demographics would require a case study that is beyond the scope of this [viewpoint].

65. The GAO study reported the poverty rate of each host community. Those figures do not prove that a community's poverty made it more likely to be chosen as host to the facility, because they do not indicate the community's standing among other communities "competing" for the LULU. Only by analyzing the community's poverty relative to that of the entire state, "service region" of the facility, or nation can one ascertain whether a community's poverty made it more likely to be chosen to host a facility. . . .

66. The largest change was a 15% increase in the relative median family income of Sumter County between 1970 and 1990.

67. It might be preferable to compare the host county subdivision (rather than the host county) to the host state, *see infra* text accompanying notes 73-84, but published data about poverty and median house value are unavailable for the county subdivisions in 1970, and data about median family income for county subdivisions are unavailable

for both 1970 and 1980. . . . Changes in the relative poverty and relative median house value between 1980 and 1990 were generally more pronounced in the county subdivisions than in the host counties. Those data do not reveal any clear trend, however: two of the county subdivisions became significantly less poor relative to the host states between 1980 and 1990, while one became significantly more poor and one remained the same. Similarly, in two of the county subdivisions, relative median housing value increased between 1980 and 1990, but in the other two, it decreased.

68. Bullard, *Solid Waste, supra* note 9, at 279-83; *see also supra* note 49. Professor Bullard's descriptions of the racial composition of the host communities do not correspond to census tract data for either 1980 or the census closest to the date the site was permitted. *See infra* text accompanying note 72.

69. Professor Bullard does not explain whether the six "Texas Department of Health Permitted Municipal Landfill Sites" and six "Browning Ferris Industries Landfill Sites" he studied cover the entire universe of sites that fall into those categories. If Professor Bullard analyzed fewer than all of the sites in those categories, his conclusions about the disproportionate siting of facilities obviously would be inaccurate. In explaining the study that served as the basis for Bullard, *Solid Waste, supra* note 9, during the course of the litigation for which the study was prepared, Professor Bullard stated that there were 76 solid waste sites in the study. Bean Transcript, *supra* note 50, at 374, 398-99. Earlier, he had submitted an exhibit analyzing 34 sites. *Id* at 399. In its decision, the *Bean* court states that 17 sites were operating with Texas Department of Health (TDH) permits as of July 1, 1978. Bean v. Southwestern Waste Management Corp., 482 F. Supp. 673, 677 (S.D. Tex. 1979) *aff'd*, 782 F.2d 1038 (5th Cir. 1986). The six sites identified as TDH sites in *Solid Waste* accordingly appear to be only a subset of sites that should have been included.

70. The three landfills that fall into both categories are the American Refuse Systems facility at 1140 Holmes Road, the Browning Ferris Industries facility at the same address, *see infra* note 71, and the Browning Ferris Industries facility at 11013 Beaumont Highway.

71. Professor Bullard counts the sites as separate landfills because the Texas Department of Health issued two permits for the landfill. Letter from Robert D. Bullard to Vicki Been (Mar. 18, 1993) (on file with author).

72. *Id.* Professor Bullard's testimony in the litigation for which he prepared the study helps to illustrate his approach to defining a "neighborhood." There, in explaining why he considered the two Ruffino sites to be located in an African-American community, he testified that although the data for the census tract in which the sites were located indicated that the tract was predominantly white, his "ethnographic" study and "field observations" of the areas showed that there was a "cluster" of African-Americans close to the site. Bean Transcript, *supra* note 50, at 382-87, 403.

73. For discussion of the problem of selecting the appropriate level of analysis for environmental justice studies, *see* Been, *supra* note 3, at 1014-15; Greenberg, *supra* note 2, at 238; Rae Zimmerman, *Issues of Classification in Environmental Equity: How We Manage Is How We Measure*, FORDHAM URB. L. J. (forthcoming 1994) (manuscript at 13-28, on file with author) (discussing various definitions of neighborhood that can be used in environmental equity studies and problems raised in selection of definition); *see also* CRJ REPORT, *supra* note 2, at 61-62 (advocating five-digit zip code areas as best unit of analysis); Zimmerman, *supra* note 22, at 7-9 (advocating municipality as unit of analysis); East Bibb Twiggs Neighborhood Ass'n v. Macon-Bibb County Planning & Zoning Comm'n, 706 F. Supp. 880, 884 (M.D. Ga. 1989), *aff'd*, 896 F.2d 1264 (11th Cir. 1989) (census tract is appropriate unit of analysis). Whatever level of analysis is eventually chosen as the most appropriate for environmental justice studies, researchers will face the additional question of how to address sites that do not fall in the center of the tract or other unit of analysis, but are instead at the border of two or more units. In the extensions reported here, when a site was at the border of a tract, the host tract and the bordering tract were combined for the analysis.

74. *See generally* Allan C. Goodman, *A Comparison of Block Group and Census Tract Data in a Hedonic Housing Price Model*, 53 LAND ECON. 483 (1977) (advocating use of "block groups" for measuring neighborhood values).

75. Studies of the property value impacts of waste facilities, for example, show effects on homes miles away from the site. *See, e.g.*, GERALD E. SMOLEN ET AL., ECONOMIC EFFECTS OF HAZARDOUS WASTE LANDFILLS ON SURROUNDING REAL ESTATE VALUES IN TOLEDO, OHIO 22 (Ohio State Univ., Center for Real Estate Educ. and Research,

Research Report No. 44, Feb. 1991) (finding that announcement of proposed low-level nuclear waste site adversely affected prices of property as far as 5.75 miles away); Janet E. Kohlhase, *The Impact of Toxic Waste Sites on Housing Values*, 30 J. URB. ECON. 1, 14-15 (1991) (finding negative effects up to 6.2 miles from toxic waste sites following announcement of area as Superfund priority site); *Cf.* Hays B. Gamble & Roger H. Downing, *Effects of Sanitary Landfills on Property Values and Residential Development, in* SOLID AND LIQUID WASTES: MANAGEMENT, METHODS AND SOCIOECONOMIC CONSIDERATIONS 350, 358 (S.K. Majumdar & E. Willard Miller eds., 1984) (finding that sanitary landfills adversely affect prices of properties on the main access roads to landfill within one mile of the landfill, but did not affect developed residential properties near landfills). Because the studies of property value impacts do not clearly establish the boundaries of the area affected by a LULU, it may be that census tracts also are generally too small to capture the impact of the LULU. The studies make quite clear, however, that the impact of a LULU is felt beyond the block on which it is located. Census blocks accordingly are less likely to be the appropriate unit of analysis than census tracts.

76. MICHAEL J. WHITE, AMERICAN NEIGHBORHOODS AND RESIDENTIAL DIFFERENTIATION 290 (1987).

77. *Id.*

78. *Id.* at 290; BUREAU OF THE CENSUS, U.S. DEP'T OF COMMERCE, 1990 CPH 3-42, 1990 CENSUS OF POPULATION AND HOUSING, POPULATION AND HOUSING CHARACTERISTICS FOR CENSUS TRACTS AND BLOCK NUMBERING AREAS, SOUTH CAROLINA (OUTSIDE METROPOLITAN AREAS) A-4 (1993). Many areas of the United States were not block numbered until the 1990 census, so comparison of block statistics across decades is impossible. BUREAU OF THE CENSUS, U.S. DEP'T OF COMMERCE, 1990 CPH 3-42, 1990 CENSUS OF POPULATION AND HOUSING, POPULATION AND HOUSING CHARACTERISTICS FOR CENSUS TRACTS AND BLOCK NUMBERING AREAS, SOUTH CAROLINA A-3 (1993). While there was an equivalent to block groups, called "enumeration districts," used prior to the 1990 census, differences between the enumeration districts and block groups make comparisons across decades difficult.

79. WHITE, *supra* note 76, at 290.

80. *Id.* When a tract grows beyond the standard size, it typically is split into sub-tracts. In the extension reported here, when a tract was split into sub-tracts, the sub-tracts were re-combined to make the comparison across decades as accurate as possible.

81. *Id.*

82. *Id.* at 293.

83. *See id.* at 297.

84. Mohai & Bryant draw circles at one and one-and-one-half mile radii from sites for their analysis, rather than using standard census units. Paul Mohai & Bunyan Bryant, *Environmental Racism: Reviewing the Evidence, in* INCIDENCE, *supra* note 40, at 163, 170-76. The CRJ REPORT, *supra* note 2, at 9, uses five-digit zip-code areas, which may be smaller or larger than census tracts, but typically are larger than census blocks or block groupings.

85. This conclusion assumes that the facilities Professor Bullard studied were a complete set of the TDH and Browning Ferris landfills in existence at the time of his study. That assumption may not be correct. *See supra* text accompanying note 69. The conclusion also assumes that proportionality should be measured by comparing the percentage of African-Americans in the host tracts to the percentage in non-host tracts. See *supra* note 2 for criticisms of that measure of proportionality.

86. A poverty rate is considered significantly higher for the purposes of this study if it is more than 110% of the rate for Harris County. An alternative method would measure the number of LULUs sited in neighborhoods whose poverty rates were within one or two standard deviations of the Houston rate. Yet another method would examine the percentage of LULUs sited in neighborhoods that fall into the bottom quartile or quintile of all Houston neighborhoods, sorted by poverty rates, median income, or mean income.

87. In the neighborhoods surrounding the mini-incinerators, relative housing values declined in one neighborhood following the siting, but increased in the other two neighborhoods. The data on mini-incinerators is of limited use, however, because all the mini-incinerators had ceased to operate by the mid 1970's and to the extent that they were not expected to re-open, any effect they may have had on property values could easily have been erased by 1980.

88. Median rents remained fairly stable in all but two of the neighborhoods. In one of the

exceptional neighborhoods, relative rents fell significantly, while in the other, relative rents increased significantly. In theory, rents surrounding an undesirable land use should fall. If there is a shortage of housing that is affordable and accessible to African-Americans and the poor, however, demand might keep the rental prices stable even though the LULU has made the neighborhood less desirable.

89. Again, this conclusion assumes that Professor Bullard included in his study all of the TDH and Browning Ferris landfills in existence at the time of his study. *See supra* note 69.

90. In the Houston subdivision of Harris County, only 45% of the population lived in the same residence in 1985 and 1990. BUREAU OF THE CENSUS, U.S. DEP'T OF COMMERCE, 1990 CPH 3-176C, 1990 CENSUS OF POPULATION AND HOUSING, POPULATION AND HOUSING CHARACTERISTICS FOR CENSUS TRACTS AND BLOCK NUMBERING AREAS, HOUSTON-GALVESTON-BRAZORIA, TX CMSA, HOUSTON, TX PMSA SECTION 2 OF 3, 843 (1993). In the areas covered by the GAO study, in contrast, the percentage of the population living in the same residence in which they had lived five years earlier was 64% in Sumter County, Alabama; 69% in Chester County, South Carolina; 50% in Sumter County, South Carolina; and 68% in Warren County, North Carolina. BUREAU OF THE CENSUS, U.S. DEP'T OF COMMERCE, 1990 CPH 3-2, 1990 CENSUS OF POPULATION AND HOUSING, POPULATION AND HOUSING CHARACTERISTICS FOR CENSUS TRACTS AND BLOCK NUMBERING AREAS, ALABAMA 360 (1993); BUREAU OF THE CENSUS, U.S. DEP'T OF COMMERCE, 1990 CPH 3-35, 1990 CENSUS OF POPULATION AND HOUSING, POPULATION AND HOUSING CHARACTERISTICS FOR CENSUS TRACTS AND BLOCK NUMBERING AREAS, NORTH CAROLINA 610 (1993); BUREAU OF THE CENSUS, U.S. DEP'T OF COMMERCE, 1990 CPH 3-42, 1990 CENSUS OF POPULATION AND HOUSING, POPULATION AND HOUSING CHARACTERISTICS FOR CENSUS TRACTS AND BLOCK NUMBERING AREAS, SOUTH CAROLINA 310 (1993).

91. The Chemical Waste facility in Sumter County, Alabama, for example, employs 300 people, 60% of whom live in Sumter County. McDermott, *supra* note 61, at 15; *see also supra* note 64.

From "Locally Undesirable Land Uses in Minority Neighborhoods" by Vicki Been. Reprinted by permission of The Yale Law Journal Company and Fred B. Rothman & Company from the *Yale Law Journal*, vol. 103 (April 1994), pages 1383–1422.

Minority Communities Are Not Unfairly Exposed to Hazardous Waste Industries

by Douglas L. Anderton, Andy B. Anderson, Peter H. Rossi, John Michael Oakes, Michael R. Fraser, Eleanor W. Weber, and Edward J. Calabrese

Douglas L. Anderton is professor of sociology and director of the Social and Demographic Research Institute (SADRI) at the University of Massachusetts at Amherst (UMass). Anderton has written extensively on research methodologies and demographic trends and is currently researching environmental equity issues. Andy B. Anderson is professor of sociology at UMass and a member of SADRI. Peter H. Rossi is S.A. Rice Professor Emeritus of Sociology at UMass and director emeritus of SADRI. John Michael Oakes and Michael R. Fraser are doctoral students in sociology at UMass and researchers for SADRI. Eleanor W. Weber is database administrator for SADRI. Edward J. Calabrese is professor of public health and director of the Northeast Environmental Health Center at UMass. In the following viewpoint, the authors contend that previous studies were drawn too broadly to accurately determine whether residents of minority neighborhoods are unjustly exposed to environmental risks associated with hazardous waste facilities. In their own study, the authors found no consistent and statistically significant differences in the racial or ethnic makeup of neighborhoods that host hazardous waste facilities. The authors conclude that waste facilities are attracted to industrial tracts and these tracts are not usually populated by more minority residents than are other tracts. The research discussed in this viewpoint was funded by a grant from Chemical Waste Management Inc.

"[Waste facilities] are no more likely to be located in [census] tracts with higher percentages of blacks and Hispanics than in other tracts."

In the past two decades, American society has become increasingly conscious that the waste products of its advanced technology can pose dangers to the health of citizens and to the viability of the ecosystem on which all depend. This concern has given rise to a number of salient policy issues centering around how best to minimize those dangers in efficient and equitable ways. This article presents new and divergent findings related to some of the equity issues in the location of hazardous waste facilities. In particular, we investigate the extent to which the geographic distribution of hazardous waste facilities may disproportionately expose neighborhoods with greater numbers of racial and ethnic minority residents to potential risks arising from such industrial activities.

Safety standards for the commercial disposal and/or long-term storage of many hazardous wastes are mandated by law. The Environmental Protection Agency (EPA) is the regulatory agency primarily charged with oversight of hazardous waste facilities. Commercial waste disposal firms typically operate several different Treatment, Storage, and Disposal Facilities (TSDFs) constituting locations at which hazardous wastes are either destroyed, stored, or held for transshipment. Some firms maintain their own facilities rather than relying on the service industry.

It is doubtful that many Americans would want a TSDF as a near neighbor and many would prefer not to be within miles of a site. Concern over the location of waste-handling facilities has provoked a political issue involving whether TSDFs, and any plausible associated risks, may be disproportionately located in neighborhoods with minority racial and ethnic groups. Inequitable exposure of minorities to environmental hazards has been labeled "environmental racism." These concerns are subsumed under the more general questions of environmental equity, which have evoked major policy attention as well as a discussion of constitutional and other legal issues in major law reviews (Chase 1993; Lazarus 1993).

The issue of equity in siting is a complicated one. To begin with, how much potential risk is generated by a TSDF has not been established nor has the relationship been determined between such risks and distance from a site. A number of epidemiological studies of areas around toxic waste sites have been carried out (e.g., Andelman and Underhill 1987; Deane et al. 1989; Grisham 1986). Most available epidemiological studies offer little conclusive evidence, although several case studies show there is some evidence of harm in proximity to toxic waste sites, enough to merit further study (e.g., Geschwind 1992; Geschwind et al. 1992).[1] As usual, the results of case studies have to be interpreted with caution. Confounding factors and differences across sites make a more general evaluation of health effects and risk assessment difficult, if not impossible. Further problems in such assessments arise because TSDFs vary in the kinds of hazardous wastes processed and in the amount of processing taking place. It is likely that the distribution of risks around a site varies accordingly.

Although most of the attention in the controversy over TSDF siting has centered around their potential negative effects, there are also potential positive ones, including employment opportunities for local residents and lowered rents and real estate prices. The net effects of TSDF siting on a neighborhood may be properly conceived of as a balance that considers negative effects as offset to some degree by positive ones.

Although in the long run we will need to know the extent to which specific TSDFs are associated with higher levels of morbidity and mortality and what are safe distances from such sites, for the present discussion our current lack of knowledge is not relevant. The current political debate over siting assumes that TSDFs generate significant effects and that those effects decrease with distance from the site.

There are also issues concerning what constitutes equity and inequity in site location. One view is that site location equity can be defined as the outcome of siting processes in which the population compositions of sites and surrounding areas played no roles. For example, TSDF sites may be chosen because of proximity to customers, real estate prices, and zoning regulations. As long as all qualifying sites have equal chances of being selected, equity is assured. That is, neighborhoods populated by high proportions of minorities would be no more likely to be selected than other areas that are equally suitable as sites. It is important to note that sites with high proportions of minorities may incidentally be more likely to be selected because they are more desirable as locations. In this view, equity is in the blindness of site selection processes to population composition of potential sites.

An alternative view of equity assumes that in siting TSDFs, a strategy should be adopted that ensures that sites with high percentages of minorities should not appear with any greater frequency than any other kind of site. Accordingly, if TSDF sites are found to be more frequently located in or near minority neighborhoods, then a condition of environmental inequity exists.

It should be noted that a finding that TSDF sites are in fact more likely to be located in or near minority areas can be interpreted as equitable or not depending on which definition of equity one adopts. However, if findings are otherwise, all definitions converge on the interpretation that the evidence does not support inequity.

This article does not take a stand on how equity should be defined. However, it does take the position that if our findings indicate that sites are not in or near areas with relatively high proportions of minority residents, then there is no evidence of inequity in siting.

Prior Studies

Three previous empirical studies of the population characteristics of the areas surrounding hazardous waste sites have received considerable public attention. The first was conducted by the General Accounting Office (GAO 1983) "to determine the correlation between the location of hazardous waste landfills and the racial and economic status of surrounding communities" (p. 2). GAO researchers compiled zip-code-level population data for areas surrounding four hazardous waste facilities in EPA Region 4, composed of South Atlantic states. The GAO found that the majority of the population in census areas containing three of the four facilities was black.

The second and most widely discussed empirical study was sponsored by the United Church of Christ's (UCC) Commission for Racial Justice in 1986 to determine the racial and socioeconomic characteristics of Americans living in residential areas surrounding commercial hazardous waste facilities (Commission for Racial Justice 1987). Like the GAO study, the UCC study used five-digit zip code areas as communities. Three population measures were central to the study: percentage of minority population[2] (blacks plus Hispanics), mean household income, and mean value of owner-occupied housing. The last two variables were employed as indicators of socioeconomic status (p. 10).

The main UCC (1987) analysis compared the 1980 population characteristics of zip code areas containing TSDFs to all other zip codes in the continental United States.[3] The UCC report found that zip code areas with at least one commercial TSDF operating in 1986 had an average proportion of minority residents twice that in areas without TSDF facilities. In addition, the socioeconomic differences between them "were not as significant as the mean minority percentage of the population" (p. 13). These results led UCC to conclude, "Race proved to be the most significant among variables tested in association with the location of commercial hazardous waste facilities. This represents a consistent national pattern" (p. xiii).

A third empirical study, conducted by Mohai and Bryant (1992), used a sample survey to assess racial biases in location of commercial hazardous waste facilities within three counties, including and surrounding the city of Detroit. The researchers employed the Detroit area study,

sponsored by the University of Michigan, to draw a household probability sample of the three counties, with an oversampling of respondents
within 1.5 miles of each of 16 commercial waste disposal sites in the
three counties. The study found that 48% of all the persons living
within a mile of a TSDF were black, compared to 39% who lived in the
1-mile to 1.5-mile zone and 18% of those living more than 1.5 miles
from a TSDF. They also found that race differences associated with distance from a TSDF were greater than socioeconomic status differences.

The three empirical studies summarized above have received considerable attention and have been influential in shaping national environmental policy. Two national conferences (Commission for Racial Justice
1991; Mohai and Bryant 1992) were convened to review research and
formulate strategies for obtaining environmental justice.

The EPA now requires data on risk to minorities to be submitted in environmental impact statements. In July 1990, the EPA formed an Environmental Equity Workgroup to assess the evidence that racial minority
and low-income communities bear a higher risk burden than the general
population and to consider what the EPA might do about it (EPA 1992,
2). In their 1992 report to the EPA administrator, the workgroup cited the
GAO report (1983), the UCC (1987) report, and the Michigan Conference on "Race and Incidence of Environmental Hazards" (Mohai and
Bryant 1992). Early in 1993, the EPA set up an Office of Environmental
Equity. In a recent (Grossfield 1993) lead story in the *Boston Globe*, Vice
President Albert Gore was quoted as saying, "Race is the single most accurate predictor of the location of hazardous waste sites."

Although it is heartening to learn that the policy arena pays some attention to empirical social research, these three studies are far from definitive. The GAO study is a collection of cases that cannot be
generalized to the entire United States. The UCC study is national in
scope but rests on an operational definition of community (zip codes)
that may be too large. The Detroit study is also a limited case study carried out in a single metropolitan region dominated by a central city that
is 76% black. We do not assert that these studies are wrong, but they are
not definitive.

Research Design and Data Sources

The analytic problem to be addressed is whether TSDF sites are more
likely to be located in or near to neighborhood communities with larger
proportions of blacks or Hispanics. To address this problem, it is necessary to define community in operational terms. Because equity issues are
ultimately concerned with potential risk or harm from TSDFs, the area

chosen for analysis should correspond to the likely areal distribution of possible harm from a TSDF,[4] but there is little solid evidence of specific harmful effects of living near TSDFs. Furthermore, TSDFs have a wide variety of potential effects (e.g., health hazards, air pollution, land opportunity costs, employment opportunities), each with unknown and, no doubt, different gradients of influence. Consequently, there are no firm guidelines on how to define areas that are subject to the potential effects of a TSDF.

In the absence of clear indications about which areal unit to adopt as a unit of analysis, the sensible strategy is to choose the smallest available areal units that can then be aggregated into larger units if necessary. Beginning with too large a geographic unit of analysis invites the possibility of aggregation errors and ecological fallacies (i.e., reaching conclusions from a larger unit of analysis that do not hold true in analyses of smaller, more refined, geographic units).

There are also constraints on the adoption of an operational definition of neighborhood that arise from the limitations of existing data sets. The only data sets that contain population composition information on all areas of the United States originate in the decennial census[5] (U.S. Bureau of the Census 1980). The smallest areal units for which detailed social and economic data are readily available in the census data sets are tracts, units that can be aggregated to larger units, such as cities, or counties.[6] Overall, census tracts have an average population of about 4,000 persons and a median land area (in 1990) of about 0.74 square miles.[7] Tract boundaries are set up by local census tract committees with instructions to "reflect the structure of the metropolis as viewed by those most familiar with it" (Bogue 1985, 137) and hence are more likely to be drawn to reflect local ideas of homogeneous neighborhoods. Because census tracts come closest to conforming to the definition of neighborhood communities, cover the places most likely to be candidates for TSDF locations, and can be aggregated, we used census tracts as basic areal units.

Prior to the 1990 census, tracts were only defined for Standard Metropolitan Statistical Areas (SMSAs), consisting of cities with populations of 50,000 or more and their surrounding counties or urbanized areas, omitting many rural areas, smaller cities, and small towns. About 15% of TSDFs arc located outside SMSAs and hence cannot be studied through a research strategy employing census tracts as units of analysis.

Our analysis is further confined to those SMSAs in which at least one TSDF is located. We compare characteristics of census tracts (and various aggregations of such tracts) in SMSAs in which TSDFs were located to other tracts in the same SMSAs in which facilities were not located.TSDFs located in portions of the country not tracted in the 1980 census (approximately 15% of all TSDFs) are not studied here, although future analyses will include them. A total of 47,311 tracts are identified in the 1980 census, containing approximately 80% of the U.S.population in 300 SMSAs (U.S. Bureau of the Census 1980). Of these, 32,003 tracts were in SMSAs of the 48 contiguous states with at least one commercial TSDF.

To carry out the analysis, it was also necessary to identify those specific tracts containing commercial TSDFs. This study includes only TSDFs that opened for business prior to 1990 and that were still operating in 1992. The tract locations of TSDFs were obtained using information maintained by the EPA and the Environmental Institute (1992), as supplemented by a telephone survey of TSDFs and computerized geocoding.[8]

We selected eight census tract characteristics for the purposes of this article.[9] Two variables are used to characterize racial and ethnic composition: percentage black persons and percentage Hispanic persons.[10] Three variables summarize the economic conditions of the population within geographic areas: percentage of non-farm families of four at or below 1979 poverty line, the percentage of households receiving public assistance income in 1979, and the percentage of all males (aged 16+) employed in the civilian labor force. Finally, three variables reflect industrial and housing characteristics of areas: the percentage employed in precision production, craft, and repair occupations and operator, fabricator and laborer occupations; the mean value of owner-occupied housing stock; and the percentage owner-occupied housing units built prior to 1960.

Analysis

We compare selected social and economic characteristics of tracts containing TSDFs to those of other tracts in Table 1. The results are considerably different from prior studies: There are slightly fewer blacks in TSDF tracts (14.5% vs. 15.2%), but the difference is not statistically significant.[11] There is a slightly larger percentage of Hispanics in TSDF tracts (9% vs. 8%), but again the difference is not clearly significant. Two indicators of economic status—percentage below the poverty level and percentage with public assistance income—do not differ, but significantly fewer males of employable age are employed in the TSDF tracts. There are also more people employed in industrial occupations in TSDF tracts (38% vs. 31%), and housing values are lower in TSDF tracts even though fewer of the houses were built before 1960.

In short, the percentages of black, Hispanic, and economically disad-

362

Table 1. Comparison of TSDF Tracts to Tracts Without TSDFs in all SMSAs

Variable	Tract Means TSDF	Tract Means Other	Cases TSDF	Cases Other	t Test	Significance Probability
Percentage black	14.54	15.20	408	31,595	–0.53	0.60
Percentage Hispanic	9.41	7.74	408	31,595	1.88	0.06
Percentage families below poverty	14.50	13.94	404	31,269	0.96	0.34
Percentage households on public assistance	9.51	9.01	406	31,306	1.12	0.26
Percentage males employed	91.75	92.73	406	31,401	–3.06	0.00
Percentage industrial employment	38.60	30.61	406	31,413	13.36	0.00
Average value of owned housing ($)	47,120.15	58,352.21	393	30,028	–8.84	0.00
Percentage housing built before 1960	55.73	59.80	406	31,317	–2.96	0.00

NOTE: TSDF = treatment, storage, and disposal of hazardous wastes facilities. SMSA = Standard Metropolitan Statistical Area. Average area characteristics are compared using t tests for means with unequal variances. The number of cases varies because some tracts had no residents with the relevant characteristics (e.g., the percentage of families below poverty level can be computed only for tracts with residential families). TSDF tracts are single tracts containing one or more TSDF sites.

vantaged in tract populations do not seem to distinguish between the tracts, but there are strong indications that the TSDF tracts are composed of residents who are working class in socioeconomic status, who are employed to a greater extent in industrial occupations, and who live in less expensive and more recently built housing.

To determine whether environmental inequities differ for large cities, the analysis is repeated for the 25 largest SMSAs, with the results shown in Table 2. For these cities, TSDF tracts have, in fact, a significantly lower percentage of blacks. However, TSDF tracts in these large cities have a significantly higher percentage of Hispanic residents. Again, TSDF tracts have significantly more unemployment and higher levels of industrial employment, with cheaper and more recently built houses.

Census tracts are smaller than zip code areas analyzed in earlier studies. To test sensitivity of these findings to the size of the area analyzed, a larger area was constructed for comparative analysis, consisting of all tracts with at least 50% of their areas falling within a 2.5-mile radius of the center of a tract in which a TSDF was located. The percentage black in these larger areas is significantly higher than in other tracts (25% vs. 14%). Hispanics constitute a higher percentage, 11% versus 7% for other tracts. Socioeconomic characteristics of the larger TSDF areas are also different. There are more families below the poverty line (19% vs. 13%), more households with public assistance income (13% vs. 8%), and lower levels of male employment (90% vs. 93%), all differences which are statistically significant in the direction prior studies suggest. In these larger TSDF areas, industrial employment remains significantly higher (36% vs. 30%), and housing is older with significantly lower average value.

These relationships are even more dramatic for the 25 largest SMSAs. Except for the value of housing, the differences between the larger TSDF areas and the rest of the tracts are at least as great as those reported for all SMSAs.

Clearly, changing the area definitions can result in radical changes in findings concerning environmental equity and may account for the discrepancy between the findings of Table 1 and prior research. Going from single tracts to aggregates of tracts caught in the 2.5-mile radius around a TSDF is, however, a considerable jump in size. To elaborate further, we use only the 25 largest SMSAs and, in Table 3, break down the aggregation into the following exclusive and successive areas around TSDFs: (1) tracts containing TSDFs; (2) tracts abutting TSDF tracts; (3) nonabutting tracts within the 2.5-mile radius around the TSDF tracts; and (4) all other tracts beyond the 2.5-mile radius within the SMSAs.[12]

The findings of Table 3 indicate that TSDF and abutting tracts are very much alike in composition and socioeconomic status.[13] It is the farther distant, nonabutting tracts within the 2.5-mile radius that contain

Table 2. Comparison of TSDF Tracts to Tracts Without TSDFs in 25 Largest SMSAs

Variable	Tract Means		Cases		t Test	Significance Probability
	TSDF	Other	TSDF	Other		
Percentage black	12.23	16.43	150	17,406	–2.18	0.03
Percentage Hispanic	13.88	10.05	150	17,406	2.25	0.03
Percentage families below poverty	12.46	13.53	149	17,211	–1.21	0.23
Percentage households on public assistance	9.23	9.64	150	17,230	–0.49	0.63
Percentage males employed	91.43	92.71	150	17,288	–2.26	0.02
Percentage industrial employment	37.08	28.95	150	17,300	7.58	0.00
Average value of owned housing ($)	55,980.13	65,764.10	145	16,323	–3.89	0.00
Percentage housing built before 1960	55.96	62.64	150	17,236	–2.68	0.01

NOTE: TSDF = treatment, storage, and disposal of hazardous wastes facilities. SMSA = Standard Metropolitan Statistical Area. Average area characteristics are compared using *t* tests for means with unequal variances. The number of cases varies because some tracts had no residents with the relevant characteristics (e.g., the percentage of families below poverty level can be computed only for tracts with residential families). TSDF tracts are single tracts containing one or more TSDF sites.

Table 3. Breakdown of Areas Surrounding TSDF Sites in 25 Largest SMSAs

Variable	Within Radius of 2.5 Miles			All Other Tracts
	TSDF Tracts	Abutting Tracts	Nonabutting Tracts	
Percentage black	12.23	15.76	32.70*	14.67
Percentage Hispanic	13.88*	14.53*	14.94*	9.32
Percentage families below poverty	12.46	14.53*	20.39*	12.72
Percentage households on public assistance	9.23	11.13*	16.49*	8.81
Percentage males employed	91.43*	90.93*	88.40*	93.26
Percentage industrial employment	37.08*	36.82*	35.17*	27.91
Average value of owned housing ($)	55,980*	53,414*	50,227*	60,012
Percentage housing built before 1960	55.96*	64.48*	78.62*	60.80
Approximate N^a	150	667	1,662	15,077

NOTE: TSDF = treatment, storage, and disposal of hazardous wastes facilities. SMSA = Standard Metropolitan Statistical Area.
a. For some variables the N is smaller because of missing values for a small percentage of tracts.
*Contrast with all other tracts (last column) is significant at .05 level.

significantly larger proportions of blacks, 32.7% in stark contrast to the 14.7% in the remainder of the SMSA tracts. In contrast, the percentage of Hispanics is about the same everywhere within the 2.5-mile radius, between 14% and 15% Hispanic in contrast to 9.3% in the remainder of the SMSA tracts.

Most other variables progressively increase or decrease when moving from the TSDF to more distant tracts. All of the socioeconomic variables show that the nonabutting tracts are the poorest in the 2.5-mile radius circle. Industrial employment is greatest in the TSDF tracts where housing values are lowest and the newest housing is found.

Further confounding any claim of national-level results, the patterns described above vary considerably within regions of the country. TSDF tracts have significantly lower percentages of persons black in the North Mid-Atlantic, East North Central, and West South Central regions (i.e., EPA Regions, 2, 5, and 67) and significantly higher percentages of blacks in TSDF tracts only in the South Atlantic region (i.e., EPA Regions 2, 3, 4) with higher percentages Hispanic only in the TSDF tracts of the Southwest (i.e., EPA Region 9). Thus higher percentages of blacks and Hispanics are each found only in TSDF tracts of a single region (i.e., the South Atlantic and Southwest, respectively) where they are most highly represented in the general population.

Finally, to confirm these findings and estimate the relative impor-

365

Table 4. Logistic Regressions of TSDF Present in an Area on Selected Variables

	Coefficient	
Variable	TSDF Tract	2.5-Mile Radius
Percentage black	−0.0009	0.0045*
Percentage Hispanic	−0.0001	0.0071*
Percentage families below poverty	−0.0210*	−0.0058*
Percentage households on public assistance	0.0078	0.0057
Percentage males employed	−0.0253*	−0.0359*
Percentage industrial employment	0.0468*	0.0229*
Average value of owned housing ($)	−0.0000*	−0.0000
Percentage housing built before 1960	−0.0107*	0.0135*
Constant	−2.4181*	−0.1677
Chi-square	186.01	1975.95
Probability > Chi-square	0.000	0.000
N	30,413	30,413

NOTE: TSDF = treatment, storage, and disposal of hazardous wastes facilities.
*Indicates statistical significance, $p \leq 0.05$.

tance of the competing associations requires multivariate analyses. The coefficients shown in Table 4 are changes in the log of the odds of the area's containing a TSDF for each unit change in the independent variable. A positive (negative) coefficient for a variable means the chance that the area contains a TSDF becomes greater (less) with increases in that variable, net of the influences of all the other variables included.[14]

The logistic regression results shown in the first column of Table 4 use being a TSDF tract as the dependent measure. Neither the percentage black or Hispanic in the tract is significantly associated with tracts containing one or more TSDFs. Most of the socioeconomic variables have coefficients that are insignificant, but the percentage of males employed is negatively related to being a TSDF tract. The percentage employed in industrial occupations has the greatest positive effect on whether an area will contain a TSDF and the percentage of homes built before 1960 has a negative effect. These findings are largely consistent with those of Table 1.

The second column of Table 4 contains results of a logistic regression for whether a census tract is within a larger TSDF area. The percentage black and percentage Hispanic within a tract are both significantly positively related to being a larger TSDF area. However, even in these larger areas, the two largest coefficients are the negative effect of percentage employed and the positive effect of percentage employed in industrial firms. All effects in the regression are again similar to those in Table 2.

Overall, the multivariate analysis supports our earlier findings. The most significant effects in each case are not those of percentage black or percentage Hispanic, but of unemployment and industrial employment within the area. For census tracts, the effects of percentage black and of percentage Hispanic are not significant. However, in much larger areas, both variables appear to be associated with the presence of TSDFs.

Conclusion

Three major implications are to be drawn from our study. First, the appearance of equity in the location of TSDFs depends heavily on how areas of potential impact or interest are defined. Second, using census tract areas, TSDFs are no more likely to be located in tracts with higher percentages of blacks and Hispanics than in other tracts. Third, the most significant and consistent effect on TSDF location of those we considered is that TSDFs are located in areas with larger proportions of workers employed in industrial activities, a finding that is consistent with a plausibly rational motivation to locate near other industrial facilities or markets. Whether or not this interpretation is correct cannot be fully sustained in this viewpoint but requires more direct evidence. Research currently under way is directed at examining the industrial composition of TSDF site areas.

Although findings vary with different geographic units of analysis, a generally consistent theme emerges. If the scope of the analysis is restricted to the 25 largest SMSAs, tracts with higher percentages of blacks are less likely, whereas those with high percentages of Hispanics are slightly more likely, to be TSDF locations. If much larger areas are analyzed, the findings change dramatically, with TSDF areas having higher percentages of blacks and Hispanics than other tracts. When these larger areas are broken down further, tracts adjacent to TSDF tracts are found to be like the TSDF tracts themselves. It is only in tracts on the periphery of the 2.5-mile radius circle around TSDFs that the proportions of black residents are significantly larger. Findings concerning persons of Hispanic origins differ, with larger proportions of Hispanics found near TSDFs in a variety of geographic comparisons. However, only in the single regions of the country in which the black and Hispanic populations are most well represented is there evidence that TSDFs are more likely to be located in tracts with greater proportions of these minorities. Certainly these minorities are not the most immediately exposed to the potential hazards of TSDFs throughout most of the country. None of these effects appears to be as consistent or significant as the finding that TSDFs are most likely to be attracted to industrial tract areas.

The analyses presented here also rest on assumptions concerning those parts of the United States that are relevant as comparisons to areas potentially affected by TSDF locations. By restricting our inquiry to SMSAs that had at least one TSDF, all of the analyses presented here compare areas with and without TSDFs only in those large metropolitan areas (SMSAs) of the United States with at least one such facility. In these comparisons, it is not our intent to define equity among social groups as merely an equal exposure to the likelihood of living near a TSDF. Instead, we have followed other researchers in seeking to assess whether the location of facilities suggests inequity in such risks. Within metropolitan areas containing TSDFs, we find no nationally consistent and convincing evidence of such environmental inequity.

We believe our findings show that TSDFs are more likely to be attracted to industrial tracts and those tracts do not generally have a greater number of minority residents. Why areas located at the fringe of a 2.5-mile radius from TSDFs should be more likely to have relatively high percentages of minority residents, we are unable to account for from the analyses presented. It appears likely that these findings reflect broader residential patterns largely unaffected by, and ineffective on, decisions of where to locate TSDFs. We are continuing to investigate this interesting question. Until that question is resolved, we must conclude that the evidence for environmental inequity is, at best, mixed in its message.

Notes

1. Several other, less detailed, studies suggest similar conclusions. In a study of 606 households located near the Stringfellow Waste Disposal Site in Riverside County, California, researchers found an elevation in disease when this group was compared to selected comparison groups (Baker et al. 1988). Types of diseases reported include "ear infections, bronchitis, asthma, angina pectoris, skin rashes, blurred vision, nausea, frequent urination" (p. 325) and other intestinal disorders. Stephens (181, 55) reports that residents of Fullerton, California, who lived near the abandoned McColl disposal site reported similar problems, including difficulties in breathing, headaches, and dizziness, and they complained of foul odors.

2. These are not mutually exclusive population categories. Hence summing them leads to some degree of double counting, especially in areas where there are significant numbers of black Hispanics, as on the East coast.

3. Some 400 zip codes were eliminated because they had no population or because they were codes for mail order firms, schools, and so on.

4. Of course, equity issues might be raised over possible benefits (e.g., employment) from TSDFs as well.

5. The census bureau routinely provides machine-readable data files at different levels of aggregation, including tracts, counties, and states. Zip code

files are available for some census years compiled by private vendors from census sources.

6. A limited amount of social and economic data are available for blocks, an areal unit which is difficult to analyze and which we believe to be too small to be useful.

7. There are considerable variations both in tract population sizes and tract areas. Although the median tract population size in the 1980 SMSAs included in the analyses was 3,861 persons, the interquartile range was from 2,601 to 5,405 persons. In contrast, zip code areas for 1980 contained, on the average, nearly twice as many (close to 6,500) persons. Tract areas, available only in 1990, also varied widely. Excluding very large outliers (tracts larger than 80 square miles) the median was .733 and the mean 3.107 square miles.

8. Although the National Resource Conservation and Recovery Act (RCRA) requires the EPA to collect and publish data on hazardous waste production, transport, and disposal facilities, it does not provide information needed for our research. Consequently, we used the latest available Environmental Institutes' (1992) *Environmental Services Directory* (ESD) as our primary source on TSDF listings. The 1992 ESD contained 454 commercial TSDFs that met the criteria of having begun operation before 1990 and being located in SMSAs that had been tracted for the 1980s census. Using a telephone survey to clarify ambiguous or missing information, we were able to geocode census tract locations of 98% (all but 8) and obtain dates of establishment for 92.5% (all but 34) of the commercial TSDFs.

9. A variety of causal arguments or hypotheses might suggest a different subset of variables. Our selection was intended only to illustrate interesting differences, to address variables already raised in prior research, and not to suggest any causal primacy of variables selected.

10. The sum of the percentages who identified themselves as Mexican, Puerto Rican, Cuban, and other Spanish persons.

11. Throughout, a significance probability of at least .05 is used to determine statistical significance. Where the significance probability is within the range of .10 to .05, qualifying phrases such as *not highly* or *somewhat* are used to convey marginal possible significance.

It should be noted, of course, that a difference can be statistically significant without being substantively significant. The difference between TSDF tracts and other tracts with respect to percentage Hispanic, for example was significant with a *p* value of .06. The actual percentage difference was less than 2%. Statistical significance only means, roughly, that we think the difference is not due to random error but rather is a genuine difference. Whether that small percentage difference is practically or substantively significant is another question.

12. This classification had to be accomplished by visual inspection of tract maps for each of the SMSAs. Hence the restriction to the 25 largest SMSAs. It should be remembered that tracts, and hence the areas produced by aggregations, are irregular in shape.

13. TSDF and abutting tracts are significantly different only with respect to the proportions of housing built before 1960, the former containing less housing built before 1960.

14. We are ignoring problems of spatial autocorrelation, a condition which can produce an error structure that is not $\sigma^2 I$. The effect is similar to autocorrelation in time series data: the coefficients are not biased but the standard errors are biased downward, leading to p values lower than they should be. However, the standard GLS solutions are not practical here because it would require an omega matrix of over $30,000 \times 30,000$. Moreover, spatial autocorrelation generally does not follow a simple structure, such as the first order autoregressive process often assumed with time series data (Anselin 1988).

Environmental Racism Subjects Minority Communities to Many Hazards

by Beverly Wright

Beverly Wright is director of the Deep South Center for Environmental Justice at Xavier University in New Orleans. The center, also known as a "Communiversity," promotes problem solving through community-university partnerships. She is the recipient of the Deblois Faculty Fellow Award for Outstanding Research in quality of life issues from the University of New Orleans. She specializes in environmental policy and equity issues, and in community organizing and occupational health. In the following viewpoint, Wright contends that recent studies strongly support the charge that minorities and the poor suffer more from toxic exposures than do others as a result of unjust policies and unequal enforcement. She disputes the view that insufficient research exists to demonstrate unjust exposure to environmental hazards. Wright also argues that disagreements between experts on the perception of unjust risk should not delay efforts to correct the problems.

"Minorities and the poor are singled out for disparate treatment in the siting of environmentally hazardous facilities and are disproportionately affected by pollution."

Environmental justice, equity, and racism are words that evoke different meanings and strong reactions from diverse groups. These concepts, with their differing interpretations, have brought the issue of disproportionate burden of environmental pollutants of certain segments of the population to the forefront of environmental concerns.

While recent studies provide strong evidence to support the charge that minorities and the poor suffer disproportionately from toxic exposures, this has always been the case. Minorities and the poor have always known that they suffer pollution in greater amounts than their white, generally more affluent, counterparts. Neighborhoods of the poor and minorities historically have been the prime targets for most nondesirable but "necessary" by-products of an industrial society. These neighborhoods are generally seen as paths of least resistance, and thus more likely targets for polluting facilities or industries.

The evidence is quite conclusive in regard to such pollutants as lead, toxic substances in the air, and pesticides, and compelling and oftentimes controversial in other areas such as hazardous waste sitings, but in general there are large gaps in the research due to a lack of data collection by race, class, and other categories.

A review of the literature shows that for at least 40 years, American children have been poisoned by lead. However, African-American children living in central cities, the suburbs, or rural areas suffer greater rates of poisoning than their white counterparts.

Lead poisoning is also correlated with income. Among African-American families earning less than $6,000, 68 percent of the children are lead-poisoned, compared with 36 percent of white children of similar family income. In families with incomes exceeding $15,000, more than 38 percent of African-American children suffer from lead poisoning compared with 12 percent of whites. Thus, even when income is held constant, middle-class African-American children are three times more likely to be lead-poisoned than their middle-class white counterparts (see Agency for Toxic Substances and Disease Registry, 1988).

It is estimated that under the new 1991 standard (10 μ/dl), 96 percent of African-American children and 80 percent of white children of poor families who live in inner cities have unsafe amounts of lead in their blood—amounts sufficient to reduce IQ somewhat, probably harm hearing, reduce the ability to concentrate, and stunt physical growth. Even in families with annual incomes greater than $ 15,000, 85 percent of African-American children in cities have unsafe lead levels, compared with 47 percent of white children (Florini et al., 1990).

The Government's Response

In the spring of 1991, the Bush administration announced an ambitious program to reduce lead exposure of American children, including widespread testing of homes, certification of those who remove lead from homes, and medical treatment for affected children. Six months later, Centers for Disease Control (CDC) officials announced that the administration "does not see this as a necessary federal role" to legislate or regulate the cleanup of lead poisoning or to require that homes be tested, or to require homeowners to disclose results once they are known, or to establish standards for those who test or clean up lead hazards (Hilts, 1991: 14).

It seems that the National Association of Realtors pressured President Bush to drop his lead initiatives because they feared that forcing homeowners to eliminate lead hazards would add $5,000 to $10,000 to the price of those homes, further harming a real estate market already devastated by the aftershocks of Reaganomics (Hilts, 1991: 14).

These events also stand as a warning to all of us who believe that "scientific evidence" alone is sufficient to resolve environmental health problems. These issues are complex, in that responses to scientific information are often compromised by socioeconomic and political factors. Their resolution will require organized responses that will entail the development of a mechanism to facilitate the collaboration of agencies and other stakeholders needed to find solutions that involve not only scientific but also political and economic interventions.

Race and Hazardous Waste

In the area of air pollution, studies have found that minorities and the poor are being significantly exposed to more elevated levels of air pollution than whites (see Gelobter, 1988, 1990; Wernette and Nieves, 1992).

The research reveals similar findings in the area of hazardous waste siting. Studies show race to be the most salient demographic characteristic for the siting of commercial hazardous waste facilities (United Church of Christ, 1987; U.S. General Accounting Office, 1983; Bullard, 1983; Bullard and Wright, 1985, 1986; Wernette and Nieves, 1992). The pervasiveness of this unethical if not illegal disregard for the health and welfare of certain segments of our population (i.e., minorities and the poor) was dramatically revealed by the 1984 Cerrell report. That report, commissioned by the California Waste Management Board in 1984 to advise the state on how to overcome political obstacles to siting mass-burn garbage incinerators, found low-income neighborhoods suitable or politically safe for the siting of garbage incinerators. Specifically, in one chapter of a lengthy technical series, the report concludes that "the state is less likely to meet resistance in a community of low-income, blue collar workers with a high school education or less."

According to the report, "All socioeconomic groupings tend to resent the nearby siting of major facilities, but the middle and upper socioeconomic strata possess better resources to effectuate their opposition. Middle and higher socioeconomic strata neighborhoods should not fall within the one-mile or five-mile radius of the proposed site" (Cerrell Associates Inc.,1984: 43). The report targeted particularly vulnerable sectors of the population, especially minority communities, for these sitings.

The Cerrell study has lent strong support to the contention of many researchers that minorities and the poor are singled out for disparate treatment in the siting of environmentally hazardous facilities and are disproportionately affected by pollution.

Moreover, a recent study by researchers at Yale University School of Medicine and the New York Department of Health gives greater urgency to the need for more attention to these issues. The study reviewed infants born with a birth defect who lived near inactive hazardous waste sites. The data suggest a small but statistically significant increased incidence of birth defects in babies born to mothers living near toxic sites (Geshwind et al., 1992).

What Determines Acceptable Evidence?

In the arena of pesticides the same scenario appears. Racial minorities, especially Latinos, are more likely to be employed as migrant farmworkers and are at increased risk of exposure to dangerous pesticides. Farm work not done by farm families is done primarily by ethnic minorities. Eighty to ninety percent of the approximately two million hired farmworkers are Latino, followed by African-Americans, Caribbeans, Puerto Ricans, Filipinos, Vietnamese, Koreans, and Jamaicans (Wasserstrom and Wiles, 1985; Moses, 1989). It is estimated that as many as 313,000 farmworkers experience pesticide-related illnesses each year (Wasserstrom and Wiles, 1985; Perfecto, 1990). Not surprisingly, Hispanic women generally show higher levels of pesticides in their milk than white women do.

There are also nearly four million public and subsidized housing units in the United States that are frequently treated with toxic pesticides to exterminate insects and other pests. These units house millions of people, including a disproportionately high number of people of color and those who are most vulnerable to pesticide exposure—young children and the elderly.

Exposure to lead poisoning, air pollution, pesticides, and hazardous waste sitings is of great concern to minority and poor communities. The problem, however, is greatly aggravated by differences between the opinions and interpretations of data by the groups affected by pollution and the governmental agencies that set and implement policy. Presently, it seems regulating agencies believe that they must produce "acceptable scientific evidence" to justify the allocation of funds to equity issues. Equally pervasive is the opinion the affected communities hold toward traditional scientific methods and government scientists. It is their belief that traditional science and traditional government will never be communities for environmental justice. A major discrepancy exists between community and government perceptions of what determines acceptable evidence. What can we glean from the history or other cultures to help us understand this dilemma?

In recent years policy analysts have come to recognize cross-national comparison as a technique for illuminating noteworthy or desirable elements of decision making in certain national contexts. This approach has proved especially fruitful in studies of science-based regulation. Comparisons between countries have helped identify institutional, political, and cultural factors that condition decision makers' use of scientific knowledge. This research has demonstrated, for example, that the analysis of evidence, especially in fields characterized by high uncertainty, can be influenced by the participation of differing classes of professionals in the administrative process, the composition and powers of scientific advisory committees, and the legal and political processes by which regulators are held accountable to the public. As a result, it is by no means uncommon to find decision makers interpreting the same scientific information in different ways in different countries (Jasanoff, 1992).

Cultural variation appears to influence not only the way decision makers select among competing interpretations of data, but also their methods of regulatory analysis and their techniques for coping with scientific uncertainty (Jasanoff, 1992: 29).

When knowledge is uncertain or unambiguous, as is often the case in science bearing on policy, facts alone are inadequate to compel a decision. Any selection inevitably binds scientific and policy considerations, and policymakers are forced to look beyond science to legitimate their preferred reading of the evidence. A number of forums on equity issues have been conducted and represent a step that can impact policy, especially in situations of scientific uncertainty. For the first time (1) high-level professionals in the administrative process are becoming sensitized to equity issues; (2) the composition and powers of scientific advisory committees now include academicians, grassroots organizers, and scientists interested in equity issues; (3) the legal and political process by which regulators are held accountable to the public is also reflecting equity concerns. This was exemplified by the Waxman hearings on lead and the recent out-of-court settlement in *Matthew V. Coye v. the State of California*. The case involved the state's not living up to the federally mandated testing for lead of some 557,000 poor children who received Medicare.

Immediate Attention Needed

These are historic times and some progress has been made; however, there are issues that need immediate attention and long-term solutions. There is great concern for communities referred to as "hot spots." These communities are painfully experiencing delays in the determination of "acceptable evidence" before their problems can be remediated or redressed.

It is easy to put numbers into a statistical model to determine that a particular risk to a certain group is statistically insignificant, but it is another thing to find case after case, for example, of cancer in one block of a small black community along Louisiana's "Cancer Alley," to smell the stench of Alsen, Louisiana, and listen to the stories of death due to cancer, cases of asthma, rashes, awful smells that cause nausea at night and insomnia, to name a few. Towns like Reiveilltown and Sunrise, Louisiana, no longer exist because the chemical plants built up to their backyards caused so much sickness, death, and overall human misery that the communities were finally bought out. But industry did not escape without a lawsuit! And in the case of Reiveilltown, vinyl chloride was found in the blood of children.

It is painful to listen to the people of Texarkana, Texas, and Columbia, Mississippi, talk about their community buyout with polluting facilities and EPA, or recite their unbelievable litany of health complaints.

Then there are the cases of West Dallas, Texas, East St. Louis, Illinois, and the South Side of Chicago to name a few. The communities that I have mentioned are mostly African-American. These citings are in no way meant to diminish the human sufferings of Latino, Asian-American, Indigenous-American, and poor white communities, but only to represent my personal experiences.

In California, the mostly Latino East Los Angeles and Kettleman City are overrun with companies trying to site hazardous waste incinerators in their communities. Kettleman City is a rural farmworker community of about 1,500 residents, of whom 95 percent are Latino. It already has one hazardous waste landfill.

Native American lands have also become prime candidates for waste disposal proposals. More than three dozen reservations have been suggested as sites for landfills and incinerators.

A Serious Problem

Disproportionate exposure is a serious problem for many communities and presents a serious challenge for regulating agencies, health providers, and environmental researchers. The question that must be answered is: *What has been the impact of disproportionate exposure from environmental pollutants on minority and poor communities?*

This question cannot be answered yet by the agencies whose duties are to protect the health and safety of the citizens of this country, because research data have not been collected by race and/or class. We presently find that government agencies, including EPA, may require investigation of exposure by race or class in the future. Because studies by race and class are conspicuously absent from most analyses related to environmental health exposure, scientific determination by government agencies along racial and class lines is still nearly impossible.

Many of the impacted communities are exposed to many toxic facilities. This of course means that residents are exposed to many different chemicals at one time. However, we have very little scientific knowledge on the cumulative or synergistic effects of exposure to chemicals. Enforcement regulations do not take this fact into consideration. For example it is possible for one small community to have many facilities releasing toxic chemicals on its citizens, but each individual facility may fall within the allowable federal limits for toxic releases. The important question of cumulative risk is absent from the equation. Moreover, what impact do the "safe" limits of exposure for individual facilities have on a community with multiple polluting facilities that are in close proximity to residents?

Regulatory compliance and enforcement are at the heart of many community environmental problems. How can the federal government ensure regulatory compliance by state and county governments? Has EPA evaluated the degree to which states or local governments are complying with environmental regulations? The experiences of many polluted communities suggest that this has not occurred. Methods for ensuring state and local government compliance must be developed.

Government Distrust

These communities want and need an *action plan* from the government. The citizens who suffer from elevated levels of pollution are seldom interested in technical risk assessment probabilities or explanations of cost effectiveness, biomarkers, biological susceptibilities, etc. What they want is protection under the law by the agencies that are charged with the management and regulation of environmental health. These communities have lost faith in the government's ability to protect them from environmental harm.

Ineffective responses to environmental problems by government have resulted in serious distrust by communities of those agencies responsible for the health and safety of the public. This distrust of government regulators is based on numerous factors, the most pervasive of which is the perception that the government acts only in the interest of the polluting industry. Moreover, government agencies responsible for regulating industry are seen as inappropriately biased in favor of particular industry risk management policies or approaches. Communities believe that government staff are not competent to deal with chemical risk issues; that government officials are deficient in skills to communicate risk information and to interact with citizens; that government officials have mismanaged regulatory programs and made highly questionable regulatory decisions; that experts and officials have lied, presented half truths, or made serious errors; and that equally prominent government experts have taken diametrically opposed positions on chemical risk issues. Also, reports of various risk numbers based on quantitative analysis of risk customarily do not match the public's perceptions of risk. This disagreement between experts and others may often be due to the public's reactions to risk statistics (Slovic, 1991). This phenomenon has created serious difficulties in the ability of policymakers to manage risk in a way that is acceptable to communities in the wake of previous ineffective responses to environmental problems.

Meeting the Challenge

The government must develop a mechanism to efficiently redress community grievances. Several academicians and grassroots environmentalists have proposed the development of regional Environmental Equity Justice Centers across the nation as a means of expediting government response to community grievances and effecting change. For example, it would appear that historically black colleges and universities (HBCUs), and other minority (Hispanic, Indigenous) institutions would represent a natural link between impacted communities and government regulatory agencies. This linkage between community groups, HBCUs, other minority institutions, and the government has not evolved due to perceptions and some real "experiences" of unequal treatment from, and access to, government agencies. Regional Environmental Equity Justice Centers housed at institutions in close proximity to impacted communities would facilitate the connection between communities and the government agencies mandated to deliver environmentally protective services to citizens. Such centers could increase the agencies' capacity to equitably deliver services.

It is important to note that these centers must function in ways that are decidedly different from traditional organizations. Remember, the centers' scientists must develop a trusting relationship with communities that have grown weary with the bureaucracy and its nonresponsiveness and are even more disenchanted with scientific studies, researchers, and their research findings. These centers should be designed to address:

1. Regulatory compliance and enforcement problems related to disproportionately high contamination of communities of color and to the unequal protection of those communities;

2. The impact of disproportionate exposure on the health of communities of color;

3. The environmental education and training needs of disproportionately exposed communities; and

4. The economic impact of disproportionate exposure on minority and poor communities.

The Deep South Center for Environmental Justice

One could conceive of a number of center models to fit the geographic needs of communities. The Deep South Center for Environmental Justice, based at Xavier University in New Orleans, is one model developed specifically for the Deep South, although it is applicable to other geographical regions as well. The center is called a "Communiversity" because the model emphasizes a collaborative management or partnership between communities and universities. The partnership promotes bilateral understanding and mutual respect between community residents and academicians. In the past, collaborative problem-solving attempts that included community residents and academicians were one-sided in terms of who controlled the dynamics of the interaction between the two, who was perceived as knowledgeable, and who was benefited.

The model represents an innovative approach for understanding and assessing environmental issues with emphasis on specific problems that exist due to the disproportionate exposure of minorities and the poor to environmental pollutants. The approach is unique in that it fosters collaboration with, and equal partnership between, communities and universities.

The essence of this approach is an acknowledgment that for effective research and policy making, valuable community life experiences regarding environmental insult must be integrated with the theoretical knowledge of academic educators and researchers. Either group alone is less able to accomplish the goal of achieving environmental equity, but the coming together of the two in a nonthreatening forum can encourage significant strides toward solutions.

The Deep South Center for Environmental Justice is a consortium of four universities—Xavier University, Dillard University, Southern University of New Orleans, and the University of New Orleans—in collaboration with community environmental groups and other universities within the region. The Center strives to achieve three objectives: partnership between university and community, interaction between program components, and legacy. It has three activity components for reaching its objectives: (1) research/policies, (2) community assistance/education, (3) primary, secondary, and university education.

Through its various programs of research, education, and community partnership, the Deep South Center for Environmental Justice will produce (1) paradigms to address environmental injustices, (2) a curriculum that can be replicated, (3) demonstration of an integrative approach to research and policy, and (4) an effective model of a community/university partnership, all to address environmental equity in a region of the country that has disproportionately borne the burden of environmental degradation.

Recommendations

1. The government must develop a mechanism to quickly redress community grievances. Administrative policies to appropriately service "hot spots" or high-risk communities should be a top priority. The Environmental Protection Agency (EPA) should be applauded for its present effort to establish an Environmental Equity Office. But this office should be adequately funded to service the needs of special populations. The last thing that this problem needs is another disadvantaged minority office with insufficient funds to address the needs of the disadvantaged.

2. Regulations should be developed to prevent this human tragedy from recurring. Federal standards should be enacted

and enforced that make it unlawful to so unmercifully burden a community with environment pollutants.

3. Synergistic effects of pollutants should be the subject of major research.

4. Regional Environmental Justice Centers should be developed around the country to investigate problems of equity and impact.

Bibliography

Agency for Toxic Substances and Disease Registry. 1988. *The Nature and Extent of Lead Poisoning in Children in the United States: A Report to Congress.* Atlanta: U.S. Department of Health and Human Services.

Bullard, R.D. 1983. "Solid Waste Sites and the Black Houston Community." *Sociological Inquiry* 53(Spring): 273–288.

Bullard, R.D. and J.R. Feagin. 1991. "Racism and the City." In M. Gottdiener and C.G. Pickvance (Eds.), *Urban Life in Transition.* Newbury Park, CA: Sage, pp. 55–76.

Bullard and Wright. 1985. "Endangered Environs: Dumping Groups in a Sunbelt City." *Urban Resources* 2: 37–39.

_____.1986. "The Politics of Pollution: Implications for the Black Community." *Phylon* 47: 71–78.

Cerrell Associates, Inc. 1984. *Political Difficulties Facing Waste-to-Energy Conversion Plant Siting.* Los Angeles: California Waste Management Board.

Costner, P. and J. Thornton. 1990. *Playing with Fire.* Washington, DC: Greenpeace.

Florini, K., et al. 1990. *Legacy of Lead: America's Continuing Epidemic of Childhood Lead Poisoning.* Washington, DC: Environmental Defense Fund.

Gelobter, M. 1988. "The Distribution of Air Pollution by Income and Race." Paper presented at the Second Symposium on Social Science in Resource Management, Urbana, IL. June.

_____. 1990. "Toward a Model of Environmental Discrimination." In Bryant, B. and P. Mohai (Eds.), *The Proceedings of the Michigan Conference on Race and the Incidence of Environmental Hazards.* Ann Arbor, MI: University of Michigan, School of Natural Resources, pp. 87–107.

Geschwind, S.A., et al. 1992. "Risk of Congenital Malformations Associated with Proximity to Hazardous Waste Sites." *American Journal of Epidemiology* 135(11): 1197–1207.

Hilts, P.J. 1991. "White House Shuns Key Role in Lead Exposure." *The New York Times.* August 24, p. 14.

Jasanoff, S. 1992. "Acceptable Evidence in a Pluralistic Society." In D.G. Mayo and R.D. Hollander (Eds.), *Acceptable Evidence: Science and Values in Risk Management.* New York: Oxford University Press, pp. 29–47.

Moses, M. 1989. "Pesticide Related Health Problems and Farmworkers." *American Association of Occupational Health Nurses Journal* 37: 115–130.

Perfecto, I. 1990. "Pesticide Exposure of Farm Workers and the International Connection." In B. Bryant and P. Mohai (Eds.), *The Proceedings of the Michigan Conference on Race and the Incidence of Environmental Hazards.* Ann Arbor, MI: University of Michigan, School of Natural Resources, pp. 87–218.

Slovic, P. 1991. "Beyond Numbers: A Broader Perspective on Risk Perception and Risk Communication." In D.G. Mayo and R.D. Hollander (Eds.), *Acceptable Evidence: Science and Values in Risk Management*. New York: Oxford University Press, 48–65.

Stark, R. 1992. *Sociology*. Belmont, CA: Wadsworth.

United Church of Christ, Commission for Racial Justice. 1987. *Toxic Wastes and Race: A National Report on the Racial and Socioeconomic Characteristics Of Communities with Hazardous Wastes Sites*. New York: United Church of Christ.

U.S. Environmental Protection Agency (EPA). 1992. *Environmental Equity: Reducing Risk for All Communities*. 2 Vols. EPA230-R-92-008 and EPA230-R-92-008A. Washington, DC: Policy, Planning and Evaluation, U.S. Environmental Protection Agency.

U.S. General Accounting Office (GAO). 1983. *Siting of Hazardous Waste Landfills and Their Correlation with Racial and Economic Status of Surrounding Communities*. Washington, DC: GAO/RCED 83–168, June 1.

Wasserstrom, R. and R. Wiles. 1985. *Field Duty, U.S. Farm Workers and Pesticide Safety*. Study 3. Washington, DC: World Resources Institute, Center for Policy Research.

Wernette, D.R. and L.A. Nieves. 1992. "Breathing Polluted Air." *EPA Journal* 18 (March/April): 16-17.

CHAPTER 8

Can Government Solve Social Problems?

Chapter Preface

Poverty and inequality are injustices that have always existed. In the past, society looked to churches and private charities to provide shelter for the homeless and food for the hungry. When the Great Depression of the 1930s struck, however, U.S. leaders were faced with the fact that churches and charities alone could not feed and clothe twelve million unemployed Americans. To help the nation's poor, President Franklin Delano Roosevelt set up such social programs as social security and the Works Progress Administration. More government programs, like Head Start and CETA (Comprehensive Employment and Training Act), were subsequently established under President Lyndon Johnson's Great Society. Through these federal programs, the U.S. government became actively involved in assisting the poor.

Many Americans believe that programs such as those started under Roosevelt and Johnson can ease the problems of today's poor. For example, John E. Schwarz, a political science professor at the University of Arizona, argues, "In 1980, one in fifteen Americans faced the desperation of poverty, compared with about one in five Americans just a generation earlier. This was accomplished, almost entirely, by the government." If government programs could cut the poverty rate from about 20 percent to about 7 percent in one generation, Schwarz and others believe, similar programs could help disadvantaged Americans today.

But other people criticize government programs for being inefficient and wasteful. Some agree with Charles Murray, the author of *Losing Ground: American Social Policy 1950–1980*, who maintains that although American taxpayers spent millions of dollars on Johnson's Great Society programs, a higher proportion of Americans were poor in 1980 than at any time since 1967. Murray's view that bureaucratic government programs are not the way to help the needy is seconded by Peter Flanigan, the founder of the Student/Sponsor partnership, a New York City charity.

He contends, "Government has a lot of money but doesn't know how to take care of people." Flanigan and others argue that because private organizations are in direct contact with the poor, these groups have a better understanding of what the poor need in the way of services.

Whether government programs can solve social problems and rectify societal inequality, or if that job should be left to private organizations, is debated by the authors in the following chapter.

Government Cannot Solve Social Problems

by Charles Murray

Charles Murray is Bradley Fellow at the American Enterprise Institute and coauthor of the controversial social policy book, *The Bell Curve: Intelligence and Class Structure in American Life*. In the following viewpoint, Murray argues that government efforts to solve social problems such as poverty, crime, and discrimination have either had no effect or have made things worse. He supports this assertion with trendlines, or graphs, that track progress before and after government intervention. Trendlines rarely show progress, he states, because government displaces the civil institutions and community organizations that do a better job of solving social problems.

"It is not that government intervention hasn't done as much *good as people think, but that it has not made* any *perceptible change in the outcomes of life that matter."*

Libertarians propose to do away with large portions of government. It is then our job to demonstrate that society would continue to function; indeed, we need to show that a world of limited government would be a better place in which to live. This demonstration cannot consist of proof, just as enthusiasts of a new government intervention cannot prove that their latest idea will work. Policy reform always means a future that is in some ways different from any past that has ever existed. But one general form of evidence is open to us.

Government intervention did not occur everywhere all at once. It proceeded in bits and pieces, directed at specific goals. The first step in asking whether we can get rid of government is this standard test: Draw a trendline showing what was happening before and after the intervention of government. Here is an example:

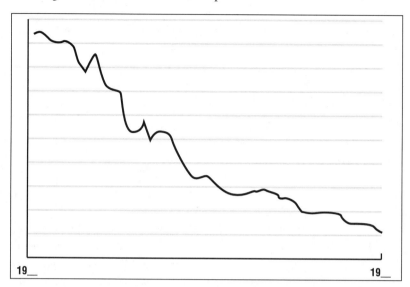

19__   19__

I will tell you what this particular trendline is about presently. The generic form—which can trend up, down, or back and forth—works for almost any kind of indicator of progress.

Poverty? Plot the proportion of Americans below the official poverty line from World War II (scholars have worked out the figures back that far) to the present, then superimpose on that graph the amount of money that government has spent trying to help the poor. Mark the trendline with the dates of major legislation to help the disadvantaged.

Education? Plot test scores or any other measure of educational achievement from the 1960s to the present. Superimpose the amount of money the federal government spent on whatever level of education interests you. Mark the trendline with points showing the landmark court decisions and legislation affecting education.

Health? Plot life expectancy, infant deaths, mortality rates for different kinds of diseases over time. Superimpose the amount of money the federal government has spent on the improvement of health in that particular area. Mark the trendline with points showing when the Food and Drug Administration (FDA) was established and when Medicaid and Medicare passed.

Safety? Plot injury rates or fatality rates for an industry. Mark the trendline with the establishment of OSHA and major events in the regulation of that industry.

Income? Plot wage rates for specific jobs. Mark the trendline with the passage of the minimum wage act, with labor union legislation, and with the landmark expansions in regulation of business.

Perhaps you are not interested in improvements for the population as a whole but in improvements for the disadvantaged—blacks, for example. Go back then and draw separate trendlines for blacks and whites. Draw separate trendlines for men and women.

The list could go on: unemployment, labor force participation, employment in white-collar jobs, crime, illegitimacy, welfare dependency—any indicator for which longitudinal data exist before and after government got involved.

Improvement Is the Exception

Suppose you have compiled several dozen such trendlines. Here is what you will find:

In a few cases improvement immediately follows the government intervention. Those will be the cases that you have probably already heard about, because they are the ones that have been publicized. To my knowledge the best examples involve the environment, showing, for example, that reductions in some emissions (but only some) steepened after federal emissions standards were set. In other policy areas there are occasional successes—college enrollment of blacks began a sharp increase in 1967, for example. Much more commonly, however, trendlines show a persistent tendency to shift in the "wrong" direction after the government intervenes. Two generalizations may be made for different categories of indicators.

Among trendlines involving social indicators—crime, the family, community, education, welfare—deterioration has been the rule and improvement is the exception. Among trendlines involving safety and health by far the most common result is . . . nothing. Whatever was happening before the government got involved continued to happen after the government got involved. Often a secular trend toward improvement continues. Sometimes the trendline looks like a random walk, bouncing around erratically, and government intervention bears no visible relationship to anything.

Failed Government Reforms

There is growing acceptance that the reforms of the 1960s largely failed, and many readers will not find it surprising that the trendline test shows that things generally got worse rather than better. But the trendline test may be extended to many of the most sacred of the achievements claimed for government programs, the ones still widely accepted as examples of programs that worked.

Didn't the New Deal end the Great Depression? Unemployment when FDR was elected in 1932 stood at 23 percent. It was as high as 19 percent as late as 1938, and still over 14 percent—still a "depression" by the popular understanding of the word—when Pearl Harbor was bombed. No prior recovery from high unemployment had taken nearly as long, nor had any other required a war to come to the rescue.

Didn't the War on Poverty at least reduce poverty? Using retrospective calculations of poverty, the trendline shows a regular drop in poverty from World War II through the 1960s, with the Johnson years accounting for their fair share, no more. Counting by decades, the steepest drop in poverty occurred during the 1950s, not the 1960s.

Didn't affirmative action at least open up professional jobs for blacks? Blacks were increasing their representation in the professions before aggressive affirmative action began in the late 1960s and early 1970s. The steepest slope in the trendline occurs in the early 1960s, before even the original Civil Rights Act of 1964. More broadly, employment of blacks in white-collar and skilled blue-collar jobs was rising at the same rate before and after the Equal Employment Opportunity Commission went into action. The single exception is clerical jobs, where a surge in government hiring drove up the numbers.

Didn't Medicaid and Medicare improve medical care? If you draw a trendline for life expectancy from 1900 to 1993, you will find that life expectancy was increasing throughout the century; after 1965 the rising trendline becomes flatter, not steeper. If you then hypothesize that the real effects were concentrated among poor people, you may draw separate trendlines for whites (disproportionately not poor) and blacks (disproportionately poor). Same result. If you then hypothesize that black life expectancy has been artificially depressed by the black male homicide rate, compute it for black women. Same result. Suppose you then hypothesize that the real measure of improvement is the *relative* black and white life expectancy. You will find that black life expectancy, only 69 percent of white life expectancy at the beginning of the century, first hit 90 percent in 1955—90.4 percent, to be precise. It never got higher than 92.4 percent thereafter. In 1993, the most recent year for which data are available, it stood at 90.7 percent—three-tenths of one percentage point higher than it was in Eisenhower's first term. . . .

Reality at Odds With Rhetoric

Let me conclude this illustration by applying the trendline test to the one case in which everyone knows that a government law absolutely, without question, saved thousands of lives: the imposition of the 55-

mph speed limit in 1974. Go back to the unlabeled trendline that opens the [viewpoint]. It represents highway fatalities per 100 million vehicle miles traveled. Could you mark 1974 on the horizontal axis?

Unlikely. Below is the same trendline with the blanks filled in. The trendline begins in 1925, the first year for which data are available, and ends in 1993. The vertical line marks the year 1974, when the 55-mph speed limit passed.

It is a picture somewhat at odds with the rhetoric you may have read about the safety value of the 55-mph speed limit. The period of the greatest change had nothing to do with government regulation. The steepest downward slope occurred in the period 1934–1949, an era when regulation of automobile safety features was nil and highway speed limits, where they existed at all, were high. The only thing that government did was build better highways as traffic increased. Meanwhile manufacturers were building safer cars—not because the government said they must but because greater safety generally goes hand in hand with improved technology in any product, whether cars or industrial machinery or toasters.

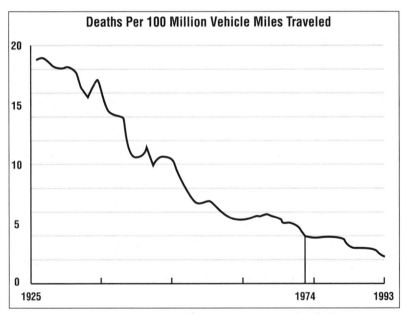

By 1974 no change in automobiles, roads, or speed limits was going to make a huge difference—another common phenomenon, whereby the first 90 percent of a problem is much easier to solve than the last ten percent. As it happened, the passage of the 55-mph speed limit made no visible difference at all. It was followed by a six-year plateau in deaths. Even more embarrassing to the supporters of the 55-mph speed limit, the trendline ends with six years of small but steady reductions in the highway fatality rate—beginning in 1987, the year Congress permitted states to *raise* the speed limit to 65 miles an hour on nonurban interstate highways.

A Simple Test, Yes; Simplistic, No

As I found when I wrote a book called *Losing Ground*, which presents many such graphs, advocates of government intervention hate the trendline test. I can hear their voices now: You can't judge the impact of something with a trendline! It's simplistic! Use life expectancy as a measure of success for Medicaid and Medicare? Outrageous!

For certain kinds of questions the trendline test is indeed simplistic. To understand many phenomena, it is essential to take several factors into account—the kind of thing that complex statistical analysis can do. Logic suggests, for example, that the 55-mph speed limit might very well produce *some* savings in lives, and I have read multivariate analyses purporting to demonstrate that it did. But statistical analyses that take many variables into account seldom make a dramatic difference in our estimates of aggregate impact. In the case of the 55-mph speed limit, the pre-1974 reductions in fatalities are too large to make the post-1974 trendline reductions look impressive, no matter how much tweaking you do.

Even after a complex analysis finds an effect, a problem remains: Statistical analysis of sociological and policy problems is a young discipline, and social scientists are still working out the kinks. The same methodology that seems rigorous when it shows a positive effect of the 55-mph speed limit from 1974 to 1986 suddenly looks much less solid when applied to the reductions in highway deaths from 1987 to 1993, when speed limits were going up—it becomes too easy to use exactly the same methodology to "prove" that higher speed limits save lives. The hard sciences can demand replicability of results as a test of validity; the soft sciences have yet to figure out adequate substitutes.

Often sophisticated analysis only makes the role of government programs look worse. For example, in the post-1965 era the government spent billions of dollars not just on Medicaid and Medicare but also on a multitude of other programs, from job training to welfare, that were intended to benefit poor people in general and blacks in particular. Insofar as they worked, they should have produced a narrowing of the gap in life expectancy independently of Medicaid and Medicare. That the raw gap did not narrow is made more ominous, not less, by detailed analysis.

For purposes of assessing large main effects in public policy, the trendline test is simple, yes; simplistic, no. If Medicaid and Medicare resulted in a significant improvement in medical care for poor people, it should show up in a measure such as life expectancy of populations that are disproportionately poor. The only thing "wrong" with the measure is that it forces policy makers to confront authentic outcomes instead of measuring how hard they are trying. Life expectancy doesn't ask whether poor people saw doctors more often or got more prescriptions. It asks whether their health improved.

Getting Along Without Government

In other words, the trendline test asks the question that the public should rightly ask. When the government engages in expensive intrusions on our lives, it does not say, "Give us 20 billion dollars and a chunk of your freedom for program X, and we will demonstrate that the impact of program X is greater than zero at the .05 level of statistical significance." The government says "Give us 20 billion dollars and a chunk of your freedom for program X, and we will make a large, obvious improvement in American life." That's what politicians promise. That's what they should have to deliver. The trendline test reveals whether they have done so. . . .

The trendline test offers an answer to the common question, "But how could we get along without program X?" How could we get along without welfare, for example, or the FDA, or antidiscrimination laws, or the Department of Education? . . . Often, my answer is that we will get along much better when the government has been pushed aside. But the generic answer is this: *Usually there is nothing to get along without.* It is not that government intervention hasn't done *as much* good as people think, but that it has not made *any* perceptible change in the outcomes of life that matter. . . .

A Return to Limited Government

Two large reasons explain why trendlines are so seldom moved in the right direction by government intervention, and both of them are important in understanding why we can return government to its properly limited role. . . .

Ineffectuality. The first reason is the simplest: most government interventions are ineffectual. The government huffs and puffs and spends a lot of money, but not much happens, because so much in a modern society has the inertia of a ponderous freight train, running on rails that government cannot shift and moving with such momentum that an out-side force such as government cannot speed it up or slow it down more than fractionally.

Displacement. Displacement is a more interesting phenomenon than ineffectuality. When a problem develops, civil society begins to develop ways of dealing with it. In the midst of that evolution a voting majority of some legislature says, "Government can do it better," and government intervenes. The government displaces the civil response that would have continued to evolve and expand if the government had done nothing.

The trendline is not immediately, visibly affected by the government intervention because, in reality, there is not much initial change in the net societal activity directed at the problem. Only later, as the government way diverges from the path that private evolution would have taken, does the world of the government diverge markedly from the might-have-been world.

Displacement also explains why government is so likely to make things worse rather than better. Government does not know how to build civil institutions (try to find survivors among the hundreds of community organizations that the federal government started during the War on Poverty). But displacement means that the government is thoroughly capable of stripping civil institutions of functions and effectiveness. One example is found in the extensive social-insurance functions served by fraternal and craft organizations. They virtually disappeared with the advent of Social Security. Another example lies in the web of parental pressures and social stigma that kept illegitimacy rare, combined with the private charitable and adoption services that coped with the residual problem. Intricate, informal, but effective, this civil system could not withstand the proliferation of welfare benefits for single mothers. Government displaces but cannot replace.

A return to limited government should not be confused with ending communal efforts to solve social problems. In a free society a genuine need produces a response. If government is not seen as a legitimate source of intervention, individuals and associations will respond. If instead government is permitted to respond, government will seize the opportunity, expand upon it, and eventually take over altogether.

To choose limited government is to choose once again to do things ourselves.

From *What It Means to Be a Libertarian: A Personal Interpretation* by Charles Murray. Copyright © 1997 by Charles Murray. Used by permission of Broadway Books, a division of Bantam Doubleday Dell Publishing Group.

Government Must Participate in Solving Social Problems

by Ruth Westheimer and Ben Yagoda

Dr. Ruth Westheimer is a psychosexual therapist who writes a widely read advice column, "Ask Dr. Ruth." She is on the faculty of New York University and a fellow of the New York Academy of Medicine. Ben Yagoda is an author, journalist, and assistant professor of English at the University of Delaware. In the following viewpoint, Westheimer and Yagoda contend that the government has an obligation to fund social programs that help families in areas such as welfare, education, child support, and jobs. Cuts in these programs, the authors argue, will add to rather than solve many social problems. They conclude that expanded government assistance—in the form of money and changes in the laws—would provide both real and symbolic benefits for families and society overall.

"If you believe government action can have an effect on the state of the family in a nation—as do both I and the Republicans who signed the Contract with America—then the government should take action."

By the time you are reading these words, the "Contract with America" may be a distant and hazy memory. But as I write them, the Contract, pledged to by the Republican Party as it took control of the Senate and the House of Representatives in 1995, is a nearly ubiquitous concept that is believed to represent a sea of change in American politics, values, and life.

Ask anyone (certainly any Republican) what the Contract represents, and I'll bet that one of the first things he or she says is "family." Indeed, the second paragraph of the Contract, in its published form, includes two sentences that are intended to sum up the significance of the new Republican majority in the House of Representatives: "That historic change would be the end of government that is too big, too intrusive, and too easy with the public's money. It can be the beginning of a Congress that respects the values and shares the faith of the American family."

I was very interested, therefore, in turning to "Strengthen Families and Protect Our Kids," the section of the Contract that explicitly deals with the family. What I found is the Family Reinforcement Act, which (again quoting from the published Contract):

> (1) protects parents' rights to supervise their children's participation in any federally funded program and shield them from federally sponsored surveys that involve intrusive questioning; (2) requires states to give "full faith and credit" to child support orders issued by the courts or the administrative procedures of other states; (3) provides a refundable tax credit of up to $5,000 for families adopting a child; (4) strengthens penalties for child pornography and criminal conduct involving minors; and (5) provides a $500 tax credit for families caring for a dependent elderly parent.

To which my response can be summed up in two words: "That's *it?*"

Families Need Government Help

Except for the first provision, about shielding children from "intrusive questioning" in "federally funded surveys," the need for which frankly escapes me, I'm in favor of all this proposed legislation. The problem is that in and of itself, it will do next to nothing to "strengthen families and protect our kids." For one thing, the specific measures tend to be either irrelevant or not forceful enough. Caring for elderly relatives at home is laudable in the extreme, and it should be encouraged. But to what extent will a $500 tax credit—amounting to a savings of not much more than $100 a year for most Americans—actually encourage this? Not much, I would submit. A $5,000 adoption tax credit is more like it, but even the $1,000-plus cash savings it would represent doesn't come close to defraying the amount of money many people spend in the course of adopting a child. So it amounts to moral support for adoptive parents— a worthy but not especially significant endeavor. And while no one could be a more enthusiastic supporter than I in putting some teeth in our system of collecting child-support payments, the Contract's provision has about as much bite as an eighteen-month-old.

Of course, the Contract deals with issues of family in another area: welfare reform. As you no doubt recall, among other things, the Contract specified that, in the interest of bolstering its conception of family values, mothers under the age of eighteen would no longer receive AFDC (Aid to Families with Dependent Children) payments for children born out of wedlock, and that states must drop families from the AFDC program after they have received a total of five years of benefits.

I have my own ideas about the relationship between the welfare system and the American family, and I will share them with you shortly. But what I want to say now is that if you believe government action can have an effect on the state of the family in a nation—as do both I and the Republicans who signed the Contract with America—then the government should *take* action.

I write this when most of the Contract is still in the legislative process, and it is unclear in what form it will emerge. But it is clear that for the time being the Contract has set the legislative agenda, that whatever does emerge will be a variation on it. And that, at least as far as the family goes, is a shame. With the national attention focused on the family, this could have been a perfect time for a broad public discussion on what is the most efficacious, most humane, and most forward-thinking way to approach family policy. That has most assuredly not happened. The Republican platform for the family is, to paraphrase Shakespeare, a lot of sound and fury, signifying not much of anything. In other words, if we're going to have a proactive, truly beneficial family policy, let's have one. Let's not just wave the family banner and then, when push comes to shove, come up with a few mild programs and a lot of empty and often divisive rhetoric.

Over the past half-century or more, government action has come, pure and simple, in the form of dollars: social programs, grants, and other forms of spending. And, in an ideal world, I would have the government generously subsidize every one of the fine profamily programs. . . . But I know that, given the current political climate, it would make no sense to expect this to happen. Nevertheless, there are far more ways the government can help the American family than are discussed in the Contract with America. . . .

As I see it, there are seven general areas in which family policy can have a truly significant impact:

1. The welfare system
2. Government regulation of business
3. The schools

4. Taxation
5. Child-support payments
6. The economy
7. A general commitment to the family

Welfare Cuts Will Not Change Behavior

I hasten to assure everyone that you are not about to read a detailed disquisition on the American welfare system. It is a complicated contentious, vexing subject, and far better minds than mine have devoted entire books to it. What I would like to do is spend a little time talking about the relationship between welfare and family—specifically, between welfare and the rise of low-income single-mother households.

Lately, the conventional wisdom (shown most dramatically in the aforementioned Contract with America) has held that the relationship is direct and causal. In other words, the fact that young, single women who have babies become eligible for AFDC *motivates* them to have babies. The corollary of course, is that if AFDC rules are changed so that payments are not automatic (or, in some cases, even obtainable), behavior will change as a result, and these women will not have out-of-wedlock babies at anything like the present rate.

A spokesman for this point of view is former Education Secretary William Bennett, who testified before Congress in favor of cutting off welfare payments for unmarried teenage mothers. "You would actually see fewer children born out of wedlock," he testified. "You would see less misery, and you would break the cycle of poverty."

I think this reasoning is full of holes, and I will tell you why. First of all, it rests on two related basic assumptions that are demonstrably false: first, that welfare payments are a significant motivating factor when it comes to poor single women having babies and, second, that when those payments are reduced or eliminated, there will be a resulting lowering of the out-of-wedlock birthrate.

How do I know these assumptions are false? Consider these facts: Between 1970 and 1993, the out-of-wedlock birthrate jumped some threefold. Yet in the same period, the average welfare benefit per family, adjusted for inflation, went *down* 45 percent, from $676 a month to $374 a month (in 1993 dollars). It would seem absurd to think that this "bonanza" (it amounts to a total of $4,488 a year—less than 40 percent of the official poverty guideline for the typical AFDC family of three) would have any kind of effect on anyone's behavior.

Also bear in mind that while the illegitimacy rate among the poor nearly doubled from 1979 to 1992, it also doubled among those who

397

weren't poor and *weren't* getting welfare checks—strongly suggesting that other forces were at work. Indeed, so skewed had the public debate about these issues become that in 1994 a group of prominent social scientists issued a joint statement that "focusing on welfare as the primary cause of out-of-wedlock childbearing vastly oversimplifies this phenomenon."

University of Pennsylvania sociologist Elijah Anderson agrees. "Many people are engaging in so many of these practices [that is, having unprotected sex before marriage] out of a sense of despair, of having no stake in the system," he says. "When people have a stake in the system, they are more careful about behavior that could in some ways undermine it."

In 1993, the state of New Jersey passed a law denying additional welfare payments when mothers already receiving aid had additional children. Previously, a mother would have gotten an extra $102 a month after the birth of a second child, and $64 a month for every child beyond that. Predictably, as of yet it has not had a perceptible effect on the rate of childbearing among these women. One woman who had a fourth child while on the program told the *New York Times*, "It wasn't planned, but I wasn't going to abort her. Sixty-four dollars is not going to change my love for my children, and if I would have aborted her, it wouldn't have comforted my soul."

The woman's reference to abortion brings up what is, to my mind, the supreme hypocrisy of many conservative politicians who favor limiting or eliminating welfare payments. I would rank the likelihood of these kind of policies affecting actual behavior as follows: Increased sexual abstinence? Virtually no effect. Increased use of contraception? Unfortunately, minimal. Increased abortion rates? Yes. For before you actually know you are pregnant everything is in the realm of the theoretical, a realm we all know most teenagers aren't very familiar or comfortable with. The moment is their world, and as for the consequences, well, why worry about them? Sitting in a doctor's office and being told that a baby is on the way, with no expectation of AFDC benefits, might be the one time when a young woman might decide *not* to go ahead and have that child.

Yet many if not most of these politicians are staunch abortion opponents. One possible conclusion is that they don't have the mental capacity to think their proposals through. Another is that they are hypocrites, or worse: In other words, abortion is morally indefensible for people like them, but for the poor, the black, the Hispanic, it's okay.

Suffering Will Grow

Another myopic aspect of these proposals is that they almost completely overlook the *fathers* of these children. Many of whom are in their twenties or older and literally could not care less about AFDC payments. The welfare-reductions-to-reduce-illegitimacy idea puts the entire burden on the woman, which is not only wrongheaded but unfair.

If these proposals won't cause a significant change in behavior, what will they cause? Robert C. Granger of the Manpower Demonstration Research Corporation, which studies welfare experiments around the country, was recently quoted in the *New York Times* on the idea of cutting off welfare benefits for mothers under eighteen. "The biggest group," he said, "would have the baby and be poorer than they would have been."

And the fact is, the main effect of these proposals would be increased suffering, as even their proponents must recognize. And it would be suffering borne primarily by children. Of the 14 million people on AFDC, about two-thirds—some 9.7 million—are children. If all the welfare provisions in the Contract with America had been passed, more than 5 million of them would have lost their financial support. . . .

I believe that cutting welfare to the extent that has been proposed would result in a level of suffering that has not been seen in this country since the Great Depression. And even though "welfare reform" has been a battle cry on almost all points on the political spectrum, I do not believe that the American people want this to happen. A recent *New York Times*/CBS News poll asked about "Government spending on welfare." Forty-eight percent of the respondents said it should be cut; 13 percent said it should be increased. But when asked about "spending programs for poor children"—which is pretty much what AFDC is—47 percent called for increases and only 9 percent for cuts. . . .

Subsidize Day Care

On February 5, 1993, President Clinton signed into law the Family and Medical Leave Act, a bill specifying that companies employing more than fifty workers must grant employees up to twelve weeks of unpaid leave annually to care for a new child or a seriously ill family member, or to recover from an illness. Unfortunately, it didn't cover enough people (only about 44 percent of women and 50 percent of men in the workforce).

And, once you read the small print, it didn't seem all that impressive. . . . (Most European countries mandate *paid* leave, of a significantly longer duration.)

But it was long overdue, and it was a start. It was, in addition, an example of the kind of proactive, profamily legislation it's possible for our government to pass. . . .

When it does, one of the first things I want our lawmakers to take a look at is the day-care industry. A recent nationwide study by researchers at four universities highlighted the poor care that is all too prevalent, especially in the case of infants and toddlers. The study found that up to 40 percent of these youngest children received "poor" care. Overall, only one in seven of the centers studied offered the kind of warm relationships and intellectual stimulation that are necessary for healthy emotional and psychological development.

It would be all too easy to draw the wrong conclusion from these findings. As Jay Belsky, a professor of human development at Pennsylvania State University, was quoted as saying in the *New York Times*, "The mistake would be concluding that only parents can care for young children and that day care is inherently problematical. When high-quality, stable care is provided, there is good evidence that children thrive."

And when is high-quality, stable care provided? By and large, when the money is there to pay for it. The national study found that the centers providing high-quality care spent roughly 10 percent more per child than those providing mediocre care. When parents can afford to pay and are willing to spend those extra dollars, everything is fine. But often that is not the case, which is why, even if it doesn't make direct grants to any other family-related enterprises or programs, the government truly needs to subsidize day care. . . .

Job Growth and Education

Of all the things that government can do to help the American family, the most significant have to do with jobs. If our people don't have the opportunity for decent-paying work, the consequences for the family are dire. After all, who can concentrate on "family values" when there is no food on the table?

"Trying to build a strong economy where a family can have jobs is the first thing," Carol Rasko, President Clinton's senior adviser for domestic affairs, told me. "If you can do that, then you can address health care, and then you can address all the other things."

I don't believe it is the responsibility of the government to furnish every citizen with a job. Yet it is the government's function to ensure that the economy is functioning properly. And our economy has some serious problems, at least insofar as our people are concerned. In the last few generations, we have witnessed a dramatic shift from an *industrial* to a service-oriented economy. That might be fine in terms of our ability to compete in the global marketplace, and it may be wonderful for your average cable-television executive, but it has had dire consequences for many of our people. As factories have moved out of the cities (to rural areas in some cases, to foreign countries in others) they have taken with them millions of relatively high-wage jobs. What opportunities are left for unskilled individuals? The most menial service jobs (that is, flipping hamburgers at McDonald's), welfare, street hustling, or out-and-out criminal activities.

The situation is obviously not good for the people of the inner cities and their families. It leads to hopelessness, illegitimacy, all kinds of pathologies (like crime, substance and domestic abuse, mental illness), and, in general, a ripping apart of the social fabric.

What can government do about it? Two areas of action come to mind. The first consists of packages of low taxes and outright grants—"enterprise zones," as they are often called—that will encourage businesses to return to the cities. The free market, as an idea, is fine, but if left completely free it will ultimately lead to the death of our cities. Sometimes the pump simply has to be primed, and this is one of those times.

The second and even more important area is education. Information and service jobs are the wave of the future, and, unlike factory jobs, they *demand* highly trained workers. We must make a dramatic, unprecedented investment in our young people so that they will be equipped to function and, eventually, thrive in this world. I'm talking about *billions* of dollars poured into new schools, into improvements in our existing schools, into computers and teachers' salaries and physical plants. I'm talking about a complete rethinking of the way we go about educating kids.

In this regard, we should be following the lead of Walter Annenberg, the former owner of *TV Guide* and ambassador to the United Kingdom, who in recent years has donated hundreds of millions of dollars to schools, many of them in our cities. He has the right idea. We as a people need to follow through on his groundbreaking work, by donating money (on a lesser level), by volunteering our time, and by *paying attention*.

All of the things I've been talking about are very practical, a diverse group of actions involving spending money and changing laws. But the importance of symbolism should not be forgotten. Perhaps as much as specific programs, it is critical that the government be *seen* as having a commitment to the family.

"One of the main things that has struck me in this job is the importance of the signaling function of public policies," says Assistant Secretary of Health and Human Services Mary Jo Bane. "They symbolize a set of values and aspirations, and they're just as important as the particular things you do. Tough provisions about child support, for example, is a statement that both parents are responsible. Even if they never deter a single young man from getting a girl pregnant, it's a very important statement about public policy. People see it on the news, on talk shows, in the newspapers, and they start to think, 'This is something I need to take seriously.'"

There are also government actions that, in and of themselves, will not have a particularly broad effect, but that will send a powerful message about the family. I'm thinking, for example, of laws relating to adoption. Everyone agrees that adoption is a very good thing: It places many otherwise unwanted children in loving homes, it is an alternative to abortion, and, in general, it strengthens the family. Yet many people who want to adopt and who would make wonderful parents often have a very difficult time doing so; for instance gay couples and individuals of one race who want to adopt a child of another race. I am enthusiastically in favor of changing our adoption laws and procedures so that these circumstances are considered as irrelevant as they are and only the truly important questions are considered: Will the prospective parent or parents love the child? Will they have the resources to care for him or her?

For an analogy to the kind of broad-based commitment I'm talking about, think of the environmental movement that began some twenty-five years ago. It wasn't just a series of legislative acts; it was a concerted *campaign*, in which every effort related to the common goal. Laws were passed, to be sure, but consciousnesses were also raised.

One thing the family movement might borrow from the "tree huggers" is the notion of the environmental impact statement. Whenever a project of a certain size is contemplated the engineers must draft a statement assessing the effect the project will have on the environment, its approval depending in part on what the statement says. How about requiring that every piece of legislation, and every major action by a regulated business, carry with it a *family* impact statement—an explanation, endorsed by experts, of its probable effect on families and children? This may have little or no practical value, but the symbolism would be enormous.

The same goes for another idea I have long favored, the creation of a new cabinet-level post devoted to the family. This would be filled by a universally respected authority who would oversee the progress of family-oriented legislation, monitor all those impact statements, and deliver an annual "state of the American family" message. As to the title this official would have, that is a no-brainer. Remember during the energy crisis when we had an "oil czar"? The family crisis is just as pressing, so by all means let's have a *family* czar.

Government Participation Is Essential to Solving Poverty

by Fred Kammer

Fred Kammer is a Jesuit priest and the president of Catholic Charities USA. In the following viewpoint, Kammer argues that an ongoing partnership between private charities and government is the key to solving poverty. Many private charities rely on government funds for their work with the poor, he states, because private contributions cannot provide for long-term needs such as housing, social services, and steady income. The government, he says, is uniquely situated to provide for these needs. Without government funding, Kammer contends, many private charities would be unable to carry out the work of helping the poor.

"Only government has the resource capacity—not to mention the political and moral responsibility—to promote the general welfare."

I recently spent an evening at Christ House, an Alexandria, Va., homeless shelter and soup kitchen sponsored by Catholic Charities of the Diocese of Arlington County, Va. In my travels across the country, I often witness the wonderful work of some of the 272,000 staff members and volunteers who make Catholic Charities the nation's largest voluntary social service network.

On that evening, I spent most of my time talking with two shelter residents. Both men had come on hard times, one from the economy and the other from a job-related injury. Both rose early for nearly minimum-wage work, were saving money for their own apartments (Christ House has a five-week maximum stay), were in debt and found it hard to make ends meet. But they were grateful for Christ House.

Christ House is made possible by church, private and United Way funding. It receives one small government grant—less than 2 percent of its budget. Forming the backbone of its soup kitchen are 1,600 volunteers who prepare and serve 35,000 meals a year. It is a wonderful program reflecting the best combination of community, church and, yes, some government funds.

Catholic Charities of Arlington has another program in Alexandria, the Martin de Porres Center. There, older adults receive meals, education and social services. From the center, outreach takes place to homebound elders, many of whom live on Social Security, supplemental security income, or SSI, and food stamps. Nearly 30 percent of the center's funds come from the Older Americans Act.

Both the Martin de Porres Center and Christ House have numerous volunteers and United Way support and are considered model community programs. That one has 30 percent government funding and the other 2 percent does not distinguish the quality of care provided.

Lacking Private Income

Few churches and charities, in fact, have the private income necessary to provide long-term housing, social services and, especially, steady income support to poor families in any number. That is a role government has played since the 1930s, when the Great Depression ended the illusion that private charity could maintain millions of poor people in decent living conditions reflective of human dignity. Now we live in a post-depression economic system where unemployment and underemployment regularly leave 30 million Americans with incomes—if any— below the poverty line.

Government plays two primary roles for such families. First, federal or state governments provide income directly through insurance or welfare programs. Included are Social Security, SSI for low-income people who are elderly or disabled, Aid to Families with Dependent Children, or AFDC, and veterans benefits. Often, when government wants to deliver services—such as child group homes, refugee resettlement or job training—instead of income, it works with experienced social service organizations.

In such programs, churches and charities play a different role than in many emergency services. Here, governments at the federal, state and local levels contract with charities to provide specialized services to affected groups. This "purchase of service" has been an essential part of government's approach to social needs for much of the twentieth century. Just as the federal government pays Lockheed to build an airplane or IBM to design a computer, it pays human-service providers, usually after competitive bidding, to provide specialized social services and care. An example would be foster-home care for infants with fetal alcohol syndrome.

An Effective Partnership

Catholic Charities agencies are proud to help people in need. It is our mission as church, as charity and as partner with community, business and government. We view our partnership with government like our participation in the United Way: helping us to meet community needs in an effective and efficient way.

Government contracts with us—as it does with the Salvation Army, Lutheran Social Services, the Council of Jewish Federations and hundreds of local religious charities—because it knows we are community-based, trusted by those we serve and scrupulous about stewardship of our resources. Governments often seek us out to deliver these services because they trust us to do the job right. We also have to be vigilant that funding by government, like United Way, foundations and individual donors, does not cause us to abandon the values that undergird this compassionate work.

Hundreds of local agency boards decide to contract with government so they can contribute to the common good and to government's responsibility "to promote the general welfare" as provided for in the preamble to the Constitution. We bring our concern for people, values, experience, volunteers and private funding to make this partnership effective. (Often, governments require a financial "match" for their contracts.) We also recognize that our private dollars stretch public dollars and allow much, much more to be done than either could accomplish alone.

Both government and religious charities then see the relationship as a partnership that helps each to be faithful to its own mission. These relationships are not without their problems, which are typical for the public-private partnerships about which we hear so much these days.

Critics of the Partnership

Recently, critics have challenged such partnerships in human and social services. On the extreme left, church-state separatists want religious charities as far away from public programs as possible. They don't want us to bring our values of human dignity, community and ethical standards to bear on services. On the far right come those who see government money as somehow "corrupting" our religious mission and religious giving. They argue that charity will be purer and more generous if government were not involved.

Ironically, these same voices on the extreme right also argue that charities—from whom they would strip all government funding—will pick up the slack if the Congress slashes both income support and social services.

The argument about government money driving out private charity is just that: an argument. Proponents produce no studies, no experiments, no proof. It is, at best, sociological speculation fueled by ideological wishfulness. If it were just speculation, think-tank theories or armchair theology, it could go unchallenged. However, supporters propose to risk the lives, health and futures of low-income families on their hunches. They feel free to do so, because it will cost them nothing to throw people in need to the vagaries of private charity. I wish they were willing to put their own children's futures or the care of their elderly parents to the same test.

Donors and Volunteers

Certainly, I know of churches and individuals who excuse their lack of concern for poor families by saying that government or United Way or some charity will do the job. But I also know that despite the fact that Catholic Charities receives two-thirds of its funding from governments, we also have wonderful donors and volunteers and expect to have many more in the future. While our government partnership has grown during the last 20 years, so too has our private giving and volunteering. In 1973, our agencies reported $139 million from nongovernment sources to support their programs. By 1993, that total had risen to $620 million. In 1981, our members reported 20,000 volunteers; in 1993, that number had grown tenfold to more than 200,000.

So while critics on the right contend that government funding will drive out private dollars and volunteers, that is not our experience. Even where government monies are far greater than in Alexandria, I find wonderful volunteers, donors and local boards working to make sure that all services, however funded, are high in quality and deeply caring.

Frankly, if the cuts proposed in the House Personal Responsibility Act were passed, we could not fill the gaps slashed in the nation's safety net. Charities certainly can do more with the help of volunteers and donors. But the government—"we the people"—should not do less.

This is not just my personal opinion. It is the considered judgment of experienced Catholic Charities leaders across this nation, echoed by the Salvation Army, the St. Vincent de Paul Society, the Council of Jewish Federations, Second Harvest, Feed the Children, Lutheran Social Services and many others. The people we serve and our services for them will be devastated.

Struggling to Meet Needs

In 1993, Catholic Charities served 10.6 million people of every social, economic, ethnic and religious background. Nearly 7 million people came to us for emergency services—primarily food and shelter. That includes 1.7 million children.

Our agencies constantly are struggling to meet the basic needs of people. We should be providing more services that help people regain self-sufficiency. Instead, since 1983 we have been forced by government cuts and the economy into the emergency food and shelter business. In 1994, we provided emergency services to about two-thirds of those we served. Compare that with the situation in 1983, when only one-fourth needed food or shelter.

Instead of using resources to help people overcome obstacles such as joblessness or alcoholism, we face working families who come to us for food when their minimum-wage paychecks won't last the week. And we provide hot meals to too many people who cannot find jobs and cannot make ends meet with government benefits.

We believe that only government has the resource capacity— not to mention the political and moral responsibility—to promote the general welfare. That begins with life-sustaining food and nutrition and includes basic income supports for those who cannot work.

Private charities work in partnership with the government. As church and as charity, we cannot fulfill the government's role in feeding hungry people or meeting needs for basic income. Even with increased giving— with or without new tax credits—we do not have the means to make up for a proposed $60 billion in budget cuts or $18 billion in cuts in food programs. We already serve 700 percent more people with emergency services than in 1981. Compare the proposed cuts, for example, with the fact that the entire national United Way effort only raises $3 billion-plus a year.

States' Shaky Record

We hear a lot of talk these days about turning programs over to the states. Sadly, the historical record raises profound doubts about the will or ability of states to protect our poorest families from the ravages of hunger and poverty. I write this as a Southerner who worked for years in Louisiana and Georgia and watched state legislatures firsthand. Despite recent political promises of a few governors, we should keep in mind the following points:

- State reforms are as yet untested and unproven in making significant improvements in welfare programs.
- As a national average, states have allowed AFDC benefits per family to decline steadily for decades.
- Many state systems of care for abused and neglected children have failed miserably and been taken over by the courts. Nationally, 100 children died in 1994 in state foster-care and child-care systems.
- Many states failed to avail themselves of the 1988 Welfare Reform Act's provisions for moving parents from welfare to work because they were unable or unwilling to put in their share of funding.
- States often have been punitive toward poor families.

The fact that food-stamp benefits increase when AFDC declines is one further reason not to turn the food programs over to state politics where they no longer will be the refuge of last resort for hungry poor families.

Federal food programs have reflected the determination of Congress that in the world's most powerful nation, children and families will not starve to death. Now, when poverty is at one of its highest levels in decades, that commitment should not change.

Jesus Christ could feed 5,000 people with a few loaves of bread and fish and, while we may try the same, it is neither sound social policy nor responsible government to put people's lives in jeopardy in hope of miracles. While there are promises that church people will come out to meet new needs created by congressional neglect, the poor already are lined up at our shelters and sometimes turned away from our overwhelmed services.

From "Compassion Alone Won't Do the Job" by Fred Kammer, *Insight*, April 3–10, 1995. Reprinted by permission from *Insight*. Copyright 1995, News World Communications, Inc. All rights reserved.

Government Programs Cannot Solve Poverty

by Marvin Olasky

Marvin Olasky is a journalism professor at the University of Texas, Austin, and a senior fellow at the Progress and Freedom Foundation, a public policy research center in Washington, D.C. In the following viewpoint, Olasky argues that in the fight against poverty, private and religious charities have succeeded where government programs have failed. He cites antipoverty efforts of the nineteenth century, before the existence of government welfare programs, when private organizations helped people work their way out of poverty. They did so, he states, by stressing family bonds, employment, and spiritual guidance. He argues that a network of charitable organizations should once again lead the fight against poverty, replacing government welfare programs that destroy lives.

"Private charities can do a better job than government."

For too long the welfare debate has been the "same old same old." Liberals have emphasized distribution of bread and assumed the poor could live on that alone. Conservatives have complained about the mold on the bread and pointed out the waylaying of funds by "welfare queens" and the empire-building of "poverty pimps."

It is time now, however, to talk not about reforming the welfare system—which often means scraping off a bit of mold—but about replacing it with a revolutionary, centrist system based on private and religious charity. Such a system was effective in the nineteenth century and will be even more effective in the twenty-first century, with the decentralization that new technology makes possible. But we must also make the right changes in personal goals and public policy.

Replacing Welfare

Why is welfare replacement necessary? Because in America we now face not just concern about poor individuals falling between the cracks, but the crunch of sidewalks disintegrating. An explosive growth in the number of children born out of wedlock—in 1995, one of every three of our fellow citizens is beginning life hindered by the absence of a father—is one indication of rapid decline.

Why is welfare replacement politically possible? Because there is broad understanding that the system hurts the very people it was designed to help, and that the trillions of dollars spent in the name of compassion over the past three decades have largely been wasted. Conservatives who want an opportunity to recover past wisdom and apply it to future practice should thank liberals for providing a wrecked ship. And liberals should support welfare replacement because, given the mood of the country, the alternative to replacement is not an expanded welfare state, but an extinct one.

Why is welfare replacement morally right? Because, when we look at the present system, we are dealing with not just the dispersal of dollars but with the destruction of lives. When William Tecumseh Sherman's army marched through Georgia in 1864, about 25,000 blacks followed his infantry columns, until Sherman and his soldiers decided to rid themselves of the followers by hurrying across an unfordable stream and then taking up the pontoon bridge, leaving the ex-slaves stranded on the opposite bank. Many tried to swim across but died in the icy water. Similarly today, many of the stranded poor will soon be abandoned by a country that has seen welfare failure and is lapsing into a skeptical and even cynical "compassion syndrome"—unless we find a way to renew the American dream of compassion.

The destruction of life through the current welfare system is not often so dramatic, but the death of dreams is evident every day. During the past three decades, we have seen lives destroyed and dreams die among poor individuals who have gradually become used to dependency. Those who stressed independence used to be called the "worthy poor"; now, a person who will not work is also worthy, and mass pauperism is accepted. Now, those who are willing to put off immediate gratification and to sacrifice leisure time in order to remain independent are called chumps rather than champs.

We have also seen dreams die among some social workers who had been in the forefront of change. Their common lament is, "All we have time to do is move paper." Those who really care do not last long, and one who resigned cried out, "I had a calling; it was that simple. I wanted to help." Some social workers take satisfaction in meeting demands, but others who want to change lives become despondent in their role of enabling destructive behavior.

We have seen dreams die as "compassion fatigue" deepens. Personal involvement is down, cynicism is up. Many of us would like to be generous at the subway entrance or the street corner, but we know that most homeless recipients will use any available funds for drugs or alcohol. We end up walking by, avoiding eye contact—and a subtle hardening occurs once more. Many of us would like to contribute more of our money and time to the poor, but we are weighed down by heavy tax burdens. We end up just saying "no" to personal involvement, and a sapping of citizenship occurs once more.

We have seen dreams die among children who will never know their fathers. Government welfare programs have contributed to the removal of fathers, and nothing can replace them.

Some would say that for the poor and the fatherless the death of dreams is inevitable, but that is not so. England in the nineteenth century recovered from its downward spiral that began in the eighteenth century. And we in the United States in the twenty-first century can recover from our recent problems, since we know a great deal from our own experience about how to fight poverty. We had successful antipoverty programs a century ago—successful because they embodied personal, material, and spiritual involvement and challenge.

A Successful War on Poverty

This vital story has generally been ignored by liberal historians, but the documented history goes like this: During the nineteenth century, a successful war on poverty was waged by tens of thousands of local, private charitable agencies and religious groups around the country. The platoons of the greatest charity army in American history often were small. They were made up of volunteers led by poorly paid but deeply dedicated professional managers. And they were highly effective.

Thousands of eyewitness accounts and journalistic assessments show that poverty fighters of the nineteenth century did not abolish poverty, but they enabled millions of people to escape it. They saw springs of fresh water flowing among the poor, not just blocks of ice sitting in a perpetual winter of multi-generational welfare dependency. And the optimism prevalent then contrasts sharply with the demoralization among

411

the poor and the cynicism among the better-off that is so common now.

What was their secret? It was not neglect. It was their understanding of the literal and biblical meaning of compassion, which comes from two Latin words—*com*, which means "with," and *pati*, which means "to suffer." The word points to personal involvement with the needy, suffering with them, not just giving to them. "Suffering with" means adopting hard-to-place babies, providing shelter to women undergoing crisis pregnancies, becoming a big brother to a fatherless child, working one-on-one with a young single mother. It is not easy—but it works.

Our predecessors did not have it easy—but they persevered. Theirs were not "the good old days." Work days were long and affluence was rare, and homes on the average were much smaller than ours. There were severe drug and alcohol problems and many more early deaths from disease. We are more spread out now, but our travel time is not any greater. Overall, most of the problems paralleled our own; the big difference lies in the rates of increase in illegitimacy and divorce. Most of the opportunities and reasons to help also were similar; a big difference in this regard is, as I have already pointed out, that our tax burden is much larger, and many Americans justifiably feel that they are already paying for others to take care of the needy.

In the nineteenth century, volunteers opened their own homes to deserted women and orphaned children. They offered employment to nomadic men who had abandoned hope and most human contact. Most significantly, our predecessors made moral demands on recipients of aid. They saw family, work, freedom, and faith as central to our being, not as "lifestyle options." The volunteers gave of their own lives not just so that others might survive, but that they might thrive.

Principles of Effective Compassion

Affiliation. A century ago, when individuals applied for material assistance, charity volunteers tried first to "restore family ties that have been sundered" and "reabsorb in social life those who for some reason have snapped the threads that bound them to other members of the community." Instead of immediately offering help, charities asked, "Who is bound to help in this case?" In 1897, Mary Richmond of the Baltimore Charity Organizing Society summed up the wisdom of a century: "Relief given without reference to friends and neighbors is accompanied by moral loss. Poor neighborhoods are doomed to grow poorer whenever the natural ties of neighborliness are weakened by well-meant but unintelligent interference."

Today, before developing a foundation project or contributing to a private charity, we should ask, "Does it work through families, neighbors, and religious or community organizations, or does it supersede them?" For example, studies show that many homeless alcoholics have families, but they do not want to be with them. When homeless shelters provide food, clothing, and housing without asking hard questions, aren't they subsidizing disaffiliation and enabling addiction? Instead of giving aid directly to homeless men, why not work on reuniting them with brothers, sisters, parents, wives, or children?

We should ask as well whether other programs help or hurt. It is good to help an unmarried teenage mother, but much of such aid now offers a mirage of independence. A better plan is to reunite her whenever possible with those on whom she actually depends, whether she admits it or not: her parents and the child's father. It is good to give Christmas presents to poor children, but when the sweet-minded "helper" shows up with a shiny new fire truck that outshines the second-hand items a poor single mom put together, the damage is done. A better plan is to bulwark the beleaguered mom by enabling her to provide for her children.

Bonding. A century ago, when applicants for help were truly alone, volunteers worked one-to-one to become, in essence, new family members. Charity volunteers a century ago usually were not assigned to massive food-dispensing tasks. They were given the narrow but deep responsibility of making a difference in one life over several years. Kindness and firmness were both essential. In 1898, the magazine *American Hebrew* told of how one man was sunk into dependency but a volunteer "with great patience convinced him that he must earn his living." Soon he did, and he regained the respect of his family and community. Similarly, a woman had become demoralized, but "for months she was worked with, now through kindness, again through discipline, until finally she began to show a desire to help herself."

Today, when an unmarried pregnant teenager is dumped by her boyfriend and abandoned by angry parents who refuse to be reconciled, she needs a haven, a room in a home with a volunteer family. When a single mom at the end of her rope cannot take care of a toddler, he should be placed quickly for adoption where a new and permanent bonding can take place, rather than rotated through a succession of foster homes.

Work Tests

Categorization. A century ago, charities realized that two persons in exactly the same material circumstances but with different values need different treatment: One might benefit most from some material help and a pat on the back; the other might need spiritual challenge and a push.

Those who were orphaned, elderly, or disabled received aid. Jobless adults who were "able and willing to work" received help in job-finding. Those who preferred "to live on alms" and those of "confirmed intemperance" were not entitled to material assistance.

"Work tests" helped both in sorting and in providing relief with dignity. When an able-bodied man came to a homeless shelter, he often was asked to chop wood for two hours or whitewash a building; in that way he could provide part of his own support and also help those unable to perform these chores. A needy woman generally was given a seat in the "sewing room" (often near a child care room) and asked to work on garments that would be donated to the helpless poor or sent through the Red Cross to families suffering from the effects of hurricanes, floods, or other natural disasters. The work test, along with teaching good habits and keeping away those who did not really need help, also enabled charities to teach the lesson that those who were being helped could help others.

Today, we need to stop talking about "the poor" in abstraction and start distinguishing once again between those who truly yearn for help and those who just want an enabler. Programs have the chance to succeed only when categories are established and firmly maintained. Work tests can help: Why shouldn't some homeless men clean up streets and parks and remove graffiti? Now, thousands of crack babies (born addicted to cocaine and often deserted by mothers who care only for the next high) languish in hospitals and shelters under bright lights with almost no human contact. Shouldn't homeless women (those who are healthy and gentle) be assigned to hold a baby for an hour in exchange for food and shelter?

Discernment. "Intelligent giving and intelligent withholding are alike true charity," the New Orleans Charity Organization Society declared in 1899. It added, "If drink has made a man poor, money will feed not him, but his drunkenness." Poverty-fighters a century ago trained volunteers to leave behind "a conventional attitude toward the poor, seeing them through the comfortable haze of our own intentions." Barriers against fraud were important not only to prevent waste but to preserve morale among those who *were* working hard to remain independent: "Nothing," declared the Society, "is more demoralizing to the struggling poor than successes of the indolent."

Bad charity also created uncertainty among givers as to how their contributions would be used and thus led to less giving over the long term. It was important to "reform those mild, well-meaning, tenderhearted, sweet-voiced criminals who insist upon indulging in indiscriminate charity." Compassion was greatest when givers could "work with safety, confidence, and liberty." Today, lack of discernment in helping

414

poor individuals is rapidly producing an anti-compassion backlash, as the better-off, unable to distinguish between the truly needy and the "grubby-grabby," give to neither.

New Emphasis

Employment. Nineteenth-century New York charity leader Josephine Lowell wrote that "the problem before those who would be charitable is not how to deal with a given number of the poor; it is how to help those who are poor without adding to their numbers and constantly increasing the evils they seek to cure." If people were paid for not working, the number of non-workers would increase, and children would grow up without seeing work as a natural and essential part of life. Individuals had to accept responsibility: Governmental programs operating without the discipline of the marketplace were inherently flawed, because their payout came "from what is regarded as a practically inexhaustible source, and people who once receive it are likely to regard it as a right, as a permanent pension, implying no obligation on their part."

In the twentieth century and beyond, programs that stress employment, sometimes in creative ways, need new emphasis. For example, instead of temporary housing, more of the able-bodied might receive the opportunity to work for a permanent home through "sweat equity" arrangements in which labor constitutes most of the down payment. Some who start in rigorous programs of this sort drop out with complaints that too much sweat is required, but one person who stayed in such a program said at the end, "We are poor, but we have something that is ours. When you use your own blood, sweat, and tears, it's part of your soul. You stand and say, 'I did it.'"

Freedom. Charity workers a century ago did not press for governmental programs, but instead showed poor people how to move up while resisting enslavement to governmental masters. Job freedom was the opportunity to drive a wagon without paying bribes, to cut hair without having to go to barber college, and to get a foot on the lowest rung of the ladder, even if wages there were low. Freedom was the opportunity for a family to escape dire poverty by having a father work long hours and a mother sew garments at home. Life was hard, but static, multi-generational poverty of the kind we now have was rare; those who persevered could star in a motion picture of upward mobility.

Today, in our desire to make the bottom rung of the economic ladder higher, we have cut off the lowest rungs and left many on the ground. Those who are pounding the pavements looking for work, and those who have fallen between the cracks, are hindered by what is supposed to help them. Mother Teresa's plan to open a homeless shelter in New York was stopped by a building code that required an elevator; nuns in her order said that they would carry upstairs anyone who could not walk, but the city stuck to its guns and the shelter never opened. In Texas and New Mexico, a Bible-based anti-drug program run by Victory Fellowship has a 60 percent success rate in beating addiction, yet the Commission on Drug and Alcohol Abuse has instructed the program to stop calling itself one of "drug rehabilitation" because it does not conform to bureaucratic standards.

Spiritual Needs

God. "True philanthropy must take into account spiritual as well as physical needs," poverty-fighters a century ago noted, and both Christians and Jews did. Bible-believing Christians worshiped a God who came to earth and showed in life and death the literal meaning of compassion—*suffering with.* Jewish teaching stressed the pursuit of righteousness through the doing of good deeds. Groups such as the Industrial Christian Alliance noted that they used "religious methods"—reminding the poor that God made them and had high expectations for them—to "restore the fallen and helpless to self-respect and self-support."

Today, the challenge that goes beyond the material is still essential to poverty-fighting. In Washington, D.C., multimillion-dollar programs have failed, but, a mile from the U.S. Capitol, success stories are developing: spiritually-based programs such as Clean and Sober Streets, where ex-alcoholics and ex-addicts help those still in captivity; the Gospel Mission, which fights homelessness by offering true hope; and the Capitol Hill Crisis Pregnancy Center, where teenage moms and their born and unborn children are cared for. They are all saving lives. In Dallas, Texas, a half-mile from the Dallas Housing Authority's failed projects, a neighborhood group called Voice of Hope invites teenagers to learn about God through Bible studies and to work at remodeling deteriorated homes in their neighborhood. During the past decade, crime rates among the boys involved with Voice of Hope and pregnancy rates among the girls have been dramatically lower than those in the surrounding community.

Private Charities Can Do the Job

We need to change our methods of fighting poverty, but we need to be clear about the reasons for change. Government welfare programs should be replaced not because they are too expensive—although, clearly, much money is wasted—but because they are inevitably too stingy in providing what is truly important: the treatment of people as human beings made in God's image, not as animals to be fed and caged.

Private charities can do a better job than government, but only if they practice the principles of effective compassion. *Giving*, by itself, we need to remember, is morally neutral. We need to give *rightly*, so as not to impede the development of values that enable people to get out of poverty and stay out. Only when the seven principles of effective compassion noted above are widely understood and practiced can anti-poverty work succeed. In 1995, as in 1895, the best programs offer challenge, not just enabling, and they deal with spiritual questions as well as material needs. In 1995, as in 1895, there is no effective substitute for the hard process of one person helping another. And the century-old question—Does any given "scheme of help . . . make great demands on men to give themselves to their brethren?"—is still the right one to ask.

From "The New Welfare Debate: How to Practice Effective Compassion" by Marvin Olasky, *Imprimis*, September 1995. Reprinted by permission from *Imprimis*, the monthly journal of Hillsdale College. Subscription free upon request.

For Further Discussion

Chapter 1

1. Sheila Collins contends that inequality is a function of capitalism—capitalism creates inequality and feeds on it. Thomas Sowell argues that human beings are themselves inherently unequal in intellect, ability, drive, and so on. Which argument is more compelling? Why? What do you think causes inequality?

2. Doris Y. Wilkinson argues that systemic racism underlies all inequality in American life, including inequities in employment, educational opportunity, health, and justice. William A. Henry III argues that inequality today may have more to do with views that favor group identity over individual achievement rather than with racism. In each viewpoint, try to find two supporting arguments that you personally agree with. Why do you agree with them? Is it possible to find valid arguments in both viewpoints?

3. Llewellyn H. Rockwell Jr. states that equality cannot exist in a free society and that attempts to guarantee equality only destroy individual liberty. John Kenneth Galbraith contends that a humane society must guarantee its citizens equality of opportunity even if it cannot guarantee equality of results. Whose argument is more persuasive? Why? What role, if any, should equality play in a free and humane society?

Chapter 2

1. Sanford F. Schram contends that culturally biased social policies and programs contribute to the poverty experienced by single-parent families. David Blankenhorn argues that poverty and other related problems result from the absence of a father in a family rather than from structural inequities. Whose argument is more persuasive? Why?

2. Myron Magnet and Herbert J. Gans both describe the factors they

view as central to the perpetuation of child poverty. Magnet blames a self-defeating, underclass culture. Gans blames pejorative behavioral labels such as "underclass." Which argument is more compelling? Why? Support your answer with evidence from the viewpoints.

Chapter 3

1. Jesse Jackson states that death penalty cases are decided more often by the skin color of the criminal and the victim than by the violence of the crime. Stanley Rothman and Stephen Powers contend that black criminals receive a disproportionate share of death sentences because of the nature of the crimes they commit, not because of racism. In each viewpoint, try to find two supporting arguments that you agree with. Why do you agree with them? Is it possible to find valid arguments in both viewpoints?

2. Authors Chi Chi Sileo and Mary Kate Cary take opposing views on the effect of sentencing laws on offenders and the public. How do their opinions differ? How do these differences influence their viewpoints?

3. Paul Butler believes that black jurors should sometimes acquit guilty defendants as an expression of their disagreement with a historically unjust legal system. Rather than correcting possible injustices, Karl Zinsmeister and Michael Weiss argue, this behavior undermines the legal system and hurts minority communities most. Compare and contrast the ideas expressed in these two viewpoints. What are the similarities? What are the differences?

Chapter 4

1. bell hooks and Glenn C. Loury take opposing positions on whether white oppression is to blame for black inequality. How do hooks's and Loury's opinions of whites differ? How do these differences influence their viewpoints? How do their views of black culpability differ?

2. Claud Anderson argues that institutionalized racism, as exemplified by the U.S. Constitution, impedes black progress. Byron M. Roth argues that individual behavior and values present the biggest obstacles to black progress. Compare their opinions, then formulate your own argument about the factors that constitute the greatest obstacles to black progress.

Chapter 5

1. Carol Moseley Braun, Michael Lynch, and Katherine Post all agree that women do not advance as rapidly as men in the workplace, but they

disagree on the reasons why. Braun argues that discrimination is the cause; Lynch and Post argue that personal choices are the cause. Which argument is more compelling? Why? Is it possible to find valid arguments in both viewpoints?

2. Myra and David Sadker believe that sexism in education deprives girls of equal opportunities in American society. Christina Hoff Sommers contends that the Sadkers' conclusions and research are flawed by bias and other failings. What evidence do the authors provide to support their conclusions? Whose evidence is more persuasive and why?

3. Jeffrey M. Leving and Kenneth A. Dachman argue that judges (and the laws that guide their actions) routinely discriminate against men in divorce and custody proceedings. Karen Winner disagrees, asserting that discrimination against women is rampant in divorce cases involving custody, property rights, and alimony. Does either viewpoint make a stronger argument? Which one and why? Is it possible that both are correct? Explain.

Chapter 6

1. Nancy J. Osgood contends that Americans stereotype and discriminate against the elderly while glorifying all that is associated with youth. Rob Nelson and Jon Cowan argue that economic and political policies have benefited the elderly and soon-to-be elderly far more than they have benefited the young. Whose argument is more persuasive? Why?

2. Daniel Callahan, Nancy S. Jecker, and Robert A. Pearlman all agree that some type of health care rationing will be needed in the near future. Callahan states that age is a sound criteria for limiting health care. Jecker and Pearlman disagree, saying that age limits are unethical and unjust. Do you agree that health care rationing is needed? Explain your answer. On what basis do you think health care rationing decisions should be made?

3. Esther B. Fein argues that discrimination prevents many older workers from keeping or finding jobs. Richard A. Posner agrees that some discrimination exists but argues that laws aimed at protecting older workers have done more harm than good—for both workers and employers. Do you agree that discrimination should be addressed? How should it be addressed and why?

Chapter 7

1. Bill Lawson states that negative views of poor urban blacks influence environmental decision making. Vicki Been contends that market forces

may guide environmental decision making in the citing of hazardous waste facilities. Compare and contrast the two views.

2. Beverly Wright contends that minorities and the poor are disproportionately subjected to environmental hazards from waste facilities. The authors of the opposing viewpoint argue that minority communities are not disproportionately exposed to hazardous waste facilities. What evidence do the authors present to support their contentions? Is one viewpoint stronger? If so, why?

Chapter 8

1. Charles Murray believes government should not try to solve social problems and bolsters his argument with evidence of past failures. Ruth Westheimer and Ben Yagoda contend that government has an obligation to help needy families and they bolster their argument with evidence of the practical needs of such families. What evidence does each author present to support his or her argument? Whose evidence do you find more convincing? Explain.

2. Marvin Olasky contends that charitable organizations are better equipped than the government to solve poverty. Fred Kammer argues that charitable organizations cannot help the poor without government help—especially money. Who do you think should help the poor? Why and how? Support your answer with evidence from the viewpoints.

Organizations to Contact

The editors have compiled the following list of organizations concerned with the issues debated in this book. The descriptions are derived from materials provided by the organizations. All have publications or information available for interested readers. The list was compiled on the date of publication of the present volume; names, addresses, phone and fax numbers, e-mail and Internet addresses may change. Be aware that many organizations take several weeks or longer to respond to inquiries, so allow as much time as possible.

American Association of Retired Persons (AARP)
601 E St. NW
Washington, DC 20049
(202) 434-2277
fax: (202) 434-2320
Internet: http://www.nassp.org/dsa/nslwaarp.htm

With more than thirty million members, the AARP is the largest advocacy group of Americans over the age of fifty. It seeks to improve every aspect of living for older people and focuses on concerns such as health care and pensions. The AARP is committed to preserving the federal Social Security and Medicare programs. The association publishes the monthly newsletter *AARP News Bulletin*, the bimonthly newsletter *Working Age*, and the bimonthly magazine *Modern Maturity*.

American Bar Association (ABA)
Criminal Justice Section
740 15th St. NW
Washington, DC 20005
(202) 662-1034
fax: (202) 662-1669
e-mail: gatelys@staff.abanet.org
Internet: http://www.abanet.org

Founded in 1920, the Criminal Justice Section of the ABA is an umbrella organization of over ten thousand members including prosecutors, private defense lawyers, law professors, public defenders, trial and appellate judges, law students, correctional and law enforcement personnel, and other criminal justice professionals. With its interdisciplinary membership base, the Criminal Justice Section works to find solutions to issues involving crime, criminal law, and the administration of criminal and juvenile justice. Its publications include the quarterly *Criminal Justice* magazine and various reference books, course materials, and legal analyses.

American Civil Liberties Union (ACLU)
125 Broad St.
New York, NY 10004-2400
(212) 549-2500
(800) 775-ACLU (2258)
e-mail: aclu@aclu.org
Internet: http://www.aclu.org

The ACLU is a national organization that works to defend the civil rights guaranteed by the U.S. Constitution. Its goal is to establish equality before the law, regardless of race, color, sexual orientation, or national origin. The ACLU publishes and distributes policy statements, pamphlets, and the semiannual newsletter *Civil Liberties Alert*.

American Enterprise Institute for Public Policy Research (AEI)
1150 17th St. NW
Washington, DC 20036
(212) 862-5800
(212) 862-7177
Internet: http://www.aei.org

The AEI is a conservative think tank that analyzes national and international economic, political, and social issues. It publishes the magazines *AEI Economist* and the bimonthly *Public Opinion*, as well as numerous papers and books.

Anti-Defamation League (ADL)
823 United Nations Plaza
New York, NY 10017
(212) 490-2525
Internet: http://www.adl.org

The ADL works to stop the defamation of Jews and to ensure fair treatment for all U.S. citizens. Its publications include the periodic *Dimensions* and the quarterly *Facts* magazines.

Brookings Institution
1775 Massachusetts Ave. NW
Washington, DC 20036
(202) 797-6000
fax: (202) 797-6004
e-mail: brookinfo@brook.com
Internet: http://www.brook.edu

Founded in 1927, the Brookings Institution is a liberal research and educational organization that publishes material on government, economics, and foreign policy. The institution produces books and papers and analyzes the legal system in its quarterly magazine *Brookings Review*.

Cato Institute
1000 Massachusetts Ave. NW
Washington, DC 20001-5403
(202) 842-0200
fax: (202) 842-3490
Internet: http://www.cato.org

The Cato Institute is a libertarian public policy research foundation dedicated to limiting the role of government and protecting individual liberties. It researches claims of discrimination and opposes affirmative action. The institute publishes the quarterly magazine *Regulation*, the bimonthly *Cato Policy Report*, and numerous books.

Center for the Study of Popular Culture
9911 W. Pico Blvd., Suite 1290
Los Angeles, CA 90035
(310) 843-3699
fax: (310) 843-3692
e-mail: 76712.3274@compuserve.com

The center is a conservative educational and legal assistance organization that addresses many topics, including political correctness, cultural diversity, and discrimination. Its civil rights project provides legal assistance to citizens challenging affirmative action and promotes equal opportunity for all individuals. The center publishes several magazines, including: *Heterodoxy*, *Defender*, and *Report Card*.

Commission for Racial Justice, United Church of Christ (CRJ)
700 Prospect Ave.
Cleveland, OH 44115
(216) 736-2160
e-mail: whited@ucc.org
Internet: http://www.ucc.org/who/am96_4c.htm

The CRJ conducts research relevant to black and other minority communities. In 1987 it issued *Toxic Wastes and Race in the United States—a National Report on the Racial and Socio-Economic Characteristics of Communities with Hazardous Wastes*, a landmark study documenting the existence of what it termed "environmental racism." In 1994, the CRJ issued an update of that report, which is available for purchase. The commission also publishes the *Civil Rights Journal*, a weekly newsletter dealing with environmental justice and other issues affecting people of color.

Competitive Enterprise Institute (CEI)
1001 Connecticut Ave. NW, Suite 1250
Washington, DC 20036
(202) 331-1010
fax: (202) 331-0640
e-mail: info@CEI.org
Internet: http://www.cei.org

The CEI is a research and advocacy group that supports efforts to make the private sector, rather than the government, responsible for protecting the environment. It believes that by politicizing environmental issues, the environmental justice movement will encourage government regulation of business, which will then limit opportunities for minorities and the poor. The CEI distributes position papers and congressional testimony. It also publishes the monthly newsletter *CEI Update* and numerous reprints and briefs.

Eagle Forum
Box 618
Alton, IL 62002
(618) 462-5415
fax: (618) 462-8909

The Eagle Forum is an educational and political organization that advocates traditional family values. To expose what it believes is radical feminism's goal to break up the family, the forum examines and disseminates its position on issues such as women in combat, family leave, child care, tax credits for families with children, and "outcome-based" education. The organization offers several books by its president, Phyllis Schlafly, including *Child Abuse in the Classroom, Who Will Rock the Cradle?, Meddlesome Mandate: Rethinking Family Leave*, and *Equal Pay for Unequal Work*. It also publishes a monthly newsletter, the *Phyllis Schlafly Report*.

Educational Equity Concepts (EEC)
114 E. 32nd St. Suite 701
New York, NY 10016
(212) 725-1803
fax: (212) 725-0947
e-mail: 75507.1306@compuserve.com
Internet: http://www.onisland.com/eec

EEC is a national organization that creates programs and materials designed to help educators provide bias-free learning environments and activities. Its mission is to decrease discrimination based on gender, race, ethnicity, and disability. Publications and materials available include vocational education videos and issue papers such as "Mixed Messages" and "Including All of Us."

Family Research Council
801 G St. NW
Washington, DC 20001
(800) 225-4008
e-mail: corrdept@frc.org

The council provides information to the public on issues such as parental responsibility, the impact of working parents on children, the tax system's effect on families, and community support for single parents. Its publications include the monthly newsletter *Washington Watch*, the bimonthly newsletter *Family Policy*, and reports and policy analyses.

Focus on the Family
8605 Explorer Dr.
Colorado Springs, CO 80920
(719) 531-3400
fax: (719) 548-4525

Focus on the Family is a conservative Christian organization that promotes traditional family values and gender roles. Its publications include the monthly magazine *Focus on the Family* and the report "Setting the Record Straight: What Research Really Says About the Social Consequences of Homosexuality."

Foundation for Economic Education (FEE)
30 S. Broadway
Irvington-on-Hudson, NY 10533
(914) 591-7230
fax: (914) 591-8910
Internet: http://www.execpc.com/~jfish/fee/index.html

The foundation publishes information and research in support of capitalism, free trade, and limited government. It publishes the monthly magazine *Freeman*.

The Heritage Foundation
214 Massachusetts Ave. NE
Washington, DC 20002
(202) 546-4400
fax: (202) 546-0904
Internet: http://www.heritage.org

The foundation is a conservative public policy research institute dedicated to free-market principles, individual liberty, and limited government. It opposes affirmative action and believes that the private sector, not government, should be allowed to ease social problems and to improve the status of women and minorities. The foundation publishes the quarterly journal *Policy Review* and the bimonthly newsletter *Heritage Today* as well as numerous books and papers.

Lambda Legal Defense and Education Fund
666 Broadway, Suite 1200
New York, NY 10012-2317
(212) 955-8585
fax: (212) 955-2306
Internet: http://www.thebody.com/lambda/lambda.html

Lambda is a public interest law firm committed to protecting the civil rights of lesbians, gay men, and people with HIV/AIDS. The firm addresses a variety of issues, including constitutional law, employment, same-sex marriage rights, domestic-partner benefits, and HIV/AIDS-related discrimination. Its publications include the quarterly *Lambda Update* and the booklets *OUT on the Job, OUT of a Job: A Lawyer's Overview of the Employment Rights of Lesbians and Gay Men* and *Stopping the Anti-Gay Abuse of Students in Public High Schools*.

Lincoln Institute for Research and Education
1001 Connecticut Ave. NW
Washington, DC 20036
(202) 223-5112

The institute is a conservative think tank that studies how public policy issues affect the lives of black Americans. It publishes the newsletter *Lincoln Review* six times a year.

National Association for the Advancement of Colored People (NAACP)
4805 Mt. Hope Dr.
Baltimore, MD 21215-3297
(410) 358-8900
fax: (410) 486-9257

The NAACP is the oldest and largest civil rights organization in the United States. Its principal objective is to ensure the political, educational, social, and economic equality of minorities. It publishes the magazine *Crisis* ten times a year as well as a variety of newsletters, books, and pamphlets.

National Council on the Aging (NCOA)
409 Third St. SW, 2nd Fl.
Washington, DC 20024
(202) 479-1200
fax: (202) 479-0735
Internet: http://www.shs.net/ncoa/polcy_st.htm

The council consists of individuals and organizations working on behalf of older Americans and promotes concern for them. It conducts research and programs on issues important to older people, such as training and placement of older workers, economic security, home services for the frail elderly, and access to health and social services. The NCOA publishes the bimonthly newspaper *NCOA Networks* and the quarterly magazine *Perspective on Aging*.

National Institute of Justice (NIJ)
U.S. Department of Justice
PO Box 6000
Rockville, MD 20850
(800) 851-3420
Internet: http://ncjrs.org:71/1/4/1

The NIJ is a research and development agency that documents crime and its control. It publishes and distributes its information through the National Criminal Justice Reference Service, an international clearinghouse that provides information and research about criminal justice. Its publications include the bimonthly *National Institute of Justice Journal*.

National Urban League
500 E. 62nd St.
New York, NY 10021
(212) 310-9000
fax: (212) 593-8250
Internet: http://www.nul.org

A community service agency, the Urban League works to eliminate institutional discrimination in the United States. It also provides services for minorities who experience discrimination in employment, housing, welfare, and other areas. The league publishes the quarterly *BEEP Newsletter* and the quarterly newsletter *Urban League News.*

9 to 5 National Association of Working Women
238 W. Wisconsin Ave., Suite 700
Milwaukee, WI 53203
(414) 274-0925
fax: (414) 272-2970
Internet: http://www.feminist.com/9to5.htm

The organization seeks to gain better pay and opportunities for advancement, eliminate sex and race discrimination, and improve working conditions for female office workers. It publishes the *9 to 5 Newsletter* five times a year as well as numerous pamphlets.

Poverty and Race Research Action Council (PRRAC)
1711 Connecticut Ave. NW, Suite 207
Washington, DC 20077-0009
(202) 387-9887
fax: (202) 387-0764
e-mail: prrac@aol.com

The PRRAC is a national organization that promotes research and advocacy on behalf of poor minorities on the issues of race and poverty. It publishes the bimonthly newsletter *Poverty & Race* and the book *Double Exposure: Poverty and Race in America.*

Southern Poverty Law Center
Teaching Tolerance/Klanwatch
400 Washington Ave.
Montgomery, AL 36104
(334) 264-0286
fax: (334) 264-0629
Internet: http://www.splcenter.org

The center litigates civil cases to protect the civil rights of poor people, regardless of race. The center's Teaching Tolerance project creates educational materials that promote tolerance and understanding and distributes them free of charge to teachers and principals. The affiliated Klanwatch project collects data on white supremacist groups. The center publishes numerous books and reports, the bimonthly *Klanwatch Intelligence Report,* and the semiannual magazine for teachers *Teaching Tolerance.*

United States Commission on Civil Rights
1121 Vermont Ave. NW
Washington, DC 20425
(202) 376-8177
Internet: http://www.usccr.gov

The commission reports directly to Congress and the president on the effectiveness of equal opportunity laws and programs. A catalog of its numerous publications can be obtained from its Publication Management Division.

U.S. Environmental Protection Agency (EPA)
Office of Environmental Justice (OEJ)
Mail Stop 2201-A
402 M St. SW
Washington, DC 20460
(800) 962-6215
Internet: http://www.epa.gov

Created by the EPA in 1992, the OEJ ensures that no segment of the population, regardless of race, ethnicity, culture, or income, bears a disproportionate amount of environmental pollution. The OEJ coordinates with other federal agencies on environmental justice issues; provides training and technical and financial assistance to the public; and serves as a repository of papers, books, and articles on environmental justice—all of which are available to the public free of charge. The OEJ also maintains a toll-free hot line to receive calls from concerned citizens about environmental justice issues in their communities. Environmental justice coordinators in all ten of the EPA's regional offices can offer further help or information.

Bibliography

Chapter 1

Clay Chandler and Richard Morin   "Two Sides of the Coin," *Washington Post*, November 4–10, 1996. Available from 1150 15th St. NW, Washington, DC 20071.

William M. Dugger, ed.   *Inequality: Radical Institutionalist Views on Race, Gender, Class, and Nation.* Westport, CT: Greenwood Press, 1996.

Richard B. Freeman   *When Earnings Diverge: Causes, Consequences, and Cures for the New Inequality.* Washington, DC: National Policy Association, 1997.

Zelma Henriques   "African-American Women: The Oppressive Intersection of Gender, Race, and Class," *Women and Criminal Justice*, 1995.

Ludwig von Mises   "Inequality of Wealth and Incomes," *Freeman*, March 1996. Available from the Foundation for Economic Education, Irvington-on-Hudson, NY 10533.

Melvin L. Oliver and Thomas M. Shapiro   "Race, Wealth, and Inequality in America," *Poverty & Race*, November/December 1995. Available from the Poverty & Race Action Council, 1711 Connecticut Ave. NW, Suite 207, Washington, DC 20009.

Madison Powers   "Forget About Equality," *Kennedy Institute of Ethics Journal*, June 1996. Available from Johns Hopkins University Press, Journals Publishing Division, 2715 North Charles St., Baltimore, MD 21218-4319.

Benjamin Schwarz   "Reflections on Inequality: 'The Promise of American Life,'" *World Policy Journal*, Winter 1995–96.

Philip Selznick	"Social Justice: A Communitarian Perspective," *Responsive Community*, Fall 1996. Available from 714J Gelman Library, George Washington University, Washington, DC 20052.
Paul M. Sniderman	*The Clash of Rights: Liberty, Equality, and Legitimacy in a Pluralist Democracy.* New Haven, CT: Yale University Press, 1996.
Thomas Sowell	"Bias Doesn't Explain Economic Disparities," *Conservative Chronicle*, July 12, 1995. Available from PO Box 11297, Des Moines, IA 50340-1297.
Stephanie M. Wildman	*Privilege Revealed: How Invisible Preference Undermines America.* New York: New York University Press, 1996.

Chapter 2

Paul A. Cleveland and Brian H. Stephenson	"Individual Responsibility and Economic Well-Being," *Freeman*, August 1995
Sheldon Danziger and Peter Gottschalk	*America Unequal.* Cambridge, MA: Harvard University Press, 1995.
Nicholas Eberstadt	"Prosperous Paupers and Affluent Savages," *Society*, January/February 1996.
Donna L. Franklin	*Ensuring Inequality: The Structural Transformation of the African American Family.* New York: Oxford University Press, 1997.
Matthew O. Hunt	"The Individual, Society, or Both? A Comparison of Black, Latino, and White Beliefs About the Causes of Poverty," *Social Forces*, September 1996.
Glenn C. Loury	"Beyond Victimhood: The Disappearance of Virtue from American Public Discourse," *Times Literary Supplement*, June 10, 1994.
Byron M. Roth	*Prescription for Failure: Race Relations in the Age of Social Science.* New Brunswick, NJ: Transaction Publishers, 1994.
Holly Sklar	*Chaos or Community? Seeking Solutions, Not Scapegoats for Bad Economics.* Boston: South End Press, 1995.
Chris Tilly and Randy Albelda	"It's Not Working: Why Many Single Mothers Can't Work Their Way Out of Poverty," *Dollars and Sense*, November/ December 1994.

William Julius Wilson   *When Work Disappears: The World of the New Urban Poor*. New York: Knopf, 1996.

Chapter 3

Jeffrey Abramson   "Making the Law Colorblind," *New York Times*, October 16, 1995.

Stephen J. Adler   *The Jury: Trial and Error in the American Courtroom*. New York: Times Books, 1994.

Robert L. Carter   "The Criminal Justice System Is Infected with Racism," *Vital Speeches of the Day*, March 1, 1996.

Edward Grimsley   "Living Up to the Promise of Equal Justice," *Conservative Chronicle*, May 3, 1995.

Gerald Horne   "On the Criminalization of a Race," *Political Affairs*, February 1994.

W.S. Wilson Huang et al.   "Individual and Contextual Influences on Sentence Lengths: Examining Political Conservatism," *Prison Journal*, December 1996. Available from Sage Publications, 2455 Teller Rd., Thousand Oaks, CA 91320.

Wendy Kaminer   *It's All the Rage: Crime and Culture*. Reading, MA: Addison-Wesley, 1995.

Randall Kennedy   *Race, Crime, and the Law*. New York: Pantheon Books, 1997.

Andrew Koppelman   *Antidiscrimination Law and Social Equity*. New Haven, CT: Yale University Press, 1996.

Patrick A. Langan   "No Racism in the Justice System," *Public Interest*, Fall 1994.

Bertel M. Sparks   "Trial by Jury vs. Trial by Judge," *Freeman*, October 1995.

Linn Washington   *Black Judges on Justice: Perspectives from the Bench*. New York: New Press, 1994.

Chapter 4

John F. Budd Jr.   "Ambition Is Not a Right," *Vital Speeches of the Day*, April 15, 1995.

Ellis Cose   "Blinded by Color," *Newsweek*, September 25, 1995.

Dinesh D'Souza   *The End of Racism: Principles for a Multiracial Society*. New York: Free Press, 1995.

Dinesh D'Souza	"Is Racism a Western Idea?" *American Scholar*, Autumn 1995.
Gerald Early	"Understanding Afrocentrism: Why Blacks Dream of a World Without Whites," *Civilization*, July/August 1995. Available from 666 Pennsylvania Ave. SE, Suite 303, Washington, DC 20003.
Peter Erickson	"Seeing White," *Transition*, Fall 1995. Available from Duke University Press, 905 West Main St., Suite 18-B, Durham, NC 27701.
Andrew Hacker	*Two Nations: Black and White, Separate, Hostile, Unequal.* New York: Scribner, 1992.
Manning Marable	"History and Black Consciousness: The Political Culture of Black America," *Monthly Review*, July/August 1995.
Melvin L. Oliver and Thomas M. Shapiro	*Black Wealth/White Wealth: A New Perspective on Racial Inequality.* New York: Routledge, 1995.
Thomas Sowell	*Race and Culture: A World View.* New York: Basic Books, 1994.
Anne Wortham	"Victimhood Versus Individual Responsibility," *Lincoln Review*, Fall/Winter 1993–94. Available from the Lincoln Institute for Research and Education, 1001 Connecticut Ave. NW, Washington, DC 20036.

Chapter 5

Annette Bernhardt, Martina Morris, and Mark S. Handcock	"Women's Gains or Men's Losses? A Closer Look at the Shrinking Gender Gap in Earnings," *American Journal of Sociology*, September 1995.
Ida Castro and Diana Furchtgott-Roth	"Question: Should Women Be Worried About a Glass Ceiling in the Workplace?" *Insight*, February 10, 1997. Available from 3600 New York Ave. NE, Washington, DC 20002.
Tom Dunkel	"Affirmative Reaction," *Working Woman*, October 1995.
Diane Harris	"How Does Your Pay Stack Up?" *Working Woman*, February 1996.
Patricia Ireland	*What Women Want.* New York: Dutton, 1996.

Jerry A. Jacobs, ed.	*Gender Inequality at Work*. Thousand Oaks, CA: Sage Publications, 1995.
Kathleen Hall Jamieson	*Beyond the Double Bind: Women and Leadership*. New York: Oxford University Press, 1995.
Elizabeth Larson and Elizabeth Toledo	"Question: Is It Time to End Affirmative Action for Women?" *Insight*, April 24, 1995.
William Murchison	"Spit Polish, Nail Polish Don't Mix," *Conservative Chronicle*, December 4, 1996.
Diane Ravitch	"In the Classroom: The Gender Bias Myth," *Forbes*, May 20, 1996.
Jennifer Roback	"Beyond Equality of the Sexes," *Freeman*, December 1994.
Catherine E. Ross and John Mirowsky	"Economic and Interpersonal Work Rewards: Subjective Utilities of Men's and Women's Compensation," *Social Forces*, September 1996.
Rosemary C. Salomone	"The VMI Case: Affirmation of Equal Educational Opportunity for Women," *Trial*, October 1996.

Chapter 6

Bernice Balfour	"The Indignity of Being Old," *Los Angeles Times*, December 13, 1995.
Christina Duff	"Profiling the Aged: Fat Cats or Hungry Victims?" *Wall Street Journal*, September 28, 1995.
Linda Ellerbee	"Should We—Must We—Lie About Our Age?" *New Choices for Retirement Living*, September 1995.
Christopher Farrell et al.	"The Economics of Aging: Why the Growing Number of Elderly Won't Bankrupt America," *Business Week*, September 12, 1994.
Betty Friedan	*The Fountain of Age*. New York: Simon & Schuster, 1993.
Leonard Hayflick	*How and Why We Age*. New York: Ballantine Books, 1994.
Constance L. Hays	"If the Hair Is Gray, Con Artists See Green," *New York Times*, May 21, 1995.
James M. Humber and Robert F. Almeder, eds.	*Allocating Health Care Resources*. Totowa, NJ: Humana Press, 1995.

Doron P. Levin	"The Graying Factory," *New York Times*, February 20, 1994.
Charles F. Longino Jr.	"The New Elderly: Myths of an Aging Population," *Current*, December 1994.
Marilyn Moon and Janemarie Mulvey	*Entitlements and the Elderly: Protecting Promises, Recognizing Reality*. Washington, DC: Urban Institute Press, 1996.
Mark R. Wicclair	*Ethics and the Elderly*. New York: Oxford University Press, 1993.

Chapter 7

Regina Austin and Michael Schill	"Black, Brown, Red, and Poisoned," *Humanist*, July/August 1994.
Vicki Been with Francis Gupta	"Coming to the Nuisance or Going to the Barrios? A Longitudinal Analysis of Environmental Justice Claims," *Ecology Law Quarterly*, Spring 1997.
Christopher Boerner and Thomas Lambert	"Environmental Justice," *Public Interest*, Winter 1995.
Robert D. Bullard, ed.	*Unequal Protection: Environmental Justice and Communities of Color*. San Francisco: Sierra Club Books, 1994.
Anthony R. Chase	"Assessing and Addressing Problems Posed by Environmental Racism," *Rutgers Law Review*, Winter 1993.
Michael Fumento	*Science Under Siege: Balancing Technology and the Environment*. New York: Morrow, 1993.
Richard Hofrichter, ed.	*Toxic Struggles: The Theory and Practice of Environmental Justice*. Philadelphia: New Society Publishers, 1993.
Kent Jeffreys	"Numbers Skewed to Claim Environmental Racism," *Human Events*, February 10, 1995. Available from 7811 Montrose Rd., Potomac, MD 20854.
David Schoenbrod	"Environmental 'Injustice' Is About Politics, Not Racism," *Wall Street Journal*, February 23, 1994.
Robert Suro	"Pollution-Weary Minorities Try Civil Rights Tack," *New York Times*, January 11, 1993.

Chapter 8

| Rebecca M. Blank | *It Takes a Nation: A New Agenda for Fighting Poverty*. New York: Russell Sage Foundation |

	and Princeton, NJ: Princeton University Press, 1997.
Sheldon Danziger and Peter Gottschalk	*America Unequal.* Cambridge, MA: Harvard University Press, 1995.
Dorothea M. Eiler	"How Government Destroys Jobs for Poor Women," *Freeman*, June 1996.
Lowel Gallaway and Richard Vedder	"What Causes Unemployment?" *World & I*, June 1994. Available from 3600 New York Ave. NE, Washington, DC 20002.
Lilian and Oscar Handlin	"America and Its Discontents," *American Scholar*, Winter 1995.
Michael Levin	"How the Free Market Can Solve the Race Problem," *Rothbard-Rockwell Report*, January 1996. Available from the Center for Libertarian Studies, 875 Mahler Rd., Suite 150, Burlingame, CA 94010.
Michael Novak, ed.	*To Empower People: From the State to Civil Society.* Washington, DC: AEI Press, 1996.
John David Skrentny	*"The Ironies of Affirmative Action: Politics, Culture, and Justice in America.* Chicago: University of Chicago Press, 1996.
Cass R. Sunstein	"Well-Being and the State," *Harvard Law Review*, April 1994.
Roger Wilkins	"Racism Has Its Privileges," *Nation*, March 27, 1995.

Index

169